AN AMERICAN EPIC

Introduction

The Relief of Belgium and Northern France

1914-1930

VOLUME I

HERBERT HOOVER

An American Epic

Introduction

The Relief of Belgium and Northern France

1914-1930

VOLUME I

HENRY REGNERY COMPANY

CHICAGO: 1959

DEDICATION

These volumes are dedicated to the tens of thousands of men and women who served in tasks which would have been hopeless without their devotion and high ideals.

These volumes are also dedicated to historians, whose job it is to fit the pieces of mosaic into the great murals of history. They will find herein contributions to their labors.

HUNGER

I come among the peoples like a shadow.
I sit down by each man's side.
None sees me, but they look on one another,
And know that I am there.
My silence is like the silence of the tide
That buries the playground of children;
Like the deepening frost in the slow night,
When birds are dead in the morning.
Armies trample, invade, destroy,
With guns roaring from earth and air.
I am more terrible than armies.
I am more feared than the cannon.
Kings and chancellors give commands;
I give no command to any;
But I am listened to more than kings
And more than passionate orators.
I unswear works, and undo deeds.
Naked things know me.
I am first and last to be feet of the living,
I am Hunger.

LAURENCE BINYON

AND I MIGHT ADD:

I am the stalking aftermath of all wars.
Pestilence is my companion.
Tumult and Revolution rise round my feet
We kill more than all of the guns.
I breed fears and hates that bring to man more wars,
From me comes no peace to mankind.
My legacy is to Children of Famine—
Stunted bodies and twisted minds.

HERBERT HOOVER

AN AMERICAN EPIC

This is the first of three volumes to record an epic of America. During this last half-century, American organizations—voluntary and governmental—have provided the margins of food, medicines, and clothing which saved the lives of 1,400,000,000 human beings, mostly women and children, who otherwise would have perished.

For thousands of years, the question "Am I my brother's keeper?" has echoed in the conscience of mankind. The American people were the first in history to accept that obligation as a nation. Never before has a nation undertaken such burdens, consciously and collectively, that human life, and even civilization, might be preserved.

Our people accomplished this task of compassion by self-denial, by longer hours of labor and greater tax burdens—and with no return other than to their own consciences.

＊　＊　＊

I make no apology for presenting a connected, detailed account of these accomplishments, for I participated in many of these efforts and I have had access to a mass of documentation hitherto not available to others. And I have had the assistance of my many colleagues in its preparation. Thus perhaps I alone am in a position to tell the whole magnificent story.

＊　＊　＊

Within a period of twoscore years, the world engaged in two total wars in which not only almost all nations on earth were involved, but in which total populations within nations—men, women, youth, and even children—were mobilized into service.

❖   ❖   ❖

Reduced production of food, medicine, and clothing is the inevitable consequence of total war. Men are drafted from farms; manufacture of agricultural implements is turned to munitions-making; fertilizers are turned into explosives; farms, homes, and processing and industrial plants are destroyed. Blockade and counter-blockade are imposed to reduce enemy nations by starvation; thousands of ships carrying supplies are sunk at sea.

❖   ❖   ❖

The end of the fighting of these wars was not peace. Old empires were fragmented. Revolutions for independence from oppression arose, and new, dynamic ideologies of society emerged. The men who led revolutions were seldom experienced in the arts of government. Weak, newborn governments seeking freedom were in desperate need of critical supplies if their freedom was to survive.

❖   ❖   ❖

Everywhere, soon after these total wars began, there was a growing shortage of food, medicine, and clothing. And soon, in order to secure a just distribution, the principal combat nations were compelled to ration supplies within their boundaries and to control overseas shipments from without.

When these total wars ended, hundreds of millions of people were faced with famine in some degree and often with its evil handmaiden, pestilence. Both wars left an inheritance of debilitated and diseased children who, without succor, would have burdened the world with dwarfed bodies and warped minds.

❖   ❖   ❖

Since the sufferings of the early Pilgrim fathers, the American people have never known famine. Even in the Confederate States during the Civil War there was enough food to maintain public health.

No one who has not seen famine with his own eyes can have understanding of its hideous reality. Mothers at every meal watch the wilting away of their children. Gaunt mothers search for scraps of food, carrying emaciated children too feeble to walk. Long streams of refugees flee from the famine areas, carrying their children and a few possessions, with many dead lying at the roadsides. Few people die directly from starvation, for disease intervenes. The hospitals and children's refuges are crowded with all who can lie on the floors. The dead lie unburied in heaps. And even worse things happen which I do not repeat here.

* * *

The relief and reconstruction that follow total wars and their aftermath of famine and pestilence do not consist of the delivery of gifts for the poor in the form of Christmas boxes tied with colored ribbons. Relief and reconstruction require the creation of huge organizations administered by men and women who are totally unexperienced in such work and who must be trained while in action. The entire process requires billions of dollars in money, the purchase of scores of millions of tons of supplies from overseas, the management of enormous fleets of cargo ships, and, at times, the taking over and managing of railways, waterways, and coal mines in areas of economic chaos. To meet the need for food, nations with a surplus must stimulate further surplus production and meanwhile reduce their consumption by the systematic elimination of waste and by self-denial. The distribution of seed to restore crops in desolated areas is a prime necessity. Reconstruction requires great supplies of tools, machinery, and railway and construction equipment. All of this requires a great organization of equipment and medicines to stop the spread of pestilence and to stamp it out. And this work requires hundreds of thousands of self-sacrificing people in every nation to save their countrymen.

* * *

Throughout these long years, American men and women have been called upon to abandon their responsible positions and their home life to administer these huge lifesaving enterprises. They never failed to respond, with little or no remuneration. The services of these Americans have been as vital to mankind as the money or the provision of supplies.

* * *

It is difficult to portray the immensity of the tasks in great famines. Statistics throw but a dim light on the scene of organization. But perhaps the reader will have a better understanding of these tasks if I relate that during the period the United States was in the First World War—from April, 1917, to the Armistice, in November, 1918— we provided the necessary margins of food, medicine, and clothing to ten nations of about 157,000,000 people. After the Armistice, we had to organize thirty-two nations with 400,000,000 people, of whom about 220,000,000 were in acute famine. And after the Second World War, to meet the world-wide famine, we had need to organize fifty nations of over 1,500,000,000 people, of whom 800,000,000, without overseas supplies, would have had less food than the prisoners in Buchenwald. Most of these 800,000,000 would have died of mass starvation or its mercy, disease.

The giving of these supplies and services from America was, in a considerable part, simple charity. From many nations the United States received obligations to repay the cost. But these obligations, in billions of dollars, were far greater than the debtors could possibly repay. We received but a small repayment on these debts, and, in the end, we abandoned all claims and forgave the debts. It is impossible accurately to enumerate these sums. A rough estimate could mount as high as fifty billion dollars. From this gigantic effort we were left with a substantial part of our national debt and thus an unending burden on the American people.

*　*　*

Many different American organizations took part in these operations over the years. I include them in this narrative. Other nations contributed within their means in these emergencies, but 95 per cent of the financial burden of these enterprises in saving human lives during both of these wars and their aftermaths was borne by the United States. Insofar as records are available, I have included an account of the contributions of other nations.

*　*　*

The record of these great American undertakings in human service contains many contributions to the history of the times. These operations were conducted in the midst of war, of revolution, of reconstruction. Through the pages of these volumes march every outstanding civilian leader and the high military commanders. The necessary exposition of economic and political backgrounds throws a bright light on many phases of history.

* * *

For twenty years I have worked part-time on the task of setting down a connected record of the work of the many organizations. I have documented it so that there can be no doubt of the facts. Tens of thousands of men and women—Americans and those of other nationalities—were associated in these tasks of unbelievable difficulty. These volumes are partly a consequence of the constant urgings of many of my former associates.

* * *

This record is concerned with what happened to civilians, and particularly to women and children. It is not an account of military action or of military men, except where their strategies and their actions affected the lives of civilians. History records many lives of soldiers saved by great acts of heroism on the battlefields. But it is not the purpose of battle to save lives.

* * *

This history of American enterprises of compassion does not suffer from a lack of documentation.

The largest collection of documents, articles, books, diaries, and records relating to these subjects is located in the Hoover Institution on War, Revolution, and Peace at Stanford University. Other sources are the Library of Congress and the libraries of the great universities. Still other essential materials are in our own government departments and the official records of the other nations engaged in total wars.

The number of these documents, books, articles, diaries, records, and reports that had to be examined during the preparation of this narrative exceeded 3,500,000. Obviously, it was impossible for me to examine personally all of this mass of information. But I have had the aid of long-time associates and my staff who have reduced the number which I had need to inspect to about 400,000 items, my home-work over the years.

* * *

To establish the authenticity of this chronicle, long and sometimes tiresome documentation must be included in these pages. There were many exciting episodes which arose in this work, and in many cases they would be incredible were they not completely documented. In giving documentation, I have introduced only the records of major importance. Since such documents are at times verbose and repetitious and contain many diplomatic superfluities, I have reduced quotations to their essential paragraphs, but have indicated deletions. Also, lest they cloud the narration of more vital matters, I have omitted scores of secondary incidents which loomed large and troublesome to our American organization at the time and involved much negotiation with governmental and private authorities. The full text of any of the documents used may be found in the Hoover Institution on War, Revolution, and Peace, or at the places indicated in the footnotes.

* * *

Part of these documents have been published. Many more of importance have not hitherto been made available to the public.

As a by-product of this work, I compiled a very brief account of a part of these American lifesaving enterprises in my *Memoirs* and in my book *The Ordeal of Woodrow Wilson*. Some minor parts of these publications must be reproduced here in order to give this connected account.

After the First World War, statistical and some documentary material relating to that war was published under the auspices of the Hoover Institution. Books have been written on some segments of these operations by the participants. But as time has elapsed, many disclosures—even with regard to the First World War—have proved previous publications wholly incomplete. Governments are slow in disclosing their records, and when these appear in later years, their import often goes unnoticed.

Publications of material relating to these subjects, during and since the Second World War, are scanty indeed. The record of one great agency, the United Nations Relief and Rehabilitation Administration of the Second World War, is extensive, but that agency covered only 20 per cent of the famine areas.

I had a hand in welding world co-operation to overcome the famine after the Second World War—the greatest in all history. From my mission to thirty-nine countries, I filled many file cases with unpublished material relating to relief activities in that war. Essential parts of this material will be found in these volumes.

* * *

An older experience of mankind lends emphasis to this narrative. The first war-created famine of which we have some record was that which followed the Thirty Years' War in Europe three hundred years ago. It is said that one-third of the population of Europe perished as a result of famine and pestilence. But because of American efforts, there has been no mass starvation or mass loss of life by pestilence following the great wars of this century. And, as I have said, this narrative will show that but for these efforts 1,400,000,000 human beings would have perished.

* * *

These American labors not only saved human lives, they saved civilization for the Western world. They erected dams against the spread of Communism.

* * *

But no amount of documents, statistics, accounts, reports of negotiations, or incidents can display the ideals, the courage, and the sacrifice of the tens of millions of Americans who participated both directly and indirectly in these great enterprises. They are the true authors of *An American Epic.*

CONTENTS

THE ORGANIZATION OF RELIEF IN
BELGIUM AND NORTHERN FRANCE

CHAPTER

FIRST YEAR

November 1, 1914 to November 1, 1915

THE RELIEF OF BELGIUM AND NORTHERN FRANCE

Germany declared war on France on August 3, 1914. Their armies of 2,000,000 men smashed into Belgium in violation of their treaties guaranteeing its neutrality. By heroic sacrifice, the Belgian army of 117,000 men delayed the German march for some days, and this delay enabled the French and British time to re-form and rally on the Marne.

However, the Belgians, under the command of King Albert, managed to hold a scrap of their homeland throughout the war. They clung to the locks at Nieuport and, by this control, flooded the inland for about twenty miles of Belgian front. Although 80 per cent of their original army had been destroyed, the King and his newly recruited men held this scrap of their country for the whole war.

The Allied counterattack on the Marne drove the Germans back to a line about four hundred miles long, stretching from the Belgian front to the Swiss frontier. Here the armies remained fixed behind barbed wire and in trenches for nearly four years, until October, 1918. Except for this little fragment, all Belgium, with about 7,500,-000 people, was occupied by the Germans. They also held, behind their lines under German hobnailed boots, about 2,500,000 French or a total of about 10,000,000 people.

Belgium and Northern France were highly industrialized areas and were dependent on imports for 70 per cent of their food, practically all of their textiles and clothing, and most of their leather and other industrial raw materials.

The British and French at once blockaded Germany and her allies. This blockade included Occupied Belgium and Northern France. The Allied armies drove the Central Powers from the sea except for their submarines and occasional raiders. In addition, the Allies extended the blockade to the neutral nation along the German and Austrian borders in order to control the exports of these nations to the enemy. One consequence was to stop imports from these countries to Belgium and Northern France.

Thus the ten million people in Occupied Belgium and Northern France were ground between the millstones of the German Army and the Allied blockade. Their plight was made worse by the invading Germans' plunder of the 1914 grain harvest and hosts of animals.

I have undertaken this publication because I alone am able to tell the whole story of the suffering of these ten million people and the organizations which enabled them to survive.

Some of the documentation, together with statistics and financial reports on the Relief of Belgium, was published under the auspices of the Hoover Institution on War, Revolution, and Peace at Stanford University in the earlier years following the war. In 1951, I included in my memoirs a brief account of the Relief.

But a connected account of this great adventure into compassion has never been published. Much of the documentation and many important actions and events have never hitherto been made public.

Also, time has disclosed much new information. This particularly applies to official governmental documents, which are universally delayed for years because of personal, security and diplomatic reasons.

Moreover, a new search through the musty files of the Relief Commission produced returns of historic importance.[1]

In the work of the Commission we had need for constant negotiations, contacts and co-operation with the Prime Ministers of Britain and France and, at times, with the Chancellor of Germany. We also

---

[1] The principal publications on the Belgian and North of France Relief are: George I. Gay and H. H. Fisher, *Public Relations of the Commission for Relief in Belgium* (Stanford University Press, 1929); George I. Gay, *The Commission for Relief in Belgium, Statistical Review of Relief Operations* (Stanford University Press, 1925); Vernon Kellogg, *Headquarters Nights* (The Atlantic Monthly Press, 1917).

had constant negotiations with all of the foreign ministers, many of the cabinet officers, top military officials and a host of lesser persons with power.

In order to maintain teamwork and to keep a record, we early established a rule in the Commission that the principal members of our staffs should dictate a memorandum covering important interviews, meetings, and incidents.

There are within these and other of their records many sidelights on the history of the times and on the great personalities of that war which hitherto have not been published.

But statistics and documents do not portray the emotions or the underlying motives of the five nations with which the Commission had to contend hourly. Nor, above all, do they express the trials and suffering of the ten million people involved.

To provide a better understanding of this narrative, I have divided it into preliminary chapters on the organization of relief in Belgium and Northern France and thereafter into the events of each of the five years. This is followed by a discussion of the winding up of the C.R.B. and an Epilogue.

THE ORGANIZATION OF RELIEF
IN BELGIUM
AND NORTHERN FRANCE

CHAPTER 1

THE BIRTH OF THE COMMISSION

I was in London a few months prior to the outbreak of the First World War, partly on a mission to secure exhibits from various governments in Europe for the Pan-American Exposition, scheduled to be held in San Francisco, and partly for my periodic visit to the offices of my engineering firm.

Immediately on the declaration of war, I had been pressed by the American Ambassador to Britain, Walter Hines Page, into managing the repatriation of some 120,000 American tourists and others in their flight from Europe. Completing this task, I had booked passage for my family and me to return home late in October.

On September 5, 1914, a committee of Belgians and Americans, under the leadership of Dannie Heineman, an eminent American engineer, was set up in Brussels to deal with food problems of that city. Ernest Solvay was chosen as Chairman and Emile Francqui as President, and two American engineers—Millard K. Shaler and William Hulse—practicing their profession in Belgian industry were members.

On September 17, through his connections in Berlin, Heineman secured from Baron von der Goltz, the German general in command in Belgium, an undertaking addressed to the American Minister in Brussels, Brand Whitlock, and the Spanish Minister, the Marquis de Villalobar, that the Germans would not requisition the food imported by the Brussels committee.

This committee dispatched Shaler, an old friend of mine, to Lon-

1

don with a credit of $100,000 to buy two or three thousand tons of food. The Belgian Ambassador in London was unable to obtain a permit for Shaler to ship this food through the British blockade. Shaler sought my advice, and I suggested that the British might permit shipments to the American Minister in Brussels if he would assume the responsibility for its distribution solely to the civilian population. To bring this about, I introduced Shaler to Ambassador Page, who promptly secured authority from the State Department for such action. Page, together with the Spanish Ambassador in London, Señor Merry del Val y Zulueta, obtained the permits for Shaler through the British Foreign Office. Until October 18—a few days before I was to return home—I thought the matter ended.

But that day, I received a telephone call from Ambassador Page asking me to come at once to the Embassy. In his office were the Belgian Minister to Britain, Emile Francqui, Baron Jean Lambert, a member of their committee, and Hugh Gibson, Secretary of the American Legation in Brussels. I had known Francqui for many years, since my North China days. It quickly developed that they had already made up their minds to urge that I take charge of the Brussels project, which might later include relief for all Belgium. They explained the plight not only of a people who had less than ten days' bread supply in the cities but especially that of the children, since the usual imports of dairy products were no longer obtainable.

I was well acquainted with Belgium, Northern France, and Germany, since the mines I had directed in various parts of the world had many of their products smelted in these countries.

While sympathetic with the Brussels committee's poignant problems, I pointed out that I knew little about food management and that I had great professional obligations to important concerns over the world, all of which were in difficulties because of the war. They insisted that the undertaking must be managed by a neutral with an administrative background. They argued further that I had had ample experience in the purchase and transport of materials around the world and that I was familiar with their country. The Belgians stated that they could provide from their Government and their banks an initial $5,000,000, with an additional $5,000,000 later. Ambassador

Page was optimistic that we could be an efficient organization which could collect tens of millions of dollars in world charity.

Mrs. Hoover and I spent a prayerful night, and next morning we concluded that duty called me to accept. I arranged with my engineering colleagues to be released from details for a few months, as we did not expect the war to last longer than that. I made but one stipulation in undertaking the Belgian mission, and that was that I would take no remuneration and would pay my own expenses. I wished neither the governments with whom I would need to deal nor charitable contributors over the world to feel that I had any personal financial interest.

At this time I had no realization that I had abandoned a constructive and remunerative profession and had entered upon the slippery path of public service. Nor was I aware of the extent and difficulties of the undertaking. Nor did I have any inkling that it would consume my energies for over four and one-half years, which were filled with haunting anxieties lest this life line to ten million people fail or that I should need to find over $950,000,000 of resources from somewhere.

ORGANIZING THE COMMISSION

Since no time could be lost, I immediately telephoned a number of my American engineer friends in London describing the situation and asking them to serve with me. I called a meeting at my office of those who accepted on October 22. There were present Colonel Millard Hunsiker, Edgar Rickard, Captain John F. Lucey, John Beaver White, Millard Shaler—all engineers—Hugh Gibson, and Ben S. Allen.

At this meeting, Gibson, Shaler, and I set forth the facts. I informed the group that the Belgians promised to find $10,000,000 and further that Ambassador Page had informed me that the British Foreign Minister, Sir Edward Grey, was sympathetic and that he had promised that his government would subscribe £100,000 to our funds.

We decided to set up the organization under the name "American Commission for Relief in Belgium." Ambassador Page had already agreed to be Honorary Chairman. Right then and there we appointed preliminary administrative officers of the Commission:

Herbert Hoover, *Chairman;* Millard Hunsiker, *Vice-Chairman in London;* Dannie Heineman, *Director in charge in Belgium, with Millard Shaler and William Hulse as Assistants;* Edgar Rickard, *Director of the London of-fice;* Captain J. F. Lucey, *Director of the Rotterdam office;* Lindon W. Bates, *Director of the New York office;* John Beaver White, *Director of Purchase and Transport;* Clarence Graff, *Treasurer;* and Hugh Gibson, *an unfailing member at all points.*

At this first meeting, John White observed that we would be han-dling large sums of money and that we should therefore secure the services of a leading international firm of public accountants to keep our books. Otherwise, he prophetically remarked, "some day some swine will rise up and say we either made a profit out of this business or that we stole the money." I enlisted the firm of Deloitte, Plender, Griffiths & Company, who accepted the task with the stipulation from Sir John Plender that they would accept no remuneration and only out-of-pocket expenses for the men they would have to assign to our offices.

Ambassador Page agreed with our suggestion that we get addi-tional American Ministers as Honorary Chairmen, and with his as-sistance we secured the American Ambassador to Germany, James W. Gerard, and the American Minister to Belgium, Brand Whitlock.

Our original idea was to make the Commission wholly American. However, within a few days we realized that the organization would be stronger if we had the patronage of the Spanish Ambassadors in London, Paris, and Berlin, the Spanish Minister in Brussels, and the Netherlands Minister in Brussels, who had already shown an interest in our work. We eliminated the word "American" from our title, and with the help of our American Honorary Chairmen we secured the additional Patrons. We also received the assurance of every assistance from the Netherlands Minister of Foreign Affairs, through whose country our supplies would have to pass. Mr. Page canvassed some of the other neutral ambassadors, including those of the Swiss and the Swedes, who, for various reasons, declined. The Spanish and Dutch officials were to prove invaluable.

It was obvious that our Honorary Chairmen could not enter into agreements with the belligerent governments which would bind their home governments, as this would involve the latter in every embarrassment that might arise. But our Chairmen became our sanctuary in times of difficulty and whenever advice was needed. They gave us the prestige and aid of their positions in introductions and in our battles.

The day after our organization meeting and its announcement in the press, a human treasure turned up in the person of Perrin Galpin, an American student at Oxford who volunteered his services, which I at once accepted. He suggested that we might enlist the American Rhodes scholars in that university. We did so and sent them at once into Belgium to reinforce our American staff of Heineman, Hulse, and Shaler. They proved invaluable.

CHAPTER 2

THE EDGE OF STARVATION

That Belgium's need was imperative was demonstrated from many quarters. A telegram from Minister Whitlock to our Secretary of State on October 16, 1914, said in part:

. . . now a grave situation confronts the land. In normal times Belgium produces only one-sixth of the foodstuffs she consumes. Within two weeks there will be no more food in Belgium. Winter is coming on and there are thousands who are without home and without hope; therefore it is necessary to extend this relief work to the whole of Belgium. . . .

The same day, Whitlock sent a further urgent telegram to President Wilson, saying in part:

In two weeks the civil population of Belgium, already in misery, will face starvation. . . .

On October 26, I received in London a message from Francqui:

My Dear Hoover:
On returning here I found the situation much more grave than at my departure. Liége, Namur, Charleroi are absolutely without flour. At Brus-

6

sels we can scarcely finish the week, and we shall be under the necessity of distributing only 100 grams of flour per inhabitant. . . .

Have still flour for four days. . . .

On October 24, an appeal come to us from the representatives of Charleroi and the Province of Hainaut. The translations were made in Belgium, and I give the essential paragraphs at length because of the light they throw on the German occupation:

While we know that much the same conditions prevail throughout Belgium we can state with bitter assurance the position of our own district.

The Province of Hainaut comprises 1¼ million people, and within a radius of 15 miles of Charleroi there are about 600,000. We are an industrial district with but little agriculture, and 80% of our food stuffs are annually imported from outside. . . . The German army imposed requisitions upon us of food-stuffs, as for instance on the 23rd of August we paid to them 120 tons of wheat, 40 tons of bread, and also large quantities of sugar, coffee, etc. The levies on our people were continued until the 6th September, when we besought the German Governor, Marshal von der Goltz, to stop the levies, and upon representation of the desperate position of our people, orders were given by him that no further levies were to be made upon us. . . . On October 13, Dr. von Sandt, Civil Governor of Brussels . . . informed us that . . . the Germans had food only for their own people and that with the exhaustion of food supplies in Belgium they could do nothing whatever for us. They advised us to go to Holland, where we applied to the Dutch Government through the Belgian Minister, and were informed by him that there were supplies in Holland only for their own needs. . . . We have established upwards of 100 soup kitchens and relief stations in the Charleroi district, within a radius of 15 miles of that city. Latterly we have only been able to make the bread allowance for one or two days in the week. . . . Of potatoes we can continue for another month. There are some meat supplies in the district, held at high prices, but if we denude the district of its animals we will have made it impossible to plant the crops.

The industries of our district are paralysed. Our coal mines are operating two or three days in the week. Our workshops are closed, our moneys are exhausted, and in the whole Province at least 800,000 people must be fed from now on by charity. The rest of the population still have resources with which they could purchase food if the food were available. . . .

Although we can sell part of the food supplies, the payment therefore is a matter of great difficulty owing to the disappearance of gold, and we trade alone in Municipal Notes, which are of little value abroad.

Our people have initiated no war. Our army has done its best to defend us against overwhelming forces. Our people at large are now on the point of starvation. . . .

> EMILE DEVREUX,
> Burgomestre, Charleroi
> EMILE BUISSET,
> Député, Echevin à Charleroi

On October 28, we received the following message from Colonel Knight, our American Vice-Consul in Liége:

In connection with the work that your Committee is engaged upon, it has been drawn to my notice how very necessary it is to arrange for supplies to be sent to Liége. The population there are in a bad way, as there is an absolute dearth of the most necessary provisions, such as flour, peas, beans, lard and margarine.

I therefore sincerely hope that you will be able to arrange for some of the first supplies you get to go through to Liége:

On October 29, we received this petition from the Town Council of Liége:

. . . the city of Liége and the neighbourhood comprising about 450,000 inhabitants are in a terrible situation with regard to the necessaries of life. . . . About eight tenths of the population belonging for the greater part of the working class have no more work, and is without any resources. The local productions have been requisitioned in August by the German Army. It has to be considered that presently there is only bread for about five days. Riots are to be feared. . . .

> ALFRED JOURNEZ,
> Deputy of Liége
> JOS. BOLORNE,
> Deputy of Liége

On October 31, the representatives of Liége sent further details:

The population of [Liége and] surrounding district amounts to something over six hundred thousand inhabitants. This includes more or less 175,000 inhabitants in Liége itself—275,000 in the industrial suburbs and 150,000 in rural parts.

. . . As the cattle have been since the beginning of the war required for meat needs, that . . . population is left nearly without food. . . . There [in Liége] quite a number of houses were destroyed and some small towns or villages entirely burnt down. . . . population in some rural localities or small towns . . . went away. . . . Some were made prisoners, some are dead, and what part took refuge in foreign countries, mostly in Holland, do not dare to come back on account of . . . the risk to be ultimately caught as prisoners. . . . It is a great wonder that such a state of things could predominate these three months already without riots, and here lays a great danger if it comes to the worst, the people will rather die fighting than starving. . . .

So, to sum up the situation, an industrial population of high efficiency is entirely cut out of work and cannot earn its food—has no reserves any more in food or saving and a rescue is immediately urgently needed, for fear that a catastrophe would be brought up by the impending starvation. . . .

PAUL STAES
EMILE DIGNEFFT
Members of Town Council of Liége

From Rotterdam on October 29, we received the following telegram from our Director in Rotterdam, whom we had sent on a mission into Belgium:

. . . We are convinced . . . that we have under-estimated the desperate condition of the Belgian people. . . .

The great and urgent necessity is for flour. If we could get about 25,000 tons of flour, we could relieve the immediate necessities. . . . The people are so hungry, and so desperate that the sight of every German incites them, and in their desperate frame of mind, seeing their children and families without food . . . they are liable to attack the German soldiers at any moment, which would mean another terrible and useless sacrifice of the Belgian people. . . .

I may well close this chapter with an appeal to the American people from the Queen of the Belgians, sent me in her own handwriting:

I have learned with gratification of the noble and effective work being done by American citizens and officials on behalf of my stricken people. I confidently hope that their effort will receive the ungrudging support which we have learned to expect from the generous womanhood of America.

We mothers of Belgium no less than the mothers of America have for generations instilled in our children the instincts and the love of peace. We asked no greater boon than to live in peace and friendship with all the world. We have provoked no war, yet in defense of our hearthstones, our country has been laid waste from end to end.

The flow of commerce has ceased, and my people faced with famine. The terrors of starvation with its consequences of disease and violence menace the unoffending civilian population—the aged, the infirm, the women and the children.

American officials and citizens in Belgium and England, alive to their country's traditions, have created an organization under the protection of their Government and are already sending food to my people. I hope that they may receive the fullest sympathy and aid from every side.

I need not say that I and my people shall always hold in grateful remembrance the proven friendship of America in our hour of need.

ELIZABETH

CHAPTER 3

THE SCENE IN BELGIUM

The conditions under which we started our work are illuminated by a letter from Francqui on November 18, 1914—a month after our meeting in London:

... our position is, I assure you, a really painful one; here we are isolated from all! There is neither telephone, telegraph nor railway.

If one wishes to send a telegram, it must first be submitted to the German authorities, and one never knows when the telegram will reach its destination. For instance, Mr. Hulse sent a wire to Mons on the 7th of November, and same only reached the person to whom it was sent 8 days later.

As to [our transport of] wheat to the different parts of the country, it is only with great difficulty, and after several days' discussion, that permission to attach one or two cars to a military train going in the direction of one or other district is obtained. For instance, for the past ten days we are endeavouring, but in vain, to send some flour to Charleroi, where there is absolutely no bread. We are refused under pretext that "so far military needs have not required the sending of a train in this direction." . . . There are hardly any more horses, as they have been requisitioned. Even if horses were to be had, it would be impossible to cart the provisions as nobody can leave the town he lives in without having a permit from the German Government. To obtain a permit eight days are required, if it be granted, because 99 times out of 100 it is simply refused.

In order to understand our position, let me mention the following cases taken from a thousand others. I have friends living at from 50 to 60 kilometers from Brussels, with whom, in spite of many efforts on my part

11

for the past two months, I have been unable to get into communication. I may also add that I know parents, who since the coming of the Germans have been unable to get into touch with their children, though parents and children are living in Belgium.

In a word those living in one town in Belgium are as isolated from the inhabitants of another town, only 20 kilometers distant, as someone inhabiting the centre of Africa is from Europe.

We are struggling against a position far more painful than if situated in the centre of China. There, at all events, there are at least means of telegraphing, carts, and means of going freely from one place to another even if slow. Here, there are nothing but continual and unforeseen troubles, inertia of every description, a chaos of difficulties paralysing everything.

I was greatly disturbed by Francqui's letter and reports from our staff that, due to the difficulties which Francqui described, the Belgians had not been able to make substantial progress in effective internal organization.

During the thirty days after the C.R.B. was organized, we had, by borrowing food from the Dutch Government and buying cargoes en route, shipped some 25,000 tons of food into Belgium and had 60,000 tons en route.

A few days after Francqui's letter, I left for Belgium to examine the situation on the spot and to aid in setting up the Belgian organization.

When I went to Tilbury to take the Dutch cross-Channel steamer to Flushing, I was held up three hours standing in line while the British Intelligence Service examined the prospective passengers. When my turn came, I was taken into a side room and asked to disrobe to the skin. My clothes and my one suitcase were searched, including the linings.

Through our Rotterdam office, I obtained a visa on my passport from the Germans to enter Belgium. When we reached the border, our automobile was held just inside a gate behind the barbed-wire fence which the Germans had completed along the whole border of Belgium and Holland. I was taken by a German sergeant into a room and again required to disrobe while every cranny of my clothes and bag was examined. In the meantime, our automobile was similarly searched.

As I passed through the suburbs of Antwerp, I saw the remnants of burned homes and buildings from the battle between the Belgians and the Germans for that city standing gaunt and naked—my first vision of the war. But even more depressing was passing through the ruins of Louvain, where its homes, its ancient church, and its university library, with its precious records of centuries, had been destroyed, not in battle, but by militarists to terrorize a free people. A helmeted, hobnail-booted German soldier stood at every crossroad and every street corner in Brussels. The gloomy, rainy, and cold day added to my depression.

The Belgians had spontaneously, as in older crises, organized soup committees in the poorer districts, and my depression was not lightened by visits to them. There were lines of children waiting for a bucket of soup and a loaf of bread, which was the food for the family.

Standing beside one of the kitchens was the devoted woman who managed the station. She remarked that the emblem of Belgium was now a soup bucket, and she added, with a touch of innate Belgian gaiety, "We Belgians make the best soup in the world." I tasted it and decided it was pretty thin and that more substance was needed. The lady emphatically but ruefully agreed.

My American colleagues and I spent several days in sessions with Belgian bankers, merchants, lawyers, and labor representatives of the Brussels committee. Our meetings took place in the board room of a leading bank, with a German sentry at the door. We continued these discussions in our hotel rooms far into each night.

The first problem was, with the aid of our Americans, who had freedom of movement, to weld the many local Belgian committees into a central organization, its work to be decentralized into provincial, city, and communal committees.

We called in statisticians, physicians, and professors. We heard for the first time strange words from the physicians and professors, who spoke of the calories, proteins, carbohydrates, and fats needed to preserve health and life. From the statistician we learned that the normal average prewar monthly imports were about 135,000 tons of wheat and rye, 9,000 tons of beans and peas, 10,000 tons of dairy products and other meat and fats, and 148,000 tons of cereals for brewing and fodder, all totaling up to over 300,000 tons monthly. At war prices and transport costs, this amounted to over $30,000,000 monthly.

An immediate problem was how far we could reduce human consumption, what imports we could eliminate, and how much and what we must import. We decided that in view of continuing German seizure of the animals, we could eliminate most of the fodder, stop the use of cereals for making hard liquor, and reduce brewery supplies.

We discussed the functions of the provincial, city, and communal committees which were being set up. We canvassed the methods of internal transport, locations of warehouses, how to get possession of the native food production, how to ration the people, and above all, where we should secure finance, even for a minimum program.

It was obvious that the volume of imports estimated at the October 18 conference with the Belgians in London was woefully understated and that we would have to do a job of mass experimentation with food. (I may interject that before we had completed the first two and one-half years, we were able to advise the world on these points.)

CHAPTER 4

THE C.R.B.

The title "The Commission for Relief in Belgium" was soon abbreviated to "The Belgian Relief" and in time further shortened to "C.R.B."—a title beloved by all its members.

The C.R.B. had six parallel tasks of organization:

(1) To build up our organization for purchase and overseas shipments of supplies;

(2) To secure adequate agreements from the Germans to protect imported and native supplies in Belgium and immunity of attack on our ships en route;

(3) To secure adequate agreements with the Allies for passage of our supplies through the blockade and liberty of action to charter ships;

(4) To organize the charity of the world;

(5) To obtain financial support from the Allies and possibly from the Germans;

(6) To build up organization of the Belgians for adequate distribution.

The building of this organization came slowly and in painful experience, as will appear in the year-by-year account of our operations.

Gradually, we were recognized by both sides as a necessity. We ultimately became a sort of neutral state making our own agreements with governments, but they both imposed stringent duties and responsibilities upon us.

THE ALLIED REQUIREMENTS

In the Allied determination that the Germans should benefit by none of our supplies or the native produce, they gradually expanded their demands on the C.R.B. controls in Belgium. They required that all food remain the property of the C.R.B. until it was issued by the communes to the people. In consequence, the American staff of the C.R.B. conducted the transportation from Rotterdam, our port of entry, and managed the provincial or local warehouses to maintain power while the food was in the possession of processors. The C.R.B. was required to account to the Allied Governments in detail for its stocks and its final deliveries. It was required to account for all financial transactions, whether its own or those of the Belgian and French committees.

The C.R.B. also was required to enforce the German guarantees and to see that the food was justly and effectively distributed to the civil population. To carry out this duty efficiently, it was necessary for the C.R.B. to maintain an American management and inspection staff of considerable size inside Belgium.

ADJUSTING ORGANIZATION TO THE GERMAN MILITARY INVASION OF BELGIUM

The Germans divided Belgium into two separate military governments. In consequence, we had to deal with two independent German authorities and we had to adjust most of our distribution organization to meet this situation.

The first, which we termed "Occupied Belgium," included about six million civilians. Occupied Belgium was controlled by a German Governor General, with local German Governors in the provinces and lesser officials in the cities. The Germans permitted some remnants of Belgian local governmental authority, such as the city councils, the courts, police, and the communes, to function. The "commune," with its Burgomaster, was the base of government and had survived many foreign dominations in centuries past.

The second area comprised most of the two provinces of East and West Flanders, with about 1,600,000 civilians. This area was a military operations zone, held by one of the seven active German armies.[1] Civilian matters came under the German Commanding General of that Army, and our organization had to deal with him in all matters not the concern of the German General Staff, whose headquarters was located at Charleville in the North of France. This region was technically known as the *Etappengebiet*, but colloquially called the "Etape." The same residues of Belgian local government remained as in Occupied Belgium, but they were much more restricted in their activities.

When we expanded to take in the North of France, we were spread over the rear of four hundred miles of trench lines held by the six German armies. Their Commanding Generals governed the civilian populations separately, except for some co-ordination by the German General Staff. There was no residue of local government authority except the municipal officials in the larger towns and cities and the *Maires* of each commune. This area contained about 2,500,000 French civilians. We were unable to get funds for this work until March, 1915, and its organization was therefore delayed until that time.

ORGANIZATION WITHIN OCCUPIED BELGIUM

Our first organizational step within Belgium was to secure co-ordination of the many local relief committees which had sprung up prior to our appearance upon the scene. In co-operation with the Belgians, we built up the *Comité National de Secours et d'Alimentation*. Colloquially, it was known as the "Comité National," or the "C.N." It was composed of leading Belgians under the chairmanship of Ernest Solvay and the effective management of President Emile Francqui and Vice-President Firmin Van Brée. Branches of this organization were set up in each of the provinces and in the city of Brussels.

[1] In addition, a small corner of Flanders was held by the Belgian Army.

Our organization in Belgium was divided into two separate functions. The French language permits separation of two ideas which are combined in our English term *relief*. One of these is *ravitaillement*, which is victualling, or food supply; the other is *secours*, that is, benevolences or charity to the destitute. These two relief functions in so large an operation obviously required different types of personnel; also, by setting them apart, we greatly simplified the accounts.

On the *ravitaillement* side, the C.N. received supplies of imported food at the commune level from the C.R.B. warehouses; to these were added local supplies from the C.N. Provincial Committees, and the rationing was done by the communal authorities. All rations and other supplies from *ravitaillement* were paid for in currency which came to provincial or Brussels offices of the C.N. The C.N. furnished cash to *secours* to purchase ration cards for the destitute, supplies for the soup kitchens and canteens for the noon-day meal for children, supplies for hospitals, fuel, and other local supplies. The Allies required that these programs be approved by the C.R.B. and accounted for to it.

Because of the suspension of Belgian governmental functions by the German authorities, such institutions as schools, colleges, asylums, hospitals, and even the financing of the courts and the police were looked after by the *secours*. Also, at times, aid had to be given in the form of loans to savings banks and building and loan associations. This organization did not develop overnight. It ultimately required a staff of over fifty thousand and much readjustment.

ORGANIZATION OF RELIEF INSIDE THE
NORTH OF FRANCE

The relief organization inside the North of France was set up in March, 1915, and was entirely separate from the Comité National in Belgium. The problems involved, as well as the insistence of the French and British Governments, required this division.

With the aid of Firmin Van Brée of the Comité National, we selected from among the residents of the North of France the members of the *Comité National de Secours et d'Alimentation du Nord de la France*—the *Comité du Nord* for short and colloquially the "C.F." The dominating personality of the *Comité du Nord* was Edmond Labbé, the rector of the University of Lille.

The German armies practically prohibited the movement of the French civilians among their armies. As a result, the Comité du Nord performed fewer functions than the Comité National in Belgium, and therefore a great many detailed responsibilities fell upon the C.R.B.

The communes formed the base of our organization. There were about 1,200, with an average of about 200 persons to a commune, and each was under a *Maire*.

The C.R.B. transported the food by barge and rail from Rotterdam to regional warehouses in each German Army district and from there distributed it to the communes. Because of the mobilization of able-bodied Frenchmen prior to the invasion, about five hundred communes were without a *Maire*. Under authorization from the French Government, we made appointments to vacancies on the recommendation of the Comité du Nord. Most of these appointive positions were filled by women, who proved to be both devoted and efficient.

The *Maires* sold the ration cards to each person in the commune for local currency and used these sums for their small local expenses and their larger burden of supporting the destitute. They sent their accounts each month to the Comité du Nord, whose headquarters was at Lille, and from there the accounts came to the C.R.B.

Because French francs soon gave out or were hoarded, each commune was compelled to issue its own currency—and each note was signed by the *Maire*. One of my vivid recollections during an automobile inspection trip was seeing a light in a communal office about midnight and finding the lady *Maire* industriously signing ten-centime notes by candlelight. This practice resulted in about one thousand different currencies. Since they were not negotiable outside the commune or municipality of issue, they proved a certain protection for the people because the Germans could not make effective use of them for the purchase of services.

By arrangement with the German General Staff at Charleville, we established our main distribution office in Lille, maintaining three or four Americans in charge, with a branch office under one or two American representatives in each of the seven Army districts in Northern France and in the Belgian "Etape."

Since we had constant negotiations with the German General Staff, we arranged to maintain an "ambassador" at Staff Headquarters at Charleville. For this formidable task I selected a distinguished scientist, Dr. Vernon Kellogg, who had received his Ph.D. from a German university. Dr. Kellogg displayed eminent qualities of statesmanship in this strange and difficult environment. He quickly won the confidence of the German General Staff in our neutrality, single-mindedness, and integrity. Dr. Kellogg was relieved periodically by another member of our staff, and for the longest interval by Caspar Whitney.

The Germans appointed two liaison officers to our office at Charleville. Throughout the war they were Major von Kessler of the Army Intelligence Service and Count Wengersky, an officer of the Reserve Army. Both were helpful men. Through them we arranged for the appointment of a German liaison officer to be attached to each of the C.R.B. district organizations. After some shifting about, these appointments came in the main from men of business experience who had been called into the Army Reserves. Most of them spoke English. Our Americans all spoke French. Much to our astonishment, these liaison officers became earnest supporters, and aides, in our work. Our American staff, among themselves, referred to them as their "nurses." On overhearing the expression, the liaison officers adopted it too.

The organization in the North of France worked more smoothly than the one under the German so-called "Civil" Government in Occupied Belgium.

CHAPTER 5

SOME NEVER ENDING PROBLEMS
OF THE C.R.B.

MILITARIST OPPOSITION

The first day of our existence we had to meet the opposition of the hard-boiled militarists in Germany, Britain, and France. All of them at one time or another opposed the work of the Commission and periodically demanded its suppression.

The attitude of the German militarists was that they would gladly feed the occupied peoples if the "illegal" food blockade were abandoned. They insisted that they could not be called upon to feed these relatives of the Allies by depriving their own women and children. They argued that the threatened starvation of these people, who were the allies of Britain and France, would, in the end, secure relaxation of the food blockade against themselves. They maintained that the opening of a door in the blockade by way of the C.R.B. weakened this pressure. They feared the C.R.B. as possible Allied spies. They were bitter toward the Belgians because the Belgians, by resisting their invasion, had delayed their attack on the Allies, which resulted in their being stalled at the Marne.

An illustration of the German militarist attitude is given in an entry in the *Journal* of Hugh Gibson dated October 14, 1914:

In the course of a visit to General von Lüttwitz [the military governor of Belgium] today, one of . . . [my] colleagues remarked that the Germans *must* keep the Belgians alive, and could not allow them to starve.

21

Lüttwitz was not at all of that mind, for he said with some show of feeling:

"The allies are at liberty to feed the Belgians. If they don't, they are responsible for anything that may happen. If there are bread riots, the natural thing would be for us to drive the whole civil population into some restricted area, like the Province of Luxembourg, build a barbed wire fence around them, and leave them to starve in accordance with the policy of their allies."[1]

The British and French militarists were also violent in their opposition to the Commission. They claimed that it was the duty of the Germans to feed their occupied populations; that they would be compelled to do so if it were not for the Commission; that the Relief relaxed the pressures of the Allied food blockade against the German people. They also claimed that our use of ships depleted their available transport. As this narrative will show, this opposition at first included Lord Kitchener, Minister of War; Winston Churchill, First Lord of the Admiralty; and Lloyd George, Chancellor of the Exchequer. However, Lloyd George later came over to our side. It will appear in this narrative that the corresponding French Generals and Ministers maintained the same attitude.

To meet the British militarists' claim that the Germans would be compelled to feed the occupied peoples, I induced Frederick Palmer, a well-known American war correspondent, to go to Germany and report to the American people. I forwarded his report to Sir Edward Grey on November 25, 1914. It said in part:

Food required to keep Belgians from starving this winter would feed five army corps a year. Any German Governor who diverts that amount from Germany's supplies will have to reckon with German public opinion. Germany is not in want of food at present. If crops are good next year she will have enough, economically managed, to last two years. But she has garnered every grain of wheat, planted big acreages, and is husbanding food stores. In case the war lasts a year her people look forward to short rations. The one valuable life, the one person to be fed, is a fighting sol-

[1] *Journal from Our Legation in Belgium* (Doubleday, Page and Company, 1917), p. 272.

dier or one who may recover to fight again. If she gives her military prisoners only enough for bare existence, will she spare any gratuities to Belgium? She will not, no matter how many governors say so.

Germany can think of Belgium only with angry bitterness. Not humanity, but do-or-die patriotism governs her emotions. They blame the Belgians for spoiling their plan of campaign. Nothing is too bad for the Belgians. Let the Belgians take care of themselves represents German public feeling. This without saying that the Germans are naturally inhumane. They are at war, their ports closed, desperate in determination not to be starved out. . . . Germany will and must think only of her soldiers. Her military commanders cannot help neglecting the people who have ruined her offensive campaign. Belgium needs food. It can come only from the outsiders. The Belgians are sure of getting it only under outside direction. . . . That is the inevitable result of military necessity in bitter warfare. Military commanders of other countries than Germany would do the same. . . . If America feeds them we know that they will be fed.

WHY THE C.R.B. WAS ALLOWED TO LIVE

It was the civilian leaders in each belligerent government at war who prevented the militarists from having their way. Aside from any feeling of compassion, there were practical war policies at stake.

These civilian leaders of both combatants were feverishly anxious either to bring the neutral nations into the war on their side or to prevent them from joining the enemy. For these purposes, they kept up an enormous flow of propaganda. But a deep sympathy for the Belgians had spread over the whole neutral world. To the Foreign Offices, their foreign policies were more important than one Relief Commission, no matter how obnoxious. It was upon this slender thread that the fate of the C.R.B. often hung.

THE MEN OF GOOD WILL

These were the arguments of our supporters to the militarists, but beyond this there was something far more inspiring in our support.

On both sides there were civilian leaders of deep religious faith and human feeling. These statesmen with vision looked forward to the day when peace would have to be made and hate stilled. It was these men in high places on both sides—such as British Foreign Minister Sir Edward Grey—who sustained the Commission at all times. In Britain, our supporters included Prime Minister Asquith, later Prime Minister Lloyd George, Under Secretary of Foreign Affairs Lord Robert Cecil, and such departmental heads as Lord Eustace Percy. On the French side, our staunch supporters included President Poincaré and Foreign Minister Aristide Briand; on the American side, President Wilson and Secretaries Lansing, Houston, and Lane. On the German side we had the unfailing support of Foreign Minister Gottlieb von Jagow and Minister of the Interior Geheimrat Theodor Lewald.

All these men helped to defend the integrity and the righteousness of the Commission from the militarists, as will be seen as this narrative unfolds. At critical times, it was the good will of these men that saved the Commission.

PRESERVED NEUTRALITY

It was vital to the continued existence of the Commission that it be maintained as a purely humanitarian body, absolutely neutral amidst this gigantic conflict of a total war. This primary obligation not only lay upon me personally but upon every member of the Commission and all its suborganizations in Belgium, and extended both to word and deed. Our opponents, the militarists in Germany, Britain, and France, stood constant watch for some misstep through which we could be suppressed. Moreover, they were not only concerned with such negative items as the prevention of military information to the enemy (thus espionage), but, as this narrative will show, at times they tried to use the Commission or its members for this very purpose. Also, we had to deal with attempts by the Germans to control our food supply in order to force the workmen of the occupied areas to work for them and, likewise, attempts by Allied agencies to use our organization to induce these workmen to boycott the Germans. Either of these actions would have made us highly unneutral and could have resulted in our suppression by the other side.

To preserve absolute neutrality was difficult enough for me and all the American members of the Commission because of our sense of outrage at the German invasion of a helpless people and the barbarities to which they were subjected. However, it was this very outrage which led us to dedicate ourselves to the alleviation of the miseries of these ten million people.

For years my dreams were troubled by that monument at Dinant, where hundreds of men, women, and children, taken as hostages, were mowed down with machine guns. The inscription on that stone memorial can never be erased from the minds of men.

Our responsibility for preserving the rigid neutrality of the C.R.B. and all of its subsidiary and allied organizations had another vital aspect. It involved the neutrality of our American, Spanish, and Dutch Patron Ambassadors and Ministers. Any failure of responsibility on the part of the members of the C.R.B. in this matter would have made the positions of the patrons at once untenable. Even if my colleagues and I had not realized all this, the constant reminders we received from our Patron Ambassadors would have kept the subject alive in our minds.

Further, it was vital to establish complete confidence in our probity and honor among the civilian departments of the belligerent governments, which were giving us their trust and aid.

Our American personnel had to have immunity in crossing war frontiers, just as our ships did in passing through the naval war. While there was no doubt about the strict watch kept upon us by both sides, their confidence in our men was necessary if our mission was to succeed.

MOVING ACROSS WAR FRONTIERS

Obviously, in the line of duty, our C.R.B. staff had to move freely across the war frontiers—back and forth to England, Holland, Belgium, Germany, France, and Switzerland and into all these countries from the United States. But crossing frontiers among nations at war was more than a tourist routine.

Every frontier was shut tight against spies. Passports, visas, interrogations, searches, and delays reduced life to its lowest level for travelers. I have mentioned in my introduction the progress on my initial journey to Belgium in November, 1914. During a three-hour wait in line to be searched, I observed favored persons being mysteriously short-circuited around this bottleneck directly onto the steamer and thus comfortably to bed. It seemed to me that some reforms were badly needed in this conduct of belligerent governments toward us. I wanted reform not only for myself but for our whole American staff.

Early in 1915, I arranged with the British, Dutch, and German Governments that in addition to the American passports we carried, we would issue a supplementary C.R.B. passport which, once visaed, would be good for all occasions and would guarantee us against being searched. To secure this concession I gave the word of honor of the organization that we would attend strictly to our own business. After that it was only on very exceptional occasions that our men were held up or searched. Only one of our men ever violated this undertaking—and to our great grief.

I was never able to win the consent of the French Government to the supplementary passport, and we wasted many weary hours waiting for and going through these tedious procedures at the French borders when our sole purpose was to save the lives of their own nationals in the North.

PASSPORTS FOR SHIPS

Our ships likewise needed immunity from search and attack at sea. In time we developed a system of "passes" issued by the agents of both belligerents at the ports of departure. Inspection was arranged either before departure or at a port of call designated for that purpose or at the destination in Rotterdam.

To save the ships from being stopped or attacked at sea, we secured agreement of both belligerents to respect our C.R.B. flag flown from the mast. And for additional protection, the sides of these vessels were marked with huge illuminated signs—Belgian Relief Commission—readable for miles. However, these protections were not infallible, as will be seen later.

THE CARE OF THE DESTITUTE

Much of the routine work of our American staff concerned the problems of purchase of food, overseas transport and railway and canal shipping to our many warehouses, processing of food, negotiation, and securing adherence to the guarantees. In the background of all these endless duties was the inspiration which came from the daily provision of relief to the destitute amid wholesale unemployment and of special services for the children, the sick, and the aged.

As the war wore on, unemployment extended to more than half of the working population, and the rigors of the food supply in Belgium (at the lowest level in the whole Western world) required larger and larger special organizations to meet the needs of the weak and the children.

THE NATURE OF FOOD IMPORTS

For a better understanding of the nature of our imports, it is desirable that I explain one phase of the regime of Continental European food. A great mainstay is bread or cereals. These comprise one-half or more of their diet, as compared to about 30 per cent of the diet of Americans.

Thus the vivid symbol of food to Europe's hungry people is bread. In times of famine their conversation turns always to the number of grams in the bread ration. They watch the announced number rise or fall with hope or despair. If the ration is 350 grams, it conveys a feeling of security. If it falls to 200 grams, it is a portent of starvation.

No bread at all brings the tragic ending of life itself. Often enough our bread ration in Belgium fell below 350 grams, but never to 200 grams.

The next important item of the European diet is fats. With bread and fats, it is possible to sustain adults in a famine-stricken area over long periods, even with considerable protein deficiencies.

THE SOUP KITCHENS

The soup kitchens were a vital part of our Relief organization. They were operated by devoted Belgian and French women and served every section of the towns and cities. The soup was an economical means of supplementing the communal ration with meats and fats. C.R.B. branches throughout the neutral world received donations of canned and packaged goods in large amounts. These donations were too irregular and not as adaptable to distribution as rations, but they were of great use in the "soups." The soup was rationed by cards and, whenever possible, was accompanied by a small extra bread ration.

SPECIAL CARE OF CHILDREN

As the war continued we soon found that the regular rations and the supplemental "soups" were insufficient for the children. The Belgian physicians reported to me that protein- and fat-deficiency diseases were becoming epidemic among the children. In the earlier days of the Relief, these doctors were not allowed by the Germans to travel about and thus investigate or meet for mutual exchanges of information. Therefore, I arranged for Dr. William Lucas, a children's specialist from California, to come to Belgium. With the aid of the Belgian physicians, he quickly found that there was a growing spread of rickets, certain glandular diseases, and tuberculosis, all of which originated or were stimulated by insufficient special fats, protein, and certain salts. In practical terms, the children needed more meat, condensed milk, sugar, and certain salts. He recommended cocoa as adding flavor as well as nourishment.

Dr. Lucas was not only to find a remedy but, from his impressive report, to persuade the Allied Governments to allow the food to pass the blockade. As a result, through the "benevolent" division of the organization, we established a system of canteens to supply a noon-day meal to infants, children, expectant mothers, and the aged. Here they received the components to make up deficiencies in the ration-ing. In time these canteens expanded until they served 2,500,000 of these special persons in Belgium and Northern France. They were directed by devoted Belgian and French women. With food relieving their deficiencies in famine, the rapid transformation of pale, sad, and wilted children into normal, chattering, active youngsters was one of the great compensations for our otherwise almost unendur-able duties. These 2,500,000 children emerged from the war even above their normal prewar health.[2]

---

[2] Our organizations for the rehabilitation of children all over Europe after the Armis-tice and the Second World War were the result of this Belgian experience. Under such organizations, scores of millions of famine-racked children were rehabilitated.

CHAPTER 6

THE CHARITY OF THE WORLD

The Commission had a dual purpose in appealing to the charity of the world. We had to have funds with which to buy food if the Belgians were to live. Equally, we had to have the support of the neutral world and the people of the Allied countries if the Commission were to live.

We had no need to describe to the neutral world the bitter plight of the Belgians. The outrages perpetrated on them were headlined daily by the press.

We prepared and issued our first appeal to world charity at the first meeting of the Commission on October 22, 1914. We were fortunate that Melville E. Stone, General Manager of the Associated Press, became our adviser and mentor in publicizing our cause. To do so effectively, Stone delegated Ben S. Allen of his London staff to work with C.R.B.

To organize the charitable giving, I telegraphed the Governors of the American States asking them to establish committees of responsible men and women to collect money and commodities for relief. The Governors organized all forty-eight states.

We also organized a committee of leading men and women in Great Britain under the leadership of the Duke of Norfolk. He, in turn, organized the countries of the British Commonwealth. The Spanish Ambassador in London arranged that his government set up a committee in Spain. Upon my appeal, the Presidents of Argentina and some other Latin American countries also established influential committees.

30

We mobilized the religious leaders of the neutral world, and were equally supported by Protestants, Jews, and Catholics. From their leaders we obtained frequent and widespread statements and support—including that of Pope Benedict XV. We secured statements of support from the heads of a score of neutral nations, including the Presidents of the United States, Argentina, Peru, Chile, and Brazil. We obtained resolutions of support from local and national legislative bodies in many nations.

Over the four and one-half years, there was a great outpouring of charity—amounting to the largest fund known up to that time. The total contributed in money and cargoes of food and clothing during the life of the Commission was:

From the United States	$34,521,026.99
From the British Empire	16,641,034.85
From Latin America and others	1,128,773.67
	$52,290,835.51

But in estimating the charitable support we received, there were even larger indirect contributions which should be included. Among them were the voluntary services of the C.R.B. staff. Our foreign exchange, our shipping, and our purchasing were done without profit by the great business houses which assisted us; these enabled the C.R.B. to hold its overhead to a total of $3,908,892.74 for the whole of its lifetime. Thus the C.R.B. handled supplies valued at about $1,400,-000,000 for less than one-third of one per cent. Any paid business organization would have required about five per cent, or about $70,-000,000, for such a service.

Beyond this, the Relief organization's successful battles with the German militarists to save and protect native food supplies secured in the war years 910,000 tons in wheat alone, to say nothing of the savings in potatoes, animal products, and other supplies amounting to an import value of several hundreds of millions of dollars.

To charity funds should also be added the profits made by the C.R.B. from sales of food to peoples outside Belgium and Northern

France, totaling $9,630,766.69, and the profits earned by sales of food inside Belgium and Northern France after the Armistice.

At the beginning of the Commission we were under the illusion that the war would be over shortly. We believed that with the assurance of the Belgian banks and our appeals to charity we could summon sufficient resources to save these millions of people from starvation.

However, during my first visit to Belgium in November, 1914, my impression of the German Army and my knowledge of the determination of the Allies made me certain that the war would last for a year or more and that the gifts we could obtain from generous people would be unequal to the task. But without the great outpouring of charity, we could not have survived the first four months. After that time we succeeded in securing subsidies from the British and French Governments. I may say parenthetically that prior to these subsidies, five members of the Commission, including the Chairman, in determination to hold this life line for these ten million people, signed their own names to purchases of cargoes en route, which on compulsory resale would have meant a loss greater than their combined fortunes—and such an event would have let the wolf through the door into Belgium.

But it was our appeal for the charity of the world which molded public opinion and enabled the Commission to maintain its own existence in many crises—and thus insured the survival of the Belgian people.

The final result of the Relief organization's four and a half years' work in maintaining the physical and moral strength of these ten million people in the heart of warring Europe was to enable them not only to survive but, the moment the war ended, to play a unique and vigorous economic part in the rehabilitation of the war-torn areas of Western Europe.

CHAPTER 7

THE PERSONNEL
OF THE RELIEF ORGANIZATION

The personnel of the responsible members of the whole organization were volunteers. Our Americans received no remuneration except for a few members after the war. A few were given an expense allowance during the war. The leaders in the Belgian membership were, likewise, all volunteers. Among the fifty thousand Belgian women who performed many important functions, some few received a free ration to enable them to serve. The astonishing minute expenditures of the whole organization—both American and Belgian—are proof of the voluntary character of the organization.

Many of the personnel served for the whole four and one-half years of the active organizations.

Many names will appear repeatedly in this narrative, and there were necessarily many shifts in their positions.

I give here the names of the principal personnel, and in a later chapter I give the whole list of the Americans. Such a list of the fifty thousand Belgians is in the records of that organization.

THE LEADING PERSONNEL OF THE C.R.B.

AMBASSADOR AND MINISTER "HONORARY CHAIRMEN" OR "PATRONS"

Walter Hines Page, American Ambassador in Britain
James W. Gerard, American Ambassador in Germany

Señor Don Alfonso Merry del Val y Zulueta, Spanish Ambassador to Britain

Señor Luis Polo de Bernabé, Spanish Ambassador to Germany

Le Marqués de Villalobar, Spanish Minister to Belgium

Brand Whitlock, American Minister to Belgium

Henry van Dyke, American Minister to the Netherlands

Jonkheer De Weede, Netherlands Minister to Belgium

Dr. Johan Loudon, the Netherlands Minister of Foreign Affairs, gave us full co-operation

HONORARY VICE-CHAIRMEN

Hugh Gibson, Secretary American Legation in Brussels 1914-1916, Secretary American Embassy in London, 1916, attached to the Department of State in Washington, 1917, attached to the Versailles Peace Conference, 1918-1919

Robert P. Skinner, American Consul General in London

Señor Don José Congosto, Spanish Consul General in London

Before listing the major administrative personnel of the Commission, I may state that most of them were engineers. At all times the men who directed our London, New York, Rotterdam, Paris, and Washington offices were engineers. The directors of our office in Brussels, except for three short periods until the United States joined in the war, were also engineers. This predominance of engineers was due to the fact that the United States had led in the technical training of administrators of enterprises. Prior to the war, there were about two thousand American engineers in foreign countries, mostly in managerial or executive positions. In such positions they often had to deal with the government officials of many different nations, and to do so successfully, they had to understand the economic life of the nation, the character of its people, and its government.

Since our staff had to be neutral and since the American engineers, by experience, were able to meet the many needs, they became our recruiting ground—and they, like the rest of the staff, were willing to serve at great personal sacrifice.

THE PRINCIPAL PERSONNEL OF THE COMMISSION FOR RELIEF IN BELGIUM

CHAIRMAN

Herbert Hoover

DIRECTORS IN LONDON

Millard Hunsiker, October 1914–March 1915
Edgar Rickard, October 1914–October 1916
John Beaver White, October 1914–September 1915
William L. Honnold, October 1915–July 1916
William B. Poland, August 1916–April 1917
Millard K. Shaler, October 1914–July 1919

DIRECTORS IN BRUSSELS

Dannie N. Heineman, October–December 1914
Millard K. Shaler, August–September 1919
John F. Lucey, December 1914–February 1915
Albert N. Connett, February–April 1915
Oscar T. Crosby, May–September 1915
Vernon Kellogg, September–November 1915 and
   July–October 1916
William B. Poland, December 1915–July 1916
Warren Gregory, November 1916–March 1917
Prentiss N. Gray, March–April 1917
F. H. Chatfield, December 1918–May 1919

DIRECTORS IN ROTTERDAM

John F. Lucey, October–December 1914
Carl A. Young, January 1915–June 1916
Walter Lyman Brown, July 1916–September 1919

DIRECTORS IN NEW YORK

Lindon W. Bates, November 1914–November 1915
John Beaver White, December 1915–April 1916
John F. Lucey, May–August 1915
William L. Honnold, September 1916–November 1918
Edgar Rickard, April 1919–January 1920

DIRECTORS IN WASHINGTON

Edgar Rickard, 1917–1919
Prentiss N. Gray, 1918–1919

DIRECTORS IN PARIS

Louis Chevrillon, January 1915–July 1919
John L. Simpson, 1918–1919

DIRECTORS AT LILLE FOR NORTHERN FRANCE

Tracy B. Kittredge, November–December 1918
William Hallam Tuck, January–April 1919
Perrin C. Galpin, May–July 1919

REPRESENTATIVES, GERMAN ARMY HEADQUARTERS AT CHARLEVILLE

Vernon Kellogg, June–November 1915 and
    July 1916–January 1917
Caspar Whitney, November 1915–July 1916
Tracy B. Kittredge, June 1916–February 1917

NEW YORK COMMITTEE

S. Reading Bertron
C. A. Coffin
R. Fulton Cutting
Alexander J. Hemphill

William L. Honnold
Melville E. Stone
Oscar S. Straus
John Beaver White

JOINT LIQUIDATORS

Edgar Rickard, January 1920–1930
William B. Poland, January 1920–1930

TREASURER

Alexander J. Hemphill, New York
November 1914–January 1920

AUDITORS AND ACCOUNTANTS

Deloitte, Plender, Griffiths & Co.

THE PRINCIPAL PERSONNEL OF THE COMITÉ NATIONAL

CHAIRMAN

M. Ernest Solvay

VICE-CHAIRMEN

M. Jean Jadot   M. L. Van Der Rest

PRESIDENT

M. Emile Francqui

VICE-PRESIDENTS

M. Emmanuel Janssen   Chevalier Emmanuel de Wouters d'Oplinter
M. Firmin Van Brée

SECRETARIES

M. J. Olyff   M. A. Henry
M. Firmin Van Brée

MEMBERS OF THE COMITÉ NATIONAL

MM. Josse Allard	MM. W. Hulse
Louis Bertrand	Baron Janssen
F. Van Brée	Ch. Janssen
Ed. Bunge	Em. Janssen
Baron Evence Coppée	Baron Lambert
E. Van Elewyck	G. de Laveleye
L. Franck	Michel Levie
E. Francqui	F. Masson
Baron A. Goffinet	Comte Jean de Merode
Max Hallet	Chev. E. de Wouters d'Oplinter
Eug. Hanssens	Alfred Orban
A. Harmignie	Cl. Peten
D. Heineman	F. M. Philippson
J. de Hemptinne	F. Portmans
C. Heynderickx	Baron Ruzette
P. Van Hoegaerden	L. Solvay
Baron A. d'Huart	J. Verhaeghe

DELEGATES OF THE COMITÉ NATIONAL ASSIGNED TO THE
PROVINCIAL COMMITTEES

Antwerp: MM. Ed. Bunge; Jos. Leemans
Brabant: MM. Maurice Despret; le Baron Leon de Steenhault de
Waerbeek

Flandre Orientale: MM. Lucien Beckers; Georges Eeckhout
Flandre Occidentale: MM. le Baron Albert Ruzette; Paul de Vuyst
Hainaut: MM. Albert Francois; Eug. Richoux
Liége: MM. Henri Le Bœuf; Herman de Woelmont
Limbourg: MM. Jos. Verwilghen; Albert Warnant
Luxembourg: MM. Alfred Bouvier; Norbert Diderrich
Namur: MM. Georges Van Dievoet; Leon de Lhoneux

DELEGATES OF THE COMITÉ NATIONAL ASSIGNED TO C.R.B. OFFICES IN LONDON AND ROTTERDAM

MM. Edgar Sengier   J. van den Branden

REPRESENTATIVES OF THE COMMISSION FOR RELIEF IN BELGIUM FROM TIME TO TIME ON THE COMITÉ NATIONAL

John F. Lucey	William B. Poland
Albert N. Connett	Warren Gregory
Oscar T. Crosby	Prentiss N. Gray

Vernon Kellogg

PRINCIPAL PERSONNEL OF THE COMITÉ DU NORD DE LA FRANCE

PRESIDENT

MM. Louis Guerin   to July 1918
    Maurice Le Blan   July 1918–July 1919

ADMINISTRATOR

M. Edmond Labbé

MEMBERS FROM THE OCCUPIED DISTRICTS

District of Lille	Senateur Gustave Dron
District of Laon	Senateur Ermant; M. Blondet
District of Mézières	M. Camion; M. Gailly
District of Longwy	M. Marc Raty
District of Valenciennes	M. Jules Turbot
District of Saint-Quentin	M. A. Gibert
District of Vervins	M. Adolphe Berteaux
District of Charleville	M. Georges Camion

CHAPTER 8

PERSONALITIES
IN THE RELIEF ORGANIZATION

Since great personalities will appear in this narrative, it is desirable at once to give some appraisal of them and their relations to the Relief organization. They include high officials of the United States, Belgium, Britain, France, Spain, and The Netherlands.

In a previous chapter I have given the forces which surrounded us and the character of the men with whom we worked. But a more intimate glimpse of their personalities is important for the record.

I may state at once that except for a few British, French, and especially German military officers, all the men with whom the C.R.B. was compelled to do business were men of personal courtesy and manners befitting their important positions.

AMERICAN OFFICIALS

AMBASSADOR TO GREAT BRITAIN WALTER HINES PAGE

Above all others, American Ambassador Walter Hines Page was the leader among the officials in the creation and support of the C.R.B. Page was one of those blossoms of American life which justify our civilization. When I say that he was a great mind, a distinguished scholar, a great editor, the soul of intellectual integrity, a man of sympathy and kindness, unbreakable in friendship, almost fanatically devoted to service of his country, I feel that I am writing the presentation paragraph for an honorary college degree. Yet this praise can be written of him with complete fidelity. He died of illness,

39

brought on by exhaustion, six weeks after the Armistice. During the four years of the C.R.B., he was an unfailing mainstay with the British Foreign Office, where his personal friendship with Foreign Minister Sir Edward Grey helped us greatly.

AMBASSADOR TO GERMANY JAMES W. GERARD

Before I met Ambassador James W. Gerard, he had been depicted to me as a typical Tammany lawyer whose appointment had been imposed upon an unwilling President by a crooked political machine. Instead of a political ogre I found a man of fine personality, of great intellectual insight, helpful, courageous, who at once inspired confidence in his integrity. When I first called at our Embassy in Berlin early in 1915, he met me at the door, saying: "We are all for you here. What can we do?"

I have recounted earlier in these pages the many dealings of the Relief through him with German officials in Berlin. He opened every German official door for us and did not leave us on the doorstep. He brought skill and, where necessary, real punch to our negotiations. At all times, until he was recalled from Germany when we withdrew all our Ambassadors to the Central Empires on February 3, 1917, he stood ready to catch the ball and run with it. Whenever he smelled danger, he acted without our having to appeal to him. He sought no publicity out of our activities but at every turn single-mindedly pressed for the success of our work.

MINISTER TO BELGIUM BRAND WHITLOCK

Brand Whitlock occupied a most difficult post. His difficulty was, however, that he was a poet by nature and a novelist by profession. During the time he served in Belgium prior to his withdrawal on our declaration of war in April, 1917, he wrote the greater part of two novels and a lot of poetry. Keenly aware of the surge of events around him, he devoted many hours a day to writing and polishing his voluminous *Journal*. Parts of it were subsequently published, and it is an admirable contribution to American literature. He was sympathetic with our work, wanted to be helpful, and when the way was pointed out, he did act.

Being a sensitive soul who shrank from the rough stuff of dealing with the German officials, he had to be prodded constantly by our C.R.B. Directors and also by Hugh Gibson, the First Secretary of the Legation. But few members of our staff ever met him. In fact, he never really knew what the C.R.B. was doing. For over two and a half years, the Legation and the offices of the C.R.B. were less than a mile apart, yet he visited our offices only once. His published *Journal* is therefore naturally deficient as an authentic record of our doings. This is not said in criticism, but merely as an indication of his dislike of dealing with the harsh realities, and relief in war is harsh.

HUGH GIBSON

Hugh Gibson, as Secretary of the Legation in Brussels, from the first moment was a part of the C.R.B. He plunged into every problem with great sense; he provided real friendship and willing aid to all of our American members. He had a superlative wit and was at all times a sunny soul, cheerful amid the greatest discouragement. We came to rely upon him for all our problems in Belgium, whether with the Belgians or the Germans.

Apparently, Gibson's energetic work, not only in the Relief, but in the other functions of our Legation, stirred up a subconscious resentment of him by Whitlock, which is only too evident in Whitlock's *Journal*. Finally, in the summer of 1916, Whitlock asked for Gibson's removal, to the great loss of the Commission. He was promptly recruited by Ambassador Page as First Secretary of our Legation in London.

To those who knew of Gibson's devotion, his burden at our Legation at Brussels, and his constant effort to protect and support his chief, it was a painful episode, and left the Minister a smaller man than he deserved to be. For Gibson was a good American. Whitlock's attacks on Gibson in his *Journal* leave a most painful impression. This injustice was proved by Gibson's rise to the highest levels in our Foreign Service.

AMERICAN MINISTER TO HOLLAND HENRY VAN DYKE

Dr. Henry van Dyke was appointed Minister to The Netherlands by President Wilson before there were signs of war in Europe. He was a literary man, a poet, and a distinguished professor of literature. He proved ill adapted to the conditions of a European war. He was always friendly to the C.R.B. but had little comprehension of the organization.

PRESIDENT WOODROW WILSON

President Wilson was an ardent supporter of the C.R.B. from its beginning. Prior to our entry into the war, he gave yeoman's service in our various crises. After our entry into the war, I was at the same time Chairman of the C.R.B., Food Administrator, and member of his War Council. He gave unfailing support to the C.R.B. in its difficulties and its finance. I have no need to describe his personality, which came to be so well known throughout the world.

THE AMERICAN CABINET

The C.R.B. had a steadfast champion in Secretary of State Robert Lansing. Again, there is no need to describe his personality, which is well known to the world.

And among our staunch supporters were Secretary of Agriculture David F. Houston and Secretary of the Interior Franklin K. Lane.

COLONEL EDWARD M. HOUSE

From the beginning of the war, President Wilson sent Colonel House upon many important missions to Europe. He was a quiet little man, a shrewd observer, and a skillful negotiator. His reliance upon the C.R.B. for information about political forces in motion and his journeys over Europe soon led to his ardent support of the C.R.B.

OUR BELGIAN COLLEAGUES

I could recite the names of thousands of dedicated Belgian patriots—men and women alike—who co-operated with us in our joint service, but space permits mention of only a few of them.

EMILE FRANCQUI

Outstanding among all the Belgians of his time was Emile Franc-qui. He had a gruff personality, but with great loyalties, affections, and devoted friendships. He was a natural administrator. His quickness and adroitness of mind were equal to any sort of intellectual battle. He had a fine sense of humor and in his many narratives about our work showed a talent for both lucid expression and dramatization.

Francqui demonstrated a devotion to his countrymen seldom equaled. He not only brought his great abilities to the Relief but in later years represented the Belgians at the Peace Conference and at every other important international negotiation. We remained affectionate friends until his death on November 16, 1935.

FIRMIN VAN BRÉE

Another outstanding Belgian who worked with us was Firmin Van Brée, First Secretary and later Vice-President, of the Comité National. He was the administrator who tied up all the strings of detail. A man of fine personality, education, and devotion, he was a favorite of all our Americans—and their friend and defender in all their troubles.

CHEVALIER EDMOND DE WOUTERS

Still another great Belgian who remains indelibly in our C.R.B. memories was Chevalier Edmond de Wouters. I had first met him in China when he was in the Belgian Foreign Service. We arranged that he be the liaison officer between the C.R.B. and the Comité National in Brussels. He was a most able man, a gentle and devoted soul—as was also his wife.

EDGAR SENGIER

Another of the outstanding Belgians associated with us was Edgar Sengier. He was a man of great abilities. He was a member of the C.R.B. and, at the same time, of the Comité National. His talents were reaffirmed by his great rise in Belgian life.

PAUL HYMANS

One of the outstanding Belgians of his times was Paul Hymans, the Belgian Minister in London and subsequently Minister of Foreign Affairs. Many of these chapters show that there was no problem we could put to him to which he did not immediately apply his full energies and his great abilities.

FERNAND BAETENS

Fernand Baetens was a Belgian and an important member of the C.R.B. in our Brussels office. After the United States entered the war, we appointed him our Director in Belgium. His ability and tact did much to make the work of our Spanish and Dutch representatives effective.

THE MEMBERS OF THE COMITÉ NATIONAL

The members of the Comité National and its provincial committees were eminent men, and although of many political facets, they formed a solid front of devotion in the service of their suffering compatriots.

BRITISH OFFICIALS

The life of the C.R.B. necessarily depended upon the support of the highest British officials.

LORD GREY

Minister of Foreign Affairs Sir Edward Grey, later Viscount Grey of Falladon, was one of the greatest statesmen in the war period. He was a man of great humanitarian spirit and a personality that won respect and affection from every associate. Without his constant defense and support, the Relief of Belgium would have collapsed a score of times. His was a difficult task because of the constant attacks on the Commission by such militarist leaders as Winston Churchill and Lord Kitchener and their successors.

PRIME MINISTER HERBERT ASQUITH

Herbert Asquith was Prime Minister of Britain when the war began. Like all British leaders, he was a man of distinguished abilities, courage, and a pleasing personality. While he did not oppose our work, he did at first oppose any financial aid for us. But through the influence of Grey and Lloyd George, he later joined in our support. At one time, when we were under much Parliamentary fire, he made an address at Mansion House in our support which silenced our critics—for a while.

PRIME MINISTER LLOYD GEORGE

Lloyd George was the most adroit political leader to rise to power in the war. He was a man with a high sense of human sympathies. As Chancellor of the Exchequer, he originally teamed with Churchill and Kitchener in opposing the Commission, but when convinced, he became a most loyal and vigorous friend of the Relief. This narrative shows that after he became Prime Minister, he never wavered in our support throughout many crises.

LORD ROBERT CECIL

Lord Robert Cecil, as Under Minister of Foreign Affairs, was one of those rare souls with great human sympathy and skill in bringing it to practical realization. He believed in our mission and gave to us every co-operation in difficult times.

THE DUKE OF NORFOLK

The Duke of Norfolk, at my request, undertook to organize the British Commonwealth for our charitable support and continued as its Chairman during the war. He always came to our defense with British officials. The devoted work of his Committee is amply evidenced by the total sums it collected in our behalf, which amounted to about $16,641,034.85.

LORD EUSTACE PERCY

Lord Eustace Percy, a member of the Foreign Office staff, was appointed by Sir Edward Grey as the Commission's liaison officer with the various British departments. His fine idealism, high intelligence, and capacity for hard work were rare in any country. His sweet personality endeared him to all the members of the C.R.B. He knew all the paths through the red tape of government. He quickly developed a friendship for the Commission, and he never flagged in supporting us among his official colleagues. Had he been a member of the Commission he could not have been more loyal to its purposes. Much of the success of the Commission was due to him.

THE FRENCH OFFICIALS

PRESIDENT POINCARÉ

President Raymond Poincaré was a leader in France for more than a score of years. One can say no more of his personality and his abilities than that he was a great Frenchman. Our relations with him were exclusively during the time he was President of France. Under the French Constitution, the power of the President of France, except in crises of ministerial change, amounted to little but friendly counsel and moral leadership. However, President Poincaré gave us all the support that his authority permitted, and he was constant in his expressions of gratitude of the French people.

PREMIER CLEMENCEAU

Georges Clemenceau came into the Premiership on November 16, 1917, and therefore after we had withdrawn our Americans from Belgium and Northern France at the American entry into the war. In my book on *The Ordeal of Woodrow Wilson*, I have described the character of the "Old Tiger" at length. He was absolutely unfailing in his support of the C.R.B., even during the low point of France during the war.

FOREIGN MINISTER THÉOPHILE DELCASSÉ

Foreign Minister Delcassé was timid in his relations with the C.R.B. He ultimately responded to the pressures of his colleagues.

FOREIGN MINISTER ARISTIDE BRIAND

Unlike his predecessor, Aristide Briand was always ready to act, and we often had the support of this courageous statesman. His personality and character stand high in world records and need no amplification here.

MINISTER OF FINANCE ALEXANDRE RIBOT

Our major administrative dealings with the French primarily involved the shifting Ministers of Finance, Food Blockade, Shipping, and other departments. We had efficient guidance from Finance Minister Ribot.

LOUIS CHEVRILLON

Louis Chevrillon, the C.R.B. Director in Paris, was our major agent in coping with the complexities of French administrative action. An engineering colleague of mine before the war, he was a man of high standing in France who commanded entry into every ministerial office and was a personal friend of Poincaré and Briand. The narrative of our entire four and one-half years is studded with evidence of his labors and his devotion.

THE SPANISH OFFICIALS

The Spanish Ambassadors and Ministers to London, Berlin, and Belgium were a mainstay of the C.R.B. They never failed in every support to the Relief which their official positions permitted—and at times even more.

AMBASSADOR TO BRITAIN MERRY DEL VAL Y ZULUETA

I cannot overstate the qualities and zeal of the Spanish Ambassador to Britain, Señor Don Alfonso Merry del Val y Zulueta. He was a man with all those fine qualities of mind and courtesy that his race produces. He supported the C.R.B. from its beginning to its end. He not only took the time and trouble to understand our purpose and our operations but was at every instant ready to join in our battles. After America entered the war, he became the great mainstay of protection for the Relief, and the account of his role during this trying period is a monument to his infinite courtesy, kindness, and courage.

MINISTER TO BELGIUM, THE MARQUIS DE VILLALOBAR

When it was necessary to use our Minister Chairmen in Belgium, we found that we could make more headway with the Germans through the Spanish Minister, the Marquis de Villalobar, than anyone else in Brussels. He was a man of unlimited courage, willing at all times to act, and he acted effectively. He had been born misshapen, with stump legs and arms and without ears and hair. His family, one of the most important in Spain, had kept him hidden away with a most unusual tutor. This tutor gave a unique education to an extraordinarily brilliant, crippled boy. In time, Villalobar was able to secure artificial parts for his deficiencies. He obtained a junior position in the Spanish Foreign Office and rose by sheer ability to the rank of Ambassador. He was most formal, always immaculately dressed, indicating little of his disabilities. He did not like Americans much. But he was devoted to the Relief and after the United States joined the war became our major support in Belgium.

AMBASSADOR TO GERMANY LUIS POLO DE BERNABÉ

The Spanish Ambassador to Germany, Señor Luis Polo de Bernabé, was always on hand to help in our behalf. After the United States joined in the war and Gerard was withdrawn from his post, he was our effective guardian in Berlin.

THE NETHERLANDS OFFICIALS

NETHERLANDS MINISTER OF FOREIGN AFFAIRS JOHAN LOUDON

Our strength in Holland came from Jonkheer J. Loudon, Minister of Foreign Affairs. Rotterdam was the port where all of our ships discharged for transport by rail or canal into Belgium. We quickly established direct relations with Minister Loudon, and he appointed a delegate to our Rotterdam office who relieved us of many difficulties.

Beyond that, he was ever ready to give instructions to our Netherlands Minister Patrons.

NETHERLANDS MINISTER TO BELGIUM JONKHEER DE WEEDE

Jonkheer De Weede, Netherlands Minister to Belgium, was one of our protecting Chairmen and always willing to help, although his attitude toward the Germans was necessarily tempered by the constant jeopardy in which his country stood. After our American staff withdrew from Belgium, he became one of the Chairmen of the Dutch-Spanish Committee which provided guardianship of the German guarantees for the C.R.B. He was a steadfast man.

THE GERMAN OFFICIALS

CHANCELLOR VON BETHMANN-HOLWEG

Bethmann-Hollweg was a typical Junker aristocrat, abrupt and positive. He did exert himself to help protect the C.R.B. from submarines.

FOREIGN MINISTER GOTTLIEB VON JAGOW

The outstanding German of high official position who was devoted to the purpose of the C.R.B. was German Foreign Minister von Jagow. He was a man of deep religious and humanitarian feeling. This record shows his frequent intervention to overrule Governor General von Bissing on our behalf.

MINISTER OF THE INTERIOR THEODOR LEWALD

Minister Theodor Lewald had served on German official missions to the United States. He was a man of humane spirit. Aside from the limitations necessarily imposed by the war, he was friendly to Americans. The German Food Administration was at times in his department. He was on our side at all points where we came in contact.

MAJOR FRIEDRICH VON KESSLER

Major Friedrich von Kessler of the German Intelligence Service was assigned by the German General Staff as the principal liaison officer between the German armies in the North of France and Eastern Belgium and the C.R.B. at their headquarters in Charleville, France.

Major von Kessler was not articulate on humanitarian matters, but on many occasions he stood up to his superiors at the risk of his future and prevented great ills from befalling the C.R.B.

Von Kessler had an assistant, Count Wengersky, a Reserve Officer. He was always helpful and especially liked the occasional supplementary ration of ham furnished by the C.R.B.

Von Kessler spoke perfect English and was entirely correct from a social point of view. His greatest service to the C.R.B. was the selection of seven liaison officers for each of our regional offices with each German Army operational area in Northern France and Belgium. These German liaison officers were all former businessmen who had been called to serve in the German Army. They all spoke English, and most of them had had business experience in the United States. When they came to understand our purpose and learn the character of the members of our staff, they practically became members of the C.R.B.

Major von Kessler, with the approval or direction of the German General Staff, did much to make our position workable in Occupied Belgium. He organized liaison officers from the German General Staff in our Brussels office to deal with Governor General von Bissing's many aides.

GENERAL VON BISSING

This narrative records our constant friction with the Governor General in Belgium, Baron Moritz Ferdinand von Bissing, and his chief aide, Baron Oscar von der Lancken. Von Bissing was a pompous, arrogant little man who disliked all Americans and resented the independence of our organization as imposed by the Allied Governments and the German civil authorities in Berlin. He wore his uniform, including his helmet and sword, at all of our meetings with him. We often speculated how he would look without these trappings.

Gibson opined of him that he was the only German general who could strut sitting down. As this text has shown, we were frequently compelled to get him overruled by the civil officials from Berlin or the General Staff at Charleville. This did not instill any affection for us in von Bissing. He oozed hate of all Americans.

Baron von der Lancken, his chief assistant in dealing with the Commission, had no enthusiasm for either Americans or Belgians.

FIRST YEAR
November 1, 1914 to November 1, 1915

CHAPTER 9

FINANCING THE RELIEF OF BELGIUM

Our financial difficulties began at the very birth of the Commission. At the Embassy meeting on the eighteenth of October, the representatives of the exiled Belgian Government had promised us £2,000,-000 ($9,600,000), and Francqui promised he would raise a loan, guaranteed by the Belgian banks, of another £600,000 ($2,880,000). The British Government, through Ambassador Page, assured us of a contribution of £100,000 ($480,000).

The Belgian Government soon reduced its promise to £1,000,000 (about $4,800,000). Francqui was unable to persuade the banks to make his loan. The British kept their promise of $480,000.

It quickly became evident that the Belgians had greatly underestimated the cost of even their minimum of needed imports. While their original estimate was about $4,000,000 a month, it was certain that the minimum for Belgium alone would be about $8,000,000 a month. Our problem was further complicated by the fact that under war conditions we had to make commitments for purchase of supplies and charter of ships at least three months in advance if we were to assure a regular stream of food to these hungry people.

It was obvious that charity could not supply these amounts and that if the Belgians were to survive, we would need financial support from the Allied Governments. On November 3, 1914, prior to my visit to Belgium, I addressed our Ambassador Honorary Chairmen on the problem, and the figure I used also quickly proved to be an underestimate. My letter was as follows:

. . . the food supply of Belgium is exhausted and . . . the problem now confronting us is of wider import than was originally expected . . . the absolute minimum of foodstuffs which will be required as from the 1st of November is 80,000 tons of cereals per month together with some amount of bacon or lard, this being calculated upon the provision of a ration per diem of 10 oz. per capitum, or considerably less than one-half of a soldier's ration. This . . . is in contrast to the normal imports and products of Belgium of something over 250,000 tons . . . per month. . . .

It appears to us that this emergency of provisioning a whole nation is of such an order that we cannot depend upon the efforts of private philanthropy for its . . . solution and that the brunt of this must fall upon the three Governments which are so critically involved in this situation . . . Belgium, England, and France. Whilst every possible device to secure private philanthropy will be used by this Commission and no doubt will [have results] . . . there still remains the fact that such a supply is not dependable and that . . . we . . . [must] have a substratum of government subventions. It is useless to tell us that when we have expended some allotment of money that we can apply for more because if this problem is to be handled we . . . [must] make arrangements . . . three or more months [in advance] and we cannot depend on the "gifts of the gods" to meet such eventualities. For transportation purposes we must charter ships extending over months. . . .

Our Ambassador Chairmen promptly indicated that they could not undertake to arrange subsidies from governments. However, they arranged an interview for me with British Foreign Minister Sir Edward Grey on November 5, 1914, to discuss the possibility of such financial help from the British. Sir Edward was most sympathetic and interested in our effort, but he had to contend with much opposition among the Cabinet, particularly the military. The essential paragraphs of the memorandum I dictated for the benefit of my colleagues immediately after our talk were as follows:

I stated to Sir Edward:
. . . The situation appeared to us so critical that we have devoted all the

energy we are capable of to securing some immediate relief, and although we have had our organization in existence scarcely ten days, we have nevertheless delivered some 4,500 tons of food into Belgium, we have some 10,000 tons which will be delivered within another ten days, and we have something like 25,000 tons in sight in various quarters of the world. . . .

This minimum of monthly requirement of 80,000 tons will involve an expenditure of between £800,000 and £1,000,000 per month, and this expenditure will be necessary over the next eight months at least. . . .

This problem therefore becomes so large as to be far beyond solution by charitable and philanthropic effort. It is one of those problems which can only be solved by a substantial substratum of government guarantee. . . . We have inaugurated . . . a vigorous publicity on behalf of the Commission, with a view to stimulating as far as possible the sympathies and help of the good people of America, Australia, Spain, Canada, and elsewhere. We have had the most gratifying response. . . .

As in all philanthropic efforts the first flow no doubt will be large, but . . . if we are to provide . . . these people with . . . constant and regular [supplies] it is necessary for us to be assured that we will have financial strength with which to carry the business on systematically. . . .

The active members of this Commission are . . . prepared to devote their time and pay their own expenses in this work.

. . . Every penny which we receive will be devoted to one purpose of securing foodstuffs and their transportation and . . . delivery into the hands of the community in Belgium. . . .

Sir Edward undertook to discuss the application with his colleagues but stated that the continued requisition of native food by the Germans made it very difficult for the British to take a favorable view of themselves contributing money, as this was in effect supplying food to the German Army.

Sir Edward stated the gift of £100,000 from the British Government to the destitute in Belgium had been paid. . . .

It will be seen that I was at this time still under the illusion that the estimated Belgian needs were correct.

As a side issue during this interview, I suggested to Sir Edward that it would be most helpful to us if he would appoint a liaison official from the Foreign Office through whom we could arrange our relations with the different British departments with which we would be dealing. I stated that such a representative would have complete access to all our records. Sir Edward appointed Lord Eustace Percy, a most able and sympathetic young man, who soon became our most devoted supporter.

The Spanish Ambassador in London, Señor Merry del Val, inquired about our financial situation. I replied:

24th November 1914

YOUR EXCELLENCY,

Señor Don José Congosto spoke to me this morning with regard to the contribution which we are hoping for from the British Government.

I am sending you copies of some telegrams that we have this morning from Rotterdam, which only emphasize the gravity of the situation with which we are faced and the absolute necessity that we should have further resources placed at our disposal. The collection of gift-food in various parts of the world is a slow business, and there is nothing that is going to save these people from sheer death but real hard cash. . . .

I do not know how we can advance the matter any further than we have done. I recently addressed a letter on the subject to Lord Eustace Percy at the Foreign Office . . . and asked him what progress was being made. He reported that he did not think there was much hope of a favourable response. Therefore it seems to me that something more must be done in the matter.

HERBERT HOOVER

Three weeks after my meeting with Sir Edward, having received no word from him concerning the conclusions reached by his colleagues, I wrote to him:

LONDON, 25 November 1914

DEAR SIR EDWARD:

With regard to the petition . . . to you on the 5th of November for financial assistance from the British Government toward this work of the Commission, I trust you will forgive me if I revert to the subject.

Although at that time I felt we were all deeply impressed with the necessities of the civil population of Belgium, every event which has happened since has . . . [emphasized] the gravity of the situation. . . . We have made some progress in the direction of the obtaining of funds, but they are wholly and absolutely inadequate to our requirements. . . .

Mr. Frederick Palmer, whom we look upon as the most statesmanlike of the American Newspaper Correspondents, recently visited Germany and at our request endeavoured to formulate some opinion as to the attitude of the Germans to the question of the feeding of the Belgians, and I send you herewith a copy of the statement which he has handed to us.[1]

HERBERT HOOVER

Determined to explore every avenue for aid in saving these people, I telegraphed Ambassador Gerard at Berlin on November 27 from Rotterdam, where I was at the moment, suggesting that the German Government contribute to the Commission:

The sympathetic attitude of the German Government toward the efforts of the American people to provision the civil population of Belgium leads me to again transgress your attention to the desirability of the German Government entering into this wide humanitarian movement by a direct contribution to our fund. The minimum required amounts to fully twenty million marks per month. . . .

I then hinted that the German Government might reap some good will by such action and continued:

. . . While the American people are responding wonderfully and generously to our appeal, the flow of charity can never supply the demand and such support can from the nature of things be only temporary.

I did not expect any handsome response from this quarter.

On December 10, I informed Ambassador Page that Francqui's proposed loan from the Belgian banks had evaporated. I also informed him that the assurance of $9,600,000 promised us by the exiled Belgian Government at our first meeting in his office on October 18 had been reduced.

Since Sir Edward had plainly indicated on November 5 that the German requisitioning of native food in Belgium stood in the way of a British contribution to the C.R.B., I enlisted the aid of Ambassador Gerard in Berlin, and on December 26, 1914, he obtained an

[1] See pages 22-23 for Palmer's opinion.

undertaking from the Germans that they would cease this practice (see Chapter 11).

Then the Germans gave the British a new reason for refusing help. In January, 1915, they began levying indemnities on the Belgian people of 40,000,000 francs a month (about $7,600,000). They insisted that the provincial governments issue bonds to the Belgian banks for this amount and that the banks discount the bonds in francs and give this money to the Germans, who used it mostly for expenditures in Belgium. The scheme amounted to an inflation of Belgian currency, as the banks had no other recourse than to the printing press. The Germans had at the time of the invasion promised that there would be no annexation of Belgium and no indemnities levied against its people. The Allied Governments were naturally indignant at this new turn of events.

Sir Edward had encouraged me to keep in contact with him, and on January 13, 1915, Lord Percy arranged another interview for me. My memorandum at the time to my colleagues on this meeting was as follows:

... [Sir Edward] stated that ... so long as the Germans continued to levy indemnities on the Belgian people the British Government could not be expected to contribute to this work.

I represented to Sir Edward that the British people had entered upon the greatest war of history for the sole purpose of maintaining the Belgian people; that it appeared to me that after this war had been fought at the enormous loss of human life and property ... it would be a cynical ending if the civil population of Belgium had become extinct in the process; that it was of little use to fight the war and find that only an empty husk remained; that if the food supplies of this Commission were to cease for a week the decimation of this people would be begun and it would be completed within ninety days.

I informed him that at our last interview he had spoken strongly as to the British inability to help us because of the ... levies [on native food] by the Germans, and that in consequence I had made representations to Mr. Gerard. ... [As a result] Mr. Gerard had ultimately been able to secure from the German Government an undertaking that no more food would be ... [requisitioned] in Belgium. I informed Sir Edward further that I felt that when we succeeded in this matter we would be entitled to support from the British Government and was disappointed that further stipulations were now raised, and that I thought it would be fair to me to know if we could expect financial support from the Government if we could succeed in these further . . . [requirements]. Sir Edward said that he considered, without committing his colleagues, that we should be entitled to such support.

RAISING MONEY BY AN EXCHANGE OPERATION

In the meantime, we had developed a plan by which we might add to our resources through setting up an exchange operation. The idea was that the Commission would accept money from persons the world over who wished to make payments to persons in Belgium. We would buy food with this money and pay the remittances out of the currency we received from the sale of rations to those Belgians who could afford to buy them. Since the Allies prohibited exchange with German-occupied areas, I had to secure their approval of this plan.

During my discussion with Sir Edward on January 13, I referred to this matter and at his request sent him a memorandum on the subject the same day. After detailing the proposal, I continued:

. . . With this end in view, I took up the question of the balances held by various Belgian banks in London and New York, and I could secure the payment to me of a considerable amount of such money as against the payment, on the other hand, of local currency in Brussels. This transaction does not amount to the importation of actual new money into Belgium, and is not in effect trading with the enemy, because such payments would be made under proper safeguards to Belgians only. . . .

The question of this exchange has an humanitarian aspect outside of the work of this Commission, in that some of the Belgian banks, having exported their balances prior to the occupation, are now in the position of no longer being able to pay out to their depositors in Belgium, thus inflicting a new order of hardship on these people. By taking advantage of this system . . . these people would be relieved. We should of course be glad to agree that any moneys coming into our hands in this manner would be used for the purchase of foodstuffs on this side, and that any payments which we make on the other side should be made to Belgians only.

HERBERT HOOVER

On January 21, Lord Percy arranged a meeting for me to discuss this exchange proposal with Lloyd George, Chancellor of the Exchequer, Sir John Simon, the Attorney General, and Lord Emmott, who was in charge of matters related to trading with the enemy. Lord Percy was also present.

I quote here at some length my usual memorandum for my colleagues. The grammar and punctuation are bad, but my defense is that it was dictated late at night with no opportunity for correction and, moreover, with no expectation that it would ever appear in print. This memorandum is, however, an important part of the record. It clearly delineates the point of view of the British militarists, particularly that of Winston Churchill, First Lord of the Admiralty, and Lord Kitchener, Minister of War. But of greater significance, it memorializes the successful conversion to our camp of Lloyd George, who had hitherto sided with Churchill and Kitchener.

. . . Mr. Lloyd George stated that he had put his veto upon the project, because he felt that, indirect as the matter was, it was certainly assisting the enemy, and that this assistance would take place in several ways. In the first instance, we were giving the Belgians more food resources with which to . . . [supply] requisitions in food by the Germans; that we were giving them more resources generally with which to . . . [support] monetary levies; and that beyond all this, in relieving the Germans from the necessity of feeding the civil population we were directly prolonging the war, which was bound to be one of wholly economic character and that economic pressure was the principal method by which the Allies would ultimately win. He expressed the belief that the Germans would, in the last resort, provision the people of Belgium; that our action was akin to the provisioning the civil population of a besieged city and thus prolonging the resistance of the garrison; that he was wholly opposed to our operations, benevolent and humane as they were; and that therefore he could not see his way to grant our request.

I pointed out that, first, as to the requisitioning of food, the Germans had given an undertaking that after the first of January no such requisitions would be made, and I read to him the undertaking which had been given to the American Minister in Berlin and informed him that we were satisfied from the many agents that we had in Belgium[2] that the Germans were carrying this out with the utmost scrupulousness. I furthermore informed him that the Germans had impressed none of our actual food. Also, I stated that I did not believe that the feeding of the civil population increased the resources which they had available for money levies; that we were introducing no new money into Belgium, but were simply giving circulation to the money already existing, and that there was no danger of the Germans taking the money which we collected for foodstuffs because that money was . . . [under the protection of] the American Minister.

On the second point, as to whether the Germans would ultimately provision the civil population, I told him that I was satisfied that they would not do so; that when we undertook this labor we undertook it with the greatest reluctance and our first move was to satisfy ourselves that this population would starve unless America intervened and converted the hitherto negative quality of neutrality into one of positive neutrality; that as proof that the Germans would not provision the civil population I thought it was desirable that he should understand the German views on this question, and I recited to him the confirmation by the German military of the current statement in Germany that there was no clause in the Hague Convention obliging the Germans to provision the civil population of Belgium; on the contrary, it incidentally provided that the civil population should support the military. I told him further, that the Germans contended that the Belgians were a people of great resources, that these resources would become valuable at once on a partial recovery of industry, that this recovery of industry could take place instantly they were given a port through which they could trade with the neutral world, that in taking the port of Antwerp and opening it to neutral ships they had given the Belgian civil population a means of provisioning themselves, but that this outlet had been blocked by the British Navy and the British must therefore bear the responsibility. Further, that the Belgian population, by continuing its hostility and its passive resistance was assisting the Allies by compelling the Germans to operate the public services, rendering . . . [factories] useless to them, also the arsenals, and requiring from them a

[2] This was prior to the death-dealing amendment to those undertakings inflicted by the German Governor General in Belgium, Ferdinand von Bissing.

considerable army of occupation; and that as the Allies do all this they must take the responsibility of these people starving. Furthermore, the Germans contend that while they have ample food supplies to carry their own people through the struggle, they have not sufficient to carry on their backs the 10,000,000 people in Belgium and France inside their lines; and that as they are struggling for national existence they must feed their own people and attend to their own military exigencies first. I pointed out that I did not offer these arguments as my own but to illustrate the fixity of mind by which the German people justify their action in refusing to feed the Belgians . . . [I] asked him if he could conceive for one moment that with this . . . conviction . . . they were right and the Allies were wrong, they would be likely to feed the Belgians. I pointed out that starvation had actually occurred in Belgium; that some, although perhaps little, riot had occurred. . . . I further pointed out the position of the French people in the Meuse Valley, who had not had our assistance and were dying of starvation although under German occupation . . . I expressed the conviction that the Germans would never feed the civil population.

He denounced the whole of this as a monstrous attitude; to which I replied that, be that as it might, one matter stood out in my mind and that was that the English people had undertaken this war for the avowed purpose of protecting the existence of small nations, of vindicating the guaranteed neutrality by which small nations might exist, for the avowed purpose of guaranteeing to the world the continuance of democracy as against autocracy in government; and that it would be an empty victory if one of the most democratic of the world's races should be extinguished in the process and ultimate victory should be marked by an empty husk. I said that the English people were great enough to disregard the doubtful military value of advantages in favor of assurances that these people should survive, and I felt the obligation went even further than mere acquiescence in our work and extended to an opportunity to the English to add to their laurels by showing magnanimity toward these people, a magnanimity which would outlast all the bitterness of this war.

Mr. Lloyd George stated to his colleagues abruptly: "I am convinced. You have my permission. I would be obliged if you gentlemen would settle the details of the machinery necessary to carry it out." Then turning to me he said that I would forgive him for running away, but that he felt the world would yet be indebted to the American people for the most magnanimous action which neutrality had yet given way to.

With this endorsement by Lloyd George, we put the exchange plan into effect. It was a good idea, but the sums received were not as consequential as we had hoped. (The total over the four years came to a little over $6,000,000.)

After my interview with Sir Edward on January 13, I had telegraphed Ambassador Gerard at Berlin through our London Embassy in order to lay the groundwork for a solution which I had in mind. It read:

LONDON, 13 January 1915

GERARD, BERLIN

Had a conference today with Sir Edward Grey on the question of the British Government and the financial support of the work of this Commission. Sir Edward said that so long as the Germans continued to levy indemnities on the Belgians . . . the British Government could not give any financial assistance to this Commission whatever, but that if the Germans would undertake that no such indemnities should be levied the British Government would consider themselves under the obligation of supporting the Commission largely. Inasmuch as the indemnities levied in Belgium at the present time cannot be yielding any very considerable actual payments it occurs to me that possibly your recent success in securing amelioration of the food levies might be extended to money also and might even be coupled with the stipulation that the British should support the Commission.

[HOOVER]

At this time our financial position was desperate. Our February 1 balance sheet showed that we had received about $5,200,000 from the Belgian and British Governments, which amount represented the actual deliveries in Belgium. However, we had been able to deliver only about 150,000 tons, while the Belgians' estimated requirements for this period were approximately 270,000 tons. Worse still, it was necessary to make contracts for purchase and transport at least three months in advance, which we had done for about 400,000 tons at a liability of about $30,000,000. Our only income against this sum was from the flow of world charity, which, by February 1, for actual cash gifts and gifts in kind en route, did not exceed $6,000,000. With the failure or inability of the Belgian Government to keep its promises, my colleagues and I were liable for payment of food purchased and the charters upon arrival of the ships in Rotterdam. Even assuming that we sold these cargoes, we would have starved the Belgians, and in addition, the loss on resale under these circumstances would have exceeded the amount of all of our combined private fortunes. We were not capitalists; we were professional men.

A few days later I resolved to go to Berlin and personally present these problems to the civilian heads of the German Government. On January 27, I asked Ambassador Page to advise Secretary of State Bryan of my intention and to urge that he encourage Ambassador Gerard to provide all possible informal assistance in my mission.

We had a powerful weapon in our arsenal—the belligerents' desire for favorable neutral opinion, especially that of the United States. I decided to wield it in full. I had in mind several alternatives which might result from my visit:

(1) If the German civil officials wanted the Relief to continue, and at British expense, they might give up their indemnity against the Belgians, since it was a comparatively small sum as war money went.

(2) The Germans might refuse to give up the indemnity but might nevertheless decide to help finance the Relief as an antidote to British propaganda in neutral nations, which constantly reiterated their general wickedness in Belgium, including the levying of indemnities on a helpless people.

(3) If I failed in regard to the indemnities, I should have convinced the Allies that we had done our best.

(4) If I succeeded in getting financial aid from the Germans, the Allies would probably not want their great propaganda theme with the neutrals—the Belgian outrage generally—weakened by a show of such generosity from the Germans.

I arrived in Berlin on February 1, 1915. Between then and February 9, Ambassador Gerard arranged interviews for himself and me in sequence with Under Minister of State Zimmermann, Finance Minister Helfferich, his Financial Adviser Herr Melchior, Foreign

Minister von Jagow, Imperial Chancellor von Bethmann-Hollweg, and Hjalmar Schacht, Chairman of the Reichsbank. Every evening, I prepared the usual hurried (and in places ungrammatical) notes on each of these interviews for my colleagues. I present these memoranda at length, not only because from these interviews came a favorable turn in the financing of the Relief, but also because they offer many sidelights on German civil officials and on some aspects of the war.

I discussed the indemnity question with almost all of these officials, but for the sake of brevity, I cite the memoranda of only the two most important meetings on this subject.

INTERVIEW WITH FOREIGN MINISTER VON JAGOW

BERLIN, 7 February 1915

At 4:30 I accompanied Mr. Gerard to call upon Herr von Jagow, Minister of Foreign Affairs. He told me he had some discussion with Mr. Zimmermann, and also with the Chancellor and with Dr. Helfferich, and that Dr. Helfferich was formulating a plan to solve our difficulties. He stated that of course the monthly indemnity on Belgium could not be abandoned, but the matter could be solved in another manner, and stated that we had better continue our negotiations which we were carrying on with Dr. Helfferich [for financial aid]. I stated that the proposals outlined by Dr. Helfferich were not agreeable to us, and that I felt that this matter did not lie entirely in the Finance Department, but lay largely in the Foreign Office, because it was a matter which concerned . . . [Germany's] good reputation abroad; that it seemed to me a great deal of a task to continue to feed the Belgians, no matter from what source money might be obtained, so long as the German Government continued to extract from these people a similar amount of money. I told him that as apparently the indemnity was only laid on Belgium after we had become well established in our work, I felt sometimes that we had been the cause of this terrible infliction. . . . He replied that the people of Belgium had enormous resources, and that forty million francs a month was much less than they could really afford to pay; that this was collected merely to support the occupying army under the provisions of the Hague Convention and that none of the money was sent to Germany; and he again affirmed that we should continue our negotiations with Dr. Helfferich, who, he stated, would help us in every possible way, as would the other members of the Government.

Discussion then shifted to other needs of the Commission. But I returned to the indemnity question, asking if I could speak frankly, and said

that the Germans were obviously anxious to win the good feeling of the American people; that they were most severe in their denunciation of . . . [American] lack of neutrality, and yet they did not take the most essential precautions to win and hold the esteem of the American people . . . [that] the Americans were pro-Belgian, and that it was . . . their view as to the treatment of Belgium by the Germans and their belief that the English were fighting the Belgian cause which led their feelings to lean so predominantly toward the English . . . that I was absolutely satisfied that in order to win American opinion Germany must mend her methods toward Belgium; that if Germany today would take a generous and grand view and would release the Belgians from their monthly indemnity, I believed it would do more to win American opinion than any other act possible. . . .

Mr. Gerard pointed out that he himself had been the vehicle through which the Germans had communicated their offers to the Belgians, after the taking of Liége . . . not only guarantees as to their national integrity, but also [against] large indemnities . . . therefore it was not much of a step to say now that when the Belgians are completely conquered they should at least be assured their national integrity . . . and that they should be free from . . . paying indemnities to the Germans.

He also reminded the Minister of the Chancellor's speech on the 4th August, in which assurances were given with regard to Belgium which had not yet been withdrawn.

In the interview Ambassador Gerard and I had with Chancellor von Bethmann-Hollweg, he positively refused to abandon the Belgian indemnities but did agree to find finance for us. My memorandum was:

BERLIN, 7 February 1915
At 6 o'clock I accompanied Mr. Gerard to a meeting with the Imperial Chancellor . . . von Bethmann-Hollweg. Mr. Gerard presented to him the essential facts with regard to our position: that the question of the feeding of the Belgians would soon get beyond the resources which we could command by philanthropy or from the assistance of the Belgian Government;

that if we were to feed the people of Northern France as well as the Belgians, we should require 40 or 50 million marks per month; and that the Allied Governments had refused to come to our assistance so long as the Germans continued their monetary levies on Belgium. The Chancellor stated at once with emphasis that the Germans would never give up this contribution, reiterating that it was absolutely impossible; that, on the other hand, they recognized the very necessary character of the work and were prepared to find some other method of financial assistance; that Germany wanted no help from the Allies in anything. That in the face of the world and of German public opinion they could not for one moment retreat from an act which they had taken under the full rights confirmed by the Hague Convention. . . .

The memorandum went on to note that I said:

. . . I had no doubt that upon my arrival in London the English Government would immediately demand to know whether the Germans had accepted our proposal, and that I would be compelled to inform them that it had not been accepted. Upon this the English would announce to the world that they had offered to pay for the feeding of the Belgians themselves if the Germans would withdraw their forced contributions from Belgium. . . . Moreover, it might release the English from all feeling of responsibility in the matter. That I felt strongly that this was a matter in which both Governments must meet half way through this Commission. He stated that he could have no negotiations with the English in any shape or form, to which I replied that we were not proposing any such negotiations but merely that each Government should assent to an arrangement with the Commission. Mr. Gerard pointed out that the Commission was absolutely the only way through which the Belgians could be kept from starvation, and that in keeping them from starvation the greatest possible military service was being done to the Germans. The Chancellor replied again that it was utterly impossible that they should give up the contribution and that he could not discuss the matter on this footing; and again affirmed strongly that German public opinion would not stand for it. Mr. Gerard pointed out that he had discussed the matter with the editor of one of the most prominent German papers, who had told him that he thought it was the proper course to take; and Mr. Gerard suggested that if His Excellency would acquiesce, he, Mr. Gerard would call in a lot of editors and lay the proposal before them and endeavor to formulate public opinion. The Chancellor said this did not suit the occasion . . . that Germany was fighting with her back to the wall, in a situation for which he could not find an English word to fully express himself—that the word "serious" was not at all adequate as a description of the position in which Germany lay at the present moment. He stated that all Germans were grateful to the Commission for the work they were carrying on, and he would pledge himself to support the Commission in every way; but he could not entertain the proposals which had been made, and begged the Ambassador not to press the point. I stated to him that in pressing this point we were pressing a point which we felt sure was one which gave the Germans a unique opportunity to demonstrate to the world their desire to be fair and generous to the Belgians, and, disregarding all that had happened, the Germans had not turned from the view which they had held from the beginning with regard to Belgium. Mr. Gerard pointed out that the Germans had consistently taken the attitude that they were not conquering Belgium, but had merely entered it as a military necessity, and that it would only be consistent with such an attitude if they did not exercise the rights of conquerors in levying the cost of occupation upon these people. I pointed out it should be the desire of every German to secure the favorable opinion of the United States toward the Germans, and that the first and primary thing necessary to obtain such good opinion was by showing the generous attitude toward Belgium. He stated that American opinion was apparently of little value, as the Americans were supplying arms to the Allies and would probably continue to do so, and that in so doing they were prolonging the war. To this Mr. Gerard replied that the position was akin to two people playing chess, where one, which he might call the Germans, stopped in the middle of the game and asked to have the whole rules of the game altered; that the rules of this game had been set down and practiced by every nation for years, and that if the rules were to be changed it could not be done in the middle of the game. . . .

Mr. Gerard again returned to the question of the indemnity and pressed the point vigorously that the Germans could well afford to, and that it was positively in their interest that they should give way. To this the Chancellor said that it is finally, and once for all, absolutely impossible. I then stated to him that no matter what proposals were brought forward, I hoped that he would bear in mind at all times . . . that our whole operations hung on a slender thread of sentiment . . . that a breath could blow away this sentiment and the Germans would be faced with ten million starving people on their hands. . . . The Chancellor replied that they recognized these points and that they would take them into consideration in the proposals which he hoped they would be able to make, and he stated that the Commission need have no fear but that a solution would be found for . . . monetary necessities, but that it could not be the solution which the Commission . . . proposed.

As for financing the Relief, discussions took many directions, all of them futile except for certain proposals by Dr. Schacht and Herr von Lumm of the Reichsbank. My memorandum of my interview with them was as follows:

BERLIN, 9 February 1915

I had a meeting at the Reichsbank at twelve o'clock and there were present Dr. Schacht, Mr. von Lumm, the Chairman and the Vice-Chairman of the Reichsbank, and . . . [Dannie] Heineman.

The meeting was called to consider the financial proposals put forward by the Finance Minister, those put forward by Dr. Schacht and others. I explained that I did not wish it to be understood that I was representing the Belgians in this matter and that as I supposed their proposals would revolve around facilitating the borrowing of money by the Belgians with which to buy foodstuffs, they must bear in mind that primarily this was a matter between themselves and the Belgians; secondarily, however, as they expected to borrow the money from American agencies, I would be glad enough to inform them of such conditions as must necessarily surround any . . . [borrowing] in America, either with or without German assistance; that they must bear in mind that the American Government had practically prohibited the making of loans to any of the belligerent governments, and that therefore this loan would have to be neutral. It could only be made neutral by virtue of being guaranteed on both sides. Furthermore, the susceptibilities of the Belgian people and the susceptibilities of the English must be taken into account, as well as the Germans; that no loan could be issued unless there was a firm agreement that the objects of the loan should be solely for the support of the civilian population; that there would be no requisitioning of foodstuffs in Belgium so long as the loan was unpaid; and, on the other side, the English would have to agree to give facilities for the engagement and passage of the ships.

The conversation lasted a long time . . . and the Chairman of the Reichsbank seemed initially much opposed to the idea; but after infinite discourse they seemed all agreed on [a proposal] . . . that if the Belgians wished to borrow fifty million dollars in America, the German Government would unqualifiedly guarantee the loan; that the Belgian Government at the Havre should be asked to guarantee the loan; that an agreement should be entered into by which the Germans undertook that there would be no food requisitions in Belgium at any time during the currency of the loan; that the proceeds either in money or food should be entirely for the civilian population, and that the English should undertake to place no obstacles in the moving of ships for this purpose; and they undertook to recommend this procedure at the Cabinet meeting which they were to attend at six o'clock this evening.

Later I was informed that Chancellor von Bethmann-Hollweg and the Cabinet had agreed to a modification which made the proposal somewhat more practical. The revised proposal was that the Germans would advance $50,000,000 to us in New York over the period until the next harvest, these advances to be ultimately an obligation of the Belgian banks. This arrangement would make it possible for the Commission to continue until the harvest of 1915, on which the Belgians could live for another three months, or until about the end of November. I did not like the plan, but I felt that my obligation was to prevent starvation; after all, it meant food, or, alternatively, it was the most valuable argument yet placed in our hands from which to press the Allies for subsidies.

Upon my return to London, I at once informed the Foreign Office through Lord Percy that even with Ambassador Gerard's help I had failed to get a relaxation of the levies but that I had developed a method of German financing of the Commission and stated it in detail. As a result of this information Sir Edward Grey wrote me a letter refusing any action by the British. His essential paragraphs were:

FOREIGN OFFICE, LONDON
22 February 1915

DEAR MR. HOOVER:
Your return from Germany, and the information you have given me as to the result of your journey, afford me an opportunity to sum up the nego-

tiations which have passed between the Commission for Relief in Belgium and His Majesty's Government, in reply to the various letters you have written me.

After reviewing the wickedness of the Germans and their refusal to abandon the indemnities, he continued:

Solely on account of this attitude on the part of the German Government, the proposed arrangement between His Majesty's Government and the Commission must be regarded as having broken down. We shall of course maintain our general favourable attitude towards your work, and our offer of financial support will remain open in the event of the German Government receding from their present position in regard to their levies in Belgium, but for the moment the idea of a direct subvention out of Government funds toward the charitable work of the Commission must remain in abeyance.

I cannot conclude this letter without expressing our appreciation of the generosity of the American people and the admirable organisation established by the Commission, which have alone made this work possible. The people of this country will, I am sure, recognise in your work a prominent example of the qualities of efficiency and public spirit which distinguish the many neutral services rendered by Americans in Europe at the present time.

E. GREY

Although this was a polite dismissal of the whole Relief of the Belgians, neither Lord Percy nor I believed even yet that the British would thrust us into the arms of the Germans for our financing. With Grey's approval, Percy arranged for himself and me to meet with Lloyd George, Chancellor of the Exchequer. I also arranged for the exiled Belgian Government's Finance Minister and Minister in London to be present. My memorandum on this discussion was:

LONDON, 17 February 1915

... Mr. Lloyd George stated that there would be a cabinet meeting on Thursday at twelve o'clock, in which the question of feeding the Belgians would come up for general review. He stated that Messrs. Churchill and Kitchener were very much opposed, on military grounds, to a continuance of our work; that his own views had been greatly altered by his discussions and correspondence with me, and that he found himself able to support us unqualifiedly in our humanitarian task. He asked me . . . how much money we had had from the British Government up to date, and I told him £100,000. . . . He reviewed some arrangements with the Belgians mentioning £300,000 in payment of Belgian railway workmen. I told him I knew nothing about the transaction at all; that from my point of view I received a million pounds a month from the Belgians to purchase food with and transmit it to Belgium, and to account therefor, and that as to what internal arrangements were made I was not interested so long as I got the million pounds a month; and that I would . . . prefer to have as little to do with such arrangements as possible; . . . that my whole approach to the problem was from a humanitarian point of view, and that I must argue the whole matter on that footing. Mr. Lloyd George asked me to review to him—in order to refresh his mind—some arguments which I had placed before him previously, as he wished to repeat them to his colleagues. He asked that I give him a memorandum, and asked how quickly I could get it to him; to which I replied that I could have it ready at half-past six. He stated that I should make it as vigorous and as strong as possible. . . . I then returned to the office and prepared the following memorandum [the essential paragraphs of which were]:

LONDON, 17 February 1915

The Right Hon. David Lloyd George
Chancellor of the Exchequer
DEAR SIR:

As to your request that I should send you a memorandum on the matters affecting the provisioning of the civil population of Belgium.

1. Except for the breadstuffs imported by this Commission there is not one ounce of bread in Belgium today. The 7,000,000 people there are at present receiving the small allowance of 250 grams of flour per diem per capita, necessitating . . . [imports of] between 65,000 and 70,000 tons of wheat per month. In addition to this the native supplies of potatoes and meat are showing signs of rapid exhaustion, and measures must be taken to supplement the bread supply which we are now providing. Of the 7,000,000 population about 1,500,000 are at present entirely destitute and are being wholly supported by this Commission, and before the next harvest over 2,500,000 people will have to be supported. . . .

I then described our method of organization and our needs

... of from £1,000,000 to £1,500,000 per month.

2. Under the agreements entered into between this Commission and the German Government there has never been any interference with the foodstuffs introduced by us. We can account to the satisfaction of any auditor for every sack of wheat from the time it leaves Rotterdam until it reaches the Belgian civil consumer, and in fact so rigorous has been our attitude on this matter that the Germans have acceded to our demand for a restitution to us from military stores for amounts equivalent to those consumed by billeted troops and by officers and men eating in public restaurants. Early in our work we undertook negotiations with the Germans to bring to an end the requisitioning of native foodstuffs, and at the end of December we reached an agreement with regard to the Occupation Zone (which comprises the most of Belgium) and since that date there have been no requisitions of native food whatever in that zone with the exceptions of one or two minor instances which were corrected upon our complaint.[3] During my recent visit to Berlin I made arrangements for the extension of this agreement to cover, so far as practicable from a military point of view, the "operation" zone, which comprises the country westward of Ghent; and . . . [because of less need] we are sending but little foodstuffs into that territory.

3. The question as to whether the Germans would themselves out of their own provisions feed the people of Belgium is one upon which I am, from the result of my observations and discussions during my recent visit to Berlin, perfectly clear and confirmed. I attach hereto a memorandum expressing the German official view of this question. I put it forward without comment as to its proper character but only as showing the feeling which permeates the entire German official mind on this question; and with this, to them, moral justification of their attitude, it seems to me hopeless to expect this service.

Of more importance than this, however, is the fact that Germany is already short of food supplies . . . and the Germans high and low emphatically state that they will not starve their own people in order to feed the enemy population.

4. I cannot too strongly affirm that unless foodstuffs are introduced into Belgium from foreign sources, the decimation of this population will be-

[3] Von Bissing's repudiation of this agreement came a month later.

gin within thirty days. Already the population is restive enough and is being held in check by the influence of the communal authorities and members of . . . [our Commission by] insistence that the food supply will stop instantly there is any disorder in the country. Futile as it might be, such disorder will certainly arise and long before a famine has decimated the people of Belgium; . . . [many] will have been slaughtered as the result of the futile outbreaks of violence.

5. The British people entered upon this the greatest war of their history for the sole purpose of maintaining the Belgian people and their national integrity. It would be a cynical thing if the land of Belgium were discovered at the completion of this task to be but an empty husk! Compared to the cost, either from a military or a financial point of view, it is not worth taking the risk that this should happen.

. . . the monetary outlay . . . is negligible beside the vast sums otherwise involved; the extension of the war through the importation from abroad to the Belgian civil population of 70,000 to 80,000 tons of breadstuff per month can amount to a lengthening of this conflict but by a few days, even assuming that the Germans would supply this bread. From an economic point of view the war will be won not by compelling the Germans to give up 6 per cent of their breadstuffs to the Belgians, but by the pressure on the other 94 per cent (that being about the ratio between the respective consumers). On the other side of the balance sheet, the Belgians are on strike; their attitude keeps a considerable number of Germans off the fighting line; their passive resistance in refusing to work arsenals and machine-shops and railways is a service to the Allies which probably amounts, when interpreted into days, to something greater than the other side of the ledger will show. Assuming that the Germans should in the last resort change their minds and feed the desperate and starving population, they certainly would only do so upon receiving in return the services of this population . . . to my mind no pleas based on military exigency can divest any of the belligerents of the moral responsibility for which they will be held responsible in history as the result of such a tragedy.

6. In the matter of public sentiment in the neutral world, I can only speak for my own country. In the ordinary course it views European struggles with a practical evenly divided opinion; but in this struggle the English people have won the undoubted sympathy of 95 per cent of my countrymen, because of Belgium, and their belief that the English people are fighting for the restoration of the liberties of this people. My countrymen, greatly affected by the situation of this civil population, have come

forward and continue to come forward with a generosity unprecedented in the history of relief work; . . . I cannot too strongly emphasize the fact that should this relief work fail to receive the sympathy and support of the English people, it would have a most serious bearing on the whole attitude of public sentiment in the United States.

7. It is not, however . . . on the above grounds that I plead the cause of the Belgian people, men, women, and children; it is on the ground of broad humanity, for which the British people have ever stood, even at their own cost; and this—one of the most critical occasions in the history of your people—is one in which we are certain there will be no failure in their magnanimity.

HERBERT HOOVER

The next day, Mr. Lloyd George asked me to call upon him again. My memorandum on what took place was very short:

18 February 1915

Had a meeting with Mr. Lloyd George at the Treasury together with Mr. Van de Vyvere [the Belgian Finance Minister of the exiled Belgian Government at Le Havre] and Colonel Hunsiker [Vice-Chairman of our Commission]. Mr. Lloyd George informed us that the British Government had decided to recommend to the French Government a budgetary allowance for the Belgian Government which included £1,000,000 per month for "Mr. Hoover's fund," but that out of this £1,000,000 per month the salaries of the railway employees in Belgium must be paid. After some discussion between Mr. Van de Vyvere and Mr. Lloyd George I gathered that the subsidy would be fixed until the end of June.

I asked Mr. Lloyd George if he had received my memorandum of the previous day and if it was of the character which he desired. He said that it was perfect except in one particular, i.e., that military observations from laymen always infuriated military men and that he had therefore used the document in the Cabinet meeting and presented to them all the points except those of military order. I told him that their decision had taken a load off our hearts, and he replied: "You have made a good fight and deserve to win out."

In the haste of dictating this account of the meeting, I omitted mention of my protest at the payment to railway employees out of any Commission funds, as that would destroy our neutral position and I could not accept this condition. Lloyd George agreed that this stipulation would not be included.

During this conference, Lloyd George told the Belgian Minister of Finance that the subsidies to the Commission would be put in the form of loans to the Belgian Government. At the latter's objection, Lloyd George intimated that he need not worry, but that it suited the Exchequer's parliamentary strategy better, as he had authority to make loans and thus this method would avoid debate from opponents of the Commission's activities. As a matter of fact, in using the term "subsidies" throughout this narrative to describe the monies provided us by the different governments, I am using the accurate word, even though they were often called "loans."[4]

With this subsidy and our estimated charitable receipts of from $1,500,000 to $2,000,000 a month, I at once asked Ambassador Page to inform Ambassador Gerard of the British subsidy and that there was therefore no need to proceed with the German plan.

[4] The Belgians did not expect to repay these "loans" and in fact did not do so, and therefore the term "subsidy" proved entirely correct.

CHAPTER 10

FINANCING THE RELIEF
OF NORTHERN FRANCE

The local manpower in the North of France had been mobilized prior to the invasion, and many civilians had fled before the advancing German armies. The population had decreased to about two and one-half million, most of them women, children, and old men.

This area normally produced a larger proportion of its own food than did Belgium, but with the destruction of many farms, the loss of manpower, the pre-invasion mobilization of work animals, the removal of many animals by refugees, and the lack of fertilizers, food production slumped, despite heroic effort by the women, children, and the aged. The immediate situation in the towns was rendered acute by the havoc of battle and the seizure of the harvest and many animals by the invading Germans. Quickly the wolves gathered at every door.

The C.R.B. had no funds for the support of the Northern French, but at my direction we furnished some supplies out of our own meager resources of charity for Belgium to the most critical area, where people were dying. But this arrangement could not continue for long without starving the Belgians.

The peril of the French was underscored in a letter to me from Ambassador Gerard transmitting information from the American Consul in Roubaix:

BERLIN, 2 January 1915

DEAR MR. HOOVER:

. . . Another matter which may interest you is brought up by our late Consul at Roubaix, who says that the civil population of Roubaix, Tourcoing, Lille, and the surrounding cities is in great need of flour. . . . Our Consul transmitted a letter from the Mayor of Roubaix, stating that 250,000 persons would be starving within a few days in those cities. . . . I transmitted this information to the Department without comment and I have since received word from our State Department, in substance as follows:

"That the British Government raised no objection to the importation of foodstuffs in Belgium under the auspices and guarantees of the Commission for Relief in Belgium, and that their attitude was the same as to foodstuffs for France; and that the question how far it is desirable that the Commission should extend its activities to districts in France, now in German occupation, seemed to be one primarily for submission to the French Government.

"In any case, the Commission would have to satisfy themselves whether they would be permitted by the German authorities to form an adequate organization in districts so close to warlike operations. . . ."

The above is the substance of the reply of the British Government to our State Department, and I transmit it to you without comment. . . .

Please command me at any time when I can be of service to your Commission.

JAMES W. GERARD

At this time we had no financial support from the Allied Governments for either Belgium or the North of France, and therefore I replied:

LONDON, 6 January 1915

DEAR MR. GERARD:

In respect to that portion of your letter of the 2d instant, relating to the position of the French people north of the German lines, we have had this called to our attention repeatedly.

We have felt that it is up to the French Government to support their own people, but we are not adverse [sic] to taking on the extra labor entailed in finding the foodstuffs and transporting them through Belgium into this section, provided of course the Germans agree; but we do feel that . . .

the French . . . should make a substantial subscription to our funds. . . . I may tell you that we already are sending some food into one section of France, but other sections we have been unable to undertake, as we have no resources with which to do so.

HERBERT HOOVER

There was no possibility of raising the huge sums needed for Northern France by appeals to the charity of the neutral world. The support which we had already gleaned from that source for Belgium was wholly insufficient for even its need. In mid-January, 1915, I presented the matter verbally to the French Ambassador in London. He was sympathetic, but he later informed me that he had failed in his efforts to secure any help.

As I have previously mentioned, on February 17, I succeeded in securing a British subsidy of £1,000,000 a month for the Belgians. At that time Lloyd George told me that he would help me with the French. To open the subject, I sent the following letter by messenger to President Poincaré of France:

LONDON, 17 February 1915

MONSIEUR LE PRESIDENT:

I deem it my duty to lay before you the position of the French civil population north of the German lines.

I then briefly described our situation in Belgium and continued:

. . . I understand [the French population] amounts to between two and three million people. The breadstuffs in this region have now been practically exhausted by the occupying army and the population and the supply of vegetables and meat will shortly be at an end. The blast of famine has already struck at the heart of certain localities and actual starvation is in progress. Representatives of these people have come over the Belgian frontier literally in scores, praying for food from our organization. We have sent representatives throughout Northern France with the approval of the German authorities and I cannot too strongly impress upon Your Excellency the extreme gravity of the situation.

Some four weeks ago we extended the boundaries of our labors to take in practically the whole arrondissement of Rocroi, as our investigation indicated that unless foodstuffs were introduced into this section the actual deaths from starvation, which had set in, would quickly decimate the population before outside arrangements could be made. . . . [I have] made representations of this situation through the French Ambassador in London, to which appeals, made in the name of the French people of Northern France, we have had no reply.

I have now again been to Belgium and have again investigated the situation in Northern France, which has now become acute to the last degree. Owing to the strain that has been put upon us I have been most reluctantly compelled to direct that no foodstuffs shall be sent over the frontier from Belgium into France after the first day of March. At the present moment 400,000 French people are being fed by this Commission, but unless we can receive financial assistance we cannot go on. . . . We have no right to take money provided to feed the Belgians and give it to the French.

I know perfectly well that Your Excellency will immediately reply: "Why do not the Germans feed the French civil population?" I have nothing to say except that, not only do they not do it, but they state emphatically that they do not intend to do it, that they have insufficient food supplies for themselves and do not propose to prejudice their own people. If Your Excellency could see the mobs of French women and children which surround every German camp from daylight to dark to gather the refuse from the German soldiers, Your Excellency would then believe that these French people will pay the last penalty unless someone comes to their rescue.

The load of work and worry carried by this Commission is already large enough, but, in the interests of common humanity, if the French Government can help us financially we will feed these people. A great many of the communes have resources in the shape of paper money and, in the case of the larger cities, ample resources in credit. We cannot, however, export either money or credit from Northern France, although we could undertake to take the obligations from these communes, ultimately handing these obligations to the French Government in discharge of advances made to us in gold.

I will not trouble Your Excellency with any description of the personnel or organization of this Commission; that is a matter that is open to investigation at all times. Nor are we seeking the labor of feeding the people in Northern France, but it happens that there is no other agency through which this service can be performed at the present time, as this Commis-

sion is alone permitted to traverse the lines of the various belligerents . . .
under international agreements which have taken a long time and much
patience to perfect. . . .

In conclusion, before taking the heavy responsibility of saying to these
people "you shall not have bread," I make this last appeal to the French
people themselves in the name of their own countrywomen and children.

HERBERT HOOVER

I had requested an old friend, Louis Chevrillon, to represent the
Relief Commission in Paris. He was a former engineering colleague
of mine and a man who enjoyed high public respect. He lit fires un-
der the French Ministry, stoked by the Senators and members of the
Assembly from the northern districts of France, who were then in
Paris.

The French were, in the meantime, considering various alternatives: one, to evacuate the population in the German-occupied area;
another, to supply food by rail from the South of France, through
Switzerland and Germany; a third, to bring in overseas food through
Marseilles, Switzerland, and Germany. Chevrillon wrote to me as
follows:

PARIS, 9 March 1915

DEAR MR. HOOVER:

. . . Confidentially, I can tell you that the alternatives are either to try to
arrange with the Commission over which you so ably preside or to bring
the whole of the population of the invaded districts into the French lines.

General Joffre has already been consulted on the subject and expressed
himself as able to transport the people into France within three days. This
of course is very confidential yet and the probabilities are that this measure
will be resorted to as a last resource; the inhabitants are anxious not to
leave all their belongings and interests at the mercy of the invader. . . . I
do not doubt that . . . the Commission ultimately [will] be asked to take
up the provisioning of Northern France.

Yours faithfully,

L. CHEVRILLON

I telegraphed Chevrillon my reaction to these ideas on March 11:

Yours March 9th. Scheme perfectly ghastly every point of view. There is in fact only one way to handle this problem and that is through this Commission. Our negotiations with Germans progressing favorably on all points required by us. . . . Swiss proposals to ship foodstuffs from Marseilles by rail wholly impracticable. We have never been able secure transport even two thousand tons a month over same Belgian railway routes by which they would need to bring ten to fifteen thousand tons monthly. Even if railway supply practicable there is serious risk by shipping foodstuffs through Germany and the comparative cost would be the difference between railway haul all the way from Marseilles to Lille as against canal haul from Rotterdam. What is more the necessity for immediate relief is appalling and any scheme provisioning through Marseilles involves long delay. We are not keen on the job but feel that the size of the problem is not recognized and can only be adequately handled in our way.

HOOVER

I went to Paris on March 20. On my arrival I asked the American Ambassador in Paris, William Sharp, to arrange meetings for me with the officials of the Ministry. He explained that he could not interfere in French internal affairs. I cited the activities of our other American Ambassadors in such circumstances—but in vain. Sharp was not inhuman, just ineffective. However, Chevrillon promptly set up an interview for me with the Minister of Foreign Affairs, Théophile Delcassé, on March 22.

Delcassé listened courteously but delivered himself violently upon the obligation of the Germans to feed the occupied populations or get out. All I could reply was that they would not do it as evidenced by the thousands already starving. I stated that the Germans justified themselves on the ground that the blockade was pinching their own women and children. They also were constantly asserting that they would feed everybody if the food blockade was taken down. The Minister finally became so abrupt in his declaration that France would never condone this gross barbarity or admit any such contention that I concluded I had been wholly inadequate in my presentation, and withdrew, not only discouraged but with a feeling of humiliation.

I returned to the Meurice Hotel . . . and started to pack my bag to return to London on the night boat. A few moments later a bellboy presented the card of M. Maurice Homberg, President of the Banque Union Parisienne. I went down to the reception room to meet an elderly and distinguished Frenchman, who spoke perfect English. He said he had heard that I was in Paris endeavoring to finance food for the French in the occupied north. He asked that I explain the matter to him. I did so, as I had now become so familiar with the political, military, and humanitarian arguments that I repeated them in my sleep. He asked what I estimated as the cost. I stated that for the French population we should have a minimum of $5,000,000 of capital for food in transit and $3,000,000 a month for current use for the present. I felt that this would provide no more than a scanty regimen, but that we might get through the balance of the winter. I also pointed out that the British subsidy was insufficient to cover the Belgians. Mr. Homberg stated that he felt sure the problem could be solved. He inquired when I was returning to London and I stated that I was going that evening unless he thought it worth while my trying other members of the French Cabinet. He thought I did not need to remain and said I would hear from him shortly. I subsequently learned that he was temporarily in the French Ministry of Finance.[1]

Chevrillon pushed the negotiations energetically, but still no money was forthcoming to us from the French Ministry. To bring matters to a head, he again arranged a meeting for me with Foreign Minister Delcassé on March 22. As two of my Belgian colleagues, Francqui and Sengier, were in Paris, I asked them to accompany me. I especially needed Francqui's explosive French language. Sengier prepared the following memorandum for me in regard to the meeting.

PARIS, 22 March 1915

Mr. Delcassé was very surprised to hear from Mr. Francqui that the Belgian Government had not notified the C.R.B. that the French Cabinet had come to a satisfactory understanding with regard to the feeding of

[1] After I had published an account of these incidents in my *Memoirs,* I discovered further documents which indicate that I had telescoped these negotiations in the *Memoirs'* text.

the civil population of the French occupied territory. The matter of settling finance being not in his sphere, it was arranged for a meeting with Mr. Ribot, Minister of Finance.

We then met with the Ministers of Foreign Affairs and Finance, together with Homberg, and Sengier again wrote a memorandum:

"Messrs. Delcassé and Ribot declared that Mr. Viviani [the French Premier] had already come to an agreement with Mr. de Broqueville [the Belgian Prime Minister] that the Belgian Government should draw and place at the disposal of the Commission for Relief, upon the credit of 250,-000,000 francs opened for the Belgian Government at the Bank of France, all sums necessary to the feeding of the necessitous population of the North of France. . . .

"In order to follow up all these arrangements, it is indispensable that Mr. Van de Vyvere should immediately place at the disposal of the Commission for Relief in Belgium a sum equivalent to one million pounds sterling, the amount necessary for the purchase to be effected without delay. Furthermore, monthly, and for the first time on 1st April next, a sum equivalent to £400,000 sterling will be . . . [furnished]."

Five days later, on March 27, a London bank official called upon me with two checks in sterling, one for £1,000,000 (about $4,820,-000) and the other for £400,000 ($1,920,000). I asked to whom we were to account for the money. He said he had no idea. Nevertheless, I took it.

Since I knew the money must have been transmitted through the exiled Belgian Government, I inquired of them as to whom we were to account. They informed me that they did not know but that they had no obligations of repayment. This façade was maintained by the French Government for about two years. It certainly did not fool the Germans, as they were well aware that the exiled Belgian Government had no such sums.

We immediately set up our own organization and a committee of French citizens to aid us. This group has already been described on pages 18-20.

CHAPTER 11

GERMAN AND BRITISH GUARANTEES
OF IMMUNITY OF FOOD FOR BELGIUM

Because there was so much interaction between the British permissions to pass food through the blockade and the German guarantees of non-interference with food supplies, they must be described together.

The Commission's problem was to secure from both belligerents agreements granting it immunity from interference. It was a slow and unprecedented process in a wholly uncharted field of international relations, for what was involved was not agreements between governments, but agreements between governments and a body of hitherto unknown men whose sponsors were neutral Ambassadors and Ministers who themselves could undertake no obligations on behalf of their own governments.

The original guarantee from the Germans had been negotiated by the Commission's subsequent Director in Belgium, Dannie Heineman, and had been furnished to Whitlock by the General then in command, von der Goltz, as follows:

BRUSSELS, 17 September 1914
To the Minister of the United States of America:
In reply to the communication which Your Excellency in behalf of the Ministry of Foreign Affairs of Belgium addressed to the Head of the Imperial Administration, I have the honor to confirm to you:
1. That the Imperial Government agrees not to levy any impost for the needs of the German Army, nor to requisition the shipments of wheat and flour destined for the alimentation of the Belgian civil population.

2. That, if contraband of war should be found in a shipment, the entire shipment would be confiscated to the profit of the Imperial Government.

3. That the civil administration of the Imperial Government reserves to itself alone the right of decision as to the distribution of the wheat and flour in the different portions of the occupied territory, according to local needs, and to supervise this distribution.

I should be glad to receive new communications from Your Excellency on this subject.

Ambassador Page had received on our behalf the following original undertaking from the British:

FOREIGN OFFICE, LONDON
20 October 1914

MY DEAR MR. PAGE:

Since our conversation this afternoon Sir Edward Grey has written to Baron Lambert telling him that we are not stopping any food supplies going to Rotterdam—from neutral countries in neutral ships—which we are satisfied are not for the use of the German Government or Army, and that we shall not therefore interfere with the food supplies for the civil population of Belgium unless we have reason to suppose that the assurance given by Marshal von der Goltz to the American and Spanish Ministers is not being carried out.

A. NICOLSON

The Germans' guarantee to Heineman was wholly unsatisfactory, as it implied their control of distribution and did not preclude their requisitioning of native food. The Germans were making such requisitions constantly. This practice, if continued, would result in our having to replace native food with imports—a Sisyphean labor on our part and, in any event, totally unacceptable to the Allies.

I have related earlier that on November 5, 1914, I had pressed British Foreign Minister Sir Edward Grey for a subsidy from his government. He at once cited the German requisitioning of native supplies as an obstacle to such support—and even to continuation of the Commission. At my request, Whitlock and the Marquis de Villalobar tried to get for us an assurance against this requisitioning from German Governor General von Bissing, but after a month of effort, they failed. Therefore, on December 5, I resolved that we would appeal to the civilian government in Berlin over the heads of the militarists in Brussels and addressed the following letter to Ambassador Gerard, describing our situation and needs:

DEAR MR. AMBASSADOR:

. . . As you are well aware . . . we are making a stupendous effort to justify our countrymen . . . in a task which has been put . . . to us.

In order to carry this out successfully, we have necessarily to receive the support of both the German and English Governments. We fully understand . . . [the points of view of the German and British Governments].

In the initial stages, the attitude of the English Government was friendly and we were even allowed to purchase a certain amount of foodstuffs in England for transmission to Belgium. Our ships were assisted by the British Admiralty and generally the British Government was helpful to a great degree. This whole attitude has, however, changed during the last week and we are now confronted with an attitude on the part of this Government which threatens to overthrow the whole of our efforts. . . . It is not that the Germans take the food which we import into Belgium, as we have been able to demonstrate the most scrupulous adherence on their part to the undertakings. . . .

The reason for this change of front has been the recurrent requisitioning of native foodstuffs by the Germans and that, where we import one ton of foodstuffs, they make a requisition for a ton of the foodstuffs which . . . simply means that by continuous requisitions on their part the Germans will secure the substitution of our foodstuffs for all of that which is now in the country. The British Government say that this indirectly amounts to our feeding the German Army. . . .

I know that this is a delicate thing . . . for you to take up, but the impending fate of these . . . millions of people surely warrants us in any endeavor which will alleviate their position. . . .

I then reported on the situation in Belgium and continued:

. . . This position is getting steadily worse, until within the next sixty days absolutely the only food supply for this whole population will be that which we can import. . . . [For the Germans] to allow these people to starve while under their . . . [military] control will raise a storm in the neutral world fifty times the volume of that which has already been created by any local destruction. It is my belief that the belligerent nation which refuses to participate in succor of these people will yet have to carry the brand of Cain as their murderers. On the other hand, any kindness held out to them in this time of dire necessity will bring with itself credit which in after history will wipe out nine-tenths of the charges of ruthlessness in war. . . .

HERBERT HOOVER

Ambassador Gerard and his Spanish colleague in Berlin secured for us a complete guarantee against the further requisition of native food. He telegraphed me this agreement on December 26 and confirmed it in writing to Arthur Zimmermann, the Under Secretary of Foreign Affairs:

BERLIN, 28 December 1914

MY DEAR MR. SECRETARY:

After my call on you last Saturday, on which occasion I was not acting officially but as one of the Honorary Chairmen of the Belgian Relief Commission, I sent to my Government and to the Chairman of the Commission the following telegram:

"Acting not officially, but as one of the Honorary Chairmen Belgian Relief Commission called today with Spanish Ambassador and Netherlands Minister on Undersecretary of State Zimmermann, who gladly and without hesitation assured us that Commanding General in Belgium will give assurances to American, Spanish, and Netherlands Ministers in Belgium that German military authorities will not make any further requisitions of food supplies in Belgium while the International Commissions are sending in food, and for a reasonable time after the last delivery. . . ."

JAMES W. GERARD

Three days later, Zimmermann confirmed the guarantee to Gerard:

BERLIN, 31 December 1914

His Excellency
Ambassador of the United States of America

The undersigned has the honor to inform His Excellency, Mr. Gerard, Ambassador of the United States of America, with reference to the esteemed note of the 28th instant, that the Imperial Governor-General in Belgium will issue without delay an order prohibiting all the troops under his command from requisitioning food or forage of any kind whatsoever which would require to be replaced by importations by the American Committee for Belgian Relief. The Governor-General will, in addition, authorize the Minister of the United States and the Spanish Minister at Brussels as Honorary Chairmen of the Committee, to convince themselves in any way which may to them appear advisable that the prohibition is observed most scrupulously. . . .

Whitlock joyfully transmitted this information to the State Department:

BRUSSELS, 2 January 1915

STATE DEPARTMENT, WASHINGTON

I have received today assurances from Baron von Bissing, German Governor-General in Belgium, that orders have been given forbidding all further requisition of foodstuffs of whatever sort in Belgian territory occupied by German troops, and that the protection thus afforded covers cattle and their food as well. He will give any reiterated assurances that we may desire on any occasion that foodstuffs will not be requisitioned, and that we may establish and maintain any kind of control that we may see fit to adopt in connection with our relief work for the civil population. Similar assurances were given to my Spanish colleague.

WHITLOCK

Before the German confirmation of December 31 reached our hands in London, Sir Edward Grey had fired a stiff note to Ambassador Page on the wickedness of the Germans generally, and the requisitioning of native food in particular, and had set up conditions under which the Commission must operate. However, the German assurance rendered this a moot question—temporarily. Von Bissing confirmed, in general, this undertaking by his government in Berlin:

BRUSSELS, January 21, 1915

With my approval the guarantee has been given to the Comité National de Secours et d'Alimentation, through the intermediary of the Foreign Office that all troops under my orders are forbidden to requisition food-

stuffs or artifically prepared fodder materials of any kind whatsoever, replacement of which must be effectuated through importation by the
Comité.

... I remark that it has been a question hitherto, in the supplies imported by the Comité, of flour and breadstuffs, rice, peas, beans, salt,
maize, and sugar, but that, in the near future, there will also presumably
be imported foddercakes and other artificially prepared fodder materials. ...

BARON VON BISSING

Von Bissing's dislike of the Americans led him into an error in his
statement. The Berlin guarantees had been given to the C.R.B. and
not to the C.N., with which the German Foreign Office would have
no dealings. Whitlock seemed to think this was sufficient and so
wrote to me on February 2.

During my visit to Berlin in early February, 1915, Under Secretary
of Foreign Affairs Zimmermann requested a memorandum from me
reviewing the Commission's problems. In the one I furnished him on
February 4, I recalled the agreement of December 31 and continued:

... [The requisition of native food] was largely abandoned by the German
Government early in January. ... The reports, however, of isolated cases
of the requisitioning of cattle, pigs, potatoes, etc., by the army since [the]
agreement was entered into, have greatly damaged the Commission's efforts to raise funds, as there has been a great outcry raised that the statement by the Commission that such requisitions had ceased was untrue. ...
The Commission, therefore, earnestly desires that the directions as to
requisitioning foodstuffs of any kind in Belgium should be made broad
enough and specific enough to cover all ... [native food]. ...

Zimmermann promised me that he would take care of it.

It was upon these German assurances that we obtained the British
subsidy on February 17. But von Bissing backed out of the agreement
in a letter of March 12 addressed to the Comité National. After reaf-
firming the guarantee against requisitioning *imported* food, he continued:

I cannot agree with your opinion that "every product obtained from our soil" is already being imported by you, and could therefore no longer be requisitioned. In particular, it is not within my knowledge that oats, straw, hay, potatoes, fresh vegetables, and sugar are imported in such quantities that my prohibition should be extended to these articles also.

If English financial circles demand a more extended declaration in the sense that the Imperial General Government exempt from requisition all foods without any distinction, necessary for the maintenance of the people and animals, which shall be produced hereafter in the country, I regret that I am not in a position to give such a declaration. . . .

The Governor General,

BARON VON BISSING

All of this meant that the Germans would continue to requisition horses, cattle, sheep, and vegetables, and it was therefore a direct repudiation of their guarantees of December 31.

On March 27, I again turned to Ambassador Gerard for help:

DEAR MR. GERARD:

. . . The real important situation, which I set out in my separate letter, revolves round our desire to protect this year's harvest in Belgium, for if the present military situation is going to continue there is nothing in God's world which will save the Belgians from extinction except their own products, and if these are going to be taken away from them we may just as well throw up our hands today as next August. We would like you to consider whether or not it would not be wise if you would have a personal discussion with the Emperor on this major question. . . .

. . . If . . . the Emperor himself would interest himself in seeing that our humanitarian efforts are carried out . . . our path would then be comparatively easy, for not only can I provide the finance until next August but the crop in Belgium would carry these people on another four months after that date. . . .

HERBERT HOOVER

In the meantime, I had begun negotiations with the German General Staff at Charleville concerning their providing guarantees against requisitions in Northern France and the Belgian Etape. There was evident good will on their part.

On April 6, the British Foreign Office, in a communication to me, reiterated its earlier demands for a German pledge not to requisition any native food or touch the coming Belgian harvest. After discussing certain matters concerning Northern France, the message went on to say:

... We really must insist that in Belgium the Germans shall scrupulously respect the produce of the next harvest. Any attempt on the part of the Germans to go back on or to restrict the application of their undertaking to requisition no more foodstuffs in Belgium; any attempt to get hold of the next harvest by indirect means; will lead us immediately to reconsider our whole attitude. We must be satisfied that the certainty of the continuance of your supplies does not enable the Germans to divert to their own use one ounce of the food which would otherwise be at the disposal of the civil population. We must be satisfied of this, not only by guarantees given by the Germans, but by adequate supervision maintained by your agents and facilitated by the German authorities. We have compromised on many points hitherto, but we can assent to no compromise on this point. . . . This is intolerable and, in the interests of the continuance of the various arrangements under which you work, I sincerely hope that you will be able to induce the Germans to abandon this impossible position.

Yours sincerely,
EUSTACE PERCY

Ambassador Gerard had not been able to make any progress toward restoration of the German guarantees of December. I again wrote to him, relaying the above British ultimatum:

LONDON, May 1, 1915

DEAR MR. AMBASSADOR:
... [The British] now say that if the Germans will make no undertaking to leave to the Belgians their harvest, the Allied Governments will have to insist that the efforts and organization of this Committee come to an end on the 15th day of August and that it should then absolutely dissolve. This would be a great pity, because if the present situation should continue into next year and even if the Belgians did retain their harvest and their local production, their breadstuffs would not be likely to last beyond the end of

October in any event. You can yourself imagine what would be the attitude of the military party in . . . [England], with whom we have had such infinite difficulties, if next autumn we should propose to re-enter Belgium and in the meantime the Germans had requisitioned or absorbed any of the native food supplies. . . . I am certain we could never again obtain approval to restart.

When I addressed you last it was with the hope that some undertaking with regard to the harvest could be entered upon . . . if the Germans would like to keep this Commission alive . . . it is positively essential that they should make, at once, a broad and sufficient undertaking with regard to the whole of the foodstuffs produced within the Occupation Zone. If we are to go on after harvest we have also got to make some sort of definite financial arrangements for our support. . . . I can only reiterate that the whole future of the business now depends upon whether the German Government will enter into such undertakings with regard to native production.

. . . You will please find enclosed herewith, copy of a purported interview with General von Bissing, which appeared in the New York *Staatszeitung* on the 12th April. . . . The inference . . . is that we are a lot of commercial pirates operating under the cloak of charity. . . . If we are to maintain this machinery in existence . . . it is . . . necessary not only to have the question of requisition settled but that General von Bissing remove the stigma which he has placed over this body of idealists. . . .

HERBERT HOOVER

On May 4, the British Foreign Office urged speedier action on German guarantees to protect the harvest and native food generally:

DEAR MR. HOOVER:

. . . Some time has passed and I have heard nothing further from you. Meanwhile we have been allowing you to send seed into Belgium, in the belief that the harvest when it comes will be used exclusively for the civil population whom you have so narrowly saved from starvation during all these months. We cannot wait much longer for a satisfactory declaration of the attitude of the German authorities, nor can I run any risk of your being able to say in the future that I did not give you sufficient warning of what may happen.

It is self-evident to me, and must be equally so to you, that your work will in all probability have to stop when the harvest matures, that is to say, I presume, about the middle of August, unless positive guarantees are forthcoming from the German authorities. . . .

In view of these probable grave results of the present uncertainty, I sincerely trust that you will be able to inform me very soon, and at any rate before the end of the present month, that you have obtained the necessary guarantees from the German authorities.

EUSTACE PERCY

As the result of my letter to him of May 1, Ambassador Gerard went into action again and addressed German Foreign Minister von Jagow:

AMERICAN EMBASSY, BERLIN
5 May 1915

MY DEAR EXCELLENCY:

At the instance of Mr. Hoover, Chairman of the Commission for Relief in Belgium, I have the honor to bring herewith to Your Excellency's kind consideration certain aspects of the work of the Commission as regards the disposition of this year's harvest in Belgium.

As Your Excellency is perhaps aware, the Commission was unable to complete definite financial arrangements in England for financing the Commission without obtaining from the Imperial Government a broad undertaking that no more native foodstuffs would be requisitioned in Belgium by the German authorities until peace was concluded, such an undertaking referring only to the Occupation Zone, not to the Operation Zone. . . .

. . . The Commission is informed by them [the Allied Governments] that, if the Imperial Government will not make an undertaking to leave to the Belgians their harvest, the Allied Governments will have to insist that the efforts and organization of this Commission come to an end on the 15th day of August and that it should then absolutely dissolve. . . .

It therefore results, in the opinion of the Commission, that, if the Imperial Government desires to keep the Commission alive . . . it is positively essential that it should make, at once, a broad and adequate undertaking with regard to the whole of the foodstuffs produced within the Occupation Zone.

Furthermore, if the Commission is to go on after the harvest, it feels that it must make some sort of financial arrangements for its support. The Commission is of the opinion that, if the Imperial Government would

comply with the request for a definite and broad undertaking with regard
to the protection of the native food supplies during the whole of the occupation of Belgian territory . . . the Commission is confident that it could
. . . [finance itself].

Mr. Hoover concludes by reiterating that the whole future of the undertaking now depends upon whether the Imperial Government will enter
into such undertakings with regard to the native production. . . .

JAMES W. GERARD

The Comité National, through the Belgian Minister in London,
had protested that the British demands were too severe. Lord Percy
of the Foreign Office wrote to me on May 26:

DEAR MR. HOOVER:

. . . I think the Belgians of the Comité National should recognize that
we are putting up a fight to preserve their harvest for them, and not object
to our action in the matter.

There is, it is true, no "bluff" about our action, as we are in deadly
earnest about stopping the whole arrangement if the necessary guarantee
is not given, but the whole value of our attitude as a means of putting
pressure on the Germans will be compromised if the Comité National
regard us as hard-hearted tyrants instead of backing our attitude up with
what influence they have in Belgium.

EUSTACE PERCY

So that everybody would know of our impending fate, I wrote Whitlock, enclosing a copy of the above letter and stating:

LONDON, 26 May 1915

DEAR MR. WHITLOCK:

I should be glad if you would communicate the following to our friends
in Brussels. . . .

From discussions I have had with the Foreign Office . . . there is no
doubt in my mind that they are . . . in earnest as regards their notice that
we must bring our work to an end by the middle of August unless some
undertaking is secured with regard to the next harvest. . . . On two suc-
cessive occasions where vital matters have been at stake, an entire change
has been obtained by me through intervention in Berlin. . . . I assume

that this course will have to be pursued again, if the stream of foodstuffs is to be kept flowing. . . .

HERBERT HOOVER

The Foreign Office next suggested that I take the entire matter up with Washington:

FOREIGN OFFICE, LONDON
31 May 1915

DEAR MR. HOOVER:

Many thanks for your letter of the 27th about the harvest. I quite recognize the difficulties you have been under as regards pushing the question at Brussels under present circumstances, but I do not think that it would be of any use to wait longer before taking the matter up officially with the United States Government. The matter is too serious to be any longer delayed—but an official communication to the United States Government should assist you in getting a favourable reply.

EUSTACE PERCY

I immediately suggested to our Director in New York that he take up the subject with an important member of the German legation in Washington known to him:

LONDON, 1 June 1915

LINDON BATES, NEW YORK:

Suggest you inform your . . . friend that we have been given absolute orders by Allied Governments to provide no food supplies for Belgium beyond August 15th unless Germans positively undertake that there be no requisitioning next harvest within Occupation Zone. I am confident there will be no retreat from this position and the whole work of Commission comes to an early end. . . . We have done all we could and it is up to them to say whether they desire the activities of this organization to continue.

HOOVER

Ambassador Gerard came to our rescue again on the vital point of the 1915 ground crops and sent me word, through the American Embassy in London, that I should go to Belgium, where von Bissing was instructed to make an agreement with us. I went to Belgium at once. Since Gerard had not raised the question in Berlin of barring the requisition of anything other than bread grains (the major ground crops), I thought it better to clinch that much first. In an interview with von Bissing's principal assistant, von der Lancken, I proposed the following formula regarding the breadstuff harvest which he said he would support:

BRUSSELS, 18 June 1915

MEMORANDUM FOR BARON VON DER LANCKEN

The Comité National and the Commission for Relief in Belgium, under the patronage of the Ministers of Spain and the United States, and the Chargé d'Affaires of the Netherlands, will continue to import, till the harvest of 1916, the necessary materials for the feeding of the civil population in the occupied territory, placed under the rule of the Governor-General in Belgium.

The Governor-General in Belgium will, on his side, leave at the disposal of the Belgian civil population placed under his orders, the produce of the harvest . . . of 1915, relating to the materials for bread-making. . . .

Since von Bissing's approval was not yet forthcoming, on June 22 I sent the following note to von der Lancken through Whitlock. After discussing some negotiations then under way for German ships and the British attitude about the harvest, it concluded:

It is perfectly immaterial to the C.R.B. whether or not these negotiations reach a successful consummation, except as to their interest in the people of Belgium . . . if it is not the wish of the German Government to facilitate this matter . . . the Commission . . . would be only too glad to retire from the entire situation, which will involve Northern France as well as Belgium.

HERBERT HOOVER

On June 25, Whitlock informed me that von Bissing had agreed in regard to breadstuffs:

The Governor-General in Belgium will hold at the disposal of the Bel-

gian civil population of the territory placed under his orders the product of
the grain harvest of 1915 used for the making of bread. . . .

General von Bissing added, however, a demand that we agree to continue imports during the harvest year, and he made no reference to
other native produce.

I submitted the von Bissing agreement and his demand to the
British Foreign Office. Lord Crewe replied to Ambassador Page on
July 7:

DEAR MR. AMBASSADOR:
. . . the Relief Commission has communicated to me the enclosed memorandum to that effect given by General von Bissing to the United States
Minister at Brussels. It would seem, however, that this undertaking is
made subject to an assurance on the part of the Commission that it will
continue to import regular amounts of foodstuffs into the territory under
General von Bissing's jurisdiction in each month until the harvest of 1916,
the distribution of the native harvest being conducted *pari passu* with the
distribution of such imported foodstuffs. In order that it may be able to
fulfil this condition, the Commission asks for an assurance from His
Majesty's Government that they will maintain in force the arrangement by
which, since last October, permits have from time to time been granted to
the Commission, allowing it to import foodstuffs into Belgium, under the
guarantee that these foodstuffs shall reach the civil population only.

His Majesty's Government are prepared to give this assurance, but they
must give it subject to certain conditions, necessitated by the experience
of the last eight months. . . .

Lord Crewe then reviewed our history and enumerated the conditions under which we could continue:

That the purchase and distribution of the harvest in Belgium shall
be under the management of the Commission for Relief in Belgium . . .
in the same manner as the imported foodstuffs, and that the Commission
for Relief in Belgium and the Comité National shall continue to administer relief in kind to the destitute as heretofore. Any agreement entered
into by, and any regulations imposed upon, the Commission or the Comité
National with regard to their activities, whether in relation to the harvest

or in relation to any other matter, shall be submitted to His Majesty's Government by the Commission for their approval, before the conclusion of such agreement or the acceptance of such regulations.

While raising the question of the continued German requisition of other native commodities, particularly animals, Lord Crewe did not at this time argue on this point, saying:

With regard to articles other than wheat and rye, His Majesty's Government cannot of course give any undertaking; and they will not permit the Commission to introduce any such articles into Belgium until an undertaking is given in regard to them by the German authorities similar to that now given in regard to wheat and rye. As, however, the Commission assures His Majesty's Government that six articles of food which it desires to import will in practice not form the object of requisitions in Belgium, His Majesty's Government are prepared on that understanding to allow the Commission from time to time to import these articles, viz.—peas, beans, rice, bacon, lard, and maize *for human consumption,* so long as the import of these articles does not represent a replacement of other articles requisitioned by the Germans. This permission shall be subject to immediate withdrawal upon determination by His Majesty's Government that the import of these articles does in effect constitute such a replacement.

As His Majesty's Government have to complain of constant and flagrant violation by the German Government of their undertaking to respect British ships carrying the Commission's foodstuffs to Rotterdam, they must insist that any further attack made on such vessels shall relieve them from all obligations under the present arrangement.[1]

Subject to these conditions, I hereby give an assurance to the Commission that His Majesty's Government will continue to give permits for the passage of its imports into the territory in Belgium placed under General von Bissing's jurisdiction.

It is of course understood that the present assurances given to the Commission by His Majesty's Government and by the German Government do not supersede, but on the contrary supplement and form an integral part of, the previous assurances and guarantees given by either government.

CREWE

[1] This referred to the German torpedoing of one of the Commission's ships, the *Harpalyce,* on April 10, 1915, which I will discuss later.

Whitlock, at my request, communicated the British terms to von der Lancken and asked the Germans to agree to the British stipulations, adding some proposals of our own:

BRUSSELS, 16 July 1915

To His Excellency, Baron von der Lancken, Brussels
YOUR EXCELLENCY:

. . . That the Comité National and the C.R.B. will continue to enjoy at all times a liberty of action in accordance with their mission and their responsibilities. . . .

That the German authorities will at no time employ the Comité National nor the C.R.B. as a means to force the population of working people, against their will and against their conscience, to employment either directly or indirectly benefiting the German Imperial Army.

That the purchase and distribution of the harvest of cereals will be made in Belgium by the C.N. in the same way as for the imported foodstuffs, and that the C.N. also with the co-operation of the C.R.B. will continue to distribute help in kind to the needy as before.

The British Government has informed us, however, that they will regretfully be compelled to withdraw permission to the boats loaded with provisions for Belgium if, contrary to the intentions declared by Your Excellency, English boats carrying relief goods to Rotterdam are attacked. . . .

The British Government has . . . declared that it will authorize the import of the following six articles besides the cereals, viz.: peas, beans, rice, bacon, lard, and maise for human consumption, as long as the import of these articles does not represent a replacement of articles requisitioned by the authorities under your orders. . . .

I have no doubt that Your Excellency will be good enough to signify your agreement with the above, and that you will at the same time confirm, in the name of your Government, as the British Government has done, the assurances and guarantees given formerly, and which are included with the stipulations above cited. . . .

BRAND WHITLOCK

On July 23, von Bissing issued the necessary decrees vesting the purchase and distribution of the breadstuff products in the Relief organization and defining the method of carrying this out. But on

August 8, he requisitioned the entire hay crop for the German Army, allowing the peasants supplies only for their own animals.

Another problem not yet solved was the German requisition of animals and vegetables. In practice, we were having to import animal products, and we insisted that food animals and their products came under the German guarantees not to requisition commodities which implied replacement by imports. Our efforts to get the Germans to observe this part of their undertaking worked part of the time.

In October, 1915, we had trouble over hay and fodder. The Germans carried out fairly faithfully their decree allowing the peasants to retain sufficient amounts of these products to feed their animals, but this did not protect the town work horses or the dairies, which depended on buying feed. With the exhaustion of these supplies in the market, the dairymen began to sell their cows and the draymen their horses, and we were about to be deprived both of milk and city transport. Early in October, I applied to the British for approval to import a small amount of grain for this purpose. There was the usual explosion, but on October 21, since the hay had all been consumed, they gave us the necessary permissions. As part of this agreement, we had to establish a rationing system for town work horses and dairy cows.

GUARANTEES IN THE ETAPPENGEBIET

The Belgian civilian population in the Operations Zone of East and West Flanders came under the control of the Commanding General of the German Army in that region, and we operated on an informal understanding with him that the guarantees given us with respect to Occupied Belgium would apply to these areas. Our relations with the German General Staff were always more cordial than those with von Bissing's administration, but it was not practical to apply to the new harvest in the Operations Zone, with its changing conditions of warfare, the method used in the Occupied Zone.

In Dr. Kellogg's temporary absence from Charleville, I instructed Oscar T. Crosby, then our Director in Brussels, to take up the harvest question with the German General Staff:

BRUSSELS, 14 September 1915

DEAR MR. CROSBY:

I understand that the German authorities in this section are requisitioning the entire harvest and that they are intending to set aside out of the harvest for the civilian population an amount of wheat which will come to 120 grams per capita per diem during the next year and that no provision has been made for the reservation to the population of fodder for their animals. The blockading governments have formally called our attention to this position and informed us that as they considered it the duty of the occupying army to set aside from the harvest complete provision for the civil population and their animals in the first instance, and that as no provision has been made for animals and only part for humans in this region, they cannot allow us to continue imports into that section. They contend that such imports amount to provisioning the German Army by virtue of replacement of foodstuffs which have been requisitioned from the population. Whether these contentions are right or wrong, the fact stares us in the face that the ravitaillement of this section is in danger of breaking down.

I shall be glad if you would at once take this question up with the German General Staff and represent to them . . . the extreme difficulty of our position standing between such conflicting interests and the hope we have in an accommodation on their part which will enable us to solve this very trying situation.

As a constructive suggestion, I have hopes that . . . the German authorities would agree to hand over the entire . . . wheat harvest at the cost to them, to the civil population, and [that] they would make sufficient reservation from the . . . oats, hay, and other fodder crops to support the animals during the winter. Such an arrangement being of course contingent on our securing the undertaking that we will be free from interference in the import of the large amount of foodstuffs which will be necessary to support the population.

I trust you will take this matter up as quickly as possible because our shipments into this section are at once imperiled.

HERBERT HOOVER

On September 14, Crosby transmitted this letter, together with some explanations, to the German liaison officer for our affairs at Charleville and subsequently reported:

BRUSSELS, 29 September 1915

The Commission for Relief in Belgium, London
GENTLEMEN:

Oberlieutenant Schroeder dictated today a note—copy enclosed . . . setting forth the determination made by the German authorities in respect to cereals in the two Flanders.

In one portion of that territory the commanding officer has issued a somewhat different program, but it is presumed that the one shown in Lieutenant Schroeder's memorandum will be made uniform throughout the territory in question.

We are now taking steps to see that the amount of wheat and rye for the bread supply, indicated in the first paragraph of Lieutenant Schroeder's memorandum, will get into the hands of the Provincial Committees so that it may be counted upon as a part of the general stock to be distributed by the Provincial Committees.

. . . Lieutenant Schroeder explains that the whole of the wheat crop in the two Flanders will be absorbed by the 120-gram ration and that the present intention is to supply the remainder of the required amount, which will be in the neighborhood of 20,000 tons for the year's program, from other sources. If, however, at any time through accident it will be impossible to deliver wheat, then rye would be furnished instead. . . .

The amount of oats per head per day for cattle was not definitely indicated by Lieutenant Schroeder. . . .

OSCAR T. CROSBY

Schroeder's note read:

The German authorities have promised to supply 120 grams of wheat per capita of inhabitant per day. In those regions where there is no wheat, they will, if possible, have it sent there, or they will supply instead 120 grams of rye.

Oats and Hay—Oats and hay have been seized by the German authorities, but producers may take therefrom for their needs up to . . . kilos per head of cattle for the year. Other foods for cattle, as for instance, maize, barley, etc., are free, can be disposed of according to desire, and can be sold, but not outside the limit of the Etapes. Maximum prices have been fixed.

The potato crop has not been seized at all, but it is forbidden to export potatoes outside the limits of the Etapes.

Prior to the arrival of Crosby's preliminary agreement, I had a stiff note from the British Foreign Office, dated September 30, in which they stipulated the same demands for the Etape as they had for the Occupied Zone. But in the meantime, our staff in Belgium had practically solved the question by the September 29 agreement, and on October 7, they secured further concessions from the Command of the Etape as follows:

GHENT, 7 October 1915

The Commission for Relief in Belgium, Brussels
GENTLEMEN:

Referring to our correspondence and conferences . . .

It has been agreed that the whole of the wheat crop of the territory shall be liberated for the civil population.

The entire wheat crop has been estimated to amount to about 40,000 tons.

In order to give the civil population for one year 120 grams of wheat per capita and per day, a round 70,000 tons will be required. Efforts will be made to bring the round 30,000 tons lacking from other territories. Where this is not possible the missing quantity will be supplied from Belgian rye. . . .

The quantities left to the Communes may be collected by the local members of the Comité National and stored in the magazines of the C.R.B. . . .

All wheat and rye seed, as well as all other crops raised here, will be left to the communes.

The oat and hay crops have been requisitioned. One and one-half kg. per head of cattle per day will be left the farmers for their own use. Owners of horses can purchase from the farmers at a fixed maximum price.

Other fodder materials as maize, barley, straw, second hay crop, bran, mangel-wurzels, turnips, and other greens have been liberated, but may not be exported from the Etapes zone. All pasturage, without restriction, has likewise been left to the inhabitants. The same applies to the potato crop.

Maximum prices have been fixed.

> *On behalf of the Etappen-Inspection,*
> *The Chief of the General Staff,*
> Ostertag, *Oberstlieutenant* [*sic*]

I informed the British Foreign Office that I considered the Etape agreement fairly reasonable, saying:

LONDON, 11 October 1915

Lord Eustace Percy
Foreign Office, London
DEAR LORD EUSTACE:

The above [Etappen] arrangements appear to me to be on the whole satisfactory in these unsatisfactory times, and they are on the whole better than the arrangements made in the Occupation Zone and represent the absolute maximum which we are able to obtain. I trust this will be satisfactory to you, and that we may, besides the usual food, also import fodder into that area for the town animals. . . .

HERBERT HOOVER

On October 21, the British Foreign Office accepted this arrangement:

FOREIGN OFFICE, LONDON
21 October 1915

[*London Director of the Relief Commission*]
DEAR MR. HONNOLD:

With reference to Mr. Hoover's letters of the 11th and 15th instant, I am now directed to inform the Commission as follows:

We will not ask the Commission to make any further demands in regard to the disposal of the native crops in the "Etappengebiet." . . .

[He concluded with a vigorous denunciation of the Germans.]

EUSTACE PERCY

CHAPTER 12

GERMAN AND BRITISH
GUARANTEES OF IMMUNITY OF FOOD
FOR NORTHERN FRANCE

I felt that it would help us to secure French subsidies for our work in Northern France if, prior to such negotiations, I could obtain adequate undertakings from the Germans to leave our imported and native food alone. Therefore, on March 9, 1915, I wrote Ambassador Gerard that any real action on our part would depend on getting such guarantees:

DEAR MR. AMBASSADOR:

. . . It is . . . necessary that we should have undertaking from German Government that these foodstuffs will not be interfered with in any manner and that we shall be allowed to place in this territory at least five American members of Commission and shall have the right to move about in full superintendence of the work of distribution. . . . As the matter is one of urgent humanitarian interest I trust that you will again lend us your kindly services and that the German Government will meet us in a liberal and prompt manner. . . .

HOOVER

The Ambassador informed me that Foreign Minister von Jagow had told him that the German Army would co-operate and had advised that we settle details of the guarantees with German Headquarters at Charleville. I had suggested that if the Germans objected to American civilians amid their operating armies, we might arrange to have the supervision of the Relief carried out by neutral army officers in uniform. On March 21, however, the German Foreign Office informed Gerard that this was not necessary.

In accord with von Jagow's suggestion, on March 18, 1915, I instructed our Director in Brussels, Albert Connett, to go to Charleville and try to work out the guarantees, including an assurance that the harvest of 1915 would be assigned to the civilian population. On March 21, Connett signed the following memorandum of agreement with General Zoellner, the Quartermaster General of the German Army, subject to my approval:

1. Mr. Hoover's telegram . . . concerning the supervision of the distribution of foodstuffs to the civilian population of the portions of Northern France occupied by the German army was produced and discussed.

2. The German army administration agree in principle that American officials in uniform act in the manner proposed as supervisors for the activities of the C.R.B.

3. The German army administration gives the assurance that in no case will the goods be claimed for the needs of the army, but that they will be solely used for the civilian population of the occupied portions of France.

4. The German army administration has requisitioned and given receipts for the foodstuffs for man and beast existing in Northern France, so that all stocks have passed to the possession of the German army administration. Therefore no stocks whatsoever any longer exist which belong to the French population, with the exception of poultry and vegetables in the gardens. To exclude any misunderstandings, the fact must therefore be stated, that the claiming for army purposes of the stocks now already requisitioned, should not be regarded as a new requisition. The most indispensable foodstuffs for man and beast have hitherto been delivered to the population by the Germans in strictly specified rations.

5. With regard to the utilization of the new crop, the German army administration has a free hand, because, by supplying seed and furnishing labor, horses, motor plows, and so on, the administration itself effects the things essential to the securing of the crop, and furnishes compensation for the use of the land and of French labor.

6. The German army administration assures the C.R.B. of the greatest liberality in regard to freight charges and will grant at least the same concessions as for the provisioning of Belgium.

The British Foreign Office at once objected to this arrangement in a letter from Lord Eustace Percy. I have already quoted in the previout chapter parts of this letter pertaining to German guarantees in Belgium. With regard to the proposed agreement for Northern France, Percy wrote:

FOREIGN OFFICE, LONDON
6 April 1915

DEAR MR. HOOVER:

Many thanks for your letter of the 29th ultimo, regarding your agreement with the German General Staff about the conditions of your work in Northern France.

As I told you the other day, the conditions of your work in these districts are not our business, but are matters for the French Government. But it may be worth while for me to point out, in connection with our recent correspondence, that this Government would regard these conditions as wholly unsatisfactory if applied in any way to Belgium.

Points 4 and 5 are of course the offending provisions. The Germans here admit that they have done in France what in effect they have recently taken steps to do in Belgium. . . .

Lord Percy then made the customary expressions of the usual British feeling about the Germans in general and continued:

. . . The fixed policy of the Germans is clearly to make larceny a title of ownership and we rely upon you to resist all such attempts at encroachment in Belgium by every means in your power.

But though point 4 is bad, point 5 is infinitely worse. . . . And the German conditions as to the French districts are . . . gravely disquieting, because they indicate an intention generously to allow you to exist provided that they are thereby enabled to take every scrap of food which the country has produced in the past or may produce in the future. . . .

EUSTACE PERCY

I instructed Oscar Crosby, who had now joined our staff to take Connett's place, to try again to get more adequate guarantees. He signed the following agreement with Major von Kessler, who had been delegated by the German General Staff to handle this matter:

BRUSSELS, 13 April 1915

1. The German Commander-in-Chief gives his consent for the C.R.B. to undertake the supply of the population of the occupied French territory with foodstuffs.

2. The German Commander-in-Chief gives the assurance that the goods imported for the said purpose will never be called upon for the use of the German Army, but shall be used solely for the French population of the occupied territory. . . .

Any goods which may not have been distributed at any time will remain at the exclusive disposal of the C.R.B.

3. The C.R.B. is authorized to appoint in the occupied territory of Northern France, American citizens as its delegates, who may, subject to the supplementary agreement No. 1 attached hereto, satisfy themselves of the carrying out of the assurance given under paragraph 2.

4. The requests to the C.R.B. for, and the distribution of the goods will be effected according to the determinations of the C.R.B., in conjunction with the German military authorities, by French trustees, who are to be nominated by the French communities, subject to the approval of the German military authorities and of the C.R.B. These trustees will represent the French communities in the transactions with the delegates of the C.R.B., more particularly in connection with accounts and payments.

5. The German Commander-in-Chief will afford every facility for the carriage of the goods to the place of destination. The goods will be admitted free of duty, and freight will be charged according to similar principles as may, from time to time, be in force for the supply of Belgium.

The transport is regulated by the supplementary agreement No. 2 attached hereto.

6. In order to eliminate doubts as to origin and destination of the goods supplied, all means of transport and storing rooms will be labeled officially by the German military authorities in such a manner as to make the goods recognizable as those covered by the stipulations of paragraph 2.

7. If military exigencies should so require, this agreement may be canceled by the German Commander-in-Chief at any time without giving any reasons, by a notice to that effect to the C.R.B. However, all goods imported by the C.R.B., then being already within the occupied French territory, shall be disposed of in accordance with the stipulations of this agreement, the American delegates remaining long enough to discharge their duties with respect to such goods, in so far as this is considered practicable for military reasons.

8. The right of the German military authorities to requisition for military purposes against "Bons" the foodstuffs for men or animals still existing in the country is in no way affected by this agreement.

Likewise, the German military authorities reserve to themselves all rights in respect to the new crop.

VON KESSLER, Major
OSCAR T. CROSBY

The supplementary agreements referred to satisfactorily facilitated the staff and transportation work of the Commission. However, the critical question of German requisitions of native food and the 1915 harvest remained unsettled. The British Foreign Office was quick to point out these deficiencies:

FOREIGN OFFICE, LONDON
21 April 1915

DEAR MR. HOOVER:

Many thanks for your letter of the 19th. The new treaty with the Germans in France is certainly an improvement on the first one, but point 8 contains the objectionable features against which I protested in the first.

As to the harvest, I know that Mr. Gerard is going to the Emperor personally about it, so I will say no more than that a settlement on this point is absolutely necessary if our present arrangements are to continue.

As to the continuance of requisitions against "bons" [obligations to pay], the provision is, to say the least, strange. In the first treaty the Germans said that there were no more foodstuffs in the possession of the population, as they had all been converted into military stores. The two statements do not tally, but both are absolutely inadmissible from our point of view.

The above is my own opinion only, but I feel most strongly about it, and I don't think anyone here is likely to feel less strongly than I!

EUSTACE PERCY

At the request of the French Chargé d'Affaires in London, I transmitted the agreements to him:

LONDON, 23 April 1915

DEAR MR. DE FLEURIAU:

With regard to the information which you asked for yesterday, I beg to enclose copies of the arrangements entered into between our staff and the

German General Staff with regard to the distribution of foodstuffs in Northern France. . . .

I then explained various organization and routine matters and continued:

I regret to say that some misrepresentation has got abroad in Northern France that this is a commercial enterprise, and I hope that no such impression has reached your Government. The whole of this Commission is carried on by voluntary effort, without remuneration of any kind. . . .

HERBERT HOOVER

Crosby not having made satisfactory progress in regard to any German pledges concerning the 1915 harvest, I now assigned Dr. Kellogg to go to Charleville and try to get an agreement with the General Staff. I joined him in July, and we reviewed the whole matter with the Germans.

The problem was far more difficult to solve than that of Belgium. In Belgium, the German Government, in effect, authorized the requisition and distribution of the crops by our organization. In the North of France, it was not physically possible for us to set up our own requisitioning system in the midst of six fighting armies even if authority had been granted to us to do so. We also had a profound distaste for searching for and seizing the peasants' produce with a German soldier at our side. There were further complications. A considerable amount of the local bread grains would have had to be shipped to Germany to be milled because there was little flour-mill capacity in this occupied territory. Beyond this, the Germans themselves had cultivated the abandoned farms and had furnished seeds and steam plowing to the remaining peasants for a share of the crop.

We finally concluded that there was only one solution for obtaining and distributing the crop to the civilian population. That was for the German Army to requisition the entire crop from the peasants and to pay the peasants for the crops they had raised, including the peasants' share of their joint operations. Then the Germans were to distribute the food as we might designate and at agreed prices, the

operation to be without profit to them. In order to simplify the operation further, we proposed that the French population's share of the
crop should be estimated and expressed in a per diem ration to be
furnished by the Germans to the communes. The problem would then
be reduced to the prices to be paid to the peasants and the prices
paid by the communes for the German ration.

However, we met with another difficulty. We had to estimate the
amount of the total crop in order to determine the size of the ration
the Germans were to deliver. We had no adequate statistical basis
on which to calculate this unharvested crop. The pre-invasion yields
provided no yardstick, since thousands of farms had been abandoned
after the invasion and lay unworked, even by the Germans. Moreover, the labor had to be performed by women, children, and the
aged, all of whom were comparatively less efficient. They were short
of animals and machinery and almost wholly lacking in fertilizers.
Furthermore, we knew that the peasants would undoubtedly secret
as much of their produce as they could, and they did so. We therefore proposed the following plan, to which Dr. Kellogg secured a
tentative agreement on August 16, 1915:

1. Beginning at latest on September 11th, there is to be put at the dis·
posal of the population of the occupied French territory the indigenous
crop:

At the desire of the Communes, per capita per day at the rate of 100
grams of flour.

2. Assuming this, the . . . Commission has declared itself willing to supply in addition thereto a supplementary ration of 150 grams of flour per
day per capita (at least).

3. The population therefore receives per capita per diem 250 grams of
flour or about 345 grams of bread. Considering the shortage of other foodstuffs this ration is not deemed too large.

4. The distribution will be made either as . . . [grain], where the possibility of milling by the population exists, or, if this is not the case, as flour.

5. With a view to economy in the use of the rye-stock, the flour distributed will be wheat flour, or whole wheat.

6. The distribution is to be based on the statistics made by the Begleitoffizier [liaison officer] of the C.R.B. delegates. The quantities thus com-

puted are to be assigned to the Communes, whenever possible, for one month in advance, under the control of these officers.

Stocks once distributed come under the same guarantee of protection as the other provisions imported by the C.R.B. The distribution of the rations is to be attended to by the Communes, but will be superintended by the Begleitoffizier. . . .

7. Payment is to be based on the requisitioning price. Thus the Communes in receipt of goods will have to pay for each 100 kilograms of flour (f.o.b.) 30 francs or 24 marks.

8. Payment is to be made in currency. City . . . [currency], etc., are only to be accepted in cases of absolute need, and only in so far as they fulfil the conditions especially prescribed for the case. Wherever possible, payment should be accepted as service of the Communes. This means of settlement is to be preferred. . . .

9. In those parts of the country where the C.R.B. cannot deliver for military reasons, the whole ration of 250 grams of flour is to be supplied from the indigenous stocks. . . .

VON SCHOELER
General Intendant of the Field Army

On September 3, Dr. Kellogg agreed with the General Staff on a method of handling the potatoes:

1. The requirements are to be reckoned at 200 grams per capita per diem. The numbers of the population established for the provisioning with bread cereals are to be taken as a basis of reckoning.

2. To begin with the requirements are to be definitely assured for six months from the date of the harvest.

The rest of the text related to administrative details.

The British complained about these agreements and again appended their views of Germans in general. Their disapproval was mostly based on a misunderstanding with respect to price and currency questions. I myself was not satisfied with certain particulars in these arrangements, and I directed Caspar Whitney, who had temporarily relieved Dr. Kellogg at Charleville, to undertake further negotiations. He succeeded in getting the Germans to agree to provide the amounts estimated as necessary for the destitute without payment.

As the year went on and the harvest was brought in, our American representatives were able to learn more about the quantity of the 1915 harvest and the actual remaining population. With this information, we calculated that the rations the Germans had agreed to furnish would require more from them than they could requisition from the peasants. This proved to be true. The total value of the food secured by these agreements, calculated on an import basis, exceeded $70,000,000. The arrangements were certainly better than the one-time French proposal to evacuate the entire population. That would have placed a burden of 2,500,000 destitute people—mostly women, children, aged, and infirm—on the free population of France. Under our setup, they remained in their homes and contributed considerably to their own support.

Various incidental problems arose in connection with the Relief of the North of France. A few samples are indicative.

On July 2, 1915, I notified the French Embassy in London of steps taken by our staff to end relief in several specified areas because of certain German actions:

DEAR MR. DE FLEURIAU:
We beg to inform you that we are this morning advised that on Wednesday last our direction in Northern France stopped the whole of the food supplies in transit to the Lille and Roubaix districts, involving about 600,000 people. This was in consequence of a threat given to the people of Roubaix by the military authorities that unless they made sacks [for sand bags] for the German army, the Germans would themselves hold up our food supplies for the city of Roubaix. Under the undertaking imposed upon us by the Allied Powers with regard to this work, we feel that it is our duty to obtain further instructions from you as to continuing the ravitaillement in view of the above incident.

HERBERT HOOVER

The German demand was withdrawn.

A much greater tribulation confronted us over the problem of forced labor, with which I shall deal later. Suffice it to say now that it involved a series of barbarities perpetrated by the Germans.

Another question, that of settling the financial arrangements with the communes, arose from a French Government stipulation through the exiled Belgian Government that we secure an undertaking from each commune to repay the French Government for the food supplied them by the Commission.

In July, 1915, I furnished the French Government, through the Belgian Finance Minister, Van de Vyvere, a complete month-by-month report concerning our organization, giving full details about its personnel and the food distribution to each district. I asked him to supply me with answers to the following questions:

1. Are we to continue the work beyond the present credit of Frs. 75,000,000?

2. Are we authorized to expend up to Frs. 20,000,000 per month after the exhaustion of the present credit?

3. Are the French Institutions satisfied to allow the financial arrangements with the communes to be settled by the Comité du Nord and that we should not, in the future, press for personal guarantees of the district committee members?

4. Will the French Government be satisfied with the method of accounting which I have proposed as between ourselves and the French Committees?

HERBERT HOOVER

Also in July, 1915, W. H. Chadbourn, now our Director in Lille, who was in London at the time, made the following answer to French Government complaints and questions concerning German violations of agreements transmitted to us by Chevrillon:

LONDON, 15 July 1915

DEAR HOOVER:

With regard to Mr. Chevrillon's letters, the last of which is dated the 13th of July, in which he inquires about the feeding of German civilians, I beg to say that I have had the direct responsibility and the most intimate contact with the whole situation in Northern France ever since the beginning, and that there never has been, so far as I know, a single German civilian or soldier who has had an ounce of foodstuff which we have imported. This proposition is a total and complete illusion on the part of somebody because there is one tribute that we can pay to the German Army and that is that they have scrupulously helped us in carrying out this part of the guarantees and no one has been so insistent that there should be no ground for complaints on this particular account as has been the German General Staff.

With regard to the other point of feeding French civilians who are at work for the German Army, we have not considered it our business to prevent these people from having food, even when they were working under duress. We have consistently taken the single attitude that every Frenchman in Northern France is to receive food; that no one else is to receive this food; that it is an obligation on us to see to it that the Germans do not prevent the French from receiving food or use the threat of suppressing our supplies as a lever to compulsory work by the French. In other words, we take the attitude that the food should flow freely to the people in Northern France; that no interruption should take place, no matter what the condition of their employment; that our guardianship consists thus of two phases: first, that no one else receive the food except the French; and, secondly, that no one interrupts the flow of food to the French. You can take it absolutely that this has been carried out to the last letter and I would add that the staff and myself who have had this matter in charge were not prepared to give volunteer effort of this kind to any other sort of control. All of us have worked absolutely for nothing; we have mostly paid our own expenses; and it is only upon the ideal set out above that we were warranted in taking the hardships and the incidental humiliation which we have supported on behalf of the French people.

W. H. CHADBOURN

CHAPTER 13

TROUBLES WITH SHIPS

At this time we needed constant use of about sixty cargo ships in order to deliver 120,000 tons of supplies monthly to Rotterdam from North American, Argentine, and Far Eastern ports.

The British required that our ships call at British ports for inspection, involving much red tape, thus inevitably making each voyage of longer duration. German agents inspected our ships either before departure or upon arrival at Rotterdam. In England, we also took on bunker coal.

Piloting more than two thousand overseas cargoes for four and one-half years during peacetime from all over the world to the ports of Holland would be only a humdrum job, but piloting them through a blockade and a submarine war in times when there was a scarcity of ships introduced totally new elements into the shipping business.

As this work unfolds, it will disclose aspects of transportation that are unique even in the history of war. We had variable co-operation from the belligerents. Slowly, guarantees of immunity for our ships were built up to meet new and stifling crises, but often the guarantees threatened to collapse under the shifting tides of war and the good or bad nature of men in a fight.

In order to procure ship charters, protect our ships from attack, and facilitate their voyages, our Shipping Director, John White, developed seven ideas. I have mentioned some, but not all, in previous chapters.

The first idea was that since both the British and the Germans insisted on searching our ships at some point, we should carry only full cargoes because part shipments made inspection difficult and implied reloading and great delays.

The second idea was that both the Germans and the British should issue passports for our full cargo ships through their officials at ports of departure and for return voyages from Dutch ports, thus saving searches en route or at sea.

The third idea was that we should fly our own flag—"C.R.B."—and mark the sides and decks with great illuminated signs, "Belgian Relief," which we hoped might make the ships immune from stoppage at sea or from sinking by irresponsible submarine commanders.

The fourth idea was that we should be given advance routes for our voyages by the belligerents.

The fifth idea was that we could charter ships of any nationality and that even our Allied-flag ships should be free from German attack.

The sixth idea was that we should be given war insurance by the Allies when we paid for it or, alternatively, that we should insure with Lloyd's.

The seventh idea was that we should be respected and even given priorities, since we were serving a great humane cause.

The following pages will show that through thickets of red tape, conflicts between the British and German orders, and obstacles normal to total war, we gradually secured all of these ideas, although, sadly, there were intermittent violations or suppressions.

SHIP PASSPORTS

As our first step, two weeks after we started work, I addressed Lord Percy at the British Foreign Office on the ship passport question:

LONDON, 8 November 1914

DEAR LORD EUSTACE:

. . . I should be glad to know if it would be a possible thing for us to approach the Foreign Office through the proper channels to obtain the following scheme, viz.: that some kind of document should be issued by the Foreign Office which would serve as a pass for our complete cargoes consigned to the Commission for Relief in Belgium . . . these passes to be sent by us to the ports where we have ships being despatched and to be there viséd by the British Consul and to be attached to the bill of lading and taken up with the bill of lading when the ship arrives. Such a document asking immunity from all British Naval Authorities would be of great encouragement. . . .

HERBERT HOOVER

The next day, the French Minister in Holland suddenly held up our ships, and, since our protests were unavailing, Ambassador Page thus queried our State Department on November 9, 1914:

SECRETARY OF STATE, WASHINGTON

The French Minister in Holland caused embarrassing situation regarding forwarding of food to Belgium saying he lacked instructions from his Government; more cargoes will arrive forthwith. Can French Government not send him instructions soon as possible to consent to transshipment through Holland as all other Governments consent?

AMERICAN AMBASSADOR, LONDON

This evoked the instructions needed.

During our first year, there was a surplus of British shipping, which we sought to charter. On November 16, I took up with the Germans the matter of their issuing "passes" and granting immunity to Allied ships when in our employ. Ambassador Page made an inquiry for me, through the State Department, to Ambassador Gerard in Berlin about the German attitude:

SECRETARY OF STATE, WASHINGTON

The Commission for Belgian Relief wish our Government to request the German Government for safe passage of British as well as neutral ships bound for Rotterdam with food for starving Belgians. Such ships will fly the Commission's flag.

Please ask German Government also for permission of military authorities in Belgium for Americans with automobiles to go from place to place engaged in food distribution. Such Americans will carry Commission's flag and have letters, each with bearer's photograph, from the Commission countersigned by Spanish Ambassador here and myself.

AMERICAN AMBASSADOR, LONDON

The German Foreign Office replied favorably to Ambassador Gerard, saying:

BERLIN, November 23, 1914

... German Government is entirely in sympathy with laudable work of American Commission for Belgian Relief. German naval forces cannot lawfully seize food on neutral ships bound for neutral ports. Germany will not interfere with any neutral ships bound for Holland with food from the United States even if food is destined for Belgium. Subject to revoke German Government agrees to permit unneutral ships also to carry food for Belgians to Dutch ports and will give same guarantee that food is put to intended uses as for neutral ships. German Government recommends that as precaution such unneutral ships carry certificate from competent American authority testifying that ship carries food for the Belgians to be brought to Belgium via Dutch ports by American Commission for Belgian Relief with the consent of the German Government and that unneutral ships also have pass which German Ambassador, Washington, will issue upon certificate above described. Inquiry made about distribution of food by Americans in automobiles.

GERARD

The British Admiralty, of which Winston Churchill was then the "First Lord," was the sanctuary of British militarists. Despite this undertaking on the part of the Germans, which we relayed to the British, the Admiralty sent out the following circular to the British War Risk Clubs, the result of which was to suspend our charters of Allied ships:

ADMIRALTY WAR STAFF, LONDON
2 December 1914

SIR:

Cases are constantly occurring of applications being made by British Shipowners as to the safety or otherwise of the route to Dutch ports.

Quite apart from the safety or otherwise of the routes, it is pointed out that the Admiralty considers it most undesirable that any British vessels should be employed in adding to the already very large supplies of grain, etc., which are flowing into Holland.

As you are aware, the Admiralty do not put an absolute prohibition on such voyages, but merely rule it out of the permissible voyages under the Insurance Scheme.

At the same time, it is hoped that British Shipowners will in future decline to carry any such cargoes, and I should be much obliged if you would circularize the members of your club accordingly.

RICHARD WEBB
Director of Trade Division

Because at this moment we could not obtain enough neutral-flag vessels, this was a blow. We then engaged in a complex negotiation through the British Foreign Office and finally achieved this amendment to the circular:

To BRITISH WAR RISK CLUBS:

In reference to my letter of the 2d instant, respecting voyages of British vessels to Dutch ports, I beg to state that the desire expressed therein was not intended to apply to ships carrying supplies for the Belgian Relief Commission.

The Admiralty, while unable to allow such voyages to be made under cover of the Government Insurance Scheme, are anxious not to hinder the work of the Relief Commission.

Will you be good enough to inform those members of the London group of War Risk Associations who are concerned in the matter.

The list of vessels probably chartered for this purpose is attached.

RICHARD WEBB
Director of Trade Division

This did not remedy our problem because without war risk coverage, we could not get Allied-flag vessels. I therefore wrote to the head of the British Board of Trade:

LONDON, 10 December 1914

The Right Honorable Walter Runciman, M.P.
Board of Trade, London

... The second matter is one of great importance to us—and that is the question of British Government Insurance on cargoes and vessels going to Rotterdam for our purpose.

Although the circular issued by the Trade Division of the Admiralty to British owners suggesting that they should refrain from going to Rotterdam was amended to the extent that the wishes of the Government did not extend to our ships, the amended circular stated that the British Government Insurance would not apply.

... the owners with whom we now have charters are compelled to take out independent insurance at Lloyd's. Furthermore, the moral effect upon the shipping world has been so great as to make it almost impossible for us to secure ships at all at any price. The rates have been advanced in an extraordinary manner for Rotterdam, and this combined with the insurance put upon us bids fair to cost us something like £30,000 to £40,000 extra over what could be done if the British Government Insurance applied to our ships as far as Rotterdam.

I have taken the matter up with the Belgian Government and they have agreed that they will undertake to guarantee the British Government against any loss which might be incurred on that section of the voyage from British waters to Rotterdam and return, and I understand they are prepared to do this without receiving any proportion of the premium, so that if the British Government could see its way to extend the Government Insurance to all our vessels to Rotterdam the effect would not only be actual in facilitating insurance but would be of the greatest moral and material benefit to us in inducing the British shipowners to give us their help.

Some time since, in an interview with Sir Edward Grey, he suggested that if an undertaking could be obtained from the German Government that ships engaged on our work would not be interfered with, it might facilitate the views of the British Government as to the extension of insurance, although he could give no undertaking in the matter. We have obtained this assurance from the German Government so that so far as the risk extends to naval action, that has been eliminated not only for the portion of the voyage from British waters to Rotterdam but also throughout the ship's whole voyage, thus to some extent possibly reducing the total risk.

I would therefore greatly appreciate it if you could reconsider the whole insurance question and see if the Government could manage to meet our difficulty to this extent. . . . Such a concession as the above would not represent any direct outlay on the part of the Government but would represent to us a material . . . [reduction in costs].

HERBERT HOOVER

On December 19, the British agreed to extend the war risk insurance on our Allied ships to and from Rotterdam—for a while.

On December 24, the Germans amplified their undertaking of November 23 concerning Allied-flag ships with detailed stipulations, but, probably out of inadvertence, they did not specifically extend "passes" to neutral ships. However, we got this amended through Ambassador Gerard, who also cleared up a misunderstanding concerning passes from Rotterdam back to Britain.

Some of our charitable gifts in kind were shipped by the donors themselves in partial cargoes to Dutch ports. Ambassador Page informed Washington of the British demands in this matter:

LONDON, 28 December 1914

SECRETARY OF STATE, WASHINGTON

The Foreign Office informs me that the British naval authorities will undertake in the future to facilitate the voyage only of such charity ships to Rotterdam as contain whole cargoes of food for Belgian relief. It is important therefore that such ships should not contain other cargo, and to secure this protection all ships for Belgian relief must be reported by Lindon Bates, the Commission's representative in New York, to the British Ambassador in Washington. After conferring with Sir Cecil Spring Rice it might be advantageous to give this arrangement wide publicity because certain societies and committees continue to ship contributions of food on ships that carry other cargo.

AMERICAN AMBASSADOR, LONDON

We had no positive assurance that the British would respect our C.R.B. flag and our markings of the words "Belgian Relief" on the sides and decks of ships in order to avoid searches at sea. But at Lord Percy's motion, Sir Edward Grey confirmed this guarantee on March 8, 1915.

Another of our difficulties was the route through the mines strewn by both belligerents in the North Sea. We had to get sailing directions from the Germans for every ship entering these areas. Furthermore, our ships from the Argentine and India needed to pass through the English Channel, for which the Germans would give us no directions.

In conversations with Minister of Foreign Affairs von Jagow on my Berlin visit, I pointed out the conflict between British and German authorities on the question of routing our ships to Rotterdam. My note of the conversation was:

I then took up the question of our steamers coming up the Channel after the 18th February, the presumable date of the submarine blockade. I pointed out that under the English regulations and the conditions of their charters, it was wholly impossible for these ships to go to Rotterdam by way of North Scotland. After some discussion the Minister promised to have orders issued of the most scrupulous care of our steamers.

Since nothing happened, Ambassador Gerard, at my request, again raised this question with the German authorities. He secured permission for us to proceed via the English Channel, but, as shown in von Jagow's reply, the Germans now refused passes for those of our ships which called at British ports. The British required us to do this for inspection purposes, and we had to call there for coal.

FOREIGN OFFICE, BERLIN
5 March 1915

MY DEAR EXCELLENCY:

Many thanks for your kind letter of the 1st instant enclosing a copy of the telegram of Mr. Hoover. Herr von Bethmann-Hollweg and I retain the most pleasing remembrance of Mr. Hoover and both he and Your Excellency may rest assured that the Imperial Government maintains its former attitude to afford the humanitarian work of the Relief Commission on the part of Germany every possible support.

We had also been informed of Mr. Hoover's anxiety through our Legation at The Hague, and I had thereupon ascertained at once through the Imperial Admiralty that ships of the Relief Commission should also proceed undisturbed by the English Channel route provided that they be recognizable by the customary insignia, which should also be illuminated so as to be plainly visible at night. The German submarines have been instructed accordingly. Herr von Mueller at The Hague will in the meantime have advised Mr. Hoover of this fact through the American Minister at The Hague.

In this connection we must naturally assume that all means will be taken to exclude the possibility of a misuse of the insignia of the Relief Commission. To this end the Imperial Foreign Office will invoke again in an official communication the kind mediation of Your Excellency to obtain from the British Government a declaration containing the assurance that only those ships that are actually in the service of the Relief Commission may carry the insignia of the Commission.

As Your Excellency will easily understand, we were unable, in view of the existing danger from mines in the war zone, to refrain from declining to issue safe-conducts to the ships of the Commission for the journey to and from England. On the other hand, we will gladly issue safe-conducts, as heretofore, to those ships of the Commission which do not touch at English points, and at the same time urgently recommend them, precisely on account of the danger from mines, to choose the northern route around Scotland indicated in the "Nachrichten für Seefahrer," No. 3161, 1914.

We believe that in this manner all the wishes of the Relief Commission, whose efforts cannot too highly be appreciated, have been met as regards sea traffic. . . .

VON JAGOW

The German Embassy in Washington followed this up by notifying our New York Director that our ships must proceed without making stops at British ports, which completed the tangle.

GERMAN EMBASSY, WASHINGTON
15 February 1915

Lindon W. Bates, New York
DEAR MR. BATES:

With reference to the recent declaration of a war zone around the English coast I beg to draw your attention to the fact that, though of course the German commanders will do their best to avoid any mistake, *every* ship entering the war zone will be in danger. Also the letters of safe-conduct which this Embassy gives to the relief ships will not remove this danger as an examination of these papers by submarines will probably not be feasible inside the war zone. I can therefore only very strongly recommend that the relief ships take the course north of Scotland indicated by the German Admiralty.

E. V. HANIEL

I immediately cabled New York that this would stop the whole works.

LONDON, 17 February 1915

RELIEF COMMISSION, NEW YORK

Please inform German Ambassador our British Admiralty and Board of Trade regulations and all our charter parties require all our ships call Falmouth for orders and necessitate proceeding direct Rotterdam through Straits, otherwise all charter parties break down and will be impossible enforce delivery. Last Monday in Berlin I discussed matter with Secretary Foreign Affairs who assured me as ships are marked and can cross Channel in daylight Germans would give instructions they not be interfered with in accordance their previous undertaking with us. Unless we can proceed as usual route entire supply to Belgium will break down.

HOOVER

Our Rotterdam office confirmed the bad news:

ROTTERDAM, 25 February 1915

HOOVER, LONDON

We have just been advised by local German Consul that German Ambassador Hague refuses to give return passes to steamers employed by our Commission, except those holding papers from American ports, and these passes are only good for return via northern route. . . . German Legation Hague refuses any kind of pass on . . . [cargoes] purchased en route. Are you guaranteeing safe return of all steamers from Rotterdam to United Kingdom ports? Will advise result of Hague negotiations as soon as possible. Three steamers have left Rotterdam for England without passes but are using Commission flag, namely: "Treneglos," "Ariel," "Rockabill."

RELIEF COMMISSION

We then telegraphed Whitlock and Gerard, asking them to help with the Germans and furnishing them with the following information:

LONDON, 26 February 1915

RELIEF COMMISSION, ROTTERDAM

. . . Utterly impossible for us to procure sufficient food supplies for Belgium exclusively from North American ports and are therefore compelled to buy floating cargoes and to engage foodstuffs from other quarters of the world, some of which are transshipped from British ports. Furthermore utterly impossible for us to deliver one pound of foodstuffs in Rotterdam if ships required to go or come north of British Islands as shipping cannot be engaged under this condition, and unless German Government is prepared to give instructions that the markings on our ships, which are visible for miles, and our flag, are to be respected in the passage of ships to and from British ports to Rotterdam engaged solely on our work, the whole business becomes absolutely hopeless. No ships will use our markings unless on our mission. We are only securing the passage of these ships by virtue of the insistence on our part that our flag will be respected under the agreements which we have with the German Government and the assurances given to me personally by His Excellency von Jagow, and if the German Government is no longer prepared to respect our flag and their undertakings to us it appears to us that our efforts must come to an end. I cannot believe that there is any intention on the part of the German Government to otherwise than assist in every way in their power this humanitarian effort.

HOOVER

Our Rotterdam office telegraphed us again that the Germans still refused:

ROTTERDAM, 16 April 1915

HOOVER, LONDON

German Embassy Hague has refused to issue safe-conduct passes to any ship touching England for coal or otherwise. German Embassy states that they only agreed issue safe-conduct passes back direct to America.

RELIEF COMMISSION

On April 18, I again had to turn to Ambassador Gerard for help, spelling out the situation to him through the American Embassy in London. Ambassador Page, on the same day, cabled an account of the entire matter to the State Department in Washington. I telegraphed a copy of Page's telegram to John White, then in Rotterdam, for the information of van Dyke, our Minister in Holland. As usual, Ambassador Gerard effected a solution of the impasse, confirmed by the German Foreign Minister as follows:

FOREIGN OFFICE, BERLIN
18 April 1915

EXCELLENCY:

In reply to your two kind communications of 17th April, I would emphasize anew that the philanthropic work of the Relief Commission for Belgium is fully appreciated as far as Germany is concerned, and that every support will gladly be lent it. Accordingly, the German submarines have now been directed to allow the ships of the Relief Commission to proceed unmolested, if they are recognizable by their marks of identification, so that a special letter of safe-conduct would not really be necessary.

However, the Imperial Legation at The Hague has now been authorized by me, by telegraph, to issue to the vessels of the Relief Commission letters of escort not only for the return voyage to America, but also for the trip to England, provided that the ships in question are required by the terms of their charter to return to England and that they take no cargo for England.

For their safety, however, and in order to avoid errors in identification, the ships in question must be strongly urged to carry by day and by night clearly recognizable marks of identification.

Furthermore, it is to be recommended to the Commission's ships, should they wish to return to America, not to call at English ports solely for the purpose of coaling, but rather to provide themselves with coal at Rotterdam.

To make this possible, we shall gladly lend our assistance that they may be able to purchase German coal in Rotterdam.

I gladly avail myself of this opportunity to renew to Your Excellency the assurance of my highest respect.

VON JAGOW

Von Jagow's "good" advice not to call at British ports was unworkable with the British, but the crisis died down—for a while.

GERMAN TORPEDOING OF OUR SHIP THE *HARPALYCE*

On my visit to Berlin in February, 1915, I asked Chancellor Bethmann-Hollweg to clarify the status of our C.R.B. flag to the German submarine authorities. To lend point to my request, I told him the story of a man who had a bulldog which he assured his neighbor would not bite. But the neighbor replied: "You know the dog would not bite, but does the dog know it?" The Chancellor agreed to instruct the submarine commanders. However, the dog did bite—many times. The first was on April 10, 1915. One of our ships, the *Harpalyce*, was torpedoed by a German submarine. On April 16, I wrote Ambassador Page the full story, including my own feelings on the subject:

DEAR MR. PAGE,

SINKING OF THE "HARPALYCE"

I want to set out my views of this business for it appears this ship after discharging her relief cargo in Rotterdam sailed for Norfolk, Virginia, at 2:30 A.M. on April 10. At 10 o'clock in the forenoon of the same day, in broad daylight, when just off the North Hinder Lightship, she was blown up in the stern without any warning whatever, and sank instantly. No boat could be launched and the Captain, Chief Officer, Fourth Engineer, Chief Steward, one European Cadet and a large part of the Chinese crew were drowned.

The ship was entitled to and received a safe conduct pass from the German Minister at The Hague before sailing, and was displaying our markings, including signs ". . . Belgian Relief Rotterdam" 5 feet by 100 feet on either side and readable for five miles.

From the evidence we sent you today this ship was certainly torpedoed and her "Relief" character must have been evident to the murderers of these innocent men engaged in a humanitarian task.

Here is a ship engaged in this work, not only destroyed in contravention of every sacred assurance of Government undertaking and of humanity but the assurances that we have universally given to shipowners and insurers that if they would engage in this traffic they would be free from attack, is blown to the winds; every contract we have made for ships and insurance based on this agreement is shattered, the work brought to a standstill, and the lives of 10,000,000 people imperilled.

I simply find myself totally unable to express in sober language a proper characterization of this action. It is absolutely in its complete barbarism without parallel in the last century. I count myself as not being given to hysterics over the abnormal events of modern warfare but if this action can be reconciled with any military necessity, or, to put it on its lowest plane, of any military advantage, then we can but abandon any hope that civilization has yet accomplished anything but enlarged ruthlessness in destruction of human life. . . .

HERBERT HOOVER

I appended for the Ambassador the complete facts of the matter, including statements from the officers of the ships *Elizabeth* and *Constance Catherina,* both of which had witnessed the sinking, as follows:

1. Sworn statement of Second Officer and Second Engineer of "Harpalyce."
2. Statement of Captain Matross of S.S. "Elizabeth."
3. Statement by Captain Kuipen of the "Constance Catherina."
4. Copy of pass issued by the German Ambassador at The Hague.
5. Copy of the receipt of the Captain of the "Harpalyce" for the markings of his ship.
6. Telegram from our Rotterdam office, showing markings which . . . ["Harpalyce"] had displayed.
7. Note Verbale of German Foreign Office to Ambassador Gerard, dated December 24.
8. Copy of telegram from Gerard to State Department re same, dated January 4, 1915.
9. Note from Spanish Ambassador, London, December 31, re same.
10. Note dated February 11 on understanding with German Ambassador, The Hague, re return passes to United Kingdom ports.

The next chapter in this incident is described in a letter I wrote to Ambassador Page on May 7, 1915:

DEAR MR. PAGE,

We have today, through Rotterdam, received the following telegram from Mr. Gerard:

> According to investigation of German authorities concerning sinking British steamer "Harpalyce," an English steamer with one funnel and four masts proceeding towards England, on the morning of April 10th, namely at the time when the Harpalyce is said to have gone down,

was sunk in the war zone between British and Dutch coasts. This steamer did not, however, carry markings of Belgian Relief Commission. It is not known whether this vessel was the Harpalyce. Accordingly the markings of the Relief Commission have not been disregarded. Gerard.

From the above description and time, and the fact that there was only one ship torpedoed that day in the North Sea, it would appear, without doubt, that the Germans admit that the "Harpalyce" was sunk by a submarine, which does away with any discussion as to whether she struck a mine or not. The outstanding question which they raise, however, is that the ship had no markings displayed. As to this, we can point to the two photographs of the ship which we have, as she lay in the dock at Rotterdam discharging, to the evidence of the officers of the ship herself and to the evidence of the captain of the ship that rescued part of the crew, who himself saw the markings of the ship shortly before she was sunk.

HERBERT HOOVER

There was little consolation in the fact that the ship was insured and the owners thus indemnified. But this was only one of the tragedies we were to endure.

WE REQUEST BELGIAN-FLAG SHIPS

In early June, 1915, John White reported to me that there were about 80,000 tons of Belgian-flag shipping which could be controlled by the exiled Belgian Government at Le Havre. He felt strongly that the Belgians should put this tonnage in our service for the duration of the war. I took the matter up through the Belgian Minister in London. The Belgian Government doubted that they had the legal authority to seize the ships and the owners protested violently because they wished to continue in their profitable trade. Although we offered to pay liberal charters, the Belgian Government concluded that it could do nothing.

GERMAN COMPLAINTS ON THE CONDUCT
OF OUR SHIPS

We had a number of complaints from the Germans to our staff in Rotterdam about the conduct of our ships. We did not wish to bother Ambassador Gerard with all our troubles and therefore addressed an answer through Minister Whitlock in Brussels:

24th June 1915

MY DEAR MR. WHITLOCK,

With regard to the constant complaints of the German Authorities as to our ships discharging small amounts of munitions or other goods into fishing-smacks, entering into ports, etc., when passing England, I would like to make a suggestion to the authorities:

1. These complaints are a complete mystification to us, because if any inimical persons wishes to carry on such traffic, it is absurd that they should do so on our boats. The cost of our freight is higher than is current even for munitions, and such method of discharging, as into fishing-smacks, is also absurd and unnecessary for anyone engaged in this business, as there is ample shipping direct to England.

If there is truth in the statements that stuff is taken off our steamers on the English coast, I am suspecting that it represents food cargo stolen by ships officers, as we have had some shortages in manifests which creates uneasiness in our minds, and it would be a great help if we could have the evidence on which these assertions are based.

2. These ships, save in case of cargoes bought afloat, are loaded under inspection of our own agents, but we would greatly welcome the presence of an agent of the German Embassy in Washington or the German Consulates at the port of loading. The German authorities could thus satisfy themselves.

3. I may mention that we have had bitter complaints from the English Government that advantage has been taken of our carrying free of charge Red Cross supplies to Germany from the United States, in the particular, that these goods are not as represented in the declarations as to their contents, and we, in a desire to continue this service for the German people, have arranged that these goods should be inspected, so that such complaints cannot be well founded.

HERBERT HOOVER

The action of Whitlock and van Dyke seemed to have satisfied the Germans and ended complaints—for a while.

THE ELEMENT OF STUPIDITY IN WAR

As a prime example of war stupidity, the record of our negotiations for German-interned ships is worth detailing here, although it continued into our next fiscal year.

After about thirty days of shipping experience, we developed, in 1914, an ideal solution for obtaining a supply of ships. I asked Lord Percy to explore the attitude of the British departments toward our chartering German cargo ships then in refuge in neutral ports. He informed me that the Foreign Office favored the idea, but was skeptical that we could get the Germans to agree.

On my journey to Berlin early in February, 1915, I discussed the matter with Chairman Ballin of the Hamburg-American Line. Ballin was a humane man and said that he would help. He was of the opinion that to put 200,000 tons more shipping on the seas in addition to the 25,000,000 tons of the Allies and neutrals should not worry the German military authorities. He declared that his company would be glad to have the earnings and proposed, in view of our charitable character, that charters would be granted on prewar terms, which would reduce our transportation costs about 60 per cent. I then went back to the British on this matter. Sir Edward Grey, on March 16, 1915, wrote to me, formally approving the idea but subject to certain conditions, as follows:

1. The title to these ships must be transferred to a firm in some neutral country. The transfer must be made in a form which would not normally entitle the ships to a change of register or to fly the flag of the neutral country concerned; and the ships must either revert to the German owners as soon as they cease to be exclusively employed by the Commission, or must in any case be recognised to be liable to be treated as German ships so soon as they cease to be so employed. A special arrangement must be made between His Majesty's Government and the neutral Government concerned by which the ships shall, for the period of their employment, be permitted to fly the neutral flag.

2. These ships shall be operated by, and the entire crew composed of, neutrals.

3. The Commission shall charter the ships from the neutral firm who shall operate them.

4. The Commission shall submit the name of the neutral firm in question to His Majesty's Government before the transaction is finally concluded.

5. The ships shall, after His Majesty's Government have finally approved the transaction and have made the necessary agreement with the neutral Government, be immune from interference on the part of His Majesty's Government to the same extent and in the same way as the ships at present employed by the Commission, so long as they are employed solely and absolutely in carrying foodstuffs on behalf of the Commission, and the Commission shall notify His Majesty's Government immediately it ceases to employ any particular ship.

6. A list of such ships in the employ of the Commission shall be furnished to His Majesty's Government and any change in the list of ships immediately communicated.

7. The Commission shall not pay for more than 4s. per ton dead-weight per month as charter money to the neutral Company and no other payment outside this sum shall be made by the Commission to the German owners. The Commission shall inform His Majesty's Government of the terms of the whole transaction before it is finally put into force.

John White went to Berlin to follow up the matter with Ballin, and they agreed on a transfer of the ships to the Royal Dutch Lloyd, together with the terms of charter and a managing agreement with the Dutch Lloyd Company, which would furnish Dutch crews. The agreement complied with all the British conditions. White telegraphed me the entire text of the contract on April 17, 1915.

The details of these negotiations dragged out interminably, but finally, on September 7, the British indicated that they would approve the contract as made by White, stating, however, that the French Government was reluctant and that I must secure their approval. On September 8, 1915, I wrote to Louis Chevrillon, our Director in Paris, as follows:

LONDON, 8 September 1915

DEAR CHEVRILLON:

I . . . [have] informed you from time to time that we were negotiating to . . . get the . . . use [of] German interned ships for this trade. These negotiations have been going on since last . . . [February] and we have finally formulated contracts, of which you will find enclosed two copies. The British Government has approved, and has asked for the approval of the other Allies, which I understand they have received with the exception of the French, and the whole matter is now held up at that point.

In a general way the price which we pay for these ships works out at about 40 per cent of the price at which we have to charter ships in the market. It will make a difference of about 4 centimes per kilo in the price of bread in Northern France. Aside from the fact that it will save us from £100,000 to £150,000 a month and thereby decrease the cost of the ravitaillement in Northern France very appreciably, it also has an important bearing from the point of view of the Allies. At the present moment we are the largest shippers outside of governments, and our entrance into the shipping market maintains the price of transatlantic shipping at fully 10 per cent above what it would be if we got out of it, and it affects the price of bread in both England and France in just about that proportion of their transport costs. Under the arrangements made the sum of money going to the Germans for the use of their ships is infinitesimal. Four shillings per ton deadweight on a 5,000 ton ship would represent £1,250 per month, and out of this practically the whole operating expenses of the ship have to be paid, and it is estimated by our shipping experts that the margin over operating expenses will not exceed £500 a month. Of this margin one-half goes to the Dutch firm which operates the ships, and one-half to the Germans, so that on a ship of this size the Germans would only be getting a revenue of £250 a month. They of course have the benefit of being relieved of the cost of maintaining their idle ships, which is the principal thing which has influenced them. They have also been greatly influenced by the humanitarian aspects of the enterprise, and we had strong support from the humanitarian elements in the German Government in our . . . negotiations with Herr Ballin.

I was wondering if it would be possible for you to stir up the French Foreign Office a little, in view of the above, and see if you could get them to signify their approval to the English Government. The matter is one of pressing importance as we are having the greatest possible difficulty in securing enough shipping for our work, and, in any event, the freight that we lose represents a considerable sum of money in which the French people are directly interested.

HERBERT HOOVER

I was utterly astonished at Chevrillon's reply:

PARIS, 6 October 1915

DEAR HOOVER:

I have had several long conversations yesterday at the French Foreign Office with the outcome that the ship question is decidedly taking a bad turn. There was a note in the handwriting of Mr. Delcassé himself giving his opinion as inclined to be adverse, and, curiously enough, a very long letter from Mr. Klobukowski, the French Minister to Belgium [the exiled Government], very strongly giving his arguments against the proposed combination.

I immediately saw one of the very high officials of the Department, but found that his conviction was also made and strongly opposed to our proposal. A note will be presented to the English Government setting out the objections of the French Government, more or less in the manner formulated by Mr. Klobukowski.

For your information, I will now present the case as set forth in this letter and such as I remember it from having had it read to me rapidly:

"In the first place it is a known fact that the Hamburg-America Company is on the verge of failure and the proposed combination might just save it. The upkeep of the boats in New York is a very considerable expense, of which that Company would be relieved.

"The boats having a neutral crew, many German sympathizers might be employed in the service, which might lead later to deplorable consequences. Also, at the close of hostilities, the boats would be scattered in such a way that many of them would be probably in home waters and therefore in a position to be immediately utilized by Germany to start at once on a career of industrial competition instead of lying in New York until they can be put in service again.

"A further reason is that the hostile press would not fail to say that the German submarine war has been so active and so successful that the Allies are obliged to take this course as the only temporary remedy to a very grave difficulty.

"Finally, the proposed combination is nothing else but 'dealing with the enemy.' The Allied Governments still consider that the work of the Commission is only tolerated under the plea of humanitarianism. The duty of provisioning and victualing the populations in a territory occupied by German troops is incumbent upon the German Government; the work is performed at the expense of the Allied nations under protest, and the idea of chartering a German fleet, of paying a German company, of relieving it from an enormous expense, of guaranteeing its ships from any attack, of putting them in perfect train for immediate action after the war is over, all this for a service which Germany should perform, cannot for a moment be entertained. No Allied Government could accept such a paradoxical position as that of a German fleet of steamers circulating freely, the only steamers of any of the belligerent governments immune from war risks or capture."

Such will be the reasons presented by the French Government in answer to the English suggestion, and I am afraid that the Foreign Office here will refuse to budge from its position unless some profound modification of the proposed arrangements is agreed upon.

. . . I do not quite understand how our French Minister at Havre came to be consulted, but it is certainly a fact that his communication came at a moment when the Foreign Office here was hesitating and clinched a decision. . . .

L. CHEVRILLON

These arguments drove us to the explosion point. How the Hamburg-America Line, a German corporation in Germany, could go bankrupt from the loss of prewar charter rates of fifty unmanned, anchored ships; how these neutral crews would be any more unneutral than those sailing three thousand other neutral ships; how this was a case of "dealing with the enemy" when we were already doing so every day to save the lives of 2,500,000 French people—all this was beyond our comprehension. Although it encroaches on the narrative of the second year, I may well report the last gasp of this effort.

The British Foreign Office again urged the French to agree. Therefore, accompanied by Chevrillon, I spent five days in Paris, from the tenth to the fifteenth of February, 1916, arguing with various French authorities, but we could not budge them.

On March 15, the British Foreign Office formally approved the contract, thinking that this would encourage the French to follow suit. But we got nowhere.

By now the Germans began to appreciate that even these 200,000 tons of shipping would provide a form of relief for the Allies and withdrew from the contract. Later, the French Government asked me if I could not revive the contract with the Germans.

Stupidity is an essential concomitant of war.

CHAPTER 14

TROUBLES WITH
GENERAL VON BISSING IN BELGIUM

We had troubles with General von Bissing. The first of these difficulties concerned restrictions on the number of our American staff in Belgium and their freedom of movement, as well as restrictions placed upon the Comité National.

The General's officials had been restricting the passes necessary for our staff to enter and move around Belgium. Together with Whitlock, I went to see von Bissing about this on February 11, 1915. Von Bissing was a small-sized man, and my impression was that without his uniform, high boots, and helmet he would have looked most insignificant. My impression of his mental processes would also be included in that term. We did not get anywhere, so the next day, I wrote him a long letter spelling out our problems on this matter in detail, the essential parts of which were:

BRUSSELS, 12 February 1915

EXCELLENCY:

In the representations which I made to Your Excellency last evening with regard to giving a larger measure of freedom of movement to the men engaged in the work of alimentation and more expedition and liberality in the issuing of passes, and Your Excellency's reply which I took to mean that Your Excellency felt that our people have already too much freedom of movement, I am afraid that I did not lay sufficient emphasis on the important phase of this work and the gravity of the situation which arises. . . .

141

After outlining British opposition to our enterprise, I repeated the original British guarantees, which stipulated

... that such machinery be set up in the shape of an organization as would satisfactorily demonstrate that these [German] guarantees would be carried out.

I then went on:

It was for this primary reason that "The Commission for Relief in Belgium" was founded and that a number of American volunteers were recruited to undertake the work. It was stipulated that in order to carry out the work without any question of doubt as to the ultimate destination of the foodstuffs ... [the] transportation and [distribution] ... should be under the members of this Commission.

It was also found that in order to secure the equitable distribution of the food throughout Belgium the members of the Commission had to take certain administrative duties. . . .

Time and again misrepresentations have been made to the English Government by ill-willed persons (and even in America) as to the attitude of the German officials in Belgium and it has only been by the explanation of the detailed supervision of our members and the completeness of our records, which show the destination of every sack ... which comes into Belgium, that we were able to keep open the road of these foodstuffs through the British fleet. . . .

We have now been engaged upon this work for nearly four months; there have been issued at one time or another a good many passes to the people engaged in this work, and I do not think that Your Excellency could point to a single instance where these passes when issued to bona fide representatives have been misused or that a single criticism can be made as to the scrupulous care with which all our relations have been carried out.

In order to obtain the character of men whose devotion to humanitarian efforts is such that they can be depended upon from every point of view we have had to operate the whole of this work with volunteers ... we could not secure for a monetary payment men of the character of those now engaged in this labor. I therefore put it up to Your Excellency that this body of men are worthy of the fullest confidence and that they are gentlemen who would scorn the imputation of espionage or other improper conduct on their part. Dependent as we are on volunteers there is necessarily more recruiting and departure of new men than would be necessary in a commercial organization.

Inasmuch as the whole body of men engaged upon the arduous labor of handling 90,000,000 kilos of foodstuffs per month are volunteers, it is hopeless for me to induce these men to remain or to secure new men if they are to be made subject to the whims of every local "Kommandantur"; and on the other hand we cannot take the responsibility of the necessary assurances to the American public who subscribe so generously, and to other interested governments, unless we have men of this character and unless we are able to carry on our daily work of supervision, inspection, and accounts with the necessary freedom of movement.

Although I feel deeply the responsibility, I am compelled to assure Your Excellency that unless we can establish a basis of confidential and friendly relations and trust from the German authorities, we shall be compelled to withdraw and the flow of the stream of foodstuffs into Belgium from outside countries must necessarily cease. . . .

I do not wish to ask for anything which cannot be properly given under the circumstances, but it does seem to me that it would be possible and entirely reasonable to detail some member of the German pass bureau, who could devote himself to our necessities, and who should have instructions to treat our applications on a very liberal and expeditious basis. . . .

HERBERT HOOVER

Von Bissing immediately replied to me through our Director in Brussels, reiterating a number of intolerable restrictions, including an order to reduce our staff. The British Foreign Office, being informed of this through their Intelligence, promptly objected. I thereupon advised Whitlock:

LONDON, 6 March 1915

DEAR MR. WHITLOCK:

I have had a severe drilling this week from the English Government with regard to our whole organization in Belgium. As you can imagine from the international disputes which have been going on with regard to provisioning the civil population . . . it seems to have occurred to the English Government to have an investigation as to whether or not we were carrying out our guarantees, and they seem to have made some considerable inquiry in Belgium. . . .

We, of course, worry on from day to day as best we can, but I think you should be advised of this rather acute situation . . .

Von Bissing, however, was adamant against Whitlock's protests. Therefore, on March 9, I telegraphed Ambassador Gerard through our Rotterdam office and sent a copy of my message to Whitlock. It said in part:

. . . We have been notified by Governor-General, Brussels, to reduce our staff in Belgium to twenty-five members by early April and that passes to these gentlemen will only be issued under great restrictions. . . . Do not believe that it can be in line with the intentions German Government toward us and trust you will take it up with them. Fundamental fact is that in order for us to give proper executive control to distribution of this foodstuff, to properly account to its donors, and above all to give credibility to our assurances to the Allied Governments . . . it is absolutely necessary for us to have the right to at least fifty people, to put any such number of staff into Belgium as may be reasonable to meet our own emergencies. Their passes must be issued directly on certificate of Mr. Whitlock and on liberal basis of movement. After four months the Germans cannot point to one single instance of lack of extreme care on the part of this Commission in maintaining an absolutely neutral and honest attitude toward them. The men who have volunteered for this humanitarian service are not engaged in espionage or similar transactions.

HERBERT HOOVER

Gerard at once obtained directions from Berlin asking von Bissing to relax. The General was amazed. At the same time, Whitlock was upset at my direct appeal to Berlin, so I wrote him a placating letter on March 18. In any event, this attempt by von Bissing to limit the American staff had been squelched—for a while.

His next effort was to try to control the Comité National. This involved two separate questions: first, the freedom of action of the Comité, and second, an attempt to use our food to force Belgian labor to work for the Germans, which I shall discuss later.

On June 26, von Bissing addressed a long letter to Whitlock. The main paragraphs, excluding those relating to labor, were:

. . . I have considered it necessary that the activity of the Comité be clearly delimited and that the mutual relations of the administration under my orders and of the sub-organizations of the Comité be regulated in such a way as to avoid the friction which necessarily was hindering the labors of the said Comité.

He then complained that Comité correspondence with its Provisional Committees was not submitted to the German authorities, that the Comité had not obtained their approval for its instructions to the communes concerning food, and that it had failed to submit monthly statements to all local German officials. Then he announced new restrictions:

Since the Comité has obtained from the communes the grant of police powers to its inspectors *vis-à-vis* the millers, bakers, etc., and since the communes have subscribed to the obligation to have the sanctions exacted by the inspectors carried out, all measures of this kind must be revoked since the administration under my orders is alone qualified to exact these measures. The supervisors of . . . the Commission for Relief in Belgium have the right to make inquiries and statements regarding the abuses committed by the millers, bakers, etc., but their right is limited to making these statements. They are allowed to communicate these afterwards to the competent authorities with request to give to the statements such sequence as these may require. . . .

The presidents of the Civil Administration shall come to an understanding with the directors of the committees in order to reduce as much as possible the price of food products.

Every tendency . . . to monopolize the distribution of relief in Belgium must be forbidden. . . .

I flatter myself with the hope that Your Excellency will share my conviction that the line of conduct thus traced for my administration will serve to guarantee a common and useful work, founded on mutual confidence, for the welfare of the Belgian population. . . .

FREIHERR VON BISSING

I failed to spark as much enthusiasm for the last paragraph as the Governor had expected. This letter was transmitted by Ambassadors Page and Merry del Val to the British Foreign Office for advice. Sir Edward Grey wrote to Ambassador Page about it on July 7. We do not have a copy of this letter in our files, but apparently, the reply to it was not satisfactory, since Sir Edward again addressed himself to Page:

FOREIGN OFFICE, LONDON
17 July 1915

My Dear Ambassador:

... Your Excellency has been good enough to transmit a copy of my letter of July 7th to Mr. Whitlock, who will therefore now be fully acquainted with the views of His Majesty's Government, and will be in a position to explain that spirit of non-interference in which His Majesty's Government intend to act, and in which they intend to insist that the German authorities shall also act, towards the Commission for Relief in Belgium and the Comité National in all matters which fall within the functions of those bodies. It is in this spirit, and not on the strict belligerent rights of either government, that the whole work of relief is based, and the introduction into these discussions of any such claims of right cannot but be fatal to the continuance of that work. It will be clear to Your Excellency and to Mr. Whitlock how far General Bissing's letter is in accord with this spirit.

I do not intend to enter into a discussion of the various technical points of administration raised by General von Bissing. It is enough to say that the decision on these points must be governed, in general, by the spirit I have mentioned, and that the decision on each particular point must be in accord with the various definite conditions which I have laid down in correspondence with Your Excellency and with the Commission from time to time since the work of the Commission began. These definite conditions represent the absolute minimum on which His Majesty's Government can allow that work to continue. In order that there may be no misunderstanding as to the nature of these stipulations I here recapitulate them. ...

1. The Commission guarantees that the foodstuffs imported shall be consumed solely by the Belgian civil population.

2. No foodstuffs shall be imported which will, in effect, replace any

foodstuffs requisitioned or purchased in Belgium by the German authorities.

3. Such commodities as may be acquired by the Commission for shipment into Belgium are to be consigned to the Commission for Relief in Belgium at their warehouses in Belgium and shall remain in the sole charge, and under complete control, of the Commission or its agents until issued to the Sub-committees of the Comité National in Belgium. These Sub-committees shall in their turn enter into sole charge and control of these commodities. . . .

He then recapitulated the permitted program of imports and continued:

7. The whole yield of the present harvest of breadstuffs in Belgium shall be acquired by the Commission for Relief in Belgium and the Comité National, and shall be held, controlled, and distributed by them alone, precisely in the same manner and under the same guarantees as the imported foodstuffs.

8. It is the duty of the Commission for Relief in Belgium to satisfy itself that all foodstuffs imported or acquired as above shall be distributed by itself and the Comité National with justice and equality over the entire civil population, and there shall be no interference of any kind whatever by the German authorities either in the sale of these foodstuffs or in their free distribution in the way of relief to those whom the Commission and the Comité National shall consider deserving of such relief.

9. The Commission for Relief in Belgium shall be maintained in its organisation and functions so long as these imports continue and shall remain under the patronage of Your Excellency and the Spanish Ambassador. The actual executive work of the Commission shall continue to be presided over by a responsible Chairman and Directors, and these officials together with all the members of the Commission shall be of neutral nationality and their selection shall in each case be approved either by Your Excellency or by the Spanish Ambassador as Patrons, or by both. The Commission shall maintain in Belgium a sufficient staff and have sufficient freedom of movement to enable them at all times to satisfy themselves that all the above conditions are maintained.

E. Grey

This being transmitted to Whitlock, he informed Ambassador Page
that von Bissing had retreated as follows:

BRUSSELS, 19 July 1915

MY DEAR COLLEAGUE:

My colleague, the Spanish Minister, and I have had two long conversations with Baron von der Lancken in reference to the note of His Britan-
nic Majesty's Government which you sent to me the other day. . . .

I am pleased to be able to inform you that we are now able to say that
the German authorities accept the principles laid down on the note, and
that the work of the Commission will therefore go on under the conditions set forth. . . .

BRAND WHITLOCK

The settlement was ratified by von Bissing on July 29, and this
particular crisis was over—for a while. I learned later that it was
Ambassador Gerard who had again brought von Bissing to terms by
means of directions from Berlin.

STILL ANOTHER BOUT WITH VON BISSING

We had another disagreeable bout with von Bissing which began
during our first year and extended into the second. As background,
I must explain that it was necessary for myself and the principal
members of our staff to cross the frontiers between belligerents in all
directions. I had pledged to our Ambassador Chairmen that none of
our Americans would traffic in any sort of information affecting military matters anywhere. Our Ambassadors had given such assurances
to the belligerents, who, however, were taking no risks and subjected
our staff to constant observation and vigorous search whenever we
crossed frontiers. Unfortunately, some of our men gave von Bissing
an opportunity to do injury to us.

On November 12, 1915, I received from Hugh Gibson, through
the code to the London Embassy, a tense demand that I come at once
to Belgium because several of our Americans were about to be ex-
pelled for espionage. He also said that von Bissing was contemplating

ousting the whole Commission. At once I crossed the North Sea, plagued both with seasickness and great anxieties. I found that Gibson had been sent for by von der Lancken and informed that five of our Americans had been guilty of espionage and that the Commission, having broken its word of honor, could not expect to continue work in Belgium. Von der Lancken refused to disclose any specific information.

I immediately concluded that we would again have to place the whole matter before authorities higher than von Bissing and decided that rather than appeal so many times to Ambassador Gerard, we would take it up with the German General Staff at Charleville, under which we operated the Northern France relief.

I believed that the General Staff realized the character of our men and strongly desired that we continue the work in Northern France, which could not be operated except through Belgium. I therefore asked Dr. Kellogg and Caspar Whitney, who then represented us at Charleville, to come to Brussels and, if possible, to bring with them their two German liaison officers, Major von Kessler and Count Wengersky. On the way up, von Kessler told Kellogg of the charges against our men. Their information had come from an American youngster on our staff in Rotterdam, whom we will call "Benedict," out of consideration to his fine family in the United States. He had set up an espionage job for himself with the German intelligence agents in that city. The youngster was a second-generation German, spoke German, and had seemed to us a perfect associate for handling our routine relations with the German authorities in Holland.

The five members of our staff alleged to be involved were Poland, our Director in Brussels, who had written a letter which von Bissing considered a personal affront; Young, our Director in Rotterdam, who had applied for a pass into Belgium for a Major Winchell of the American Salvation Army and had made the bad joke in the presence of "Benedict" that Winchell was a member of that Army's intelligence service; and three of our men in Belgium, who had come to the Rotterdam office in connection with their work and whose minds "Benedict" had probed for their opinions of the Germans, thereupon reporting their chatter to the German authorities.

Present at our meeting were Kellogg, von Kessler, Wengersky, Captain Uhl, also an officer of the German Intelligence, and myself. Dr. Kellogg made the following hasty and somewhat ungrammatical memorandum of what took place. I quote it extensively because it sheds light on some of the events of war:

BRUSSELS, 2 December, 1915

Mr. Hoover stated he was glad to have the opportunity to go exhaustively into the whole situation; that the relations of the Commission with the Staff in the north of France had always been so cordial and the Staff engagements so justly and liberally carried out, the Staff attitude so open and frank, that he felt he could be frank even to brutality. That the situation in Belgium was becoming intolerable and that the ravitaillement of Northern France must collapse with that of Belgium. He sketched briefly the history of the Commission and its relations to the General [von Bissing] Government, laying stress on the fact that while Governor von Bissing's attitude was correct, if not cordial, he was surrounded by an absolute pack of bureaucratic underlings whose sole desire and mission seemed to be to seize anything in Belgium and dress it up in some form designed to attract the Governor's attention to themselves and their energies. That it was patent that the utmost jealousy existed among these departments, and that we were the shuttlecock with which they beat each other over the head, hoping the Governor would notice their valiant conduct. He sketched the relations, first when the C.R.B. and the C.N. were under the Civil Department: how their control had been seized by the Political Department last June from the Civil Department, on the impeachment of [that] committee's bad political activities; how this was but an incident in the war between von Sandt and von der Lancken, and how von der Lancken had been put to it ever since to justify his representations to the Governor at that time. That we had been subjected to intolerable destructive inquisition, no remote helpfulness in attitude, and how gradually this was degenerating into violation of the spirit of the agreements.

He sketched the attempts to manipulate the relief, in violation of the undertakings about forcing labor through control of relief, and pointed out that the Commission would not go on one minute if it were to become an implement to force the population, against its will and consent, to work for the German Army. That to use the control of men's food to force the civilian population to disloyalty to its government was a thing we would not stand for on humane grounds, to say nothing of the international undertakings upon which we were founded.

He took up the Poland incident as an example of bureaucratic tyranny and incompetence and gave them a sketch of this transaction and the notorious letter involved. They read the letter, and [von] Kessler remarked that its contents were innocent and justified and that it was in text and character far different from that represented to him by the [Brussels] authorities. Hoover pointed out that if experienced men such as Poland were to be jerked out of the country on the breath of an arrogant clerk, in this manner, we would have to chuck the job at once. Hoover went into the incident of the three men and the failure to get any reasons for the attitude about them. He pointed out the hopelessness of obtaining men of character and honor if they were to be treated in this way. He stated that the heads of the business had a right to know what the charges were. Von Kessler said that he had heard several items, one of which was that information was conveyed verbally by these men to Young at Rotterdam as to the September offensive and through this route to the Allied Governments; that Young had proposed to introduce two spies into Belgium with Commission passes but had been stopped by protest of his American colleagues. He said he was unaware of the details but that in our position spread over the whole rear, the Staff were greatly disturbed by these reports. He said they had the utmost confidence in Hoover, Kellogg, Whitney, and most of the men, but that such matters as this transcended every food question.

Hoover agreed and stated at once that the matter must be gone into to the very bottom; that they would find him more Catholic than the Pope on the slightest breath of justifiable suspicion; that from his point of view he required no such evidence as was needed in law courts but the ground for reasonable suspicion would be sufficient; he expressed his absolute horror at the idea that [any American] would jeopardize the lives of 9,000,000 people by such conduct, for it must genuinely reflect on the neutral character of the Commission. He expressed his absolute disbelief that there was a word of truth in it and stated he believed that it was a tittle-tattle produced by von der Lancken in accord with his general attitude. He suggested that any capable German officer be given the dossier and that this officer and Hoover should jointly hold an inquiry to establish, not guilt, but reasonable suspicion.

Von Kessler also said there was some complaint about a Major Winchell that Mr. Young had applied for a pass for, and gave the impression that they believed that he was an Allied agent. Mr. Hoover explained the circumstances of his belonging to the Salvation Army, etc., and that . . . [Young] had made the foolish . . . [joke that] he might be the head of their intelligence service, which joke had poor results. He stated he believed it could be proved to be absolute nonsense. . . . [As to other men mentioned, they had not] arrived from America until after the date of the great offensive. Von Kessler agreed that more data should be given.

On the main issues von Kessler stated that he and his superiors had taken the matter up energetically with General von Bissing and recommended him to create a special department to look after the C.R.B. . . . and that it had been done, and that he had brought Captain Uhl from the Staff to take charge of our relations to this department. We all expressed pleasure at this arrangement, learning incidentally that Captain Uhl had been chosen because he was a good American resident of Santa Barbara, California. Von Kessler said that Wengersky would remain in Brussels for a fortnight to get the new bureau running. Mr. Hoover mentioned that Captain Merton had turned up, saying he was going to be associated with us; that we liked him and hoped it would be so. Von Kessler said it would be arranged as we wished.

Hoover then elaborated on the indivisibility of the C.R.B. and the C.N. in all departments, the fears and suspicions on all sides as to proposals made by the General Government, and the disastrous results that would follow to food and tranquility, and hoped the new department would meet these matters in an intelligent manner. This, von Kessler and Uhl assured us would be the case. . . .

With von Kessler's help, we quickly disposed of the charges against Young, Poland, and the Salvation Army major as nonsense. We sent the three others to work in our London office, as they were given to chatter. We immediately sent "Benedict" to London, where, upon a hint to Scotland Yard, his passage to the United States was so expedited that he was placed on a ship for home within twelve hours. However, on his way to the ship, he poured out to his escort a new and highly detailed story to the effect that we Americans were all working for the Germans. This tale being transmitted to the Admiralty, we had to cope with it later.

Major von Kessler settled these questions with von Bissing. He quickly established what we had long wanted by way of the posting

of German liaison officers in our Brussels office. Since these new men
were members of the General Staff, they could influence von Bissing.
All this having been arranged, I had a peace conference with von der
Lancken, my memorandum of which was as follows:

BRUSSELS, 4 December 1915

Von der Lancken said he was glad to tell me that the Governor had
decided to set up a new committee, comprising representatives from
each—the Political, Finance, and Civil Departments, together with an
officer from the General Staff, which would take over all questions relating to the C.R.B. and C.N. [and designate capable liaison officers to work
with us]. . . . He stated he had sent for Poland and that incident was now
out of the way happily. . . .

CHAPTER 15

COERCION OF BELGIANS
TO WORK FOR THE GERMANS

On a trip to Belgium in June, 1915, I learned, from our C.R.B. Director, William B. Poland, and our inspection staff, of an "underground" activity of an Allied military department through the Belgian exiled Government at Le Havre. One of its purposes was to subsidize the Belgian railway employees and other skilled mechanics with monetary allowances so that they would not work for the Germans. The Belgians had every moral and patriotic right to embarrass the Germans by any device they could invent, and it was none of the C.R.B.'s business. But there were phases of it which bothered us and which could endanger our whole service to the Belgian people.

In our view, this activity was foolish and would invite reprisals. These men and their families would be fed under our rationing system whether they worked or not, and the Germans had ample manpower of their own to conduct any critical railway operation needed for military purposes. Our fear was that if the Germans believed the C.R.B. was connected with it, they might raise serious questions about our fidelity to our undertakings to preserve rigid neutrality. At once we made a record of protest in Belgium, and later at Le Havre, which might clear our skirts if any such charge arose. However, the Germans never mentioned it to us.

But von Bissing quickly began a series of measures—to coerce the Belgians to work for the Germans—which did concern us. On June 26, he addressed a letter to Minister Whitlock, one paragraph of which was:

Concerning the relief to be granted to those out of work, the presidents [of our Relief provincial committees] shall take care that the latter do not hinder the resumption of work by the laboring population. *Moreover, relief cannot be given to workmen who refuse remunerative labor.*

This made food for the Belgian workmen contingent upon working for the Germans.

The information of this action came to the British Foreign Office, and on July 17, Sir Edward Grey notified our Ambassador Patrons in London that no food would be allowed to go into Belgium if used for these purposes of coercion. This being communicated to our Minister Patrons in Brussels by our Patrons in London, they, on July 29, secured the following modification from von der Lancken:

That the Governor-General . . . [will] never make use of the Comité National to force the Belgian population to employ itself in the service of the German Army contrary to the stipulations of the Hague conventions.

This was not entirely satisfactory, but we concluded to await further developments, which came rapidly.

On August 14, von Bissing took more severe steps by issuing a decree providing for imprisonment of Belgians who refused to work for the Germans. It read:

BRUSSELS, 14 August 1915
ARTICLE 1
Anyone who without adequate reason refuses to undertake or continue labor in the interest of the public, for which he is called upon by German authorities and which is in the line of his professional activity, shall be punished by detention or imprisonment for not more than one year.

In particular, any reason for such refusal based on international law is to be accepted as adequate.

ARTICLE 2
Article 2 of the Decree of 19th November 1914 (*Gesetz- und Verordnungsblatt für die okkupierten Gebiete Belgiens*, No. 17, p. 57) is replaced by the following regulation:

Whoever undertakes, by force, threats, persuasion, or other means to restrain others from undertaking or continuing labor in the interest of the public, for which he is called upon by German authorities and which is in the line of his professional activity, or labor for German authorities or for contractors executing contracts for German authorities, shall be punished by imprisonment for not more than five years.

ARTICLE 3

Anyone who knowingly aids or abets a refusal to work which incurs punishment in accordance with Article 1, by furnishing support . . . or in any other manner, shall be punished by a fine of not more than ten thousand marks, in addition to which a sentence of imprisonment for not more than one year may be imposed.

ARTICLE 4

If communes, unions . . . or other organizations aid or abet refusal to work as described in Article 3, the penalty shall be imposed on the leaders.

ARTICLE 5

Sums of money which are proved to be destined for the support of the persons designated in Article 1 shall be confiscated for the benefit of the Belgian Red Cross.

ARTICLE 6

The German military courts and the German military authorities have jurisdiction in these cases. . . .

The decree then provided for the exceptions stipulated in the Hague Conventions. Article 5 indicated that the Germans were aware of the extra payments to the workmen by the underground.

When these decrees reached the British Foreign Office, Sir Edward Grey blew up in a letter to Ambassador Page:

FOREIGN OFFICE, LONDON
22 September 1915

MY DEAR AMBASSADOR:
. . . On August 14th and 15th the Governor General of Belgium issued two decrees which were published in the *Gesetz und Verordnungsblatt* at Brussels on August 22nd. These decrees impose severe punishments on

workmen who refuse to give their labour to "works of public interest" or who, being in receipt of either public or private relief, refuse to accept work offered to them. Similar penalties are imposed on persons, "communes, associations, or other groups" who, "by the distribution of relief or by other means," "favour" such refusal to work. The decree of August 14th is to be enforced by the military tribunals. The decree of August 15th imposes automatically imprisonment for a fortnight to six months on all who, having refused work, become a charge on either public or private relief.

Both these decrees contain a clause exempting from their operation those cases where refusal to work is based on considerations admitted by international law, and I am well aware that the German authorities will claim that this exemption is a sufficient fulfilment of their promise quoted above. They will also doubtless claim that the word "favour" implies a deliberate use of relief for certain objects and does not apply to the assistance given by the relief committees of the Comité National. Unfortunately, the German authorities cannot expect, in view of their known actions in such matters, that any reliance should be placed on the interpretation to be given to such vague phrases by their military tribunals. The report recently published by the Belgian Commission of Inquiry (9th Report, August 6th) on the methods of coercion applied by the German authorities to the railway workmen at Luttre has revealed the German policy in such matters, and it is alleged on good evidence that, in order to give effect to that policy, the relief committees, communal soup-kitchens, etc., have in many cases been forbidden to give relief to classes of workmen whose labour the German authorities desire to enlist in their service. It is, however, unnecessary to rely on such allegations, since, by the decree of August 15th itself, the mere grant of relief to a workman renders that workman liable to imprisonment on the ground that he has in the past refused employment.

It is unnecessary to recapitulate the account given in the report above-mentioned, or to dwell on the measures of deliberate starvation, imprisonment, deportation, and torture to which these workmen have been subjected. This, it must be assumed, is the "law of nations" which is referred to in these German decrees and to which the relief committees are to be subjected, and this is the interpretation to be placed on the "Hague Conventions" and on the phrase "the service of the German Army" in Baron von der Lancken's letter. If any Belgian workman, knowing the wide ex-

tent of the needs of the German army and the manner in which every industry in Germany is already devoted to the task of supplying it, should
refuse to work in industries indirectly essential to the maintenance of that
army, relief is to be denied to him and starvation and imprisonment await
him.

I feel that, were this correspondence to be published—and it will, I fear,
soon be my duty to ask Your Excellency's consent to its publication if
present conditions continue—the people of this country would draw from
it the conclusion that no further assistance should be given on their behalf
by His Majesty's Government to a relief organisation whose activities are
in danger of being so controlled by the enemy.

In face of the grave alternatives before which the whole work of relief
is thus placed, I feel obliged to ask you to be good enough to draw the
attention of the patrons of the Comité National at Brussels once more to
the facts I have stated, in order that they may take the necessary steps to
satisfy themselves both now and as time goes on, that the German authorities abstain from all interference in the work of relief which those authorities themselves have so recently promised to leave free and untram-
melled. . . .

In conclusion I must again call attention to what I said in my letter of
July 17, that this work could not be based on the strict belligerent rights
of either Government. Your Excellency knows that the Commission is enabled to exist solely by the assistance given to it by His Majesty's Government, and His Majesty's Government having so far gone beyond their
duties and renounced their rights, they cannot tolerate that they should
be met in this matter by an assertion of rights on the part of those who
have renounced their duties.

I have sent an identical letter to the Spanish Ambassador, and have furnished the Netherlands Minister with a copy at his request.

E. GREY

Protests from the British Foreign Office had little effect on von
Bissing.

As a sidelight on the history of the war, but more specifically as a
real human document, I give this instance. On October 25, 1915, the
operators and workmen in the Lessines Quarries were convicted of
refusing to work and sent to jail by a German Military Court. The
quarrymen appealed to von Bissing as follows:

EXCELLENCY:

We learn that you have directed an inquiry into the facts as a result of which a certain number of directors and assistants as well as numerous quarrymen of Lessines were recently condemned to prison by a War Court for refusing to work.

. . . the position taken by them is not only sanctioned by the rules of International Law but also by Article 1 of your Decree of 14th August 1915.

For more than a year all operations have been suspended in the Lessines quarries and great misery prevails among the working population of that city and the adjacent villages. Further, masters and workmen would embrace with joy the opportunity to resume work which would not be opposed to their patriotic duty.

This was our attitude at the first. We so declared it on 21st August to Mr. Martini, Berg-Assessor at Mons. We told him that if sufficient guarantee could be given that the product of the quarries would not be employed either directly or indirectly for military purposes, we were convinced that all difficulties would be easily settled. Unfortunately, the guarantees we asked were refused us without discussion . . . we have received proof that the macadam of Lessines is shipped toward the German lines.

Under these conditions our refusal to work is legitimate, as we stated above, through Article 52 of regulations concerning laws and customs of war, and through Article 1 of your Decree of 14th August 1915.

Also, may we count upon the equity of Your Excellency, to have justice done to our fellow-citizens, recently sentenced. . . .

We are ready to endeavor to induce the workmen to resume work if formal assurance is given us that no product of the Lessines quarries will be acquired or requisitioned for any military purpose whatever. . . .

. . . we venture to draw the attention of Your Excellency to the treatment inflicted upon the recently sentenced directors of Lessines.

They are under a régime of hard labor, which is particularly serious on account of the age and state of health of several of them. . . .

. . . we dare to hope that Your Excellency will see fit . . . to intervene in order that the treatment to which our friends are subjected, may be mitigated.

> *The Masters of the Lessines Quarries*
> except Jacquemin, Vanderveede and new quarry owner

Von Bissing was adamant in the face of this prayer and replied:

BRUSSELS, 5 November 1915

The memorandum of 25th October 1915 concerning the refusal to work at Lessines has not altered my opinion on the subject.

The opposition of the operators and the workmen to my efforts to settle the question of work and to effect the well-being of the population is not justified by the Convention of The Hague.

The operators should recognize my efforts to induce the workmen to earn a regular salary (see my Decree August 16) and had better demand the protection of the military power to force the recalcitrant men to work. . . .

I have no guarantee to give that the product of the Lessines Quarries shall not have a military application and I must reject this requirement. . . .

. . . the penalties imposed are just because they are not counter to Article 52 of the Hague Convention and the culprits were warned of the penalties they incurred in refusing to work. . . .

BARON VON BISSING
Governor-General

But worse was to come.

CHAPTER 16

AN INTERLUDE
OF AMERICAN POLITICS

In October, 1915, there occurred an incident which loomed dangerous at the time. It contained a great tragedy, but in the end, it strengthened our organization.

The Director of our New York office at this time was Lindon W. Bates, an old friend and engineering colleague of mine. His eldest son was en route to join our staff in Belgium when he was drowned as a result of the German torpedoing of the *Lusitania* on May 7, 1915.

John White, our Director of Shipping, who had gone to New York on business in September, soon after began sending me word that Bates was acting in a strange manner. He stated that Bates blamed the Relief for the loss of his son; that he was in communication with the State Department, and some Senator in Washington, denouncing the Commission as a national danger; that we were acting in violation of the Logan Act of a century before, which prohibited American citizens from taking part in negotiations with foreign governments on international affairs.

All this impressed me very little at that moment because our negotiations were not on behalf of the United States but on behalf of a private, neutral organization sponsored by neutral Ambassadors and Ministers. However, it seemed that Senator Lodge, a violent critic of President Wilson and the State Department, was developing a sensational story.

The Commission was peculiarly dependent upon good American opinion, and this might well be disturbed by any such denunciation,

since Americans were resolute to keep out of any European entangle-
ments. On the urging of Ambassador Page and Melville E. Stone, the
General Manager of the Associated Press, I very unwillingly sailed
for New York on October 16, 1915. Ambassador Page and Mr. Stone
had opened the doors of the State Department and the White House
to me. On my arrival at the State Department I was hailed with a
grin and asked if I were "prepared to spend a thousand years in jail."

The President was most considerate, expressed his great satisfaction with what we were doing, and asked if he could be of any help.
I suggested two things: that he might issue a statement expressing
his confidence in the Commission, and that it would be helpful if he
would request a group of leading citizens in New York to constitute
a Committee to take charge of our New York office. He did both. The
Committee's members were Robert Fulton Cutting; Alexander
Hemphill, Chairman of the Guaranty Trust Company; Otto T. Ban-
nard, Chairman of the New York Trust Company; S. R. Bertron, a
leading New York Democratic leader; Oscar Straus, former Secretary
of Commerce; Melville Stone; and John White of our own staff. The
appointment of the Committee was announced by the White House.

Through Mr. Stone, a dinner was given me by the leaders of the
press. They agreed to act in our protection.

Mr. Straus of the New York Committee suggested that I call on
Senator Lodge in Boston. The interview was not very satisfactory.
Mr. Stone arranged for me to call on former President Theodore
Roosevelt at Oyster Bay. He was most cordial and assured me that
he would take a hand if necessary.

Mr. Bates was persuaded to retire peaceably, and I was able to
return to London without anxieties for the Commission, but in sor-
row at the tragedy of my old friend. As for Senator Lodge, this narrative will show that he continued in opposition to many of our subsequent activities.

CHAPTER 17

A STATISTICAL SUMMARY—
AND SOME KIND WORDS

Our arrivals of food and other supplies at Rotterdam for the year November 1, 1914, to November 1, 1915, were as follows:

	Tons of Food and Supplies
1914:	
November	21,234
December	57,862
1915:	
January	69,733
February	77,283
March	98,979
April	110,485
May	132,998
June	80,171
July	83,334
August	48,374
September	68,752
October	134,474
Medical and other supplies for the Commission	129
	983,808

During this year the shipments from Rotterdam were:

	(Metric Tons)	
	Belgium (12 months)	North of France (8 months)
Wheat, Rye and Wheat substitutes.......	413,913	79,974
Flour	140,736	12,521
Meat, Bacon and Ham....................	13,908	7,236
Lard and Lard substitutes...............	5,038	3,200
Corn (Maize)	111,987	2,350
Rice and Rice substitutes...............	48,192	14,991
Peas and Beans........................	25,889	6,413
Yeast materials	3,337	....
Coffee	211	632
Condensed Milk	2,258	527
Soap	1	78
Clothing	1,799	....
Miscellaneous (mostly for children)......	34,834	1,273
Totals	802,103	129,195
Stocks in hand in Rotterdam.......	52,510	
Grand Total	983,808	

To these amounts should be added the native produce that we saved for Relief uses by agreements with the Germans.

But cold statistics do not express the sufferings of people or their anxieties for their future. Nor do they acclaim those who died on sea or land for the millions who were saved.

KIND WORDS FROM BRITISH OFFICIALS

I may well add to this account of the C.R.B.'s first year some extracts from an address by Lord Curzon of the British Cabinet on October 15, 1915, at a meeting in London (at Mansion House) convened by our British Committee, of which the Duke of Norfolk was Chairman. The purpose was to stimulate British contributions to the Relief, for which the Lord Mayor had delivered an impressive appeal. After describing the situation and the need, Lord Curzon said:

... You alluded, my Lord Mayor, to the work in this respect which has been undertaken by the Neutral Commission, and here in passing do let us, as indeed we cannot fail to do, pay our tribute to ... Mr. Hoover, an American gentleman ... who voluntarily charged himself with this great organization and has successfully pursued it to this hour. I believe you spoke no more than the truth when you indicated that this is one of the most striking achievements which we can find anywhere on record. This is the first time in history that a whole people has been fed by a private organization ... the task of purchasing [the food], of engaging shipping and transporting it to Europe, of landing it in Holland ... of preparing it for distribution and finally of distributing it amongst the seven millions of people ... is an absolute miracle of scientific organization. Every pound of food and supplies is accounted for and you have the remarkable fact that at this day bread is fetching no more in Antwerp or in Brussels than it is in the city of London. And when it is remembered that the bulk of the work ... is voluntary work, is work gratuitously given by those who take part in it, that again distinguishes it from almost any previous attempt of the kind.

Hitherto, in political history you almost always find public relief, on a large scale at any rate, associated with extravagance and scandal. But in this case and I think in this case almost alone, it has become synonymous with economy and efficiency combined.

This meeting resulted in large British giving and provided much-needed support for the C.R.B. against the opposition of the British militarists.

SECOND YEAR
November 1, 1915 to November 1, 1916

INTRODUCTION

We entered the second year of Relief on November 1, 1915, in a climate of apparent calm all along the line—with guarantees, finance, ships, and food moving to the Belgians and French—but the slender balance which we had to maintain between two powerful empires at war gave us no certainties of a placid year. And we had none.

Again for the sake of clarity, rather than risk the confusion of a chronological narrative, I discuss our activities according to subject, despite some overlapping of time.

CHAPTER 18

FALSE CHARGES
BY THE BRITISH MILITARY

In a country overrun by the German Army and with the added irritant of a sentry posted at every corner, there were bound to be many minor infractions of our food guarantees. As I have stated earlier, the Allied military authorities maintained an effective intelligence service in the occupied areas to watch over us, and constant and usually exaggerated reports of minor leakages of relief supplies went back to the British and French military departments. Those agencies were violently opposed to us from the start and made life miserable not only for us but for those in the British Foreign Office who were our steadfast friends.

Many of the supposed infractions were the doings of an extensive black-market which had sprung up in smuggled goods. This black-market drew its strength from the high prices of food outside the rationing systems in both Germany and Belgium, and its practitioners included nationals from Holland, Denmark, Sweden, Norway, Belgium, and even from England, the latter operating, by night, in craft across the Channel. The black-market sales were mostly to the Germans and were naturally encouraged by them. There were also sales to well-to-do Belgians. For the black-marketeers and smugglers, the favorite transportation routes to Germany were through the Dutch and Belgian canals.

Under pressure from both the Allies and Germans, the Northern neutrals were compelled to divide their meager surplus—mostly animal products—between the Allies and the Germans and, in the early

171

years, were not legally allowed to export to Belgium. The C.R.B. interest lay mainly in the smuggling through Holland.

To make sure that we kept track of any possible leakages to the Germans, to assure just distribution among the Belgians, and to make certain that there was no corruption anywhere, we had in our first year set up a Bureau of Inspection and Control. It was operated jointly by Americans from the C.R.B. and by Belgians from the Comité National. When infractions involving Germans were discovered, they were reported to local German authorities, who usually acted very judicially. When they involved Belgians, they were handled through the Comité National provincial agencies and the offenders were hauled into local Belgian courts.

Our C.R.B. men soon found that they were having difficulty with the Belgians in this joint operation. The Belgians were naturally loath to expose their countrymen, especially in times when both privation and temptation were so great.

In order that we should be able to cope with the flood of Allied complaints, I proposed, in January, 1916—and Francqui accepted—a separation of the C.R.B. inspection from joint operation with the C.N. Our men were to report their findings to the C.N. and to our American Director in Brussels. They recruited a staff of trustworthy Belgians, whose names they never disclosed, to help them in their investigations.

These energetic American youngsters, under the leadership of Joseph C. Green, at once undertook to get to the bottom of the black-market activities in and around Belgium. They established contacts with "patriotic" Belgian black-marketeers and smugglers, whose code of morals forbade them to deprive their own countrymen of food. These men co-operated with our staff in locating actual or supposed leakages from Belgium and Northern France to outside countries.

Thus set up to guard against infractions, we were able to meet head-on the deluge of accusations by the British and French espionage staffs concerning alleged violations of guarantees. The Allied agents were unknown to us and had little understanding of our organization. A great part of their complaints consisted of records of black-market operations and of canal-boat movements in and out of

Belgium and Holland. I can best illuminate the British complaints by giving a few samples.

Sample No. 1: On December 16, 1915, Lord Percy, for the Foreign Office, sent me a list of infractions and at the same time notified me of a reduction in our import permissions—presumably as a reprisal against the Germans, although only the Belgians were hurt. After enumerating the quantities of authorized import commodities, Lord Percy wrote:

> In view of action by the Germans which appears *prima facie* to infringe their undertakings, and in view of grave doubts which have arisen as to whether certain of these imports do not in effect constitute a replacement of articles bought or otherwise taken by the Germans, it is necessary to restrict your activities for the moment.

He then named certain commodities which were to be suspended, and added:

> I do not want to close this letter without saying, what you already know, that these restrictions on your activities arise out of the exigencies of the situation and imply no loss of confidence in you or the other members of the Commission.
>
> EUSTACE PERCY

Lord Percy's expressions of confidence in the C.R.B. did not appear to add to the Belgian diet, and the Germans took no fright.

Our reply to the Foreign Office after investigation of their list of complaints was to remind them that the Belgian ration ran from sixteen hundred to eighteen hundred calories, often only 50 per cent of the British ration, and that people in such straits were not given to handing over generously the C.R.B. food to Germans. We demonstrated in detail that black-market operations accounted for most of the complaints.

Sample No. 2: We were providing a huge number of small tins of condensed milk to more than 2,500,000 children in their special canteens for a noon meal in Belgium and Northern France. On December 28, 1915, the British claimed that the Germans were gathering up our empty tin cans for their metal content and promptly applied pressure on us via a letter from Lord Percy:

FOREIGN OFFICE, LONDON
28 December 1915

DEAR MR. HOOVER:

I am sorry to involve you in so many difficulties, but . . . I must trouble you.

. . . as to the condensed milk. Our people are firm on the point about the return of the empty tins. The danger does not arise from the amount of metal in the tins but from the tins themselves. Germany is very short of tins, so much so that she is sending out empty tins to be refilled with preserved meat, etc., in neutral countries, and is collecting empties high and low.

Now I quite see that this means a considerable amount of new organisation on your part, but the re-collection of these tins should present no huge difficulties in itself. Each commune can collect them fairly easily from the consumer each time the latter applies for a new ration, and all the way up the chain from the communes. . . .

Meanwhile, can you take steps to have the Commission in Belgium and France keep a careful eye on the Germans and stop them at once if they try to collect tins from house to house as they are doing in Germany itself?

EUSTACE PERCY

He further stated that they were holding up one of our ships, the *Livingstonia,* pending a solution of this question.

The French added to this complaint by asserting that the Germans were throwing the C.R.B.'s small condensed-milk cans across the trenches—loaded as hand grenades.

We undertook to recover the tins. Since the Germans controlled our transportation, we had to secure their approval for the collection and transport of the tins, especially from the midst of their armies operating in the north of France and the "Etape." The Germans said amid laughter that the amount of tin on these little cans did not interest them, and they added that the supposed hand grenades were a variety of their soldiers' trench humor, as the empty cans were loaded with rocks and, in any event, could not be fitted with firing devices except at impossible expense. They raised no objection to our installing a system requiring the communal authorities to deposit ten francs with us against each can issued to them. We returned the deposit when we got back the empty can. The burden of accounting by the canteens and the communes was exasperating, and the difficulty of transportation by trucks and barges was another burden, but we got the tins back and deposited them in Holland.

Sample No. 3: On January 21, 1916, the British military authorities lodged a complaint with the Foreign Office which they expected to be our doom. The report stated that we had brought about 25,000 tons of rice into Belgium, which, in turn, had found its way into Germany. Lord Percy wrote:

FOREIGN OFFICE, LONDON
21 January 1916

DEAR MR. HOOVER:

A most unsatisfactory position has arisen with regard to your importations of rice into Belgium. In recent conferences with me you have estimated the monthly amounts which you wish to import at 5,000 tons. In September, October, and November last, however, you shipped from Rotterdam much larger amounts—namely 13,064, 9,361 and 11,735 tons, respectively. . . .

As I told you some time ago we were much disturbed by exports of rice from Belgium to Germany via Holland in October and November last. We now discover that this is due to the sale by the Relief Committees in Belgium of portions of the stocks with which you had provided them and to the purchase of these stocks by the Germans.

As you know, I have frequently warned you against any accumulations of stocks in Belgium for fear of some such incident. I need not emphasise the serious nature of what has occurred, undermining as it must, our whole confidence in the watertightness of your system.

I must therefore ask you for a statement of the full amounts of rice thus sold by the Committees, and we shall expect to hear within a month that the Germans have handed over an equivalent amount of rice . . . Until this happens, you must import no more rice into Belgium, and if it does not happen within a month we shall reconsider, not only the question of rice imports but the question of your imports as a whole, since it will then be evident that we cannot rely either upon the efficiency of your organisation in Belgium nor upon the respect of the Germans for their own pledges.

For the moment, your importations of rice into France may continue, but only on the absolute condition that you accumulate no stocks there whatever, and if we do not receive satisfaction within a month, this also will be reconsidered.

EUSTACE PERCY

My colleagues were exasperated at the absurdity of this charge because we had never handled any such quantities of rice. But it offered us an opportunity to discredit the British Intelligence with the Foreign Office. We launched a vigorous and exhaustive investigation covering the entire gamut of C.R.B. activity. We brought to London every bill of lading of every canal boat and railway car which had, on the records of the Dutch Government, passed over its frontiers. We brought the receipts and the accounts of our warehouses of destination and the receipts of every one of the four thousand communes. We had them audited by our public accountants, who were British, and offered to place them in the hands of any other responsible auditors whom the British might appoint.

The matter boiled down to a failure of the accounts to cover 400 tons during our fourteen months of operations in which we handled 1,200,000 tons of food. There was no evidence that even this amount reached the Germans.

The smuggler allies of our Inspection staff informed us of a few communal committees which had sold rice at black-market prices and had bought potatoes, which had greater food value, from the same sources. Our informants insisted that they had sold the rice in Belgium. It amounted to a total of about ten tons. My report to the Foreign Office on these complaints was as follows:

LONDON, 8 February 1916

DEAR LORD EUSTACE:

EXPORT FROM BELGIUM OF OUR IMPORTS

This matter has now been under rigorous investigation in Belgium and I send you some of the data.

(1) The bills of lading of the 18,000 odd tons totals of goods shipped from Rotterdam after the 1st September have been inspected and the only

items of a character at all related to our imports were: rice, 855 tons; beans, 14 tons; corn flour, 10 tons. Of this total quantity [of 879 tons], it appears that a considerable amount was gathered from prewar [Holland] stocks, and there is constantly some rivulet of these supplies across the frontier from Holland.

Judging by the instances which our people have been able to . . . [track] down, it appears a good deal less than one-half could have come from our imported material; thus approximately 400 tons have leaked away from a total of 1,200,000 tons [of food] imported.

(2) We find that some of the local committees, finding the fabulous price at which they could sell rice, have done so entirely in innocence of heart and have invested the money in potatoes, thus getting larger value for their destitute with the same funds. They have all been soundly lectured on this subject, and further the entire inspection staff in Belgium is being changed from the joint control of the Comité National and the C.R.B. to the sole control of the C.R.B.

Furthermore, it appears that all this [black-market] stuff was gathered up by one German firm, newly established in Belgium for the export of commodities which are not in question, such as wine. The German authorities, in order to show fair play, are putting this firm out of action so far as dealing in any commodity which we may import is concerned.

I think you may take it that these measures will settle the business once and for all and that the strenuous tone of your note calling attention to this matter has done a world of good; still, I do not feel that in the midst of our other difficulties and complexities the matter merits further pursuit.

HERBERT HOOVER

Sample No. 4: On January 25, 1916, still another sort of complaint issued from the Foreign Office—with concurrent action on their part. This was an assertion that the Germans were feeding huge herds of cattle on Belgian pastures.

FOREIGN OFFICE, LONDON
25 January 1916

DEAR MR. HOOVER:

Our attention has been drawn to a notice in the *Cologne Gazette* of December 14th last stating, with reference to a communication made by the German Government to the Budget Committee, that in the spring of

1915 eighty thousand head of cattle were sent into Belgium to be pastured there and that similar action will be taken in the spring of 1916.

As you are aware, the German Authorities have requisitioned the crop of oats and hay in Belgium. If there is sufficient pasturage in Belgium to support eighty thousand head of German cattle, any lack of meat in Belgium must be clearly due to the action of the German Government and, in the presence of this fact, His Majesty's Government must hold the German Government responsible for the supply of meat to the population of Belgium.

Moreover, the Commission for Relief in Belgium is now allowed to import no fodder except maize to an amount of twenty thousand tons a month. As part of the resources of Belgium are apparently to be devoted to the maintenance of German livestock, a proceeding equivalent to the export of fodder which we have demanded shall cease, His Majesty's Government will be obliged to reconsider the permission given for the importation of this amount, and we must therefore ask you to import no more maize for fodder purposes until the situation is cleared up.

There is no objection to the importation of maize for human consumption being continued.

EUSTACE PERCY

We replied that our investigation showed this alleged situation to be almost wholly a fabrication. It had a remote and small basis in fact in that the Germans temporarily pastured a few hundred beef cattle in Belgium which were en route for slaughter by their armies at the front.

Our investigation of many other complaints of leakages proved that the offenders were smugglers and black-market operators. These minor incidents were infinitesimal in proportion to the volume of supplies which we handled for 10,000,000 people. I have gone into the subject more than would otherwise be necessary because it was part of the background for a subsequent action taken by the Commission.

CHAPTER 19

THE BRITISH REFUSE
US MORE FOOD THROUGH
THE BLOCKADE

A much greater problem confronted us in Belgium than the petty transactions related in the preceding chapter. By December, 1915, it was evident that with the seasonal exhaustion of native supplies, we would have to import much more food into Belgium if we were to maintain an average ration of about 1,800 calories per diem per person, which, even so, was only about 60 per cent of normal for either themselves or the British. Therefore, on December 21, I asked the British for an increase in blockade permits from the then total of 80,000 tons a month to the following tonnage per month:

Wheat (or flour)	54,000
Lard	7,000
Bacon	3,500
Rice	5,000
Condensed milk	1,000
Beans and peas	4,000
Maize	20,000
Sugar	2,000
Coffee	2,000
Soap	1,000
Potatoes	10,000
Salad oils	400
Preserved meats	1,500
Preserved fish	400
Cocoa	1,000
Oleomargarine materials	1,000
Butter	500
Dried fruit	100
Linseed cake	10,000
Cheese	2,000
Total	126,400

In addition, we required more medical supplies, clothing for the destitute, and gasoline and automobile supplies for staff use. This request evoked an explosion from the British by way of a letter from Sir Edward Grey to Ambassador Page:

FOREIGN OFFICE, LONDON
31 December 1915

MY DEAR AMBASSADOR:

On various occasions I have felt obliged to address lengthy communications to you as patron, in your unofficial capacity, of the Commission for Relief in Belgium. A very critical situation has now arisen regarding the affairs of that Commission, and I must therefore put before you briefly the views of His Majesty's Government.

The Foreign Minister then lengthily reviewed the evil conduct of the Germans in Belgium from the beginning of the war and went on:

The result of this process has been clearly seen in the last few months. The Commission, which had expected to be able to reduce its activities after the harvest, has increased them. It has made a series of new requests for import permits in respect of various fresh articles of food, and it has largely increased its importations of bacon and lard. It is planning to import large quantities of clothing for the destitute. This gradual expansion cannot continue, and within the last few days, as Your Excellency is aware, His Majesty's Government have felt themselves obliged to suspend temporarily the importation of various articles into Belgium by the Commission. The time has therefore arrived when the whole work must be placed on a more clearly defined basis. . . .

They are therefore about to lay down a programme of imports for the Commission which will be regarded as final. However long the German occupation of Belgium may continue, this programme will in no circumstances be expanded. Further, His Majesty's Government must make the following stipulations, which appear to be the minimum necessary to safeguard the livelihood of the Belgian people:

1. The export of all foodstuffs and substances fit for use as food, whatsoever, including livestock and fodder of all kinds, and also all fertilizers, seeds, and agricultural stock of every sort, shall be absolutely prohibited from the territory administered by the Governor-General of Belgium to

any destination whatever, with the one exception that the Commission for Relief in Belgium may be allowed to export to Northern France, for distribution there by them, foodstuffs of which there is a clear surplus over and above the present or future needs of Belgium.

2. The export of all articles of clothing and of all raw materials for their manufacture shall be prohibited except to neutral countries, and then only after full provision has been made for the present and future needs of the civil population, including the destitute.

3. None of the articles above mentioned shall on any account be used by the German Army of occupation in Belgium.

4. These prohibitions shall be rigorously maintained without exception of any kind.

5. The Commission shall be allowed to exercise any control over the stocks mentioned in the preceding paragraphs which may be necessary in order to conserve them for the future, or make them available for the present needs of the population.

If these steps are not taken His Majesty's Government will hold themselves entitled to reconsider their whole attitude towards the Commission. . . .

E. GREY

We were fully cognizant that Sir Edward's action arose from pressures of the British and French military departments. But in any event, on February 23, Sir Edward reduced this application from 126,400 tons to 68,150 tons. This was 12,000 tons less than our meager imports prior to our application. The permits were to be as follows:

	Tons
Wheat	54,000
Yeast	250
Bacon and lard	2,400
Peas and beans	3,000
Maize and meal	8,000
Condensed milk	500
Total	68,150

Some medical supplies for the people and gasoline for our C.R.B. cars were allowed. We naturally protested verbally over this reduction, and our final reaction will appear later.

NORTHERN FRANCE

We were importing about 35,000 tons of food and supplies per month into the North of France at the end of our first year. On December 21, 1915, I presented to the British Foreign Office for submission to the French Government a request to increase this amount to 48,000 tons a month at a cost of about 24,000,000 francs per month. At the direct request of the French Foreign Office, I prepared a memorandum setting forth our progress and organization and asked that the French Government approve our proposals made to the British Foreign Office, stating:

The whole situation as imposed by the approaching winter and the gradual exhaustion of summer supplies has been the subject of a very intimate study by the American staff in consultation with the French district committees, and the following program of minimum food supplies has been drawn up. . . .

After listing these requirements, I went on:

. . . this represents the minimum supplies which will . . . maintain the population in health. It will be noted that the supply is entirely below that generally advanced by dietary specialists as required to support life . . . yet the Commission feels that this is all that it can hope to deliver . . . in view of the present position of the shipping world. . . .

I then described the over-all structure of the Commission and the dimensions of our task and reviewed the financial support we had received for the North of France. I also requested more ships, written approval of our methods of accounting, and a ban by the French Government on various speculators who were shipping small amounts of food through Switzerland and selling them in the black-market.

The French authorities transmitted this report back to the British Foreign Office. But the British did not approve of an increase in imports for Northern France:

FOREIGN OFFICE, LONDON, 27 January 1916

DEAR MR. HOOVER:

We have received from the French Embassy a memorandum which I enclose herein, and which I understand was drawn up by you and Monsieur Chevrillon, dealing with your organisation for relief in Northern France.

I am directed to inform you that the general financial and other principles set forth in this memorandum are approved as a basis for your work.

We cannot at present extend this approval definitely to the programme of imports which was embodied in this memorandum, but I will communicate with you further on this point.

We shall conclude, unless we hear to the contrary, that your organisation in Northern France will be conducted on the lines set forth in this memorandum in the future without material alteration.

EUSTACE PERCY

To stimulate our zeal in control, the British specified the quality of the soap we were to import into the North of France, with the idea that variety would not be useful to the Germans if they should take it, saying:

FOREIGN OFFICE, LONDON
2 February 1916

DEAR MR. HOOVER:

Without prejudice to the list we shall finally and permanently fix, the Board of Trade will probably now instruct the International Commission to allow the export by you of your 1,000 tons [of soap] a month for Northern France. But as this authorisation depends absolutely on the soap being of the *hard* variety not containing ingredients fit for military purposes (the kind you now are buying here, I think), we want it to be understood for the present that you will buy *all* your soap in this country in order that we may be able to say at any time that we *know* that the soap is of the right kind.

I feel all these various small stipulations must give an undesirable impression of lack of confidence in you, but I beg you to believe that this is not at all the case and that it is merely a question of our being able to vouch for things of our own knowledge and not on hearsay.

EUSTACE PERCY

Lord Percy might have added—and he did, verbally—that the agency to whom he wished to "vouch" was the Admiralty.

Having got nowhere in obtaining either the ships we needed for furnishing supplies to Northern France or the increase in permissions for imports, absolutely necessary if the population were to be kept alive, I went to Paris on February 9 for a weary round of interviews with most of the bureaucracies concerned. I made the usual memorandum for my colleagues:

LONDON [18 February 1916]

Thursday, 10th February 1916

Arrived Paris three o'clock in the morning via Dieppe; went with Chevrillon at ten to call on Lieutenant Serruys at the War Ministry, he being the delegate of the General Staff to keep track of our operations. . . . discussed shipping question. . . .

At eleven o'clock went with Chevrillon to see Monsieur Gout, Foreign Office (he being the link with the Marine Department). . . .

We discussed shipping matters, which I detail elsewhere in this narrative, and I then insisted

that we must have immediate tonnage or disaster must result. He agreed we should see General Staff and Prime Minister.

At four o'clock went with Chevrillon to see Monsieur Chappsal, Under-Secretary in charge of the ravitaillement of civil population of France. . . .

At 5:30 I saw Monsieur Nail, Under-Secretary (Marine).

He agreed that we must have more shipping, and we urged

. . . immediate action, which could only be done by strong measures at governmental hands—in forcing tonnage to accept our mission.

Friday, 11th February 1916

10:30—Went with Chevrillon to see Monsieur Metain, Minister of Labor; briefly recited our difficulties, principally shipping. . . .

5:30—Called with Chevrillon on Monsieur Sembat, Minister of Public Works, he, jointly with M. Thierry, being in control all questions of mercantile shipping and M. Sembat representing the French Government in joint councils with English on shipping questions. We . . . strongly urged our necessities. . . .

Saturday, 12th February 1916

5:00—Called on Monsieur Berthelot, Under-Secretary for Foreign Affairs, who had M. Kammerer with him (the latter being in the Finance Department—Foreign Office link). [We again expounded on our shipping and food difficulties] . . . insisting vigorously that the job was primarily the concern of the French people and if they would only come out of the shell of "we do not object" and take on a formula of "we insist," things would go better. He agreed we must be saved somehow.

Sunday, 13th February 1916

4:00—Motored with Chevrillon to Chantilly, and discussed matters with General Staff. Colonel Buat and Captain Marsal received us and we went over a multitude of grounds, military, political, financial, shipping, etc. They agreed that the principle of a minimum food supply just sufficient to supplement native supplies must be maintained, but they were strong on the minimum. . . .

. . . I stated that it seemed absurd to us, an American body, that we should be at constant trench warfare with the French and British General Staffs over this work. That we were in constant battle over imports absolutely vital to preserve the life of French people and we were prepared to surrender and let them do the job if they could do it better. That we were always in an equal quarrel with the German Staff over native food—and we were getting very, very tired and worn. This caused some [interest] . . . I am satisfied we will have better co-operation.

Monday, 14th February 1916

At 5:30—Went with Chevrillon to the Elysée, where we were received by President Poincaré. He stated that he had asked me to call, as he wished to express the appreciation and admiration of the French people for the work we were doing on behalf of their northern countrymen. He stated that he had kept himself in touch with the work and said that he was filled with admiration for the efficiency and the ability with which it had been administered; that it had now become an enormous enterprise and one of great complexity. He had fully realized the pressure we were under from the people in the North to increase the supplies, and the still greater pressure we were under from the different Allies to reduce them; also the difficulties we were constantly getting into with the Germans in our endeavor to protect the native food supply. He said no one expected us to reach the ideal in any of these directions. I told him that our whole desire was to keep the population alive and in health until the war was over; that this meant a good deal of privation, especially to those classes who had always had more than sufficient, and that it had necessarily meant a good deal of complaint from them. I also stated that we were in jeopardy of total failure owing to the lack of shipping and I felt that a more direct support of the Commission from the French Government would be of great assistance. He stated that the Council had already discussed the matter fully and made direct representations to the British Government, hoping to thus afford a solution of our shipping and other difficulties.

Mr. Chevrillon told him that the question of maintaining food supplies to the people in the North was one of vast military, political importance, but that this phase of the question was obviously not for discussion with a neutral; that my attitude was wholly that of the humanitarian aspect, but from the French point of view these weighty factors must not be overlooked. The President said that he fully realized the importance of these phases of the matter, that they had been thoroughly ventilated from time to time in the councils of the French Government; that, of course, the humanitarian aspect must in the end dominate all questions; that the French people were fighting for their existence and the existence of the French nation embraced the two and a half millions of Frenchmen in the North.

He rose and again stated impressively that he wished to convey to me the thanks of the French Republic.

Returned to London, Tuesday, 15th February 1916.

On February 23, the British Foreign Office, under pressure from the militarists in Britain and France, instead of approving our increased imports to Northern France, informed us of a reduction in our monthly supplies, by about 5,000 tons, to 30,000 tons per month. It was a great shock to us—and to the people of Northern France.

The native ground crops were practically exhausted at this time of the year. These reductions of food to Belgium and Northern France were far below the level at which we could maintain public health. The effect was a program 50 per cent short of the minimum needs of fats and proteins.

We had no taste for being an instrument of slow starvation, and by the end of February, 1916, we—who had, after all, taken on our heavy burdens voluntarily—became, to use a British expression, "about fed up" with these obstructionist attitudes. The action I took as a result is reported in a later chapter.

CHAPTER 20

MORE TROUBLES OVER SHIPS

Another of our growing discouragements during the first four months of our second year was the total lack of co-operation from the French, the Belgians, and the British in obtaining ship charters for the Commission. The total Allied and American tonnage afloat at this time was about 23,500,000 tons. The total European neutral tonnage was about 6,200,000 tons, of which they needed about 2,000,000 tons to transport their own supplies. Aside from the tonnage in use by the Allied Governments for war and supply services, the British, French, and Belgians had over 5,000,000 tons of shipping engaged in commercial trade in the Pacific, Indian, and South Atlantic oceans. While that was desirable in order to sustain their economic life, it did seem to us that our tonnage requirements should be regarded as a negligible drop in that bucket. We needed at this time a reliable fleet of 250,000 to 300,000 tons of cargo shipping if we were to maintain the lives of 10,000,000 people.

WE TACKLE THE FRENCH

I have already related my experience with the French in the previous chapter. They had promised ships but delivered none. They had established a special food fleet of their own flagships and neutral charters to supply unoccupied France. They had turned down the opportunity opened up by the C.R.B. to charter the German refugee ships and now refused to transport supplies with their own fleet for their own people in the north.

To lessen somewhat the apparent harshness of this criticism, I must mention that the military situation at this time was running against them; however, what we needed was little indeed from Allied and neutral totals.

WE TACKLE THE AMERICANS

We learned that the American Navy had a number of cargo ships for coaling and supply service and that many of them were idle in reserve, since we were not at war. We thought that they might be assigned to us, returnable at once on demand. Our New York office felt that the Navy might be criticized by the Congress for assigning some of them to us and therefore obtained the following House resolution on January 6, 1916, through the kindness of Representative George A. Loud:

WHEREAS the people of the United States, through various relief organizations, in compassion for the destitution of needy people of Europe, caused by the war now raging there, have contributed and are contributing large amounts of money, materials, and supplies for their relief; and

WHEREAS for the ocean transportation of such relief materials and supplies a large portion of the amounts so generously contributed has heretofore been paid: Therefore be it

Resolved, That such materials and supplies shall, during the present calendar year be transported in the auxiliary ships, to wit, colliers and supply ships, of the Navy, without cost to the relief organizations: Provided, That such materials and supplies shall be in suitable cargo lots, and that the loading and discharge of such cargoes shall conform to such regulations as the Secretary of the Navy shall deem necessary to carry out the intent of this resolution: Provided further, That not more than one-fourth of the tonnage of all such auxiliary ships of the Navy shall be used at any one time in such service.

I then appealed to the Secretary of the Navy, Josephus Daniels, for the use of these idle ships. He replied:

NAVY DEPARTMENT, WASHINGTON
14 February 1916

Mr. Herbert Hoover
SIR:

I have given careful consideration to the subject of transportation for Belgian relief supplies in Navy colliers to Belgium, as requested in your letter of 10 February and a telegram of 11 February from Mr. Bertron.

After consultation with regard to the matter, and after due deliberation, we have decided that it is impracticable to authorize the use of Navy colliers for this purpose.

I regret exceedingly that conditions make it impossible for us to aid you in your deserving work.

JOSEPHUS DANIELS
Secretary of the Navy

WE TACKLE THE BELGIANS

It seemed to us that the exiled Belgian Government at LeHavre had a major responsibility in all of this tonnage difficulty. I have already told of my first effort to secure some of their ships. John White now obtained full information about this fleet through one of his friends, a British ship operator. White found that the Belgians had twenty-six cargo ships which flew the Belgian flag and were subject to requisition by the exiled Government at Le Havre. There were twenty-five more cargo ships, owned by the Belgians (the Belgian Lloyd Line) but registered in Britain. Part of the latter had been requisitioned by the British Admiralty, and some of these had been assigned to the French. Upon investigation, we found that a considerable part of both varieties were engaged in commercial trade. We decided to appeal more vigorously for a substantial part of these Belgian cargo ships. I wrote Chevrillon, our Paris Director, asking that he devote himself to the matter. My letter summarized the situation:

LONDON, 19 January 1916

DEAR CHEVRILLON:

... we find that there are about twenty-five Belgian ships flying the English flag which would be suitable for our purposes, and there are about twenty-six Belgian ships flying the Belgian flag ... which would also be suitable. Belgian-owned ships which fly the British flag ... are at present requisitioned by the British Admiralty. Through the Belgian Legation here we have put up an urgent request that the English Government should requisition the remaining fifteen such ships, in order that they might terminate legally all their outstanding contracts and charters, and that immediately afterwards they be released [to us]. ... Furthermore, we have telegraphed this morning to the Belgian Government at Havre, [again] urging them strongly to requisition, on their own account, the twenty-five ships which fly the Belgian flag, and are therefore subject to Belgian law, that they should then release the ships from requisition, subject to the owners entering into a reasonable contract with us, we undertaking that if the Belgian Government should require any of them for military purposes we would hand them over at once. This amount of shipping, together with such neutral ships as we could engage, would solve our whole problem, and this looks to be the only immediate solution. ...

HERBERT HOOVER

Having no word from the Belgians that they would requisition their flagships, I telegraphed the Belgian Prime Minister at Le Havre:

LONDON, 26 January 1916

According information received ... it is probable that friendly arrangements can be made between the Belgian shipowners and ourselves for the chartering of Belgian vessels for the Commission. In order to allow the Belgian owners to break their existing contracts, it is urgent that a bill should be passed making it legal to requisition Belgian ships without a moment's delay. Each day's delay means one day for Belgium without bread. ...

HOOVER

Three days later, Chevrillon reported on his efforts to secure the Belgian-flag ships which were in the French service:

PARIS, 29 January 1916

DEAR HOOVER:

. . . I have, within the last two days, called at the various ministries, Admiralty, War, Foreign Office, Public Works; and although I find all earnestly interested in the question of a prompt solution of our difficulties, I find no inclination to give a blind support without more information than that which I possess. I have therefore cabled you yesterday as follows:

"Belgian [ships] scheme favorably considered, but Government will not recommend blindly, without knowing to what extent will affect military necessities. Insists on full list of ships in order to examine which can possibly be spared, as even those under British flag may be working for French military account."

. . . I have, however, the positive assurance that in the instant I can lay before them a list of the ships to be requisitioned, with the particulars of each, and the exact number of ships needed by the Commission to complete its fleet, our matters will be attended to with prompt despatch. . . . I am meanwhile trying to obtain a recommendation from the French Government of the requisition of Belgian ships by the Belgian Government provided that as each ship is requisitioned the . . . Government is allowed to accept or refuse requisition according to military necessities. This is the best I can do at present. . . .

CHEVRILLON

This seemed to us to be sheer evasion by the French, since they had been told a dozen times that we needed these fifty Belgian cargo ships and had been given all details.

The British refused us the Belgian-owned ships flying the British flag, and I so informed our Paris Director:

LONDON, 3 February 1916

CHEVRILLON, PARIS:

Am informed that decision here has been adverse to use by Commission of Belgian-owned ships flying British flag, which forces us back practically solely on Belgian ships flying Belgian flag. These at best could deliver only about 300 grams food per diem to Belgian population alone, and I fear we shall have to take decision these ships be confined to service of Belgians

and full responsibility providing shipping for French population must rest
on French Government who primarily Government most concerned.

HOOVER

Finally, on February 6, 1916, the Belgian Government did requisition the Belgian-flag ships, and ultimately we got them into our service. They satisfied only about 30 to 35 per cent of our needs.

Since we had information that the British-flag Belgian-owned ships
were being partially employed in commercial trade between neutral
ports in the Pacific, I appealed to an old shipping friend in London,
Shirley Benn, who was also a member of Parliament and was on several shipping councils. He requested a written memorandum, which
I furnished on February 4. After describing our operation in general
and giving vent to some indignation, I said:

Now, after all this violence, I wish to make a constructive suggestion.
In the first place, of the Belgian-owned ships under the British flag, some
twelve or fourteen are at present requisitioned by the Admiralty. On the
other hand, some ten or twelve of these ships are free and engaged in general trade. It cannot therefore concern the Admiralty particularly if the
ships which are free from requisition at present are handed over to us. . . .
This, I believe, could be accomplished by the Food Committee without
bothering the Admiralty. Furthermore, we have fourteen voyage charters
of English ships arranged for future dates, carried over some four months,
and if we could have an assurance that these charters would not be requisitioned away from us this would also help.

Again, I may mention that on this general question there are a good
many British ships plying in the Pacific between neutral ports, and there
are even some ships on the list we asked for which are trading between
neutral ports, and it does seem to me that, in all these circumstances, it
must be of some interest to the Allies to feed their own people rather than
facilitate outside trade.

The Belgian . . . [Government has] a feeling that if they requisition the
entire shipping flying the Belgian flag for our purpose, this shipping could
be devoted to feeding the Belgian population; but this leaves the French
population of two and a half million people dependent on a few British
charters which we have and such neutral charters as we may pick up, and
of course the Belgian shipping does not provide enough tonnage for even
a minimum bread supply for the Belgians alone. My only right of com-

plaint in this matter is not personal but purely on behalf of the ten million people whose very existence is imperilled and the last I want to do is to give offense in the advocacy of their interests. So do not allow any one to take my sentiments as being in the slightest of an unfriendly character to the interests of the situation as a whole.

HERBERT HOOVER

Several days later, I telegraphed Minister Whitlock through the American Embassy to inform Francqui that the Belgian Government had requisitioned the Belgian-flag ships but that we had made no progress in regard to the North of France:

LONDON, 8 February 1916

MINISTER WHITLOCK, BRUSSELS:

The Belgian Government completed the Law of Requisition last Sunday and it is now in force. The necessary requisition orders are going out today for all the ships flying the Belgian flag, of which there are nineteen. They are badly scattered all over the world, and it will take at least two months to get the whole fleet into action on our behalf. We shall, however, be able to get deliveries from some of the ships within the next thirty days.

This fleet will give us . . . [under] 60,000 tons per month in Rotterdam and with a certain number of neutral charters, which we can no doubt get at some price, we shall be able to deliver at least an undercurrent of food supply [for Belgium]. . . .

The second part of our shipping program, that is, the securing of Belgian-owned ships which fly the British flag, has met a curt refusal from the Control Committee. . . .

I may mention that Lord Curzon is chairman of this committee and is at present with the King of the Belgians, who has been asked by Mr. Hymans [the Belgian Minister in London] to take the matter up with Lord Curzon.

Furthermore, I have informed the French Government formally, that shipping under the Belgian flag will be unable to entirely supply the Belgian people, and that reluctantly we have been compelled to take the decision that we cannot ask the Belgian people to starve in favor of the French, the responsibility for the people in Northern France is primarily that of the French Government and that unless they can furnish us shipping we have to decline to continue. This attitude has produced a perfect storm in Paris, and I am going tomorrow to see if I can direct the hurricane so as to secure the second stage in our shipping program.

HOOVER

In late January, the British Government had requisitioned *a Belgian-flag ship already in our employ.* I protested through Hymans, and he received the following reply:

FOREIGN OFFICE, LONDON
22 February 1916

Monsieur Paul Hymans
Belgian Minister, London
SIR:

I have the honour to acknowledge the receipt of your note of the 10th instant . . . regarding the requisitioning of the S.S. "Flandrier" chartered by the Commission for Relief in Belgium.

I have laid this whole question before the competent authorities and I have the honour to assure you that it is the policy of His Majesty's Government to give to the Commission for Relief in Belgium such facilities for obtaining tonnage as are possible in present circumstances. But I wish to lay before you, for the consideration of the Belgian Government, the very great difficulties, and indeed dangers, to which the Allied Governments are exposed by the present extreme shortage of shipping. His Majesty's Government are in the position of having in large measure to supply the urgent needs of the other Allies. . . .

. . . and while everything possible will be done . . . I trust you will represent to your Government the great difficulties in which His Majesty's Government are placed. . . .

(For the Secretary of State)
MAURICE DE BUNSEN

In commenting on this to the Foreign Office, I suggested that a large number of Belgian-owned ships under the British flag were engaged in private trade, not in the British military shipping program, and that there was neither rhyme nor reason for this when the Belgian people were starving.

It is useless to speculate on the reasons for all these arbitrary actions. I was convinced at the time—and gathered verbally from Lord Percy—that it was militarist pressure on the Foreign Offices, applied with the hope that it would make our task impossible. As far as preventing starvation in Belgium went, our efforts were successful.

CHAPTER 21

A PROBLEM INSIDE BELGIUM

By February, 1916, there had developed a problem in human relations and emotion which involved the C.R.B. and the Comité National.

When the Relief was organized fifteen months before, Belgium was in economic chaos, starving, and subjected daily to oppression from the German Army. Gradually, we had built up the moral and physical strength of the C.R.B. and the Comité National. Through the efforts of the two organizations and their Minister Patrons, many oppressions had been relaxed, economic life was greatly restored, and the people, until then, were being provided with enough food, medical supplies, and clothing to keep them alive.

Under Francqui's leadership, the Comité National, from its inception, included leaders from all political groups, all of whom showed an unfailing unity and solidarity in their dedication to the great emergency of their people. Likewise, the organization of the Comité du Nord under the leadership of Labbé and its devoted divisional heads had revived the spirits of the French. It was a great satisfaction to us that we had contributed to building the forces which sustained the morale, the spiritual strength, and the courage of the Belgian and French peoples.

In Belgium, the Comité National had perfected their organizations to such a point that much less supervision by the C.R.B. was necessary. We in the C.R.B. rejoiced at any sort of relief of our responsibilities and fully supported a greater assumption of them by the

Committees. However, the Allied Foreign Offices had a different view. Their view was that the Comité National and the Comité du Nord were prisoners of the Germans. As I have stated, the Allies insisted that the C.R.B. must administer, under its own name, the transportation, warehousing, processing, and district release of supplies from its warehouses to the communes. And since the C.R.B. was the repository of the Allied subsidies, they insisted that it must rigidly account for both food and expenditures, including the monies received from the sales of food and other supplies in Belgium, and that it must maintain a strong American inspection staff over the work of the Comité National and the Comité du Nord and make constant reports to the Allies. All of this could be nothing less than irksome, especially to the Belgians—that a wholly unimportant group of American youngsters should be imposing orders on the efficient and able local committees. The Belgians felt that they were not subjects of the Allied Governments and that they had made great sacrifices in the Allied cause and should be treated accordingly.

The sympathies of our men—and my own—were entirely with the Belgians. No human being could pass by the ruins of cathedrals, of universities, of whole villages, of homes and places where civilian women and children, as civilian hostages, had been mowed down with machine guns, or witness the spectacle of a free people, whose every street and highway fell subject to the hobnailed boots of German soldiers, without indignation.

We in the C.R.B. felt that greater responsibility should be recognized by the Allied Governments and assigned to the Comité National. However, in the latter part of February, 1916, some bright mind in the Comité prepared an elaborate set of rules and regulations setting up our respective relations, the effect of which would considerably diminish the responsibilities of the C.R.B.

We welcomed the idea. However, I feared that the authorities in London and Paris would construe it as a limitation of their requirements of the C.R.B. We did not report it to the Allied Governments, hoping that we could work matters out ourselves and feeling that peace would soon come to the world again. Nevertheless, ignoring the difficulty did not quiet it.

CHAPTER 22

THE C.R.B. RESIGNS AND RESUMES

By the end of February, 1916, the various embarrassments besetting the Commission were becoming wholly intolerable to my colleagues and to me. The chief members of our staff were volunteers who had abandoned their careers, were paying their own expenses, and were carrying on an enormous task of purchasing, transporting, and distributing huge quantities of supplies, as well as providing their guardianship and accounting, in the middle of a war. All of this required working twelve hours a day, seven days a week, and it brought many personal dangers, as well as constant, bitter, and unnecessary discouragements. To help make clear the major step which the C.R.B. now took, I must briefly review the impasse we had reached.

First, the exiled Belgian Government at Le Havre was paying little heed to our pleas for the use of their Belgian-owned but British-registered ships.

Second, although we were trying to save the Northern French, at their own Government's request and expense, we were given not a single cargo vessel from the considerable French fleet, and, out of sheer stupidity, French officials had prevented us from securing German refugee ships which might have been used for the relief of the French people.

Third, Brand Whitlock, the American Minister in Brussels and a fine American, was not the type of man for the rough-stuff into which he had been precipitated. He was too sensitive a person to be American Minister amidst such suffering and tragedy. He shrank from battles with von Bissing and resented the constant pressures for action applied by us and by his First Secretary, Hugh Gibson. In February, 1916, he secured Gibson's removal from Brussels—to our immense loss.

Fourth, the Germans had, through von Bissing, repudiated their agreement of December, 1915, not to requisition native food in "occupied" Belgium. Although the civil authorities in Berlin and their military authorities in the North of France were co-operative, in Belgium itself we were subjected to a great deal of Governor General von Bissing's arrogance and anti-Americanism.

Fifth, the British, acting also for the French, had reduced our permits of food imports to a point where the peoples for whom we were responsible would shortly be starving. These cuts included the supplies for soup kitchens and even supplies for our canteen system which were vital to the lives of the children. We were thus being forced to become instruments of slow starvation, not only of adults, but also of children.

Sixth, there was an inherent conflict between the responsibilities imposed upon the C.R.B. by the Allies and the very natural feelings of the Belgians in Belgium.

Seventh, the British Military Intelligence was constantly feeding the Foreign Office stories of trivial or mythical infractions or violations of the guarantees by the Germans, and we were constantly being hectored and harassed as if we had some evil intent.

Eighth, an incident with the British Admiralty fueled our discontents. In January, 1916, the Chief of the British Naval Intelligence, Captain Hall, requested me to call on him. He asked many questions bearing on German military operations in the Relief areas. I told him that we were pledged to neutrality, that we collected no military information and knew nothing of what was going on in any German Army. He pressed me, arguing that inasmuch as the Relief was being supported by the British and French Governments, it was my duty to aid their interests. I flatly declined on the ground that my responsibility was to ten million starving people and that my staff and I, on our honor to our Patron Ambassadors, had pledged ourselves to do nothing of the kind for either side.

Some weeks later, I learned from an intimate friend that a Naval Intelligence agent, representing Captain Hall, had called upon him and others of my friends, making extensive inquiries about my private business, my character, and had even inquired if it were possible that I could be a German spy. I complained to Lord Percy, who simply hooted. But he later informed me that the subject was getting very "troublesome."

Ninth, all of these matters came to a head in the latter part of February, at which time Francqui and Baron Lambert of the Comité National, together with the Spanish Minister to Belgium, the Marquis de Villalobar, came to London. Hugh Gibson accompanied this delegation. He informed me that they had been considering a plan by which the exiled Belgian Government would take over the purchase and transport of supplies and the Comité National would take over all the operations in Belgium, thus retiring the C.R.B. I at once held a session of our available C.R.B. leaders, and we determined to welcome the plan. In any event, we concluded that it offered an opportunity for a showdown, which might lessen the plight of the ten million people for whom we had so great a responsibility.

With the approval of my colleagues, I addressed a letter of resignation to Ambassador Page, expressing our sympathies for the Belgian plan, and I sent copies to all of our Ambassador and Minister Patrons:

LONDON, 24 February 1916

DEAR MR. AMBASSADOR:

I have recently had several conferences with my American associates in regard to the general situation of Belgian relief work, and we have together reached the conclusion that the time has arrived when the Allied Governments should consider whether it is not possible for them to transfer to a Belgian organization the guarantees and responsibilities which we have thus far carried and enable us to withdraw from the work without thereby entailing any hardship or suffering upon the Belgian civil population; the presence of the leading spirits in the Comité National in London seems to offer an appropriate moment for raising the question.

. . . the Commission for Relief in Belgium was initiated in your Office on

October 18, 1914, to meet a very critical emergency. . . . At that time the country was in a terribly disorganized and demoralized condition. The occupied territory was entirely deprived of the ordinary facilities for transportation, communication and travel, and the Belgians could not hope to effect an adequate organization for themselves. It was, therefore, essential that some neutral agency, possessed of liberty of movement and freedom from the severe measures imposed upon a conquered people should undertake the initial work and bring order out of the reigning chaos.

Thanks to the devoted services of a large corps of American volunteers and to our diplomatic patrons, we were able to build up an organization which has grown steadily in efficiency, and have been able to meet the conditions imposed by the Allied Governments and carry out the guarantees which we have assumed from time to time.

Conditions of life in Belgium have materially improved since the beginning of our work, and the Belgians themselves now enjoy a larger liberty of movement than at any time since the war began, and as their freedom of movement has increased they have taken a larger share in the work and in the relations with the German authorities. When the work began, it was, of course, utterly out of the question to expect the Belgians to create and perfect the necessary organization; now that it has been perfected—so far as seems possible under the abnormal conditions which exist—there would seem to be no inherent reason to prevent the Belgians from assuming entire control of the work and carrying it on. This would enable the members of the Commission to bring their activities to a close, with the assurance that the Belgian people, in whom they take so friendly an interest, would not suffer by the cessation of their labors, and it would at the same time leave us free, individually and collectively, to turn our efforts in other directions where there is need for our activities and such abilities as we may possess.

I know that it is unnecessary for me to tell you that neither I nor my associates would for one moment consider the step I have proposed were it to involve the cessation of the work which has gone on so far. We have considered for some time, however, that the original and imperative need for our continued efforts no longer exists, and in August last I proposed to the Comité National an arrangement by which they could take over the entire work. Yielding to their urgent request at that time I consented to continue, but it now seems to me that an occasion has arisen when we may again broach the subject without fear of endangering the relief of the Belgian people. . . .

Since the name of the "Commission for Relief in Belgium" is bound up with the financial responsibility which my associates and I have assumed, we should expect to dissolve the Commission . . . in other words, the affairs of the Commission for Relief in Belgium will be completely liquidated and it will cease to exist.

I would, therefore, be grateful if you would present this matter to the interested governments and ascertain whether they would be prepared to transfer the guarantees and responsibilities to the Comité National in such a manner as to ensure the continued feeding of and relief of the Belgian civil population, so that my associates and I may conscientiously withdraw from the great work in which we have been privileged to play a part during the past.

HERBERT HOOVER

The first to protest was Ambassador Page, who wrote:

LONDON, February 25, 1916

DEAR MR. HOOVER:

My understanding of the organization and operation of the Commission for the Relief of Belgium is this:—

That it came into being around you and at your suggestion and in response to your impulse to do this urgent work of philanthropy;

that, since nobody knew how big it would grow to be nor how long it would be needed, you yourself took command. The gentlemen you called in understood and accepted your leadership and kindly gave their help;

that the Commission never had any legal existence, and that the Governments which have had important dealings with it have had these dealings with you; and that you alone are financially responsible for its moneys and that therefore you must be in supreme control.

All the work of the Commission has been voluntary and has been under your sole direction; and membership on the Commission can be accepted only on this condition, since the body has no legal existence.

The work could not have been done in any other way and it is now, of course, too late (and unnecessary, besides,) even to discuss any change in this organization—so long as you continue the work.

WALTER H. PAGE

After a visit by the Belgian Minister in London to the Foreign Office, Francqui joined in the protest in a letter to Ambassador Page:

LONDON, 26 February 1916

YOUR EXCELLENCY:

Mr. Hoover presented to me yesterday evening a copy of the letter which he addressed to Your Excellency on the 24th inst. In this communication Mr. Hoover expresses the wish to dissolve the Commission for Relief in Belgium, for which he suggested substituting the Comité National of Belgium.

Your Excellency . . . knows better than anyone with what disinterestedness, what devotion, your compatriots have come to the aid of the Belgian population. You know also that without the active leadership of Mr. Hoover it would have been absolutely impossible for us to continue the provisioning and assistance of the Belgians; also you will not be astonished when I insist, not only in my own personal name, but also in the name of my colleagues and in that of all my fellow-countrymen, that Your Excellency should use your kind influence on Mr. Hoover that he should abandon the idea set out in his letter of the 24th inst. . . .

E. FRANCQUI

The Spanish Minister to Belgium, the Marquis de Villalobar, had been in contact with the Foreign Office. Sir Edward Grey, on February 28, after disposing of other questions which the Minister had asked, wrote to him:

. . . Mr. Hoover, with whom I am obliged to deal in close co-operation in all such matters . . . [is,] in his capacity as head of the Commission for Relief in Belgium, the only person directly and personally responsible for the manner in which the whole work, both inside and outside Belgium, is carried on. If I may express one further hope, it is that all parties concerned in this matter, realising the impossibility of holding personally responsible either the diplomatic representatives of neutral Powers or the citizens of a noble and unhappy country under foreign domination, will take into full account the heavy burden of responsibility resting on this great neutral

Commission and will in every possible way lighten that burden by making its responsibility as easy to discharge as possible.

E. GREY

Grey also addressed Ambassador Page as follows:

FOREIGN OFFICE, LONDON
13 March 1916

MY DEAR AMBASSADOR:

I have carefully considered your letter of February 25th enclosing a letter from Mr. Hoover, regarding the possibility of the retirement of the American Commission from the direction of the relief work in Belgium.

I quite appreciate the desire of the Commission to divest themselves of the burden entailed by this work, which they have borne for so long, but I must state clearly that His Majesty's Government can only allow the work of relief to continue if the entire responsibility for it both inside and outside Belgium is borne by neutrals who, having complete freedom to come and go, and having no official position limiting their personal liability, can in fact be held responsible for the carrying out of the various conditions upon which His Majesty's Government have insisted. The American Commission is the only organisation which fulfils these requirements, and His Majesty's Government therefore feel obliged to insist that either the whole work should cease or the American Commission shall continue to direct it as heretofore.

I shall be glad if you will convey these observations to Mr. Hoover, and ask him to reconsider his views in the light of these contributions.

E. GREY

The Germans also reacted unfavorably to our proposed withdrawal. Ambassador Gerard later informed me through his courier that he had mentioned the matter to the Minister of Foreign Affairs, von Jagow, who had emphatically declared that his country would not agree to the Relief's being conducted by the Belgians and had further expressed the complete confidence of the Berlin authorities and the General Staff in our organization. The Ambassador also informed me that he had taken the occasion to remind the Foreign Minister that General von Bissing was not holding to his agreement of December, 1915, not to requisition any more native Belgian food and that this had added to our difficulties. Von Jagow promised to examine this question again. No doubt it was Gerard who thus brought about a sudden change in von Bissing's attitude a little later.

After prayerful conferences with my colleagues and after having received many promises of better co-operation, we agreed to carry on, with the hope that we had cleared the air.

CHAPTER 23

A VICIOUS ATTACK
BY BRITISH MILITARISTS

The requests that we continue and the promises of better co-operation did not include the British Admiralty, who now seemed to renew their determination to wipe us out. Their first volley in this renewed campaign was another and more extensive list of complaints concerning German seizures of food intended for the Belgians. The Foreign Office wrote:

FOREIGN OFFICE, LONDON
11 March 1916

DEAR MR. HOOVER:

A report has reached us that the Germans are taking half of the food imported by the Commission into the district of Ghent. It is said that they are giving this food to their soldiers and are also sending it in part to Breslau. I should be glad if you would make an inquiry into this question because, although I know that this kind of story is a common one in Belgium, this particular account comes to us from an unusually trustworthy source, and it refers to the military zone in Belgium where I have always felt some doubt whether your control is sufficient to secure the safe disposal of your imports.

As you may shortly be going to Belgium there are one or two other points of a similar nature which I should like you to inquire into.

In the first place, I have statistics of shipments from Belgium to Germany via Holland for the two months November 28th to January 27th. These shipments contain the following items:

On one boat 150 tons of rice and 150 tons of coffee.

206

On two other boats an aggregate of 1,700 tons of coffee, rice, and beans.
On another boat 400 tons of coffee, rice, beans, and flour.
On another 450 tons of coffee, rice, beans, and oil nuts.
Two further boats carried 1,200 tons of rice and beans, and 300 tons of rice, respectively.

These figures suggest a grave suspicion not only that shipments of Belgian native stocks, such as coffee and oil nuts, are being exported freely, which of course we knew before, but also that the leakage of your rice from Belgium, of which we have had evidence, is combined with a corresponding leakage of beans.

Finally, we have had a report that one particular mill owner in Brussels, by name Vuylsteke, is using the oil extracted in milling your grain for sale for the Germans for munitions purposes, and we are told that Vuylsteke is working in close touch with the Germans.

You will, of course, regard all this information as strictly confidential so far as it might betray the source from which it came.

EUSTACE PERCY

I at once submitted this matter to our inspection staff in Belgium. From their smuggler friends they came back with details of the origin and destination of each of these supposed transgressions. They were solely black-market operations, and the supplies had originated in Holland, Denmark, and even Britain.

On March 14, the Foreign Office, upon a complaint from their Military Intelligence, cut off our imports of clothing to Belgium, which consisted largely of second-hand clothes donated through our charity committees over the world. Their reasons were:

FOREIGN OFFICE, LONDON
14 March 1916

DEAR MR. HOOVER:

There has just been brought to our notice a decree issued by the German Government in Belgium commanding the seizure of all raw or manufactured wool. All the stocks of these articles must be declared to the German authorities by the 15th of February under heavy penalties, and the whole must be sold to the German purchasing association at Brussels *(Kriegswollbedarf-Aktiengesellschaft)*.

. . . this particular condition, creates the very gravest situation, and we have no choice but to take appropriate measures at once. We must there-fore ask you to stop absolutely, until the revocation of the decree, all im-ports by you of clothing materials into Belgium. . . .

EUSTACE PERCY

We, of course, pointed out to Percy that there were practically no sheep left in the occupied territory and that the wool stocks were infinitesimal, and we obtained a protest against the German action by our Minister Patrons in Belgium. This was a minor item, however, of Admiralty actions.

Soon after the spasm of good will following our resignations, Lord Percy informed me confidentially that British Naval Intelligence had sent the Foreign Office a long series of charges against the C.R.B. and against me personally and had demanded my removal. Percy revealed that the charges included reflections on my personal integ-rity, accused the C.R.B. and me of working in the German interest, and expounded the notion that in any event the Relief was an aid to the Germans and a great military and financial cost to the British. Also, these complaints had asserted that I had large private interests in Germany, was an undoubted German spy, and generally was de-livering the Relief food to the Germans.

Percy said that to the Foreign Office this was complete nonsense but that Sir Edward Grey was greatly concerned lest these charges influence the Cabinet. He suggested that I appear before some sort of inquiry at which Captain Hall would represent the Navy. I stated that I would do no such thing, that I was not a British subject, that even if I were I would not stand for an inquisition by such a crooked bunch as the Admiralty Intelligence had so often proved to be. But Percy came back and urged that it would avoid the publicity of an attack on the Commission by the Admiralty and would help Sir Ed-ward in his support of us if he appointed an outstanding King's Bench Judge, Justice Sir Sidney Rowlatt, personally to investigate our entire enterprise. Feeling quite indignant, I informed Ambassa-dor Page of the whole matter, including the constant misrepresenta-tions and complaints by Admiralty Intelligence and Captain Hall's bald attempt to question me on German military operations.

Certain matters in Belgium demanded my immediate attention. The reduced food supply in Belgium and Northern France was producing heartbreaking hardships. I was determined, therefore, to make a re-estimate of their situation on the spot. Ambassador Page undertook to see that there was no action in these matters until I returned.

In the meantime, Lord Percy asked for a memorandum—which he could show to Justice Rowlatt—concerning methods we used to safeguard against leakages to the Germans. I directed our staff to prepare it, and they sent it on April 5. Upon my return from Belgium, Ambassador Page advised that in view of the importance of the matter at stake and the undoubted friendliness of Sir Edward Grey, I had better see the Justice. It was an unpalatable performance for an American who thought his service should be enough of an answer. However, I answered his questions. I opened my private files and accounts to him and instructed the solicitor of my engineering firm to tell him anything he would like to know about me personally or my private business.

While we were in the midst of all this, Ambassador Page requested that I give him a note reviewing the whole affair—and up to date, too—for his record. After reviewing my conversations with Captain Hall and the rumors he had put in motion, I said:

April 12, 1916

DEAR MR. PAGE:

. . . I was informed that the reports mentioned at the Foreign Office had been referred to Mr. Justice Rowlatt for consideration, and I was asked if I would see him with regard to them. My first impulse was to refuse . . . but I felt that I should submit to anything that came along lest some word or action of mine should add further misery to the overload that these millions of helpless people in Belgium already have to endure. I saw Mr. Justice Rowlatt, and in all matters affecting the affairs of the Commission I was able, I believe, to give him such information as he wanted. If he is not entirely satisfied, I trust the Government will appoint someone to make a rigid investigation into all the Commission's offices and into our multitudinous records.

I thoroughly recognize that anyone thrust into such a position of public responsibility as I hold—especially considering the delicate international problems involved and the large sums of money employed—must be prepared at all times to submit to any open and competently conducted investigation. We have endeavored to provide all the safeguards that honesty of intention and desire for competency can devise and we welcome any such investigation.

On the other hand, both as an American citizen and as Chairman of the Commission for Relief in Belgium, the whole of whose work rests on good faith in all its dealings, I feel I have the right to demand a distinction between such investigation into the conduct of this work and a personal inquisition wherein I am summoned to answer anonymous attacks upon my private character. Mr. Justice Rowlatt raised questions outside the work of this Commission, of course, without disclosing to me their origin or specific bearing. With some natural diffidence, when accused on obviously malicious and entirely anonymous grounds, I could not, naturally, attempt any adequate defense.

The form of inquiry adopted bordered upon a presumption of guilt and necessity to prove innocence. I do not resent any inquiry into my private life, so long as it is done fully and so long as I have the ordinary rights of justice and the facilities of evidence. . . .

It seems to me that if such things were to be considered by serious men, I could have had such an opportunity for answering with the production of the evidence and accusers, instead of detectives being employed to interview my old . . . [clients] and communications being made to my friends of old standing.

As you know, I willingly went to answer the interrogatories of the judge appointed, although, despite the most courteous action on his part, the whole proceeding is one of deep humiliation. It does seem hard that one must, in the interest of the work itself, submit to a personal inquisition merely because, at your request, I have sacrificed what are to me important business affairs to serve the Allies in ameliorating the misery of the war.

If the inquiry results in a favorable report, I presume that, except for the feeling of humiliation, the matter is ended. If, on the other hand, there is any reserve in it, such reserve can only arise from incomplete inquiry; and I feel that it is due to you and to my colleagues, as well as to myself, that the matter does not rest there, and that further steps be taken to produce the authors of this outrage and to call upon them to meet me, that the thing may be gone into to the very bottom.

HERBERT HOOVER

The Ambassador informed me that he had previously seen Sir Edward and had called his attention to the fact that the good faith of himself and of all the American Ambassadors and the Minister Patrons was involved and that no steps should be taken without prior consultation with him. Further, he had demanded to see the Admiralty charges, which presumably were laid before Justice Rowlatt. He also had a meeting with Sir Sidney. I gathered from Page that he had used some vigorous language, including comment on the fact that the neutral Ambassadors should have been consulted before any such injustice was launched.

Page secured the copy of the charges and also a copy of Justice Rowlatt's report for me to see. It appeared that a considerable part of the charges was based upon allegations by "Benedict" to the police while he was being escorted out of the country after I had fired him from the Rotterdam office as a German spy (see Chapter 14).

"Benedict" had related a strange story. One of his charges accused me of being a German spy. Another alleged that I had large financial interests in Germany and that I had employed a Captain Merton in our Brussels office who was an official in these "interests." The Justice found that I had no such interests but that before the war I had been merely a "vendor" of minerals to German smelters.

The Admiralty had furnished the Justice with a long list of "leakages" of Belgian food to the Germans, which was asserted as proof that I was working for their interests. These charges were detailed to Sir Sidney by a Lieutenant Commander of the Navy named Wyatt, an assistant of Captain Hall's. Lord Percy had informed the Justice that these charges were fictitious and that in any event they had been dealt with by him and the Commission.

Among the charges by Wyatt was the old one about the nonexistent 25,000 tons of rice (see Chapter 18). The Justice's conclusions about the "leakages" were:

1. At the present time there is no ground for believing that the articles imported by the Commission are not applied for the relief of the people for whom they are intended.
2. At no time during the existence of the Commission have these articles

been misapplied in the sense that the benefit of tnem has been intentionally diverted from the people for whom they were intended, but it is proved that in the autumn of 1915 certain rice imported by the Commission was not consumed by those people, but was sold for their benefit or by the people themselves. Other leakage of the same kind may have occurred before the preventive organisation of the Commission had reached its present development.

3. The Commission has throughout, in good faith, endeavoured to secure that these articles should in every case be actually consumed by the people for whose relief they were intended. The amounts imported have not exceeded what can fairly be accounted for by such consumption. Consequently any amounts not actually so consumed can only have been a very small proportion of the total imported.

Sir Sidney's exhaustive report to Sir Edward Grey, which Lord Percy allowed me to read, completely vindicated both the Commission and me.

Since the Admiralty had been spreading its charges in many quarters, our friend the Duke of Norfolk, Chairman of our British Empire Committee, arranged a public meeting under the sponsorship of the Lord Mayor of London at the Mansion House. Prime Minister Lloyd George spoke. He said in part:

. . . At the request of His Excellency my friend Dr. Page, Mr. Hoover undertook the work, and formed, under the auspices of the American and Spanish Diplomatic representatives, what is now known as the Neutral Commission for Relief in Belgium. A noble friend and colleague of mine, Lord Curzon, has described Mr. Hoover's work as "a miracle of scientific organisation." That, I believe, is not an over-statement. With the people in Northern France, which is occupied by Germany, added to those in Belgium, Mr. Hoover and those associated with him have had to provide, and are providing every day, food for over nine million persons, 5 millions of whom are practically destitute. (Hear, hear)

My Lord Mayor—the enormous volume of shipping and food supplies rendered necessary, naturally brings the operations of the Neutral Commission under the closest supervision of the Admiralty and the War Office here. I am glad to be in a position to say on behalf of those Departments of His Majesty's Government, that we are convinced that the relief food reaches the Belgians and the French, and reaches them alone. (Cheers)

I am desired to express on behalf of the Government our deep gratitude to Mr. Hoover and to those American citizens who have so nobly given up their time and their occupations without recompense, and to a large extent without recognition, to this work of purchasing, shipping and distributing the supplies, which alone enable the population of Belgium to keep body and soul together (cheers). It is one of the finest achievements in the history of human and philanthropic organisation. (Cheers)

Ambassador Page received the following letter from Sir Edward:

FOREIGN OFFICE, LONDON
16 May 1916

MY DEAR AMBASSADOR:

In your private note of March 23d last you were good enough to send me a copy of a letter from Mr. Hoover stating that the Commission for Relief in Belgium would be willing to continue their work of relieving the civil population of Belgium. In the last paragraph of his letter Mr. Hoover observes that it is hopeless to carry on this work without the daily co-operation of various departments and agencies of His Majesty's Government, and he says that, in agreeing to continue, it is on the clear understanding that this co-operation shall continue also.

I think that the Commission may perhaps desire to receive some assurance from His Majesty's Government on this point, and I therefore beg that you will be so good as to make it clear to Mr. Hoover and those associated with him in this great humanitarian work that it is the desire and intention of His Majesty's Government that various public departments connected with the work should co-operate with the Commission in the closest possible way.

I am happy to [be] able to say that the Commission [will] continue to enjoy the complete confidence of His Majesty's Government, and I should like to add my own personal tribute to the admirable organisation which they have evolved, and to the tireless energy of all its members, who are so devotedly carrying out their difficult task.

E. GREY

The French also joined in our vindication by way of a letter from their Ambassador in London:

EMBASSY OF FRANCE
IN LONDON
July 3rd, 1916

MONSIEUR HOOVER:

. . . M. Briand has charged me . . . to inform you how much the French Government is indebted to you for the activity, the devotion and the courage with which your colleagues and yourself have come to the help of our unhappy populations.

Believe me, Sir, with the assurance of my highest consideration,

PAUL CAMBON

All of this only amounts to an account of military morals in the war.

CHAPTER 24

MORE FOOD
AND BETTER GUARANTEES

Notwithstanding the assaults of the militarists, we were not neglectful of our obligations to ten million very hungry people. Taking advantage of the promised support from the Allied Foreign Offices, we asked for increased import permits and more subsidies.

There had been no reason for the British and French Foreign Offices' reduction of food supplies at the end of February, 1916. There was, at this time, abundant overseas food available in the world. The action taken by the British and French certainly did not frighten the Germans. Indeed, it gave them the opportunity to charge the British and French with starving the Belgians and Northern French.

As I said in the last chapter, I personally went to Belgium to make a re-estimate of the situation on the spot and to give as fresh a report as possible to the Foreign Offices. With the reduced food supply, the Belgians' daily regimen was as follows:

Total grams per diem 394.0
Total protein 49.1
Total fats 39.5
Total carbohydrates 256.1
Total calorific value 1,552.0

The total of 1,552 calories per person per diem was about 50 per cent below the normal consumption of the Belgians and about 50 per cent below what was being consumed by the British at the time.

Worse still, the ration was entirely too short on protein and fats. Even if a diet were balanced, a per-person average of 1,552 calories would mean that large segments of the population would get only 1,000 calories because a minimum of more than 2,500 calories had to be given to people engaged in heavy physical labor or the very wheels of life would stop. Of the total food supplies, substantial amounts had to be assigned to the soup kitchens and the children's canteens. But the reduction in imports "debilitated" the soup and the canteens.

I again returned to the necessity of increasing imported supplies to Belgium and the North of France in a letter to Lord Percy at the Foreign Office:

LONDON, 5 April 1916

DEAR LORD EUSTACE:

BELGIAN PROGRAM OF IMPORTS

I wish to put before you the result of my investigations into the food position in Belgium as the result of my recent inspection. I may say that I had the advantage of discussions with the whole of our forty American district and staff managers, as well as with the Belgian committees and authorities. As a result we earnestly recommend the following changes in the permitted reports: . . .

I then urged an increase from the previously allowed monthly program of 68,150 tons for Belgians to 75,750 tons, this additional quantity to be used mostly for the needs of children. I also urged:

We strongly recommend that all cereals be made interchangeable as we simply cannot arrange precise shipments, and specific limitation on individual cereals has the effect of frequently decreasing the ration. . . .

WE SECURE BETTER GUARANTEES
FROM THE GERMANS

From the information given me by Ambassador Gerard in the wake of the C.R.B.'s "blowup" (see pages 204-205), it appeared that the Germans were anxious for us to continue our work. Therefore, as a first step in assuring a more liberal attitude from the British on imports, I felt that this was an opportune time to secure re-establishment of the Germans' agreement of December 25, 1915, not to take any native food. Von Bissing's repudiation of that undertaking was one of the causes of our troubles with Allied import permissions. To satisfy the British, I again demanded that the Germans prohibit exports of any food from the occupied territory and that they stop requisitions of native food.

The negotiations were taken up by Villalobar and Whitlock with von Bissing's regime. To aid them, I sent them samples of what we had to confront in the way of British complaints. However, the negotiations with von Bissing in Brussels by our Minister Patrons were getting nowhere. I took advantage of a returning American Embassy courier to inform Ambassador Gerard in Berlin of von Bissing's attitude and suggested that perhaps he could stir up things without creating "feelings" in either our patron Ministers in Brussels or in von Bissing. As usual, the Ambassador acted at once and ably. To my astonishment, the Ministers in Brussels suddenly succeeded in effecting our demands all along the line—no doubt due to Ambassador Gerard.

On April 14, 1916, a long document of agreement with our demands was received by Whitlock and Villalobar from von Bissing via Baron von der Lancken, his chief assistant. After an opening exposition of von Bissing's good will and kind conduct, it contained the following essential paragraph relating to exports of food from Belgium:

. . . In accordance with the general import of the assurances last given the Government which Your Excellency represents, the Governor-General will resume and complete the measures already taken in this direction by new instructions *forbidding the exportation from the territory of the General Government of foodstuffs (including animals), produce, and fodder, serving for human alimentation and animals. He will forbid, moreover, the exportation from said territory of seeds, fertilizers, and agricultural supplies.* This prohibition will apply only to products of Belgian origin, it being especially understood that products of German origin which are now in the magazines of the military government may be exported. . . .

The paragraphs prohibiting the requisition of native food were:

The Governor-General will give also to the Military Commissariat of the General Government, to ensure the success of the enterprise *(pour les effects consequents)*, instructions no longer to requisition, or buy freely, in the occupied territory of Belgium, for the needs of the army of occupation, any of the products mentioned above. As your Excellency has certainly been convinced in the course of the recent negotiations, the Governor-General attaches greatest importance to the creation of a definite and clearly understood situation. It is therefore with great satisfaction that I have inferred, from the note which His Excellency the Minister of Spain was so kind as to send me, that Your Excellency, in the capacity of representative of your Government, will not consider occasional purchases of these products made individually by persons belonging to the army as contrary to the engagements entered into by the Governor-General, provided that these purchases are not at all systematic *(aucunement systématique)*, and are not made for the account of the Military Commissariat.

Having thus extended the scope of the obligations entered into by him previously toward the three neutral Powers, for the territory which he governs, the Governor-General is persuaded that, on its side, the Government which Your Excellency represents will assume toward him the guarantee that the British Government will henceforward definitely renounce the practice of interfering by requisition of ships, or in any other manner, with the ravitaillement of the civil population in Belgium. . . .

The final paragraph was:

The Governor-General has noted with satisfaction that Your Excellency will see to it that the work of Secours and Alimentation placed under his patronage be kept strictly within the limits traced for its activity. This will permit the Governor-General to give, as in the past, all his aid and all his protection to the Comité National and the Commission for Relief in Belgium under the patronage of Your Excellency, in order to permit the members of these two organizations to continue the work which they have been doing up to the present with such devotion in their humanitarian and charitable enterprise, destined to lighten for the population of Belgium the weight of the sufferings occasioned by the war. . . .

LANCKEN

On May 6, Sir Edward Grey accepted these agreements in a memorandum attached to a letter to Ambassador Page. The key paragraphs concerning our work were:

. . . It will . . . be necessary, in the interests of all parties concerned, to set up some form of control over the native produce of the forthcoming season similar to that arranged in 1914 in regard to breadstuffs, such control to include all the livestock and dairy produce in the country; the bodies entrusted with this control will be in the best position to determine what commodities are in excess of the needs of the population.

His Majesty's Government are further glad to note the Governor-General's declaration that he will give orders . . . [as to food] requisitioned or purchased for the use of the occupying army. In return for this assurance His Majesty's Government now agree to raise no objection to the incidental purchase by individual soldiers of Belgian native produce, provided that such individual purchases are not in any way systematic and do not, in fact, come in any way within the purview or control of the quartermaster's department or any other military authority. . . .

. . . the Commission for Relief have recently pressed upon me extensive proposals for the increase in the present rations. After a careful examination of these proposals and acting on the assumption that the undertakings given by the Governor General in Belgium will rapidly be carried into effect, His Majesty's Government have decided to increase the rations in the sense desired by the Commission. It will of course be understood that the continuance of the rations on the higher scale must be dependent on the exercise of a control over native Belgian produce on the lines indicated above.

WE SECURE INCREASED PERMISSION TO IMPORT

Finally, on May 10, the British formally agreed to the increase of supplies to Belgium.

FOREIGN OFFICE, LONDON, 10 May 1916

HERBERT HOOVER,
SIR:

With reference to your letter of the 5th ultimo putting forward various proposals for an increase in the present Belgian ration, I am directed by

Secretary Sir Edward Grey to state that, after full consideration of the matter, His Majesty's Government have agreed to the revised programme as suggested by you, viz.:

Four thousand tons of bacon and lard per month [instead of 2,400 tons], 5,000 tons of rice [for which there was no previous allowance], and 1,000 tons of yeast materials per month [instead of 250 tons].

No objection will be raised to making all cereals interchangeable, provided the actual imports of maize are not allowed to exceed 8,000 tons per month and provided it is clearly intimated to this Office on each occasion when it is proposed to substitute one cereal for another. The rice will of course be cleaned rice. . . .

MAURICE DE BUNSEN

In a letter from Sir Edward Grey to Ambassador Page of June 14, the British notified us that they had lifted the embargo on our imports of clothing for the Belgian destitute.

With these backgrounds, the question of securing protection of the 1916 harvest became a routine formality in the negotiations with von Bissing by our Minister Patrons in Belgium. It was effected by a decree from von Bissing on July 8 giving authority to the Relief organization to take and distribute the crops in the Occupation Zone. The arrangements we made for the Operations Zone in Flanders are detailed later in the discussion of Northern France, since they were settled through the German General Staff.

I could not but think that our American rebellion had contributed to clearing the air on all sides—British, German, and Belgian—for a while. In any event, the various crises relaxed.

TROUBLE WITH COWS

We had been trying for some time to build up special dairies to provide milk products for the children's services. Our organization had purchased hundreds of milch cows from Holland and had rescued some serviceable cows from the slaughterhouses. However, von Bissing waved a forbidding hand, as is shown by the following note from Emile Francqui:

28 June 1916

The Governor General has just advised the C.R.B. and the C.N. that, until further notice, the importation of milch cows from Holland to Belgium and the North of France is not desirable and that . . . it would be necessary for them to make a special request to the "Vermittlungstelle" in each case.

As you know, in order to supply our children's canteens with milk, we imported from Holland several hundreds of milch cows. The Ministers Protectors received the assurance of the German Government that these cows, bearing a special mark, could not be requisitioned.

These cows are located in the industrial centres and it is in the communes to which they were sent that the products supplied by them for the alimentation of children are employed.

On two occasions also we have already imported several head of cattle for the slaughter houses in Brussels, the meat thus supplied being used in the preparation of the soup for the people.

The letter went on to say:

Bruhn, who directs here the German political department, has declared that his Government knew that England was going to take energetic measures with the Dutch Government to prevent the exportation of foodstuffs to Germany; but, he added, "before such measures take effect, the German Government itself has quite decided to buy in Holland for Germany all that it can procure. It is for that reason that the German Government puts obstacles in the way of making purchases [of cows] in Holland for Belgium and the North of France."

On June 30, Lord Percy requested that we write him another essay on our methods of preventing leakage of food, which he could again show to the British militarists. We did so, but it contributes nothing new for this narrative. It seemed to keep them calm for some time.

To comfort the Foreign Office, I began sending them copies of every report of leakages discovered and investigated by our American inspectors, the details of the exact movement of every car or canal boat and its contents, from the Dutch ports to its destination, the receipts from warehouses, the record of issues from the warehouses to food processors, and the receipts of each commune.[1]

I AGAIN APPEAL FOR MORE IMPORTS
FOR THE BELGIANS

On April 5, 1916, I had recommended to Lord Percy proposals for increasing the C.R.B. imports. On May 10, the Foreign Office agreed to the revised program. But even with the increase, the Belgian food imports remained heartbreakingly below the need. On September 15, 1916, I sent a report on the situation to our Patron Ministers in Brussels, asking them to intervene. The essential paragraphs were:

DEAR MR. MINISTER:

As the result of a general inquiry by the C.R.B. representatives as to the native food outlook, we are convinced:

a) The potato crop which last year proved insufficient for the population will next year be much worse, as the crop is 30 per cent below that of last year.

b) The breadstuff crops are fully 20 per cent under last year.

c) It is now proved that Belgian cattle which normally lived largely upon cereal fodders cannot be fattened on green feed. The cattle have therefore, owing to absence of fodder imports, failed to take on consequential weight during the summer. The meat supply will be much less than heretofore. . . .

. . . The industrial classes already show greatly decreased vitality, increased tuberculosis, and other bad signs.

In consequence of all this, the imports of food must during the winter rise to much larger quantities than anything we have hitherto contemplated, and this in the face of the highest prices the world has ever known.

HERBERT HOOVER

I followed this with an urgent request to the British Foreign Office

[1] Those interested will find all this in a complete statistical record of the Commission published by the Stanford University Press on June 20, 1925: *Statistical Review of Relief Operations,* by George I. Gay.

for increase of permits for Belgium to 87,000 tons a month. I again pointed out that there was a great deficiency in both protein and fats in the diet of the people and that the health of the children was degenerating; I proposed additional imports to enable us to expand our special extra meal for children and the infirm. My report to Lord Percy read:

October 7

DEAR LORD EUSTACE

. . . The whole of the native breadstuffs are in control of the Relief Organization and are combined with the native wheat, and a rigid bread ration is issued to the entire population. The other imports are issued upon a ration *(carte de ménage)* to a more limited number of people who are presumed unable to secure native supplies or in any event only partial supply. In addition the Relief Organization supplements the diet of more destitute members of the *carte de ménage* class by public feeding through soup for adults, by canteens for infant children, and by serving a meal each day in the schools. Approximately 6,000,000 people have a *carte de ménage* and 2,820,000 receive supplementary help through public kitchens.

II

In the consideration of a revised import program for the coming year, three outstanding new factors must be given weight:

a) As shown by Dr. Lucas' investigation, the industrial and minor commercial adults and the children over five years of age have been steadily underfed during the past year, and while their vitality has not been lowered to the breaking point, they cannot face another year on such a margin.

b) The new potato crop is 30 per cent to 40 per cent short of last year. The available local breadstuff harvest in the Occupation Zone is diminished by about 25 per cent, although this is compensated for by the larger German guarantees in the Etappen. The local meat supplies are again most seriously reduced, and the local fat supplies are also much diminished.

c) The considerable filtration of Dutch fish, cheese, etc., has almost ceased by virtue of the German prohibitions.

After giving a rough estimate of the native food supplies available prior to the next harvest, I also provided these statistics concerning the greatly decreasing meat supplies:

From these data and our other investigations we are convinced that the total meat killed does not now exceed 3,500 tons per month for the whole of Belgium, and on an even distribution this would be less than 17 grams per capita, per diem, or less than one ounce, but as the price of meat has risen to from Frs. 8 to 12 per kilo and there is no physical possibility of an even distribution, it simply means that the producers and well-to-do classes get the whole of this meat, less the amount which we buy at these high prices for the soup kitchens (for which we need about 800 tons per month).

Fats.—Fat supplies, outside those contained in the above meat, have now been reduced to a very low ebb. As shown above, there is a steady diminution in the number of animals; but of equal importance is the fact that Belgian animals are largely dependent upon cereal fodder, which has been for months non-existent. The meat, fat, and butter and milk producing capacity per head is therefore greatly reduced. The . . . [total tallow] collected by the German Fat Central, which requires the total tallow from all abattoirs, average less than 50 tons per month. If we assume the outside figure of 500,000 milk cattle still left (against 1,000,000 before the war), the theoretical dairy fats available in butter and cheese are now less than 1,000 tons per month. . . . Some further theoretical fats may be estimated for the skimmed milk . . . through the Relief Organization [it reaches] the children only. . . .

. . . This deficiency of the available food supplies, as brought out by the above figures, represents a monthly shortage in:

	Tons
Protein	5,400
Fats	1,800
Carbohydrates	18,450

I again proposed that the food imports be increased from the previous level of 75,500 tons to 86,986 tons, with a better proportion of fats and proteins. And I added:

. . . the above total [is] estimated [to] cost . . . £2,069,200 [monthly, of which] approximately £330,000 is due to the increase in imports proposed.

The cost of the whole program has been materially affected by the great rise in prices during the past five months, this rise representing roughly about £400,000. Out of the total of £2,069,200 the Commission hopes to be able to obtain about £150,000 per month from charity and commercial exchange, and therefore the need from subsidies represents about £1,900,000, or an increase of about £900,000 over the present . . . [level].

Shortly after the end of our second year, the Foreign Office decided that we were to have permits to import amounts which were only four hundred tons below my recommendation:

FOREIGN OFFICE, LONDON
11 November 1916

DEAR MR. HOOVER:
. . . in regard to the increase in the Belgian ration, I now transmit to you herewith a complete revised table of all your rations in order to put the situation on a clear basis. . . .

RELIEF IMPORTS FOR BELGIUM

	Metric Tons
Wheat	59,000
Maize	8,000
Rice	5,000
Peas and beans	3,000
Meat	500
Fish	850
Bacon and lard	5,686
Cheese	500
Condensed milk	1,000
Cocoa	350
Coffee	1,100
Yeast materials	1,000
Soap	1,000
Clothing and clothing materials	
Medical supplies (not including rubber goods)	

For the Commission's staff

Petrol	20,000 liters
Lubricating oil	1,000 liters
Mineral transmission grease	100 kilos
Motor car accessories	

THE GERMAN ARMY VIOLATES THE GUARANTEES

These concessions from the British had been obtained in the face of slight weakening by the Germans in the matter of complying with their own guarantees. The amounts taken were small in comparison with the totals of food, and it soon became evident that it was not the fault of von Bissing's government. The German Army was overriding his undertakings in the Occupation Zone.

On October 23, 1916, on the basis of information furnished by our Inspection Staff, the Minister Patrons in Brussels protested, citing five small shipments out of Belgium to German destinations by German Army agents.

We could not allow small leaks to start. Therefore, on November 1, a protest from the Patron Ministers to von Bissing contained the following passages:

. . . it now becomes necessary to call attention to the fact that infractions of these undertakings, especially of those pertaining to the non-requisitioning, wholesale purchasing and exportation of native foodstuffs, are becoming frequent and serious. Indeed there is sufficient evidence on which to base the statement that there is a systematic attempt under way to help supply the needs of the Military Authorities in the occupied territory and the needs of the civil population in Germany by large purchases and exportations of the native food products.

Since the middle of September, cases of infractions of the guarantees as to indigenous foodstuffs are reported in numbers greatly exceeding those of earlier times. It is also to be noted that the quantities involved in these cases, especially in those of exportation, are rapidly increasing in importance. . . .

Despite this breach of principle, the Foreign Office, because of confidence in our Inspection Staff and the vigorous protests made to the Germans by our Minister Patrons, granted us the further increase in supplies on November 11.

CHAPTER 25

OUR BATTLE TO SECURE
THE 1916 HARVEST
IN THE NORTH OF FRANCE

The battles we fought over the 1916 harvest so aptly portray the sidelights on the war and the problems with which we had to contend that I document them at great length lest the narrative be otherwise unbelievable.

Late in February, 1916, the C.R.B. had secured some minor concessions from the German General Staff. On February 19, it was agreed that the German contribution to the flour ration should be based on 125 grams of wheat, in effect a small increase because of high milling, and that the Germans should ship potatoes from Germany in order to maintain the daily ration of 200 grams. On February 21, they agreed to supply garden seeds and promised that there would be no requisitioning of garden produce. On February 25, they consented to furnish the population with all ground-crop seeds for the harvest of 1916. At this time the General Staff also declared their intention to requisition all crops from the 1916 harvest but promised that negotiations with us concerning its disposition would be taken up before the harvest.

In March, the French Government began insisting to Chevrillon that the 1916 harvest should be put on the same basis as was current in Occupied Belgium, where the Relief organization collected the crops and distributed them. To his letter on the subject, I replied:

LONDON, 18 March 1916

DEAR CHEVRILLON:

... As to the general question of the protection of native foodstuffs in Northern France on the same basis as the occupied territory in Belgium, there are [several differences]. . . . as Northern France is wholly within the Operations Zone there is no definite form of civil government, but simply the decentralization of six different armies, whose control of the civil population is quite independent of each other, and who are never disposed to act in concert except by way of recommendation from the General Staff, which they do or do not carry out in detail as they see fit. . . .

The French Foreign Office should recognize that it is utterly impossible . . . the native food supply could be set up in the actual Operations Zone of the army . . . by neutrals, in the same way as it is possible under the civil government in Belgium.

As to the requisitioning of French wheat. . . . This affair in fact falls into four classes: first, land planted by the Germans and harvested by themselves; second, abandoned land for which they hired French workpeople on the basis of advancing them seed and animals for a share of the crop; third, sections where they advanced seed and ploughed the land with their steam ploughs, giving the peasant a right by virtue of some labor and land ownerships, to a share of the crop; fourth, cases where the peasants raised their own crops without any relations with the Germans. All these involved different relations. . . . I visited Paris in July last and in company with you called on Mr. Humbert and stated to him . . . that we wished the views of the French Government as to its attitude and on this question as affecting continued ravitaillement and their requirements in the matter. We were unable to get any view whatever and gained the impression that nobody cared. We were compelled to take up the question with the Germans without the strong support which I was solicitous to obtain, and we did the best we could under the circumstances.

HERBERT HOOVER

On April 1, I addressed Major von Kessler, who represented the German General Staff, concerning the German requisitions of animals and animal products:

LONDON, 1 April 1916

MY DEAR MAJOR VON KESSLER:

There is one matter in connection with the ravitaillement of Northern

France in which it appears to me a new situation has gradually developed and which I would like to raise with you, in the hope that you can, as always heretofore, find some solution of a favorable nature. This is the question of the remaining native food supplies in the country in the shape of cattle, milk, butter, chickens, eggs, rabbits, etc.

The native supplies have undoubtedly diminished to a very low ebb and while it is our impression that they are not, in actual amount of food, of very great importance from a military point of view, they have become of great importance to the civilian population as the final margin on which they can eke out an existence by way of supplement to the ration which we are able to import. . . .

Requisitions to an amount which at one time represented only the surplus have through the decrease in supplies generally now amounted to almost the whole of certain articles.

. . . I am extremely keen to avoid any possible criticism as to our operations degenerating into a replacement through imports. . . . of the native supplies absorbed by the occupying army. . . .

Also I understand that milk and butter from native cattle are requisitioned and purchased for the troops. The local milk supply is now far under that required for the children and infirm. We have tried hard to secure by import a sufficiency to maintain these classes, but the demand on the world's milk supplies makes it hopeless, even had we sufficient transport, to do more than we have already done, and even with the local milk and butter these supplies are far below the needs of the people.

We wish to make an effort to remedy this to some extent by the establishment of milk herds on behalf of the most necessitous communes through the importation of cows from . . . Holland, but this effort would come to but little result unless the milk supply already in the country could go to the civil population.

I recognize fully the stupendous difficulties arising out of any attempt to reserve such native food supplies to the population during military occupation, but if requisition were abandoned and if the purchase of native food supplies were limited to the occasional purchases by soldiers from local sources, it would be all that any practical person could assume would be possible. . . .

HERBERT HOOVER

This letter proved to be more educational than productive.

After a heartbreaking inspection on the ground, I again addressed the British Foreign Office to transmit to the French Foreign Office a request asking for permission to restore previous imports and even increase that level for the North of France. My report was:

LONDON, 5 April 1916

DEAR LORD EUSTACE:

NORTHERN FRANCE PROGRAM OF IMPORTS

I have been to Northern France to investigate present conditions. There have been three causes in operation militating against our revictualment of this region.

1. Reduction of permitted quantities, as per your direction of February 23d.
2. Failure of native food supplies.
3. Shortage of overseas transport.

I detailed the reasons why we needed an increase from 29,700 tons per month to 36,800 tons to assure the Northern French a reasonable protection from starvation. I then stated that I and four members of our American staff had made a survey of three city areas of 1,260,000 people and gave these details:

Meat.—We found the meat shops all closed and there had been no fresh meat on sale nor any distributed in the district either through shops or markets for 10 days, with three exceptions:

a) The shops that have recently and openly sold dog meat, now closed by the authorities.

b) A little [smuggled] Dutch meat, which reached Roubaix. Only two sides were exposed for sale in the whole town, the vender demanding an average of Fr. 12 per kilo, bones and all—about 5 shillings per pound [$1.25].

c) Some meat that had been obtained by special exertions [of the Commission] for the soup kitchens.

... during 12 days of 16, in one commune, there had been no meat or ... [fat] base whatever to the soup. We are doing our utmost to get a small amount of meat ... for the soup kitchens. ...

Incidentally, two of our party endeavored to obtain dinner in Lille, and after visiting four restaurants which had no meat, they found one where the proprietor was able to offer a single chicken at Fr. 16 [$3.20].

The potatoes throughout the region are absolutely exhausted. One hundred kilos were offered in the Valenciennes market and sold for Fr. 85 (£34 per ton, as against £4 normal). The German authorities originally supplied 200 grams per capita per diem, but as the exhaustion of the supplying districts extended farther and farther afield, in both Belgium and Northern France, these shipments became first intermittent and finally negligible. We tried to get some potatoes from Holland, but failed. The food value of the small quantity of potatoes desired is of course of less importance than its value in preventing the spread of scurvy.

In every case among the numerous provision shops visited the shelves were absolutely bare. . . . The total number of food animals seen in our whole journey was four cattle and fourteen chickens. The population receives no milk and butter supplies, and a package of [smuggled] Dutch margarine sold recently in Lille for Fr. 16 [$3.20] per kilo. We saw no vegetables in the markets apart from a little celery and a good deal of dandelion leaves.

It is obvious that the population are dependent upon our imported ration, and it is clear that the March basis will not support life. The mortality statistics for the city of Lille for the past four months show an increase from 20 in December to 42 the first 25 days of March. Sickness has increased far beyond what the figures for mortality so far indicate and will be reflected in the more serious mortality statistics of later months.

In Roubaix riots broke out in one of the poorer communes upon the announcement of the reduction in the ration, and I am informed by the German authorities that they removed 2,000 men from the town to work for them in order to preserve tranquillity. They stated that these men have been sent to other districts to work on the roads.

There are no consequential leakages in the distribution. The goods all go to the communal magazines under seal and the mayors themselves report their arrivals and quantities to the American district managers and they, in turn, to our central organizations. Every household has a *carte de ménage* issued by the committees, and this card entitles the holder to purchase or gift of the ration. The ration is posted publicly everywhere. As the population must starve or get the ration, they get it. Moreover, as it is less than life can endure upon, they do not part with it. The people are free to complain to the American district managers, and the Americans are in constant motion visiting the people. An indication of the tenacity with which the people cling to their pittance lies in the disparity in price of free lard (when obtainable), which is Fr. 15 per kilo, against our lard ration, where sold, at Fr. 2.20 per kilo.

In conclusion.—I feel my entire inability to draw for you an adequate picture of the unutterable depression and despair of these people. We are the only link to their kindred and their allies, and we are thus the only mouthpiece by which they may express to you their prayer for more help. My colleagues and myself feel that when the result of our representations last month was a reduction in their food instead of an increase as pleaded for, we have today to recognize that we have but proved our incapacity as their advocates.

The Allies have not fought this war, nor do they intend to fight it, on the basis of abandonment of solicitude for the helpless; yet we, who for over a year have been ceaselessly endeavoring to alleviate this mass of misery, are now forced to appear as an instrument of torture, since daily we must refuse the pleadings of a people whose sufferings will yet be told in terms reflecting neglect for which we are now daily blamed.

HERBERT HOOVER

As a result of this prayer, the Foreign Office agreed to our increased program:

FOREIGN OFFICE, LONDON
11 April 1916

Herbert Hoover, Esq.
SIR:

With reference to the letter addressed by you to Lord Eustace Percy on the 5th instant, pointing out the scarcity of certain foodstuffs in Northern France as a result of the recent reduction in the ration, I am directed by Lord Robert Cecil to state that His Majesty's Government have decided, in view of the considerations urged in your letter, to agree to the increases for which you ask, namely three thousand three hundred tons of flour, one thousand six hundred tons of bacon and lard, and two thousand two hundred tons of rice per month.

His Majesty's Government further agree that all cereals shall be made interchangeable, including wheat.

His Majesty's Government must however insist that the German authorities should furnish the two hundred grammes of potatoes per capita per diem as originally promised.

EYRE A. CROWE

On May 10, the German General Staff agreed to the protection of any dairy herds that we might assemble or bring from Holland. We succeeded in establishing several small dairies for the children.

Constant in our minds was the aim to secure an undertaking from the General Staff that the 1916 harvest, and all other native produce, be reserved for the French civilian population. At my direction, our staffs at Charleville and Brussels again urged this vigorously upon the Germans. They were not able to report much progress, and on June 13, the French Government began to exert pressures on us, through Chevrillon, our Director in Paris, who wrote to Honnold, our Director in London, as follows:

PARIS, 13 June 1916

DEAR MR. HONNOLD:

. . . I am advised from the Foreign Office that the French Government intends to take measures in order that the Commission should obtain from the Germans the full French crop for the benefit of the French civil population. I am, at once, setting all the influence I can in motion to oppose this, as I know perfectly well that no weapon can be put into your hands to obtain this from the Germans unless it be more suffering for the unfortunate populations under German rule, and I do not believe that the Germans accept this unless the French Government goes to the length of actually stopping all relief. I believe I am right in this, but would like to have your views. . . . They . . . consider that a strong attitude is the proper line to take and that the Germans will also give in in Northern France if we threaten stoppage of relief unless they allow the full French crop for French needs. I would be glad to have your views on this.

L. CHEVRILLON

In a letter of June 13 to the French Foreign Office, Chevrillon endeavored to get the French Government to take the responsibility for stopping relief if its demands regarding the 1916 harvest could not all be secured:

... In March 1915, Mr. Hoover came to Paris with the object of organizing the ravitaillement in Northern France, and to take instructions from the French Government which he did not succeed in obtaining. The Commission then did its best and succeeded in that Northern France might retain approximately one-third of the total harvest. Having only as sanction for imposing its demands on the Germans a threat of . . . [starvation], it did not deem it proper to undertake a responsibility which is not within the province of a neutral commission devoting itself to a philanthropic work.

Considering the German participation in the agricultural work in Northern France, it seems at first sight certain that we will not obtain the totality of the harvest for the civil populations; further, each time we exact a new concession from the Germans, we always knock up against the German argument of the food blockade which serves them as a pretext in refusing to discuss the obligation by the occupying authorities to feed the people. My feeling is that, despite the desire which one may have to increase the proportion of the harvest set aside for the alimentation of the civil population, the proportion which we have today, representing 7,500 tons of wheat monthly (viz., 90,000 tons per annum), does not fall far short of the maximum which we could obtain; and, in these circumstances, I ask you kindly to consider that the only weapon in our possession is a menace to interrupt the ravitaillement, commencing to enforce same.

I do not know whether you will gain a clear idea of the lamentable situation in Northern France today, and to what degree of misery the population is reduced. To increase their hardships would be to incur the responsibility of an increase in mortality which I cannot describe precisely but which would certainly be considerable in view of the fact that the statistics for the month of March show that under existing conditions and through insufficient alimentation the rate of mortality in Lille has risen from 17 to 40/1,000.

I believed it to be indispensable to expose to you the above-mentioned observations in order to clearly demonstrate the eventual consequences of a new intervention. The Commission is entirely disposed to re-commence negotiations on the basis which it will suit the Government to formulate, but should plainly refuse to undertake the carrying out of a sanction which would compromise the existence of the populations of whom it has charge.

L. CHEVRILLON

Several weeks later, the British Foreign Office gave us a blast from their side, addressed to Ambassador Page:

FOREIGN OFFICE, LONDON
7 July 1916

MY DEAR AMBASSADOR:

The Allied Governments have been carefully considering the question of the disposal of the harvest in the regions of Belgium and Northern France under German occupation [Army operations] where the Commission for Relief in Belgium is carrying on its work.

The Allied Governments feel obliged to demand that throughout the whole of this territory the same principles shall be established and observed as are now recognised in the zone of Belgium under civil administration, namely, that the whole harvest and all produce of the soil whatsoever in Belgium and in Northern France shall be reserved in their entirety for the civil population.

The details as to the precise measures necessary to collect, control, and distribute the native crops may be settled by the Relief Commission, but the arrangements finally made must carry out the principle stated above, which the Allied Governments regard as an absolute condition of the continuance of the work of the Commission.

ROBERT CECIL

The next day, the Foreign Office transmitted to me the demands of the French Government with regard to the coming harvest, which amounted to a retreat into a pious hope that we could continue the previous basis with the Germans, but with a willingness to compromise on whatever we could get and a refusal to take the responsibility for ending the Relief. The essential paragraph of the letter was:

FOREIGN OFFICE, LONDON
8 July 1916

DEAR HOOVER:

I enclose for your private information a note prepared by the French Government for your confidential guidance in these negotiations. I should like to see you about this whole question some time, but meanwhile you will understand the private character of this note which is for your own eye and not for communication to anyone else.

EUSTACE PERCY

To this letter Lord Percy attached a note from the French Foreign Office reciting in detail various alternatives which we should propose to the Germans. In no sentence did they authorize us to stop the Relief if their plans did not work. But they were not as well acquainted with the Germans as we were. We had to be very positive.

On July 11, I asked Ambassador Gerard to take up with the Berlin authorities the reservation of the crops in Northern France and the Belgian Etape:

DEAR MR. GERARD:

By this mail Dr. Page will be forwarding you a despatch from the British Government, dated 7th July 1916, in which the Allied Governments demand that the whole produce of the soil in Belgium and Northern France shall be reserved entirely for the civil population. This demand does not relate to the Occupation Zone in Belgium, but only to the Etappengebiet in Belgium and to the occupied area in Northern France. These two areas are under the direct control of the German Army . . . and as before we have to rely upon you and your own individual exertions with the Staff in this matter. . . .

I then described the different ways by which the German Army was connected with agricultural production in Northern France, continuing:

. . . any scheme under which the harvest should be physically taken over by the relief organization in this area is almost unthinkable from a practical point of view. Therefore, it would appear to me that the basis of discussion should take the form of the German authorities furnishing to you an estimate of the harvest of various commodities and the proportion which they consider has been raised by the result of their exertions. . . . In any event, if you would be good enough to take the matter up with the German Government and impress upon them that we are having the usual time to defend the Relief, and that we shall be able to save it in these regions only by close co-operation from them . . . .

I shall go into Belgium in the course of the next ten or fourteen days and would like to be advised by you as to whether I should go to Berlin to take up the matter there or whether I should intervene directly with the General Staff at Charleville. At least it will have prepared the way for detailed discussion if you are so good as to take up the matter with the authorities at Berlin in advance and thus give them some time for consideration.

HERBERT HOOVER

Ambassador Gerard wrote the German Foreign Office as follows:

BERLIN, 18 July 1916

His Excellency, Dr. Helfferich,
     Imperial Secretary of State for the Interior and Vice Chancellor
MY DEAR EXCELLENCY:
     Our Ambassador in London has received a letter from the British Government, of which a copy follows. I have also received a letter from Mr. Herbert Hoover, stating that he will come to Berlin to confer with whoever has charge of this matter or would go to Charleville to confer with the officers of the General Staff there. I spoke of this matter yesterday to His Excellency Herr von Jagow and, if you remember, he called you on the telephone and then informed me that you would be very glad to confer with Mr. Hoover on the matter.

As I understand it, the demand now made by the Allied Governments does not relate to the occupation area in Belgium, but to that territory known as the Etappengebiet and to all of the occupied area in Northern France. These two areas are, I believe, under the direct control of the General Staff.

I understand, of course, that in Northern France the German Army of Occupation has taken over and cultivated large areas and has further furnished seeds, additional labor, horses, etc., to the peasants.

Possibly the discussion should take the form of the German authorities furnishing to Mr. Hoover and to me an estimate of the harvest of the various grains and the proportion of these which they consider has been raised as the result of the work of the German Army or by its assistance. This refers to the occupied territory in Northern France.

With regard to the Etappengebiet in Belgium, I understand that the problem there is simpler, because the German Army has taken no part in planting or otherwise producing the harvest . . . Of course, the Commission for the Relief in Belgium is very anxious that the relief should go on and that the importation of food should not be stopped by the Allies, and therefore hopes that some arrangement can be arrived at, satisfactory to all parties.

I am simply setting out these facts in this letter in order that your assistants may be considering the matter before the arrival of Mr. Hoover. I am telegraphing Mr. Hoover that you will take up the matter with him, and I think he will be in Berlin in about two weeks. . . .

JAMES W. GERARD

The German reply to Ambassador Gerard was:

BERLIN, 25 July 1916

MY DEAR EXCELLENCY:

I have the honor to acknowledge receipt of your esteemed letter dated July 18th, to which you were kind enough to append the Note of the English Foreign Office under date of July 7th addressed to the American Ambassador at London. The question of supplying the territory of Northern France occupied by German troops and of the lines of communication in Belgium concerns the chief military authorities in the first place. To the latter I have therefore transmitted Your Excellency's communication and inquired where, according to their idea, the conference desired by Mr. Hoover should most expediently be arranged. . . .

HELFFERICH

Having thus laid the groundwork for dealing with the General Staff, I joined Dr. Kellogg at Charleville on August 1. We had long conferences with the liaison officers, Major von Kessler and Count Wengersky, and finally with the German Quartermaster General, von Sauberzweig. The Germans insisted that the only practical base of organizing the matter was for them to requisition all the crops produced by the peasants themselves and to add to this quantity the amounts to which the peasants were entitled from working their

partnership farms with the Germans and then give a per diem ration
to the civilian population, either through us or directly to the communes, as we might wish. By way of trying to impress us with the
impracticability of any other course, they invited us to visit the hin-
terland of the armies to see what it was like. We motored for some
time over the army supply lines, and then they suggested that we
might like to take a look at the Battle of the Somme, which was raging at that time. I made an immediate note of this visit which I later
summarized in my *Memoirs:*

We motored for several hours to a point near a hilltop observation post
in the forest, a distance back from the forward trenches and a mile or two
away from the main roads. During the last few miles an occasional shell
cracked nearby but the ingenious camouflage of the road—to the extent
of a false parallel—seemed to give protection to our route. At the post the
constant rumble of artillery seemed to pulverize the air. Seen through
powerful glasses, in the distant view lay the unending blur of trenches, of
volcanic explosions of dust which filled the air where over a length of sixty
miles a million and a half men were fighting and dying. Once in a while,
like ants, the lines of men seemed to show through the clouds of dust.
Here under the thunder and belching volcanoes of 10,000 guns . . . the
lives of Germans and Englishmen were thrown away. On the nearby road
unending lines of Germans plodded along the right side to the front,
not with drums and bands, but in the silence of sodden resignation. Down
the left side came the unending lines of wounded men, the "walking cases,"
staggering among cavalcades of ambulances. A quarter of a million had
died and it was but one battle in that war.

The horror of it all did not in the least affect the German officers in the
post. To them it was pure mechanics. The battle had already been raging
for days. Not one of the Germans showed the slightest anxiety. They said
that the British were losing two to one—butting their heads against a
stone wall. And that was true. It was all a horrible, devastating reality, no
romance, no glory.[1]

It was obvious that in the midst of such operations it was only the
Germans who could collect the crops, and on that basis the problem
resolved, as was the case of the previous year, into an estimate of

[1] *Memoirs of Herbert Hoover,* Vol. I, p. 193.

what the base amount that they would ration to the civilian population should be. I had obtained from the French authorities in Paris an estimate of what the amount should be, and I had also obtained an estimate from our American staff and their French colleagues on the ground. The Germans also produced one. They differed widely. The estimate of the French Government amounted to practically normal production—and therefore was without sense. Our estimate was that we should receive more bread grains than was obtained from the 1915 harvest. It exceeded the German estimate by more than a thirty-million-dollar value based on import costs.

One difficulty in the negotiations had arisen from the fact that a French commercial group was shipping small amounts of food to Northern France through Switzerland, with the approval of the French Government. These supplies amounted to less than 2 per cent of the need and were sold at high prices to individuals and communes. It disturbed our whole rationing system. Quartermaster General von Sauberzweig had an idea that this practice could be amplified, thereby eliminating the nuisance of having the Americans about.

While Major von Kessler was inclined to settle on our estimate, the General was obstinate, arrogant, and generally overbearing. Finally, I suggested that since Ambassador Gerard had initiated the matter with high authorities in Berlin, von Kessler, representing the German General Staff, should accompany Dr. Kellogg and myself and discuss the problem in Berlin. The Quartermaster General at once decided that he would go along. I give a summarized account of what happened from my memorandum at the time:[2]

Dr. Kellogg and I duly arrived at the Esplanade Hotel. There, on the following morning, we met General von Sauberzweig and Major von Kessler. There was no food shortage at the Esplanade although there could be a shortage of cash to pay the price of it. The officers informed us that they would take our matter up in conference with the ministers and other authorities and meet us at the hotel later. We were disappointed not to be

[2] *Memoirs,* Volume I, pp. 193-95. Dr. Kellogg made his own notes and expanded on the currents around the negotiations, mentioning no names, in a small book entitled *Fighting Starvation in Belgium* (Doubleday, Doran and Co.). The two accounts agree in the important particulars.

allowed to present our cases ourselves, especially as we knew Minister [of the Interior] Lewald would be there [and would be friendly to our cause].

At four o'clock the General and the Major returned. . . . The General seemed upset and promptly ordered a whisky and soda. The Major, who spoke perfect English, gave us the news of the conference. It was bad. The authorities had decided that they would make no compromise with our estimates. Worse still, they had discussed the whole question of abolishing the Commission. The Major said that it looked bad for us. He added that several of the generals had made violent speeches directed at us. Only [Minister] Lewald spoke for us. Our espionage case and matter published at this time in the British newspapers had roiled them; most of them had determined that they had better throw out the Commission and blast the British for the blockade generally. They said it was no worse for Belgians and French to starve than for Germans to starve. We naturally disavowed any responsibility for the remarks of the British and French. We urged the whole case of the Belgians and Northern French over again. The General took his nth whisky.

Then there came one of those unforgettable episodes. After we were told that the relief was probably all over, von Kessler apologetically mentioned that the General was greatly broken up by the news he had just received that his son had been permanently blinded in a gas attack on the Western Front. I expressed sympathy for this tragedy. The General, who had still another drink, then went into a monologue about the war. [Kellog and von Kessler translating.] He said that civilians were messing into it too much and that it was no longer a soldiers' war with manly weapons. Civilians had made these poison gases. They were engaged in many activities which they should keep out of—probably meaning us.

He grew vehement on the starving of German women and children by the blockade, "and then, there was the case of that Cavell woman." He seemed to want to elaborate on that. We expressed interest. He said she had organized an espionage group of a thousand Belgian women. He said he had warned them. He had punished some of them mildly. They would not stop. He was compelled as a soldier to make an example and stop it. He had her tried, she confessed, and as a soldier he was compelled to execute her to protect the German army. He had been "painted as a monster all over the world." He said he was "called a murderer; a second Duke of Alva." The neutral peoples think "I am the most infamous of men."

I had thought von Bissing, the Governor of Belgium, was responsible for the horror of Miss Cavell's execution. But I confirmed afterward that it was this General von Sauberzweig. He was temporary military Governor at that time.

As he mumbled along I had a thought. The General obviously did not like the kind of publicity he had received in the neutral world. The Relief was apparently about to blow up. I said to Dr. Kellogg that I wanted to make a further statement to the General about the whole relief matter and asked him to translate fully. I said that the conclusion of the German authorities would mean death for millions of people, mostly children; that as he was responsible officer he would be portrayed to the world as a monster infinitely bigger and blacker than the picture they drew of him after the Cavell incident. . . . And as my temperature rose I emphasized this theme so strongly that Kellogg hesitated to translate my language, and said so. But Major von Kessler injected that he would translate. And he did it with no reservations. It [later] appeared that he had been fighting our battle all day and was himself in no good humor. The General made no immediate reply. Then suddenly he remarked that there might be something in what I said. Whether it was the threat, the whisky, or his grief, or the human appeal that had moved him, I do not know. He directed von Kessler to inform Minister Lewald that he thought the negotiation ought to continue. He would be obliged if the Minister would take the matter in hand and settle it.

We broke up at once and with von Kessler went to the Ministry. Lewald seemed relieved to hear von Kessler's authorization.

We quickly settled with Lewald[3] that our estimate should be adopted and that it should be later fixed as a ration from the Germans to the French civilians through the Commission or directly to the communes as we would specify. The Minister proposed to put this in a letter from himself to Ambassador Gerard and to show us a draft if we would wait. The draft was everything I could have wished, except that one-third of the text was devoted to the inhuman effect of the blockade on German women and children and was obviously intended for publication. I requested him to change a line

[3] I might note here that Theodor Lewald had represented Germany at various American expositions and on other missions and knew the United States favorably. Thirty years later, just after World War II, he called upon me when I was in Berlin. He was then a haggard old man, obviously very hungry. I took some satisfaction in arranging through General Lucius Clay that he and his wife receive adequate food.

which implied the Commission's commendation of his views—as it would make my job more difficult with the British. He returned in a few moments and said approximately, "Let us cut out that whole part anyway—we will answer the British with bullets."

Kellogg and I took the letter to Ambassador Gerard and told him of our experience. On his advice we left Berlin within an hour, lest the generals reverse the civilians again. I wrote a note of thanks to the Minister of the Interior, to which he replied:

BERLIN, 9 June 1916

DEAR MR. HOOVER:

For your friendly lines I wish to express my sincere thanks. I . . . [was] very pleased to see you again after so long a time, and to discuss with you the details of the great Relief work which you have called into being, and which you direct with an ability which is recognised on all sides.

THEODOR LEWALD

The details of our settlement with Minister Lewald emerged in the following agreement between Kellogg and von Kessler:

BRUSSELS, 26 August 1916

Major von Kessler declared it to be the intention of the German authorities to increase, from October 1st, 1916, the ration of flour and potatoes of the civil population of the North of France and the Belgian Etappen to 200 grams of flour and 400 grams of potatoes per person per day, this being an increase over the flour ration at present provided of 100 per cent, and over the potato ration of 100 per cent.

Major von Kessler further declared it to be the intention of the German authorities to continue to reserve to the civil population the garden fruit and vegetables and to make certain other reservations to the civil population of poultry, eggs, pigs, rabbits, etc., as will help to ensure a supply of fresh meat to the people.

Director Kellogg declared it to be the intention of the Commission for Relief in Belgium to continue the ravitaillement of the North of France and the Belgian Etappen along the lines of the present ravitaillement but with certain changes in the amounts of flour and other foodstuffs in order to make the whole ration, German and C.R.B. combined, the most advantageous one from the point of view of the nutrition of the people.

The increase in the German ration of flour, for example, would allow the C.R.B. flour ration to be somewhat reduced, and the money and tonnage thereby saved devoted to the increase in the amounts of certain other foodstuffs provided, as bacon and lard, dried peas and beans, etc., and especially to the obtaining and providing, if possible, of fresh or preserved meats.

Director Kellogg also declared it to be the intention of the C.R.B. to endeavor to obtain an increase in its funds devoted to the ravitaillement of the North of France in order to meet the additional needs of the people for the coming winter.

These declarations are hereby accepted as the basis of an agreement between the German General Staff of the Great Headquarters and the Commission for Relief in Belgium as to the conditions of the further ravitaillement of the civil population of the North of France and the Belgian Etappen, that is, from October 1st, 1916, until later agreement.

VON KESSLER
V. L. KELLOGG

On our calculations, this base of supplies from the Germans would fully equal the amounts which they could requisition from the peasants of Northern France. The animals—chickens and all—were so far gone as to account for little, so we did not pursue this aspect of the matter. Later, when we had secured confirmation of the agreement by the Allied Governments, I expressed my appreciation for von Kessler's great assistance:

BRUSSELS, 19 September 1916

DEAR MAJOR VON KESSLER:

I am glad to confirm to you, as I have already stated verbally to Count Wengersky, that the Allied Governments have agreed with the Commission for Relief in Belgium to accept the arrangement settled between yourself and Doctor Kellogg on August 26th, and they have facilitated our securing a considerable increase of resources on the basis of this arrangement. We now have available an increase of between seven and eight million francs per month—in addition to the twenty millions previously; and furthermore have an indeterminate sum at our disposal to pay for fresh meat, cheese, and butter if they can be secured from Holland.

We are also replacing the saving on imported wheat in the Etappen by increasing the other supplies to this section.

I wish to express my personal appreciation of the spirit of co-operation shown by the German authorities with us in so adequately augmenting the much needed supplies to the French people and the Belgians in the Etappen.

HERBERT HOOVER

On my return to London, I took up with Chevrillon the minor shipments of food through Switzerland by what were really black-marketeers:

LONDON, 12 August 1916

MY DEAR CHEVRILLON:

. . . I have been in Belgium and Berlin, endeavoring to come to an arrangement with regard to the . . . [crops]. It has proven an extremely difficult and disagreeable negotiation in every particular, and difficulties and disagreeableness have been materially increased and the whole position jeopardized by the continued action of the French Government in giving permission to ship through Switzerland. . . .

. . . it seems to me hardly fair to us, in the midst of a negotiation of this kind, that we should be placed in the position we have been. . . .

I do not think that anyone could be more solicitous for the welfare of human beings than our group have been for the welfare of the people of Northern France . . . we would like to have a larger supply of food, more money, and more ships . . . that thereby life should become much more endurable . . . but it does not appear to me to be fair to us to ask us to continue in this work without our being considered the absolute pivot on which the whole ravitaillement hangs. . . . We have no desire for a monopoly. We have encouraged in every manner every stream of foodstuff into Northern France.

I then stated that we could not continue unless the French Government required that such minor streams of supplies be consigned to us.

One of our perpetual troubles in the North of France was the insistence of the French Government that the communes give us their periodic written obligations to pay the Government for these supplies. This was a most tedious business, and our delegates and the Comité du Nord found it irksome to collect the obligations from twelve hundred communes each month. Finally, I instructed our delegates and our office to cease to bother with such details because it was solely a French matter and I did not believe they would ever be paid anyway. In any event, if the Allies won the war, the French Government could collect from the communes.

Another of our chores was the payment of French Government allowances to the wives of soldiers and former pensioners. The Germans raised no objection to this, and the payments were made by the *Maires* from the sale of rations.

My next activity for the North of France was to obtain the increased imports for which we had asked and additional finance. To pave the way, I advised Chevrillon:

LONDON, 24 August 1916

DEAR MR. CHEVRILLON:
The steady increase in necessities for the North of France together with the extraordinary rise in the prices of foodstuffs during the last month, renders it necessary to reconsider the entire financial problem involved in the relief of the people in Northern France.

I then gave the statistical situation, and continued:

... present negotiating with the German Government . . . may result in diminishing our requirements for imported wheat to about 15,000 tons a month or a saving of, say, £300,000; but the condition of the population is such that we must undertake at once the importation of meat and other supplies. Two thousand tons of meat per month would cost about £160,000 per month, and other supplies needed will restore the demands to the full figure of requirements, or at least Frs. 33,000,000 per month. As you are aware, our present monthly subsidy is Frs. 20,000,000, which at present sterling exchange yields approximately £710,000 per month. You will notice that we overspent during the quarter ending 25th July, but we were able to do this as we had some money in hand as a result of our being unable to deliver the full program during the winter, owing to the shortage of shipping. It appears to me therefore that if we are to continue to keep the population going, it will be necessary at once to increase our subsidy.

I am wondering whether you would be good enough to lay this before the French Government for their consideration.

HERBERT HOOVER

In order to advance these negotiations for more food and more money, I went to Paris on August 27. I explained our proposed settlement with the Germans to the officials of the French Foreign Office. They approved it.

The British and Belgian officials decided to come to these conferences. I prepared this memorandum about the meetings for my colleagues:

PARIS, 28 August 1916

I left London for Paris on 24th August, arriving on Friday morning the 25th at Havre, where I lunched with Mr. Berryer, Minister of the Interior of the Belgian Government, and Mr. Vandervelde, Minister of War. I informed them generally as to the shortage of the Belgian subsidies, owing to the rise in prices, and of the demands for more foodstuffs.

On Friday night I went to Paris.

On Saturday morning at 9:30 had a meeting with Lord Eustace Percy and Lord Granville at the British Embassy. Discussed the question of increased food supply in the North of France and the abolition of the various new committees which have risen. . . . At 10:30, with Lord Granville, Lord Eustace Percy, and Mr. Chevrillon, called upon Mr. Margerie . . . [at the Ministry of] Foreign Affairs . . . also present [was] Mr. Laroche.

Had a long discussion, during which Mr. Margerie outlined the necessity for more food for the people in the North, their constant demands made to obtain it, the desire of the French Government that they should have a more liberal supply. . . .

At this point they discussed the shipments from Switzerland and agreed that we

. . . must have a complete monopoly in order to deal competently with the German authorities. I stated that there was a tendency to overestimate . . . but that, eliminating the hysteria in the matter, the people did require a further supply of foodstuffs, for which permits had not yet been granted to us by the English Government (especially fats and protein); that the curtailed ration on which we were operating was undoubtedly too low, and that the sensible thing to do was to put us in a position both as to permits, finance, and shipping, to competently care for these people. A prolonged discussion took place in which the English representatives insisted strongly upon the maintenance of a controlled monopoly, the elimination of the other schemes. Finally Mr. Margerie drew out three questions for me to reply to in detail, requesting that we should draw up a complete memorandum for discussion at a meeting to take place on the 28th at ten o'clock.

In the afternoon at 3:30 I again attended at Mr. Margerie's office and met Mr. Kammerer together with Mr. Laroche, to discuss the financial aspects of the French relief. I outlined to them the increased cost owing to the rise in the price of food and the cost of the additional shipments, and stated that it would be useless to talk of further food supplies or even of the maintenance of the present supply, unless we were assured of at least 35,000,000 francs per month. They considered this was possible of arrangement, and it was left that I should incorporate this in the memorandum to be prepared for Monday morning. I also presented the outstanding accounting questions and it was agreed that my views thereon should also be put into the memorandum.

On Sunday at ten o'clock I attended at the British Embassy with Lord Eustace Percy and Mr. Chevrillon. Chevrillon and myself drafted up a memorandum from the Commission embracing the questions put by Mr. Margerie and the proposals of the Commission, and Lord Eustace Percy drew up the views of the British Government.

On Monday at ten o'clock we attended at the Ministry of Foreign Affairs, there being present Mr. Margerie, Mr. Laroche, Lord Granville, Lord Eustace Percy, Mr. Chevrillon, and myself. We read through the memorandum which had been prepared. After prolonged discussion the French representatives accepted the views expressed in the Commission's memorandum, and it was left that they should consult the Minister of Finance to arrange for an increased subsidy and that the English representatives would put it up to their Government that the French Government was insistent upon the proposals of the Commission being accepted.

They accepted our proposals as to accounting.

The memorandum referred to was only a review of the situation in the North of France, the imports and rations proposed, the regulations of shipments sent through Switzerland, an increased program of imports, and an estimate of additional finance required by the Commission amounting to thirty-five million francs. This program of imports had been boosted, by the French officials, far above what I believed would be accepted by the British—and they did refuse, vigorously. However, the French Government provided the increased subsidies.

I reported Dr. Kellogg's final agreement to Lord Percy on September 4, estimating that we would secure 340,000 tons of bread grains through the Germans. I also reported that we were to have all the potatoes that the Germans could extract from the peasants both in Northern France and the Belgian Etape.

That same day, I transmitted the documents to the French Government through Chevrillon and urged that they engage neither in criticism nor exultation over the agreements.

On September 20, in consequence of our arrangement with the Germans, we reduced our imports of grain and increased our imports of cocoa, phosphates, and meats, essentials for the extra meal a day in our canteens for the 500,000 children, expectant mothers, and aged, and for supplies for the asylums for waifs and orphans.

A week later, I wrote to Chevrillon:

LONDON, 28 September 1916

DEAR CHEVRILLON:

We are of course pretty anxious about the French subsidy. I found when arriving in Belgium that the potato crop in the North of France and the Belgian Etapes had proved very much less than the Germans had anticipated and probably will only furnish 60 per cent of the quantity which they [estimated]. . . . Also the grain crop has not realized on harvest what they anticipated. Altogether the bargain was one which we could not have gotten through if we had been a month later with it. They were therefore very restive under the contract, and Kellogg and all our people were insistent that we must confirm the agreement and give them no time or loophole for escape. . . .

We secured a thousand sheep in Holland and shipped them into Northern France as a first installment, and the gratitude of the people is beyond description, as this was the first meat any of them had tasted in five months.

We are still negotiating with the Germans with regard to the [import of] Dutch foodstuffs, and Kellogg is rather confident that we shall get a permit for the importation of at least 5,000 sheep a month and some other products from Holland. . . .

HERBERT HOOVER

On November 18, I received the following letter from the Executive Head of the Comité du Nord:

BRUSSELS, 18 November 1916

MR. CHAIRMAN:

It had been my intention to take the opportunity of your presence at Brussels, to convey to you, in the name of the Lille District Committee, our feelings of deep gratitude.

The population "ravitaillés" by the Commission for Relief in Belgium are unanimous in recognizing that thanks to you they have been able to bear privations of all sorts imposed by circumstances, not only as regards the feeding of the masses, but also for clothing, fuel, and feeding of small children, etc. . . .

Always ready to give satisfaction to the best of your ability, you have continued to increase the quantity and varieties of the foodstuffs, and you have also facilitated the purchases in Holland of the representatives of the large towns of the district.

What would have become of us without the American Commission? Such is what everybody is saying, which shows in its simplicity how appreciated are the services rendered by your organization over which you preside with so much activity and devotion.

Please accept in the name of the Lille District the expression of our deep gratitude.

LABBÉ

CONTINUED TROUBLES OVER SHIPS

The drastic British cut in our permitted imports into Belgium and Northern France of February, 1916, was terrible in its effects on the people, but it did temporarily relieve the pressures for ships. By August, however, we were again in shipping difficulties, and I once more took up with the Belgian authorities the problem of the Belgian-owned ships operating under the British flag:

LONDON, 18 August 1916

Administration de la Marine Belge, London
DEAR CAPTAIN BULTINCK:

With regard to our conversation of today on the needs of the Relief Commission in shipping, I beg to say that . . . we have as yet been unable to secure the necessary supplement to the Belgian fleet for the fourth quarter and from thence forward it seems to us that the only solution of the needs of the Relief Commission is to obtain from the Belgian Lloyd further ships for our regular employ, beginning with the fourth quarter of this year. . . .

We are receiving complaints from the Bunker Committee that we are disorganizing the neutral chartering market by our extravagant bidding for shipping, and we are quite unable to do otherwise as we must have the ships and the only way to prevent this disorganization by having our independent bidding on the market, is to put into our hands sufficient regular shipping from the Belgian Lloyd. We simply cannot take the responsibility of leaving Belgium and Northern France without food supply so long as we can obtain neutral ships at any price. . . .

251

Unless we can obtain some assurance that we shall have a regular line of shipping . . . we were compelled to go out and obtain ships at some price . . . unless our energies die out we shall get them some way, but it is much better that we should be put beyond the necessity of being a disturbing factor to the whole shipping world.

HERBERT HOOVER

We were advised that most of these ships were engaged in commercial trades, and I therefore tried to interest the Foreign Office in securing for us these Belgian-owned ships:

LONDON, 8 September 1916

DEAR LORD EUSTACE:

. . . The twenty ships we have in our constant employment flying the Belgian flag, should deliver approximately 60,000 tons per month, leaving 44,000 tons to be provided. . . . If we could get the twelve Belgian Lloyd ships which fly the British flag . . . to add to our regular fleet, we would only need to go into the neutral market to secure about four or five voyage charters per month. . . . It seems to us obvious that there would be a drop in neutral rates by removing our competition, and the same neutral ships would be available to the Allied Governments that are available to us.

HERBERT HOOVER

We never did get these Belgian-owned ships—and we necessarily continued to torment the Allied shipping agencies with our competitive bidding for neutral ships. However, saving money is not a universal habit of governments in war.

CHAPTER 27

GERMAN COERCION OF
BELGIAN WORKMEN
AGAIN INVOLVES THE C.R.B.

The continued German coercion of Belgian workers to go into their employ was to develop new troubles for the C.R.B. As a sample of these activities, I summarize a report to our Brussels office from the C.R.B. representative in the Province of Namur, C. M. Torrey, which illustrates the methods used by the Germans:

NAMUR, 29 March 1916

GENTLEMEN:

Regarding the question of attempts by the military occupants to force Belgian workmen to do repair and construction of a military or semi-military nature on the railroads. . . . On the 7th of February 1916 a summons to these three and to eleven other able-bodied men of Rochefort . . . came from the office of the German Kommandantur, commanding the men to present themselves at Jemelle, a village two kilometers away, where railroad repair and construction shops are situated. Following this demand, the fourteen presented themselves the same day at Jamelle. . . . When all had gathered there at 8:00 A.M., a German officer evidently in charge of the shop asked them to work, describing the labor generally as that of repair, and offering as payment 3 marks 60 pfennigs a day . . . the men . . . seemed to agree substantially that the work demanded was either directly military . . . or indirectly . . . connected in general with the main purpose of the Germans' use of Belgian railroads.

This request . . . was immediately refused by each of the fourteen. . . . February 8th, they were taken . . . to Namur. . . . In Namur they were first put into prison . . . and kept there thenceforward on a diet (they tell

253

me) of bread and water. Finally on February 25 their formal examination and trial was held, at which they were condemned to a month's imprisonment. . . .

Mr. Torrey continued with several other cases.

    I enclose herewith copy of German affiches on the subject. . . .

C. M. Torrey

On October 4, 1916, Lord Grey, the British Foreign Minister, asked our Ambassador and Minister Chairmen for their opinions on whether or not the Germans were violating their undertakings. His letter to the Secretary of the American Embassy read:

Foreign Office, London
4 October 1916

Dear Mr. Laughlin:

    1. You will recollect the communications which I felt obliged to address to you on various occasions regarding the question of forced labour in Belgium.

    2. As you have been kind enough to assume, together with the United States and Spanish Ministers at Brussels, the function of supervising for the guidance of the governments concerned, the carrying out of the guarantees under which the Commission for Relief in Belgium works, I shall be glad if you could inform me whether, in the opinion of the Patrons of the Commission . . . the guarantees given by the Germans to respect the liberty and conscience of Belgian workmen are being duly carried out.

Grey of Fallodon

On October 20, I received a directive from the British Foreign Office through Lord Eustace Percy which, in effect, was a proposal that the C.R.B. should use food pressures to stop coercion. Lord Percy said:

Foreign Office, London
20 October 1916

Dear Mr. Hoover:

    I want to draw your attention to Lord Robert Cecil's recent answer in the House of Commons to a question as to the distribution of foodstuffs in Belgium in connexion with the German labour policy. Lord Robert laid down in that answer that the Commission worked on the following principles:

1. The Commission supplies nothing to any German civilian.

2. The Commission supplies nothing, except bread, to any Belgian who earns enough to feed himself from native supplies.

3. Any workman working for the Germans under coercion must be maintained by the Germans entirely, without any assistance whatever from the Commission.

You should take this as a direction to the Commission on which they should model their action.

As you know, the Press at the present moment is full of the accounts of the coercion of Belgian workmen and their deportation to the place where the Germans wish them to work. These are two points in connexion with this that you should bear in mind.

First, if deportations take place, it does not matter whether they take place to Germany or to other parts of the occupied territory, since under the third rule set out above you will have no further responsibility for them. If, therefore, deportations take place on any large scale under any general decree of the Governor-General, it will become necessary to consider whether your importations should be proportionately reduced, and as it will be impossible for us here to judge accurately the extent to which any such decrees are being enforced at any given moment, or will be enforced by the time that any one of your shipments reach the ultimate consumer in Belgium, it will become necessary for us, in order to meet the pressure of public opinion here, to make a rough general reduction in your ration probably out of all proportion to the actual number of workmen coerced.

Secondly, to judge from the Press reports—and indeed from the necessities of the situation—all coercion of labor in Belgium is bound to be based upon the criterion that men who fall under your relief owing to unemployment are liable to be coerced. Now, all relief, whether in kind or in cash, given in Belgium arises from your importations and is made on your responsibility. Therefore, this criterion amounts to a statement that a workman renders himself liable to enslavement by the mere fact of accepting relief from you. This is clearly equivalent to the use of your relief as a means of coercing workmen against their conscience, and therefore constitutes a clear and deliberate violation of the German guarantees.

You should be guided by these considerations in dealing with this very serious and dangerous question.

EUSTACE PERCY

These stipulations to the C.R.B. were impossible to impose. We could not discriminate among 7,500,000 Belgians on just who was to receive relief and who not. If these workers lived at home, this idea was futile, since we could not starve their women and children. I was certain that Percy did not want to jeopardize our neutrality by any such action but was merely making a record for consumption among British officials. We, however, could not permit the use of food in such a manner.

As was shown in Chapter 15, von Bissing had agreed with our Patron Ministers in Brussels that food should not be used to coerce workers to work for them contrary to the Hague Conventions. Since Minister Whitlock at this time was unwilling to take vigorous action, Dr. Vernon Kellogg protested to Governor General von Bissing as follows:

BRUSSELS, 20 October 1916

Among the undertakings given by His Excellency the Governor General to the Protecting Ministers is one which provides that the German authorities will not make use of the institutions of the relief work for the purpose of compelling the Belgian populations to work for the service of the German Army. Until recently this undertaking has been rigorously lived up to. . . . Recent happenings, however, give grave cause to fear that measures . . . are in open contradiction to the intention and even to the wording of the undertaking. It is common knowledge that demands are being made upon unemployed, and even employed men, to work for the German army. The most conspicuous examples of these measures now under way of enforcement are in the Belgian Etappen, but there are in addition specific cases in the territory of the General Government, for example, in the province of Luxembourg and in the region of Tournai in the province of Hainaut. . . .

In the Luxembourg, orders have been issued which prevent the civil population from continuing to labor at certain public works established by the civil authorities of the province and the representatives of the Provincial Committee (which itself is but a suborganization of the Comité

National). Further orders prevent the men thus thrown out of employment from being employed by private persons. These men are then invited by the German military authorities to work for them. . . .

In Tournai the situation is even more serious. Direct demands have been made upon large numbers of men to take up work for the military authorities. On the refusal of these demands the men have been interned in camps, practically as prisoners, and put upon a ration of bread and water. . . . If . . . the Commission for Relief in Belgium should accept this situation without protest, they would be permitting an indirect infraction of the undertaking between the General Governor and the Protecting Ministers, and would even be a party to the punishment, by a limitation of the food rations, of these Belgian men. . . .

All together, the incidents and conditions which are apparent today in various parts of Belgium seem to indicate a definite purpose on the part of the military authorities to force parts of the civil population to work in the service of the German Army. . . .

V. L. KELLOGG

There was here, in fact, a clash between the Allied Military Departments, coaching and subsidizing the Belgian underground, and the British Foreign Office. The latter was determined to preserve the neutrality of the C.R.B. and thus the lives of these ten million people.

Lord Grey (formerly Sir Edward Grey), the great statesman he was, raised a clear voice on the whole subject in a long directive to the C.R.B. concerning responsibilities which, on transmission to our Patron Ministers in Belgium, gave them a directive regarding our authorities in control of any Relief organization participation in the "underground." I condense it somewhat because it comprised more than three thousand words under fifteen headings, including a detailed history of the C.R.B., which I omit. Lord Grey said:

FOREIGN OFFICE, LONDON
20 OCTOBER 1916

DEAR MR. AMBASSADOR:

. . . It seems obvious that only a neutral organisation under the powerful protection which the Commission for Relief in Belgium enjoys, could have been or can be in a position to make agreements of a binding character with belligerent governments and officials, and to secure the fulfilment of those agreements. Such agreements . . . must be supported, not only by the influence of the neutral governments involved, but also by public opinion in belligerent as well as neutral countries. Such agreements, if made on behalf of a Belgian committee under present political conditions, would have no such support. . . .

His Majesty's Government do not conceive that the vast quantities of money and foodstuffs required can be protected in overseas transport and internal distribution unless they are the absolute property and under the absolute control and administration of such a body of neutrals; and the responsibility of this body must extend to the maintenance of a distributing organisation of such character as shall in itself minimise the possibility of leakage. . . .

Beyond this, again, it is a fact inherent in any military government imposed on territories occupied by force of arms, that there can be no expectation of rigid justice and fidelity in the distribution of relief, whether of food or money, unless the administration of the whole work is participated in at every point and absolutely controlled by an independent neutral body such as the Commission for Relief in Belgium. . . .

The Commission must maintain in Belgium an entirely independent organisation, composed of responsible and capable Directors and Managers, responsible directly to the Chairman of the Commission and numerous enough to secure the adequate representation of the Commission and the execution of its duties throughout Belgium. Whilst in a general way the Comité National and its component sub-committees must of necessity bear the labour of the detailed distribution, both it and its component committees must act as the agent of and on behalf of the Commission. . . .

The Commission for Relief in Belgium must itself purchase the foodstuffs and transport them into Belgium within the quantities fixed by the Allied Governments, and these foodstuffs must remain the absolute property of the Commission until they are delivered by the Communal Committees to the final consumer. . . . Moreover, as large quantities of foodstuffs are sold in Belgium and the monies realised therefrom are applied to the department of "Secours," His Majesty's Government require that the responsibility of the Commission for Relief in Belgium shall, in the same manner and for similar reasons, extend to the handling of these monies no less than to the distribution of food, the various branches of the

Comité National acting in this matter also as agents of the Commission in its name and with its full knowledge and consent.

... His Majesty's Government must insist on the general and independent responsibility of the Commission to see that such form of organisation and distribution shall be maintained as will secure that all foodstuffs and relief shall be distributed and administered with justice and equity and shall reach their destination with the minimum possible risk of leakage. . . .

In the accomplishment of these objects, His Majesty's Government attach the greatest importance to the Bureau of Inspection and Control, which must independently satisfy itself that the whole relief organisation is functioning properly in all the particulars above set out. . . . The Commission must continue, both in and out of Belgium, the Bureau of Audit, under independent Accountants, who shall from time to time audit the essential accounts of the whole relief organisation; also a Bureau of Statistics, which shall be in a position to supply to the Protecting Ministers adequate data as to the food collection, transport, and distribution. . . . Beyond this, it appears to His Majesty's Government that the assumption by the Belgian committees of separate responsibilities towards any of the authorities or any independent action on their part could only compromise and endanger their members, and I must again repeat that on no other conditions than those laid down above can His Majesty's Government permit food importations into Belgium.

... I shall be glad if Your Excellency will communicate the above to the principal members of the Commission for Relief in Belgium and, through your colleagues in Brussels, to the principal members of the Belgian Committees in Belgium, and I shall be glad to receive your assurance that the above principles are fully understood and that the whole organisation is conducted upon these lines.

GREY OF FALLODON

All of which implied that the C.R.B. must require the Belgians in the Relief organization to remain neutral.

There is a vast amount more documentation on these subjects which at the time seemed threatening to our continued existence. I omit them because they add little except details about these clashing forces.

My colleagues in the C.R.B. and I had no liking for any part of these conflicts among the Allies, which added to those we already had from the Germans. We had enough work and worry to obtain finance, food, ships (and to protect them at sea), and to secure equitable distribution in the midst of the occupying armies of more than two million men. It seemed to us that the lives of ten million human beings were more important than these secondary issues, mostly insolvable by the C.R.B.

Lest Minister Whitlock should be unduly disturbed in the midst of all this, I sent him a note, the last sentence of which was: "By patience I believe we may worry through to the end somehow."

CHAPTER 28

FINANCIAL TROUBLES

I have from time to time in this narrative of the second year mentioned our financial troubles. During the early months of 1916, we were receiving about a $4,800,000 monthly subsidy from the British for the Belgians and about $1,000,000 a month from world charity. Also, we received about $3,000,000 a month from the French Government for the North of France.

Prices of food and transport steadily increased, and by the summer of 1916, we had to secure more financial support for both Belgium and the North of France.

WE MAKE A NEW APPEAL FOR CHARITY

We inaugurated a more vigorous drive for charity on behalf of Belgian children. I addressed a letter to His Holiness the Pope, bespeaking his influence with the great Catholic membership in the United States. I received the following reply:

THE VATICAN, October 27, 1916

The Honorable Herbert Hoover
London
Illustrious Sir:

Your esteemed pages, dated October 19th, duly reached the august hands of the Holy Father, in which you explained the very sad situation of the thousands of Belgian children suffering through insufficiency of nourishment and formulated a proposition of your meritorious committee to supply to each child, thanks to the generous aid of the children of America, a supplementary meal each day.

I am pleased to signify to you that His Holiness, benevolently impressed with the situation described and with the great appropriateness and nobility of the proposition, has deigned to send his venerable Letter to His Eminence Cardinal Gibbons, warmly recommending to His Eminence, and by his means, the American Episcopacy and Clergy, to favour and second in every way, the prudent initiative of the Committee.

Also as a further sign of the loving interest of the August Pontiff for the success of this effort, he has furnished to its needs an offering of ten thousand Lire, which he has sent to the above named Eminent Cardinal Archbishop of Baltimore.

Expressing to you, Sir, and by your courtesy, to all the members of the Committee, the high satisfaction with which His Holiness sees develop their indefatigable and generous activity in aid of Belgium, I have pleasure in assuring you of my distinguished and sincere esteem.

Your servant,

P. CARD. GASPARRI

(Secretary of State to His Holiness)

We also secured the co-operation of the leaders of all the other religious faiths in the United States. We reorganized our state committees, directing their appeal on behalf of our rehabilitation of children. We obtained several millions of dollars in subsequent months.

WE AGAIN PRESS FOR GREATER
GOVERNMENTAL SUBSIDIES

We opened a campaign for an increase in our subsidies from the Allied Governments with a preliminary letter to the Belgian Minister in London in order that the exiled Belgian Government should initiate the action with both the British and French:

LONDON, 24 August 1916

DEAR MR. HYMANS:

... with the extraordinary rise in food prices the past few months, our authorized import program is going to cost over £1,700,000 per month; and in addition to this the Belgian people, as you know, are in need of and are asking for ... additional ... imports which will cost a further £300,000 per month. In other words, we are in imperative need of a secured income of £2,000,000 [about $9,600,000] per month, or the doubling of our present subsidy. The income from charity is erratic and uncertain. ...

After the fall elections [in the United States] we may perhaps, by increase of our American [charitable] receipts, reach a total of say £100,000 a month; and our commercial exchange brings us in £25,000 to £30,000 per month ... which is simply a margin of security. ...

HERBERT HOOVER

The British Foreign Office had held up a reply to our requests for an increase in financial aid pending decisions on internal matters in Belgium, but ultimately we partly succeeded:

FOREIGN OFFICE, LONDON
27 October 1916

H. C. Hoover, Esq., London
DEAR SIR:

I am now able to inform you that the Cabinet have decided to approve an increase in the subsidy for Belgian relief to £1,500,000 per month.

A. W. LIDDERDALE

The French also increased our subsidy to about $4,800,000 a month.

AN AMERICAN LOAN

In October, 1916, the British and the French confidentially informed me that it was becoming most difficult to secure further loans from American banks and therefore difficult for them to find the dollar exchange to finance our purchases overseas and to pay for transportation in neutral ships. They stated that they would give us ample notice before the end. I suggested that possibly the Commission, with British, Belgian, and French guarantees, and aided by the great sentiment in the United States for its work, could float a loan in New York for $150,000,000. They were enthusiastic over my making an effort. I made an inquiry of our Director in New York of such a possibility:

LONDON, 5 October 1916

Financial position of relief particularly Northern France has become extremely grave. Would like have early telegraphic views our New York colleagues on probable success issue short term notes for relief purposes. . . .

I then outlined the amount we proposed and the possible guarantees which could be arranged. Our New York office replied in discouraging terms:

NEW YORK, 8 October 1916

HOOVER, LONDON

Proposition receiving earnest consideration notwithstanding your suggestion comes at most inopportune time inasmuch as market is flooded with foreign offerings and negotiations for further large loans are pending. However, it may be possible to meet in some degree your wishes, but if so it will probably be for smaller amount and on less favorable terms. . . . Suggest you confer with H. P. Davison [of J. P. Morgan & Co.] who is now in London.

RELIEF COMMISSION

I at once discussed the matter with Davison, who was very encouraging. I replied to New York:

LONDON, 15 October 1916

RELIEF COMMISSION, NEW YORK

It is our idea that a loan to be called the American Relief Commission Loan should on sentimental and national grounds receive the support of the whole American banking community, who should donate their services free even to include underwriting if it should be considered desirable to underwrite. In this form it should not conflict with any other finance and would represent a truly American backing to America's greatest philanthropic effort. Have seen Morgan and Davison, both of whom evince great interest. They have discussed matter with Government here and will discuss matter with you on Davison's return.

HERBERT HOOVER

On December 26, I received the following from our New York office:

Bankers ready to act on loan soon as formal request received [from the Governments involved]. They reiterate transaction will be undertaken without expense to Relief, this being their Christmas expression of appreciation to you.

CHAPTER 29

STATISTICAL SUMMARY
OF THE SECOND YEAR

Despite serious losses of our ships at sea, troubles over finances, the problems of keeping the Germans to their guarantees, passing through the British blockade, and our difficulties with the Foreign Office, our major purposes during the C.R.B.'s second year were undefeated.

As of November 1, 1915, our stocks on hand in Rotterdam amounted to 52,910 tons, and from November 1, 1915, to October 31, 1916, we received the following amounts of overseas supplies for Belgium and Northern France:

	Numbers of Cargoes	Tons of Supplies
1915		
November	40	96,212
December	32	72,240
1916		
January	43	106,933
February	51	97,896
March	52	75,697
April	56	63,100
May	60	112,428
June	51	114,735
July	76	115,195
August	86	164,014
September	88	160,803
October	84	121,069
Total	719	1,300,322

During our second year of operations our shipments comprised the following tons of commodities:

	Belgium	North of France
Wheat and Rye	660,362	215,103
Flour	3,076	3,426
Meat ⎫		
Bacon ⎬	17,013	11,766
Ham ⎭		
Lard and Lard Substitutes	24,774	18,443
Corn (Maize)	120,265	19,197
Rice and Rice Substitutes	60,301	45,426
Peas ⎫		
Beans ⎬	9,933	10,511
Yeast and Materials	6,211	691
Coffee	——	12,404
Condensed Milk	2,010	11,972
Soap	——	8,135
Sugar	——	13,729
Clothing	1,316	840
Miscellaneous	685	1,357
Total	905,946	373,000
Grand Total		1,278,946
Plus stocks on hand, October 31, 1916		68,698

In addition, we had been able to save large native supplies from requisition by the Germans. In wheat, the amount was 388,000 tons; there was also a large additional tonnage of potatoes and animal products (although no accurate figures were available, the total would probably have amounted to more than 600,000 tons).

We lost about 44,000 tons of food at sea, with many tragedies to courageous seamen. The ship losses and their cause for loss were as follows:

Sunk by German submarine torpedoes:
    S.S. *Ryndyk* with 5,230 tons of food
    S.S. *George Embiricos* with 5,270 tons of food

Sunk by mines:
S.S. *Ulriken* with 3,077 tons of food
S.S. *Ellewoutsdijk* in ballast
S.S. *Leto* with 4,990 tons of food
S.S. *Maasdijk* in ballast
S.S. *Hendon Hall* with 6,188 tons of food
S.S. *Friland* with 7,366 tons of food
Damaged and partial loss:
S.S. *Althamas* with 6,134 tons of food
S.S. *Levenpool* with 6,543 tons of food

But no one died of starvation during the year—and the children were fully cared for.

THIRD YEAR
November 1, 1916 to November 1, 1917

INTRODUCTION

The third year of the C.R.B. was an even more desperately troubled one. To see the events of this narrative more clearly, the reader will need a brief background of the atmosphere and events in which we worked.

In November and December, 1916, the Germans had started the hideous deportations of men from Belgium and Northern France to work in their factories.

On February 1, 1917, they declared their unlimited submarine war. They torpedoed some of our ships, and others, en route, fled into British ports for refuge. We had to stop shipments until we could restore the guarantees.

These actions blew up our imminent loan of $150,000,000, the completion of which I had arranged in New York the week before.

We secured a restoration of the Relief, the British, on February 9, having agreed to the German demands that our ships proceed direct to Rotterdam without calling at English ports of inspection. The Germans reaffirmed their guarantees a little later, but they continued to torpedo our ships, and it was not until February 24 that we were able to start loading ships again. In the meantime, a total of 200,000 tons of food, for which the Germans would give no guarantees of immunity of attack, was marooned in British ports. The loss of this food and that on torpedoed ships brought a period of extreme suffering to Belgium and Northern France.

On April 6, the United States declared war. We substituted Dutch and Spanish personnel for our American staff in the occupied territory but continued supplies up to the Belgian frontier.

271

Also on April 6, I was requested by the President to come to Washington to head the United States' food activities. I accepted on condition that I could continue to conduct the Relief. I returned to Washington on May 5 and was appointed United States Food Administrator.

On July 15, 1917, the Congress gave authority to the President to impose an embargo on exports and imports. It was not until August 10 that the Food Control Act was passed, which enabled us properly to control production and price profiteering and to organize the systematic provisioning of supplies for the Allies.

Because of excessive exports prior to the embargoes and the effects of drought on our 1917 harvest and animal products, we had no statistical surplus of food for the harvest year from July, 1917, to July, 1918. The amount we could now export depended on the amount by which we could reduce our American food consumption and stimulate production. We established a priority on food exports to Belgium, and we exacted shipping for the Belgians from the neutrals as a condition of our furnishing food to them.

We lost our Patron American Ambassador, Gerard, in Berlin, through his withdrawal on February 3, 1917, in protest at the unlimited submarine war. Minister Whitlock was withdrawn from Brussels upon our declaration of war on April 6, 1917.

Our remaining Patrons were the American Ambassador in London, the Spanish Ambassadors in London and Berlin, and the Spanish and Netherlands Ministers in Brussels. They redoubled their efforts in our behalf.

Had it not been for our stouthearted Directors in New York, London, Rotterdam, Brussels, and Paris, the C.R.B. would have gone on the rocks irrecoverably time after time during the different crises through which we passed. Those Regional Directors in constant service during the year were William Poland, Edgar Rickard, Vernon Kellogg, Prentiss Gray, John White, William Honnold, Walter Brown, and Louis Chevrillon.

As in the case of other years discussed in this memoir, I have, for clarity, arranged the ensuing chapters by topics, which on occasion overlap chronologically.

CHAPTER 30

GERMAN DEPORTATION OF BELGIAN AND FRENCH WORKERS TO LABOR IN GERMAN FACTORIES

Early in our third fiscal year, the Germans took the final step to force Belgian and French workers into German factories by means of wholesale deportations. When they began, in November, 1916, I was in Brussels, and I urged Minister Whitlock to make a general protest against the entire deportation infamy. He was loath to act, so I sent him a strongly worded letter:

BRUSSELS, 8 November 1916

MY DEAR MR. WHITLOCK:

Reports this morning from all over the country show seizure of men right and left regardless of employment, including members of our local committees and employees. I fear it is the beginning of the end.

It is worth your considering uttering a full and strong protest with all the vigor of which you are so capable.

This is a greater issue to the Belgian people than anything since the invasion and they look to you as to America for some strong action.

It may result in nothing, but it will have put the American stamp on it in indelible terms, and if we do nothing else for Belgium we will go down in a blaze of indignation at this, its worst of any trials since the first agony.

HERBERT HOOVER

Whitlock believed that making such a protest lay beyond his duties and that it might endanger the Relief. He may have been right. Nevertheless, Ambassador Page, on my information, took the matter up with Washington. As a result, our State Department took a strong stand and issued the following statement to the press:

273

WASHINGTON, 15 November 1916

In consequence of the deportations from Belgium, the State Department has directed Mr. Grew, its chargé d'affaires in Berlin, to discuss the matter personally with the Imperial Chancellor.

Mr. Grew is requested to inform Herr von Bethmann-Hollweg that such deportations cannot but have a most unfortunate effect on neutral opinion, particularly in the United States, which has the welfare of the Belgian civilian population very much at heart.

These instructions are the outcome of a long report from Mr. Grew stating that he had discussed the situation informally and unofficially with Herr Zimmermann, who admitted that the definite policy had been adopted of enforcing the labour of Belgians in cases where they refused to work voluntarily, on the ground that so many had refused to work that the strain on public charity had become intolerable.

The deportations are viewed here not only as a violation of international law, but in a certain degree as a violation of Germany's assurances made to Mr. Gerard in June, which, though relating to the deportation of French women from Lille, Roubaix, and Turcoing, are felt to be applicable to the present case.

The protest by the State Department had little effect.

When the deportations began, they were presumably limited to the unemployed *(chômeurs)*, and certificates from their employers were supposed to give them immunity. Further, it was agreed by the German authorities that the Belgians employed by the C.R.B. would be immune, and for their protection, we issued a certificate card to them.

A few of our C.R.B. staff reports to our Brussels office indicate the procedures. Gardner Richardson, our representative in Antwerp, reported on November 15, 1916, as follows:

The taking of chômeurs to Germany from the province of Antwerp has been going on this week. Four thousand men are called every day to present themselves at the railroad station, and of this number up to date, from the closest calculations we have been able to make, 5,856 have been sent to Germany. This is from the city of Antwerp alone and does not include the country districts.

When the men present themselves at the railroad stations the Germans make every effort to induce them to sign contracts to work. . . .

In general every pressure is brought upon the men to sign, but in most cases the Belgians have refused to do this. Those who present certificates that they are employed in general are released, but those who have no certificates are put on trains and sent to Germany.

One hundred and three men employed in the guano factory of Ohlendorf were all sent to Germany in a block, some of the workers being fifty years old. . . .

GARDNER RICHARDSON

Our C.R.B. representative in Brabant, R. A. Jackson, reported:

15 November 1916

Yesterday, 14th November, I went to Court–St. Etienne to attend the taking of Belgian men by the Germans. . . .

The men were brought in by a long path to a "filature" some distance from the town. The women and children therefore were not present. All men who stated themselves to be sick were examined by a doctor, and a certain number were thus released.

The others came on to the filature—to an open space between two buildings—where they presented themselves and their papers, such as cartes d'identité and cards from the Meldeamt, together with any certificates of one sort or another which they might possess. They were on the whole very decently treated by the Germans, but they were usually too frightened or confused or embarrassed to be very intelligent, as proved by the fact that often when told to go "à gauche" which was the way out and to liberty (though they perhaps didn't know it) they took the other path, which led to Germany. . . .

Various burgomasters and employers were present to urge special reasons for exemption, or to give assurance that certain men were actually and regularly employed. The Germans certainly really tried to take the young and unmarried men without employment, rather than others. They released many young men who were employed in usines, and on farms, or who were small cultivateurs on their own account.

But toward the end of the list, when perhaps they were afraid they would not get as many men as required, they took a number of factory workers for whom their employer, Mr. Henricot, gave assurance that they were regularly employed. . . . I believe certain workmen employed elsewhere were also taken.

Later . . . I learned that two of the De Broux workmen, who had cards from the C.R.B., had been taken. I protested. . . . He said we were lucky that so few were taken, that no one is irreplaceable. . . .

My impression is that the officers had orders to take so many—1,000, I believe—men, and that when they thought too many were being let off, and that there might be difficulty in completing the number, they felt obliged to take a larger proportion of those who presented themselves, workers or not.

R. A. JACKSON

A report from another of our representatives in Brabant reads in part:

17 November 1916

As requested by Director Gregory, I was present at the requisition of men at Wavre on Wednesday, 15th November. . . .

Arriving at the square, after some difficulty, I found Mr. Foreau, of the Brabant provincial committee and Regional President of Wavre. . . .

I learned that the cards which we have issued were actually in the hands of . . . those who had been duly listed by the regional president as engaged in the work of . . . [the Relief].

These men were grouped together and they were later placed by the German officers with the town officials near the head of the column into which the men were formed. . . .

As Wavre was called first, I joined the C.R.B. group in the Wavre column and went with them . . . and remaining there for some time, together with Mr. Foreau. . . .

. . . I was able to observe the examination of all the men from Wavre. . . . I gathered still more information later by mingling with the people. . . .

. . . those who claimed release on account of sickness were led to a room for medical examination. . . .

All the rest passed at once into a room where four or five German officers examined them. . . .

From this room, they were sent to an adjoining room . . . guarded by soldiers and presumably escorted to the train for deportation.

It was impossible for anyone else to approach the train and no one was allowed to see the men after this separation. . . .

The majority of those who were taken were young men but a good many were over 40 years of age and some over 50 . . . a considerable number were men of family. . . .

The requisition was not confined to men without work. . . . Railway employees especially were among the number taken.

. . . The examinations were made rapidly and the decision "à gauche" or "à droite," quickly made, was final. No discussion was permitted save in a few instances. . . .

There was no disorder, and no attempts at resistance were made, the men being hurried through in single file like animals. . . .

There was a host of such reports from our staff all over Belgium, but the above are indicative.

On November 22, Lord Grey requested the United States Government, through Ambassador Page, to exert pressure on Germany to stop the deportations. I give that portion of his request relating to deportations:

FOREIGN OFFICE, LONDON
22 November 1916

MY DEAR AMBASSADOR:

1. I venture to ask Your Excellency to transmit a message from me personally to Your Excellency's Government in regard to a matter of which you have fuller knowledge and which you can more fully explain than would be possible for His Majesty's Ambassador at Washington to do, were I to transmit the message through him.

2. The recent deportations from Belgium . . . cut at the root of the guarantees on which the whole relief work in Belgium is based, and, while His Majesty's Government are no less keenly anxious than in the past to fulfil their duties toward the populations of the occupied territories, it will be clear to Your Excellency that it may at any moment become materially impossible to continue a work the basic guarantees of which have been destroyed. I should therefore be grateful if you could communicate by telegraph to your Government a personal appeal from me that they will exert themselves at Berlin and Brussels to see that this great work of international benevolence and co-operation which I think Your Excellency will be able to assure your Government has never been used by His Majesty's Government for any but purely neutral purposes, and which they have

indeed regarded as of inevitable military advantage to their enemies shall not be endangered or destroyed by acts which it is impossible for the Allied peoples to countenance or tolerate. . . .

GREY OF FALLODON

The United States Government again officially protested to Berlin:

WASHINGTON, 29 November 1916

The Government of the United States has learned with the greatest concern and regret of the policy of the German Government to deport from Belgium a portion of the civilian population for the purpose of forcing them to labor in Germany, and is constrained to protest in a friendly spirit but most solemnly against this action, which is in contravention of all precedent and of those humane principles of international practice which have long been accepted and followed by civilized nations in their treatment of noncombatants in conquered territory. Furthermore, the Government of the United States is convinced that the effect of this policy, if pursued, will in all probability be fatal to the Belgian relief work, so humanely planned and so successfully carried out, a result which would be generally deplored and which, it is assumed, would seriously embarrass the German Government.

On December 5, the British, French, and Italian Governments jointly issued the following press statement:

. . . The Allies must warn the world of what is about to take place. As their own situation grows more desperate, the Central Empires intend to tear up every guarantee on which the work of the Relief Commission rests. They intend to cast aside all their promises, and to use Belgian foodstuffs and Belgian labor to support their own failing strength. The work of the relief which neutrals have built up for two years is about to lose its foundation, and is in danger of falling.

As soon as the financial resources of the Belgian Government were exhausted the Allies provided sums for the continuation of the work. They have furnished the Commission with shipping and all other necessary facilities. Further, they have done their utmost through the neutral Commission to protect Belgian industry from the disastrous consequence of invasion.

The Allies have only stipulated that the Germans should equally draw no advantage from the operations of the Commission; that they should not seize either imported or native supplies, and that the distribution of relief should not be used for the purpose of coercing Belgian workmen against their conscience.

The statement then reviewed the guarantees which had been violated, and continued:

... as it will be impossible for the relief work to continue if its basic guarantees are destroyed, they appeal to the civilized world, not on their own behalf, but on that of the innocent civilians who cannot protect themselves, to see that this great work of international benevolence and cooperation which has grown up in the midst of war, and for which the Allies have advanced the money, shall not be endangered by treachery or destroyed by violence.

On December 29, the State Department asked for my opinion on the effect of the American protests:

WASHINGTON, 29 December 1916

AMERICAN EMBASSY, LONDON
Department would be glad to have Hoover's opinion for its confidential information regarding continuance of Belgian deportations, whether there has been any change in the policy of the German authorities since the protest of this Government on November 29.

LANSING

I replied to Lansing that things were worse:

LONDON, 2 January 1917
There has been no apparent change in German policy since the President's protest, deportation continuing on a large scale—now apparently three to five thousand per week. Despite assertions made to the President, no distinction is made as to whether deportees are unemployed or not and in fact there seems a definite policy to secure all members of certain trades, and the desire to secure these and other skilled labor leads press gangs to deliberate choice of those in actual employment. Moreover, they have taken altogether, up to 15th December, over 700 persons employed by the Commission, despite the exhibit of credentials and their specific agreement with us to the contrary and against our protest. Furthermore,

our American members have witnessed the taking of several thousands, particularly from Flanders to Northern France, and together with local French people, are now being forced to work for the German Army in the preparation of timber and fascines for the trenches. Refusal to perform such labor here has been met with refusal of food and other brutal acts. It is also reported to us from what we believe to be reliable sources that Belgian and French civilians have been required to work on trench construction in Northern France, and certain deportees have been recently returned wounded by shellfire. Of the deportees to Germany, some 300 have been returned to the Hainaut Province, of whom a part were apparently returned because physically unable to work, but the remainder maintain that they were returned because of their steadfast passive resistance to pressure, although they were . . . refused food over a considerable period and were ultimately returned for their recalcitrancy. Their appearance confirms this.

Altogether, the assurances given the President that only unemployed were taken, and that they are not employed on military work or brutally treated, are absolutely untrue, not only before but since the assurances were given. It does appear that the civil government in Brussels has made some efforts to prevent brutality . . . but they appear unable to control the military press gangs or effect any remedies. . . .

I am now convinced that the . . . [Allied] Governments will take no action against the Relief as a consequence of these deportations, as they are convinced that stoppage of relief would be no remedy, and, they generally recognize, would only accentuate the misery.

The hourly witnessing of these outrages and the prayers to the Americans from a people now in a state of complete terror, since Americans have been so peculiarly their protectors during the past two years, make it difficult for us to control the natural feeling of our staff and we can only hope that no untoward incident may occur. . . .

I suggested that perhaps a personal and confidential note from the President to the German Government might do some good and added

. . . that if Germany is genuinely anxious for peace she can scarcely hope for sympathetic sentiment to grow abroad to that end coincident with these acts, and that a total cessation of the deportations and forced labor and the return of the deported Belgians and French to their homes would be not only an act of great magnanimity but also of the greatest assistance in the promotion of peace sentiment.

On January 27, 1917, at Ambassador Page's request, I replied to a query from Secretary Lansing:

DEAR MR. SECRETARY:

I am convinced that the following facts could be established by any independent enquiry which was given sufficient facilities for free investigation:

That 90% of the Belgian Deportees are taken by force against their will and conscience;

That acts of the greatest brutality take place in recruiting and transport;

That a large portion of the workmen recruited were actually in employment when taken;

That over one thousand employees of the Relief Organization have been taken, despite the presentation of the credentials agreed upon with the German Authorities;

That on refusal to work all the Deportees are put under great pressure by reduced food and threats;

That some Belgians and large numbers of French civilians are required to work in the preparation of military works in the North of France, and upon refusal to do so have been treated with the utmost brutality.

In general, I do not know that there is any advantage in giving specific instances. Almost volumes of such reports lie in the Embassy in Brussels, if they have not already reached your hands. In any event, such detailed disclosures [if made public] are dangerous [to relatives].

There is one point in connection with all this which I do not think has been generally understood, and that is: the Belgian people are entirely seized with the fact that labour of any kind which they perform for the Germans is of assistance to their enemies. In consequence, great numbers of them are resolute to the point of death in refusal to perform such labour. The Deportees are regarded as martyrs and are not expected to ever return.[1] The reflex of this is a state of terror in the population beyond anything which has been known during the last hundred years.

It is useless for me to emphasize these points to you, despite my deep feeling in the matter. Its premeditation and dimensions make it the great-

[1] The number of deportees who returned to Belgium and France after the German surrender in November, 1918, exceeded 700,000. This was not the total deported, however, because many had died in Germany.

est crime against human liberty which the world has witnessed since this war began.

HERBERT HOOVER

While these exchanges between governments were going on, the C.R.B. was engaged in a running battle to prevent the deportation of our Belgian employees, who, von Bissing had agreed with our Patron Ministers in Brussels, would be immune. I can summarize the result of this undertaking from a report of our Brussels office on December 30, 1916, stating:

The number of our men taken up to date in the different provinces is as follows:

	Men taken having cards	Men taken entitled to cards but not having received them
Hainaut	453	—
Namur	250	15
Luxembourg	234	9
Limbourg	30	—
Brabant	24	39
	991	63

On January 10, 1917, our Minister Patrons in Brussels vigorously protested the violation of the German understandings not to deport our Belgian employees. Minister Whitlock reviewed the circumstances of these 991 deported employees and concluded his protest:

His Excellency von der Lancken will certainly realize . . . this state of affairs is contrary to the assurances which have been given to the Minister Protectors.

Mr. Whitlock . . . is confident that His Excellency the Governor-General will be good enough to give him the assurance that the members, employees, and workpeople of the . . . [Relief] already deported into Germany will be repatriated as soon as possible and that the necessary steps will be taken to assure that in the future no more members . . . will be deported.

As far as I know, none of them were seen again until the war was over.

CHAPTER 31

WITH LORD GREY'S ENCOURAGEMENT
WE MAKE A MAJOR DECISION

As the war went on, our multitude of difficulties in food, supply, shipping, and finance had steadily increased. And, in addition to all these difficulties inherent in events, there had been demands that we stop the Relief in consequence of the deportations.

Thus deportations presented us with a major decision. Should we risk the lives of ten million people with a declaration to the Germans that we would terminate the Relief if the deportations were not stopped? We had tried every measure of persuasion and every measure of pressure of neutral opinion. Nothing less than such an absolute declaration on our part would stand any chance of success, but what if it failed?

It seemed to me that in these difficulties we had need of advice and assurance from higher authority before we took any irretrievable steps. I laid the problem before our Ambassador Patrons Page and Merry del Val. They opposed our making any such demand. They suggested that I consult Lord Grey, the British Foreign Minister.

The interview with Lord Grey took place in early December. We canvassed the problems presented by the deportation and the other difficulties of the Relief. The Ministers stated that their information confirmed our reports that the Germans were adhering to their agreements not to take the imported food, that we had protected the harvests, and that the occasional taking of native food was, in its isolated instances, comparatively trivial in view of the large quantities we were handling.

In weighing our problems, I pointed out the importance of the Relief in American and neutral public opinion, since it had been a profound demonstration of great devotion and generosity of the British to a helpless people. Lord Grey said that he regarded this phase as highly important. He advised that we take no risks and that we continue the Relief.

We discussed our financial problems. Lord Grey was aware of the statement to me from the Treasury—through Eustace Percy in October—which said that it could not do much more to provide dollars to the Commission for our necessary purchases in the Western Hemisphere. He asked how much our needs were in this exchange. I told him that our total outlay was now running at the rate of more than $150,000,000 a year, of which about two-thirds was in dollars and the balance in sterling and francs. He stated that the British now had the added burden of finding either dollars or Latin American exchanges for the Italians and French.

He was aware of our proposed loan from New York bankers and inquired about our progress. I was able to give him an encouraging report and stated that I was leaving for New York in early January to settle on the details.

In closing, he remarked that he thought the Admiralty had exhausted their pinpricks, expressed his admiration for the way we had conducted the Relief, and assured us of his continued support. But through an overturn of the Asquith Ministry, he retired from office a few days later, to our great loss.

THE RELIEF LOAN

I have related that late in our second year we had conducted negotiations for an American bank loan to the C.R.B. of $150,000,000, to be guaranteed by the British, French, and Belgian Governments. I was delayed in my departure for New York by the slowness of the Belgians and the French to settle details. I finally sailed on January 15.

On my arrival in New York, we made rapid progress with our loan negotiations. The bankers agreed to underwrite the loan without profit to themselves. On January 31, I called on President Wilson, who expressed his great interest in our work and his good wishes on the success of our loan. The bankers asked me to help launch the loan with a public address and arranged for me to speak at noon on February 1 to a large meeting of the New York Chamber of Commerce.

In this speech I described our organization and our problems— but they are being related in these pages. The address was just about my first considerable oratorical effort since the one I delivered during my school days, some thirty years earlier, under the title "Rome Was Not Built in a Day." In view of what was going on in the world at the moment I began that speech, it had approximately the same importance as the earlier one.

CHAPTER 32

THE GERMANS'
UNLIMITED SUBMARINE WAR

On January 31, 1917, the Germans declared unlimited submarine war on all shipping of every nationality approaching Allied ports.

On February 2, I received in New York the following memorandum from the German Embassy in Washington. To me, the crucial paragraph was:

From February 1, 1917, sea traffic will be stopped with every available weapon and without further notice in the following blockade zones around Great Britain and France, Italy, and in the Eastern Mediterranean. . . .

The notice went on to define in detail the zones where ships would be sunk without warning. The Germans' declaration closed all our approaches to Rotterdam from British ports. The orders did provide a passage through the German mine fields in the North Sea—on condition that the ships proceed from neutral ports directly to Holland without calling at British ports. The Germans further provided that neutral ships near their destinations "will be spared during a suitable time" (later defined as no later than February 4 and thus, as far as we were concerned, a deadline of forty-eight hours).

We also received on February 2 the following from our Director in Brussels, through our Rotterdam office, confirming, in more detail, the German declaration:

286

ROTTERDAM, 1 February 1917

Relief Commission, London.

This morning the . . . [German] authorities called in conference the Protecting Ministers and ourselves and gave us following message:

"It goes without saying that the Imperial Government has no intention whatsoever of standing in the way of the humanitarian work of the ravitaillement of Belgium, but the Imperial Government must insist that the C.R.B. will send its ships outside of the forbidden zone. It is understood that ships which find themselves on the first of February in the forbidden zone can leave the zone by taking the most direct route without fearing unlooked-for attacks and that the ships which find themselves in English ports can leave them, up to the evening of February 4th and can traverse forbidden zone by the most direct route. Nevertheless the C.R.B. is instructed in the most pressing manner to turn by immediate advice, all ships on route toward the routes situated outside of the forbidden zone. The ships which do not follow such instructions will navigate at their own risk and peril."

Ministers have sent urgent appeals to their respective governments, but you must give immediate notice ships on route as above. . . .

WARREN GREGORY

This was no help to us. All of our ships en route were required by the British to call at a British port for inspection, and at that time British ports were the only place to coal for the return voyage. The cross-Channel Dutch line which the German orders permitted to operate had no consequential cargo capacity.

President Wilson broke off relations with Germany on February 3, which implied the recall of Ambassador Gerard from Berlin and Minister Whitlock from Brussels. An arrangement was made for Whitlock to remain informally in Belgium for a while, but Gerard left Berlin at once, and our only effective contact with Germany was through our Spanish Ambassador Patron in Berlin, the Spanish Minister in Brussels, and the Dutch Ministers in Berlin and Brussels. All passenger services were suspended across the North Atlantic, and I could not reach Europe, which I urgently needed to do.

From New York, on February 2, I instructed Mr. Poland, our Director in London, to consult with our Patron Ambassadors and the

British Foreign Office and to inform our Rotterdam office and myself of any conclusions reached. He advised me as follows:

LONDON, 2 February 1917

After conference with British Foreign Office and Ambassador Page, Ambassador [Merry del Val] will communicate Berlin reference German regulations relief shipping calling attention to [the fact] that . . . One-fifth our tonnage originates in English ports by purchases in United Kingdom. German regulations totally eliminate this tonnage, which cannot be obtained overseas under present conditions. Also number of ships have sailed destined for British ports, which will arrive within next few days . . . which would break down ravitaillement. Also necessary [for] vessels touch English ports for coal. For these reasons German authorities earnestly petitioned to allow to continue present guarantees of safety to vessels protected by marks and German safe-conducts from and to United Kingdom ports, Rotterdam, and overseas. . . . [Poland instructed Rotterdam to] Assure people of Belgium and France that Foreign Office expects . . . [relief] to continue without serious interruption and that they must not be unduly alarmed. . . .

At my request, our Brussels office informed me of the status of our food stocks in Belgium. They comprised 227,000 tons of grain, 9,000 tons of meats and fats, and 12,000 tons of sundries. Our Rotterdam stocks at this time totaled about 64,000 tons. Our stocks in the North of France were 33,000 tons of grain, 8,200 tons of meats and fats, and 5,000 tons of sundries. Without further overseas food, we thus had about 358,000 tons of supplies available, or, considering its dispersal, we had about sixty days' supplies.

On February 1, we had nineteen ships at sea. Two of them had passed inspection at British ports and reached Rotterdam. Fifteen of them were either in British ports for inspection or nearby, and, upon the demand of their owners, the Admiralty ordered them into British ports, which they reached safely.

On February 3, despite all its illuminated "Belgian Relief" markings, the Germans, without notice, torpedoed one of our ships, the *Euphrates,* outside the prohibited zone. There was only one survivor.

The wickedness of this sinking added to my sleepless nights. It was days before I could shake off the harrowing scenes of those courageous sailors who had trusted the Germans' guarantees of safety. I was to be haunted with more such tragedies of torpedoed ships, each bearing German passes and guarantees of immunity from attack. Two days later, February 6, our ship the *Lars Kruse* was torpedoed outside the prohibited zone. The crew escaped in lifeboats.

During these anxious days, my colleagues and I were in constant touch by cable over the problems involved in continuation of the Relief. They were:

(1) Since the United States was no longer a restraining force on the Germans, should we hand over the whole Relief operation to the Dutch and Spanish Governments?

(2) Could permission be obtained from the Germans and British for our ships and stocks in British and French ports (some 188,000 tons of supplies) to proceed to Rotterdam?

(3) Could permission be obtained from the British for our ships to proceed directly from American and other ports outside the war zone to Dutch ports, with inspection by British authorities at ports of departure?

(4) Since Belgian coal was useless for bunker purposes, could we obtain it from Germany?

(5) If the United States declared war, could we maintain the Commission's service up to the Belgian frontier?

(6) Would the Allies consent to such action and continue their subsidies in event of withdrawals of the American staff from Belgium and Northern France?

In any event, one thing was clear: we would have to reach some understanding concerning the protection of our ships before we sent any more of them into this milieu. We therefore gave directions not to load cargoes or buy cargoes en route until there was more daylight on the situation. We also directed that we should keep our staff on the job in Belgium and Northern France as long as possible.

I consulted Secretary Lansing by telephone and arranged for the following cable from our State Department to Ambassador Page, giving the Secretary's view and my view at that moment and my instructions to our staff:

STATE DEPARTMENT, WASHINGTON
3 February 1917

American Embassy, London:

Department would be glad if you would express to the British Government the strong feeling of this country and of the Government that the relief of the Belgian and occupied French population must in any event continue, for this country will wish to show no less interest in this great work of humanity than has been shown during the last two years by the British and the French Governments, [even] should it become impossible for the Americans to remain in Belgium and in control.

Hoover considers it desirable that if necessary the work of relief should be taken over by the Dutch Government, a transfer which could probably best be negotiated by the Belgian Government and American Minister at The Hague. We have telegraphed Whitlock asking him to remain at his post and asking him to secure from the German authorities, for members of Relief, the treatment of diplomatic and consular staff. Mr. Hoover desires you convey following message to Poland and Kellogg:

"Think it extremely desirable for all members in Belgium to remain at their posts even after the departure of diplomatic and consular staff, if Germans will guarantee their freedom to depart if situation becomes entirely untenable. Wish you to take Mr. Page's advice in all matters and to consult freely with Belgian and British Governments particularly on the following questions: First, if any change in sailing directions of ships afloat, such change, if any, to be issued by British Admiralty; second, whether and by what route ships at present in Rotterdam and Atlantic ports should sail. If new British mine field does not interfere, represent to British Government strongly desirability of taking route outside war zone at the present time.

"Ask Spanish Ambassador if he will communicate through Brussels and Berlin that as British mine field and necessity to bunker in the United Kingdom and conditions of charter and insurance render Falmouth Channel route the only practicable passage, the Germans should agree at once to respect relief ships on this route and issue passes to this end . . . all departures are held up [in the] meantime. . . ."

LANSING

With the disorganization of the Relief shipments, the portent of the recall of the American Ambassador from Germany, and the general sense of alarm that the United States might soon become involved in the war, it was necessary to suspend the $150,000,000 loan. The project was never resumed.

CHAPTER 33

GETTING OUR SHIPS
IN MOTION AGAIN

We immediately undertook three simultaneous negotiations to get our ships in motion: first, with the British—to allow our ships to proceed directly to Rotterdam without calling at British ports; second, with the Germans—to assure no submarine attacks; and third, to open a route for our sixteen cargoes in British ports to proceed to Rotterdam. At that moment we had 120,000 tons on board ships in Britain and 68,000 tons of stocks in Britain and France, making a total of 188,000 tons of marooned supplies.

Four days after the declaration of unlimited submarine warfare, I instructed Mr. Poland, our Director in London, to seek the aid of our Ambassador Patrons in Europe in these negotiations. Ambassadors Page and Merry del Val presented our proposal of direct sailing to Rotterdam from neutral ports to the British Foreign Office on February 6, 1917. On February 9, Poland advised me that the British had approved, subject to guarantees of safety by the Germans. His cable was:

LONDON, 9 February 1917

HOOVER, RELIEF COMMISSION, NEW YORK

British Government has agreed that Commission ships in or outbound need not touch at United Kingdom ports, but for your confidential information must touch at British ports elsewhere such as Halifax or Bermuda or West African Coast. Merry del Val through Spanish Ambassador Berlin and our Rotterdam office through German Legation Hague and

292

Brussels office and British Foreign Office through King of Spain are asking German Government on basis concession British Government that boats not required touch United Kingdom to modify German regulations as follows:

1. All relief vessels clearing overseas ports or Rotterdam subsequent to February 1st and which do not touch at United Kingdom ports shall be furnished safe-conduct passes by German authorities and when protected with Commission signs and marks shall be allowed to approach or leave Rotterdam by either north or south routes through German danger zones and overseas without molestation.

2. Relief steamers now in U.K. and steamers which cleared overseas ports before February 2d and which may arrive later furnished safe-conduct passes and unmolested to Rotterdam or overseas.

3. All vessels in No. 2 allowed touch U.K. ports unmolested.

4. All relief ships carrying U.K. purchases protected between Rotterdam and U.K. both directions.

5. German Government to arrange for coal for relief ships at Rotterdam.

RELIEF COMMISSION

We at once requested the Spanish Minister in Brussels, the Marquis de Villalobar, to give us his aid. He replied that he would go at once to Berlin. On February 13, we received word from him that he had in writing from von Bissing's Government a pledge that the Germans would not interfere with Relief vessels if they did not call at British ports.

Villalobar urged my return to Europe. The important paragraphs of my reply to him were:

NEW YORK, 14 February 1917

. . . Under present situation I cannot leave here [as a matter of fact there were no passenger steamers operating], but we are unceasing in our labor to obtain the re-establishment of the Relief. . . . this can only be accomplished if the German authorities are prepared, first, to allow our staff to remain as before or [if necessary] accept some other neutral body in Belgium and Northern France on the same basis of freedom of movement and relations to distribution as hitherto enjoyed by our staff. . . . Furthermore we must have a safe lane opened to our [marooned] ships into Rotterdam. . . . The whole of our service is paralyzed until we can guarantee the immunity of these ships [in British ports], and our resources are being consumed in enormous penalties and demurrages right and left. . . .

HERBERT HOOVER

On February 18, 1917, the Spanish Ambassador in Berlin secured an undertaking of protection to our ships, subject to certain conditions from the German Undersecretary of Foreign Affairs as follows:

. . . the Government attaches particular importance to the continuation without interruption of the work of ravitaillement of Belgium and the occupied territory of France. However, this desired continuation is in no way hindered by the proclamation of the war zone of January 31st. . . .

1. . . . The vessels still on the high seas will be obliged to take the course to the north of the Shetlands outside the war zone. Free transit across this zone, especially by the Channel, will not be conceded, to my deep regret, for reasons of a military nature, especially as the Allies might abuse this concession for their own ends.

2. As regards vessels still in English ports, they would have been able to leave these ports during the respite up to the 5th of February, had they not been hindered by the British Government. In the meantime, the Imperial Government begs you to furnish them with a detailed list of the vessels in question and the ports in which they are at present.

3. Safe-conducts cannot be delivered in the future except on the condition that the vessels take the course north of the Shetland Islands outside the war zone where no danger from the operations of the German Navy will threaten them.

4. Foodstuffs purchased by the Commission in England can only be sent to Flushing by the paddle-wheel boats of the Dutch Line to which a special permission has been granted.

5. To make bunkering possible to the vessels of the Commission, Belgian pit-coal will be furnished to them at Rotterdam.

The Imperial Government is persuaded that it will not escape the perspicacity of the Royal Government that further concession to the wishes of the Relief Commission would be incompatible with the German military measures dictated by present circumstances. . . .

The German undertaking did not solve our problem of marooned food in England and France. Moreover, Belgian coal was unsuitable for steamship purposes.

However, with this crack opened by the British permissions and the German reassurance, I started such neutral ships from the United States as we had under charter on February 24, 1917.

Our troubles were by no means over. The submarine sinking of ships of all nations continued right and left, with losses running as high as 800,000 tons a month. We had great difficulties securing insurance and charters from neutrals, and Allied-flag ships were no longer available.

On March 2, Poland reviewed further difficulties ahead of us:

LONDON, 2 March 1917

MY DEAR HOOVER:

. . . When we attempted to despatch vessels from Rotterdam the German authorities refused to give absolute guarantees against submarine attack until March 5th, indicating very clearly that our position was correct in considering the north-about route unsafe.

The situation as to United Kingdom cargoes is very grave. . . . By messages received today, the Germans are proposing methods by which these vessels may be moved across, but the British Government . . . [in their] pinch for food . . . insists that at least some of our vessels be unloaded. . . .

Our next great difficulty is in regard to insurance. Lloyds and the Companies have cancelled their arrangements effective March 4th, and despite every endeavor which we have made with the Government, we have not been able to make an arrangement yet for their taking over insurance on hulls and cargoes of neutral vessels. . . . I anticipate the gravest difficulty in obtaining any neutral charters for Rotterdam, as ship-owners consider it very much more hazardous than trips to the United Kingdom; in addition to which, owing to the very serious lack of tonnage for the Allies, we are finding many open . . . obstacles. . . .

POLAND

DEALING WITH OUR MAROONED FOOD

Villalobar had, on February 11, obtained the following pronouncement from the Germans concerning the food marooned in England:

". . . concerning the merchandise bought in England, the German Government will only consider this question on the condition that this merchandise will be transported to Holland by the Dutch boats which regularly constitute the service [from] Holland [to] England and by no other. This line of boats will be respected by the German Government."

The idea of transporting 188,000 tons of food in 100-ton lots twice a week did not appeal to us.

While we were still trying to get German safe-conducts to Rotterdam for our ships marooned in British ports, the British authorities decided that the marooned ships should be unloaded. They were needed for Allied sea transport. On February 27, Poland asked for more time from the Foreign Office. The next day, however, he was told to unload the ships. We ultimately sold the food to the British Government at the then prevailing prices. Our purchase contracts for food in Britain and France had to be canceled. The sale of this food brought a total of $2,913,076.27, of which $575,420.47 was net profit. Later, I will discuss the use which we made of this money.

The Spanish Ambassador in London had tenaciously urged the Germans, through Madrid, to give us permits to sail our marooned ships from Britain. On February 28, the Germans agreed, subject to conditions. This statement was not received by the Ambassador until after the matter was already rendered moot by the British decision to unload.

MORE GERMAN SUBMARINE SINKINGS

We had started such ships as we could get from American or other ports direct to Rotterdam on February 24 with German safe-conducts. On March 8, one of these ships—the *Storstad*—was sunk by a submarine. Two members of the crew were lost.

Despite their assurances and their issued safe-conduct passes, the Germans apparently did not issue orders to their submarines until March 13, when they informed our Rotterdam office as follows:

> THE IMPERIAL GERMAN EMBASSY
> THE HAGUE
> 13 March 1917

All submarines at sea after the 15 March have instructions concerning the security or safety of traffic lanes in the North Sea.

Since the situation *outside* of the blockade area is exactly the same as before February 1st of this year a further explanation on the convoy passes is not necessary, for which the Imperial Embassy would first have to obtain an authorization from Berlin.

The Imperial Ambassador
by von STUMM

This was a mystery to us, since they had been issuing safe-conduct passes from Washington for nineteen days. Ambassador Merry del Val induced the Spanish Ambassador in Berlin to make a strong protest over the destruction of the *Storstad,* but it had no effect.

We were obviously becoming short of food in Belgium and Northern France. The German Government now blamed the Commission for this shortage, as is shown in the following letter from Poland to the Spanish Ambassador in London:

March 16, 1917

YOUR EXCELLENCY:

I beg to acknowledge your letter of March 15th, conveying the information that the German Government attributes the shortage of food and reduction in rations in the occupied territories to the Commission for Relief, the German Government adding that they "do not understand the delay in the departure of these vessels when the Imperial Government have guaranteed a safe route to Rotterdam."

In answer to this I beg to say:

In a communication which you were good enough to forward me on March 14th, the German Government states that attached to the proclamation of January 31st, establishing the war zone, was a note giving a respite to February 13th, which applied to Relief vessels and would have enabled them to reach Rotterdam instead of being interned, as they were, in United Kingdom ports through lack of German safe-conducts. The fact is that we received no such notice either from the German Legation, from Rotterdam or through the Spanish Embassy, London, or the Swiss Legation, London, but, on the contrary, were repeatedly warned that vessels would proceed at their peril after February 5th. . . .

POLAND

The Spanish Ambassador similarly nailed this German statement in this reply to Poland:

LONDON, 22nd March 1917

DEAR MR. POLAND:

Untoward circumstances of various kinds have prevented an earlier reply to your letter of 17th inst. on the above question.

According to your Director in Rotterdam, Baron von Stumm stated in conversation on February 21st that he assumed that advice as to the use by Relief ships of the Channel route to Holland up to February 13th last had been given to the Commission for Relief in Belgium through this Embassy.

As a matter of fact I was telegraphing myself on February 5th and 8th to the Spanish Government at the demand of the Belgian Minister in London begging them to obtain a free passage for the Relief ships through the Channel, and at your own request I did so again on February 10th transmitting the contents of the Memorandum enclosed in your communication of February 9th, clause the 2nd of which requests the same concession. On February 10th the Spanish Government telegraphed to me that they were forwarding the request to Berlin and on the 15th of the same month they sent me a telegraph from our Minister in Brussels announcing that the German Authorities refused.

Neither before nor after did I receive any intimation of the kind alluded to by Baron von Stumm.

A. MERRY DEL VAL

On March 21, the Spanish Minister at The Hague telegraphed Merry del Val:

The German Government is prepared to permit all the ships of the Commission for Relief in Belgium at present in English ports to go to sea the 1st May 1917 and to permit them to traverse the forbidden zone by routes yet to be determined without risk of attack from the Imperial Navy on the following conditions: the Commission for Relief must declare before 10th April 1917 under engagement on their part if England is in accord to let these boats go to sea with their cargoes the 1st May 1917 and what ships' names and distinctive signs will want to use the offer to depart and where these ships are. The routes that these ships must follow will be communicated by the Imperial Government as soon as it is in possession of the reply to paragraph one. It is to be noted that security against the danger of mines cannot be guaranteed even on the 1st May. An urgent reply is desirable in view of the terms fixed by the Imperial Government. Have communicated same telegram Madrid.

AGUERA, *Spanish Minister*

This message having been conveyed to Poland, he replied to Merry del Val on March 24:

YOUR EXCELLENCY:
... The Imperial German Government must realise that when, despite its declaration of desire to co-operate in arrangements for the despatch of the food detained in United Kingdom ports in Relief vessels, safe-conduct passes to Rotterdam for such vessels are withheld until May 1st, a period of three months after the declaration of the danger zone on February 1st. ...
In addition to [the 120,000 tons on marooned ships] we have contracts for further deliveries of 68,000 tons of general produce for future deliveries in the United Kingdom. All this produce is urgently needed in Belgium and France and, as we have repeatedly explained [to the Germans] from the very first days of the "blockade," the people are suffering for lack of these commodities. ...

POLAND

Poland gave Ambassador Merry del Val information about four small vessels which, by persistence, he had persuaded the British to allow him to retain, hoping to use them for cross-Channel transport. They had a total of about six thousand tons of food aboard. The Ambassador negotiated with the Germans to allow these ships passage to and from Rotterdam to Britain; they argued the matter for nearly two months. We finally gave up on April 4.

On March 21, Poland protested through Merry del Val about German submarine attacks on two more ships, the *Tunisia* and the *Haelen*:

March 21, 1917
YOUR EXCELLENCY:
I beg leave to enclose herewith copy of a telegram received from our Rotterdam office which gives the details of the attack, outside the limits

of the German danger zone, upon two of our Relief vessels, the *Tunisia* and the *Haelen,* which sailed from Rotterdam after midnight March 15th, provided with specially endorsed German safe-conducts guaranteeing immunity from submarine attack.

These vessels were outward bound in ballast, accompanied by three other Belgian vessels which have not yet been heard from.

There can be no question as to the reliability of the information which is, in addition, confirmed by newspaper reports from other sources.

I beg that Your Excellency will be kind enough immediately to communicate through your Government with the German authorities at Berlin and from them demand, in the name of the Commission, a complete statement in regard to this occurrence. We should be advised:

1) What conclusion is to be drawn from the declarations which the German Government have made of their desire to have the work of the Commission continue, in view of the action which they have subsequently taken.

2) What value we should place upon their safe-conducts and guarantees of immunity for our vessels from submarine attack.

3) In the event that the German Government actually desire the Relief work to continue and do not wish us to consider their guarantees valueless, will they state specifically and at once how they propose that Relief vessels can navigate to and from Rotterdam in safety from submarine attack.

4) It will be evident that unless complete assurance is given by the German authorities concerning these points, they will, by their own actions, have terminated the work of Relief. . . .

POLAND

The German reply to the Spanish Ambassador concerning the torpedoing of the *Tunisia* and *Haelen* was as follows:

LONDON, March 31st, 1917

W. B. Poland
SIR:

By a telegram from our Ambassador in Berlin the Spanish Government has learned that the German Government, in view of the representations made as a result of my telegram of March 21st on the incident above-mentioned, has replied that they have no knowledge of any attack by submarines against ships belonging to the Commission and that they have given every possible guarantee. . . .

A. MERRY DEL VAL

The effect of all this on the Belgians is indicated by a letter I received from Francqui which, due to delays, was not received until the end of March, although its date was February 24, 1917:

MY DEAR HOOVER:

. . . There is perfect confusion here; the greatest uneasiness reigns although we have entire confidence in your personal energy. We feel the liveliest satisfaction in the thought that you will not abandon the Belgians and that you will continue to look after them, even if you are obliged to remain in America on account of the blockade.

Our fears are justified. We have foodstuffs for but a few weeks; rice becomes rare; we have been obliged by prudence to reduce the bread ration, and the working classes are deprived of potatoes. In the industrial centres famine commences to be felt.

In these cruel circumstances everybody counts on you and hopes that you will finish by finding a system to continue to send us foodstuffs by Holland. . . .

You will see that the assistance of your indefatigable activity and of your mind so capable in finding practical solutions is more indispensable than ever.

If the Belgians were to learn that you had ceased to consecrate yourself to their relief, they would certainly suffer severely in their body through the distress to which the suppression of all . . . [foreign] revictualing would fatally condemn them, but their moral sufferings would be much deeper and more painful at finding themselves abandoned by a friend in whom they had placed all their confidence and their last hope.

E. FRANCQUI

CHAPTER 34

WE HAVE A BOUT
WITH VON BISSING
AND ITS REPERCUSSIONS

The previous chapters indicate that there were sufficient troubles to keep our energies and our minds busy. But there were coincident troubles which I relate in this chapter in order not to confuse the reader with our major purpose of restoring the movement of food to Belgium and Northern France.

Ten days after the start of the German unlimited submarine war, a storm blew up from a new quarter. On February 11, the Marquis de Villalobar cabled me that our entire American staff in Belgium and Northern France, totaling about seventy-five Americans, had to be reduced to five or six. He said:

The German Government has notified us that they could no longer authorize American subjects to continue in the service of the C.R.B. in the North of France and in the provinces of Belgium. The German Government consents to allowing five or six Americans to continue to reside in Brussels in order to assure the service of the central administration. The German Government will be very happy to see the C.R.B. continue its activity in Holland, England, and America, on condition, however, that C.R.B. boats will strictly observe the indications laid down by the new blockade and will take the Northern Route for Rotterdam. . . .

In the face of the deportation of our Belgian staff, it was a certainty that we could not carry out our responsibilities to the Belgian people or the Allied Governments under any such restrictions as these. We would be deprived of all our staff outside Brussels and would be forced to operate hopelessly in the dark. But I was convinced that the author of this new maneuver was just von Bissing, acting without any authority from the German Foreign Office or the German General Staff.

To call von Bissing's bluff, I instructed our Rotterdam office to notify him, through our protecting Ministers in Brussels, as follows:

... in view of communication from German Government [in Brussels] to you through Lancken that Americans can no longer exercise their functions in Belgium and Northern France, please notify the German authorities and Comité National that as under these conditions the American members of the Commission can no longer carry out their responsibilities and undertakings with the other interested governments and toward the peoples of France and Belgium, the American members officially withdraw from participation in the work of the Commission for Relief in Belgium and from the relief work in France. ...

HOOVER

AMBASSADOR PAGE ADVISES THAT WE QUIT

In view of von Bissing's action, Ambassador Page took the drastic view that we should quit the whole works. He cabled the State Department:

LONDON, 12 February 1917

SECRETARY OF STATE, WASHINGTON

Director Gregory at Brussels informs Commission for Relief in Belgium that von der Lancken, Civil Governor of Belgium, has reported to him that the German Government will no longer permit American members of Commission to exercise functions in Belgium and Northern France. Hoover and his American associates can in my judgment pursue only one course, namely, inform the German Government immediately that every American retires, get all American members out of Belgium and France in whatever way their exit can best be managed by Gregory, with whom Poland is conferring by telegraph, and close the Commission's business immediately in Belgium and France and liquidate it as soon as possible.

We shall have to leave to the decision of the British, French, and German Governments the work for the future. Americans can now retire with clean record and make dignified exit without parley, leaving the onus on the German Government.

I regard it as of the very highest importance that Hoover announce retirement under German order emphatically and immediately. Further discussion may lose the present tactical advantage.

I await Department's instructions to me to retire as Patron of Commission which I hope will be given.

Please inform Hoover of the contents of this telegram and your instructions to me.

PAGE

I did not agree with Page's recommendation because not only did I feel that von Bissing was bluffing, but I also believed that through our negotiations we could restore our ship immunities, concerning which we were making progress at the time with both the British and Germans. I so told Secretary of State Lansing in Washington on February 14 and 15.

In London, Spanish Ambassador Merry del Val went into action promptly, and the German Foreign Office informed the Spanish Ambassador in Berlin that they did not hold with the von Bissing order. Key paragraphs of their communication were:

IMPERIAL FOREIGN OFFICE
Berlin, February 18, 1917

To His Excellency Monsieur Luis Polo de Bernabé
    Ambassador of Spain.
Monsieur l'Ambassadeur,

... the Imperial Government is also actuated by a lively desire that the humanitarian work of the Relief Commission of Belgium should continue. Although the Government of the United States has broken off diplomatic relations with Germany the work of ravitaillement, based on the agreements concluded at the same time with the Governments of Spain and of the Netherlands, can evidently continue its benevolent work. The Imperial Government has no intention of forcing the members of the Commission to suspend their work and to leave the occupied territories. They think on the contrary, that it would be useful if these gentlemen remained provisionally at their posts, even while considering the possibility of their replacement, in case of need, by other neutral agents suitable to the work. Further, nothing will prevent that certain of the American members remain in Brussels for the management of the Commission.

With a view to settling this question, negotiations have been set on foot by the General Government in Belgium directly with the Protecting Ministers of the commission. These negotiations have had as a result that the Americans will remain at their posts until further orders, the question of the introduction of other neutral agents into the Commission, in the first place to assist the Americans, and subsequently to replace them, is reserved for the present. . . .

In the hope that these measures will assure the continuation of the work of Relief without hindrance, I take this opportunity to renew to you, Monsieur l'Ambassadeur, the assurance of my highest consideration.

ZIMMERMANN

Von Bissing himself now backed down, as is shown by a telegram to our London Office from Brussels:

ROTTERDAM, 15 February 1917

RELIEF COMMISSION, LONDON

Brussels advises:

"We have had today a meeting . . . [attended by] von der Lancken, Villalobar, Whitlock, Bruhn, Rieth, Francqui, and Gregory, and which was held concerning your telegram of the 12th instant. It has been agreed that our delegates may remain as heretofore and with the same privileges. However, it is possible that later it may be necessary to place delegates of other nationalities on military fronts. In consideration of this, the Protecting Ministers and Gregory suggest that we keep on our regular work as heretofore and consequently we will not close our accounts unless we receive other instructions from you."

RELIEF COMMISSION

I at once sent these instructions to Brussels through Rotterdam:

LONDON, 15 February 1917

RELIEF COMMISSION, ROTTERDAM

Advise Brussels in view changed attitude of German authorities . . . American staff requested to remain at their posts long as possible but notify German authorities this action taken solely on understanding that representatives' functions, activities, circulation, communication continued in full. . . .

A myriad of confusions arose over this action. I had not wanted any publicity because I expected that von Bissing would be ordered to retreat and I had instructed our London office to send my reply to von Bissing only to our Spanish Patrons in the hope that their action would stop him. However, our London office had sent it to all of our Patron Ministers and the British Foreign Office. It was immediately leaked to the press, which instantly demanded a statement. I was in Boston at the time and could do nothing more than verify the message, since I had not yet received the cable telling me that von Bissing had been overcome. Thus the confusion was compounded.

Several reactions ensued before we could get the matter straightened out. First, the French and British embraced the opportunity to blame the Germans for killing the Relief. Foreign Minister Briand of France issued the following statement to the press:

[PARIS, 14 February 1917]
At this moment when the German Government is forcing the American representatives of the Spanish-American Commission of Relief to leave the invaded lands and to abandon the task to which they have dedicated themselves with so much devotion, I desire you to express to the Central Committee of the Commission in London, the recognition and gratitude of the Government of the Republic for the humanitarian work which the American representatives of the Commission, with the devoted collaboration of the Spanish representatives, have carried out, in saving the unfortunate French populations from famine. I do not overlook with what disinterestedness the Commission has successfully administered a most complicated and difficult work, which has necessitated constant and methodical efforts. The devotion of the Commission, of the bankers and contractors to the Commission for Relief in Belgium, who have refused all remuneration, is also known to us. It is to be hoped, for the sake of our unhappy compatriots of the North of France, that this great international work of benevolence may be able to continue to the end of the war. It is to this end that the generous efforts of the King of Spain, to whom the Government of the Republic has just appealed, are at the present directed.

If, as we like to hope, His Majesty Alphonse XIII succeeds in making the voice of humanity heard in Berlin, we are sure that the services of the Americans of the Commission for Relief will be continued in the same devoted way, in the work of purchase and transportation, thus still contributing, with the co-operation in the country of other neutral representatives who will come to replace the Americans, to the humanitarian task which they now perform.

Of all the acts of charity which now stand to the credit of the Americans and which earn our deepest gratitude, the work of the Commission for Relief is among those which are dearest to us, since they are working for the sake of those French people who add to all their other misfortunes that of temporary separation from their mother country, and who have to suffer bondage to the enemy.

BRIAND

Lord Robert Cecil, Under Secretary of Foreign Affairs, joined in these encomiums—and condemnations—with a press statement:

LONDON, 14 February 1917

The withdrawal of the Americans from participation in the work of the Commission for Relief in Belgium and the withdrawal of Mr. Page and Mr. Whitlock from their position as Patrons of the Commission, will be very sincerely regretted by the Allied Governments.

The Commission still goes on in the hands of its other neutral members, but you know how, in practice, the organization of the Relief Commission both here and at Rotterdam and in Belgium and Northern France was created by, and in practice, depended upon Mr. Hoover and his American colleagues who, for more than two years have sacrificed every personal interest to their great humanitarian enterprise. It is they who have dealt daily and hourly with the Foreign Office here, with the German authorities at Brussels and with the German Headquarters in Northern France. They have been the constant intermediaries in a series of most arduous international negotiations, and it is they who have built up the elaborate system of guarantees which has made the continuance of the work possible for twenty-eight months and which stands today as a bulwark between the Belgian people and their invaders.

Now, I am not going to pay any tribute to their business organization or their efficiency, wonderful as these things have been. The mere fact that for twenty-eight months they have kept alive ten millions of people without a single serious hitch in the machinery of purchase, transport, and distribution shows what their organization has been. But this any observer can judge as well as I. What I want to say is this:

When the first proposals were made in October 1914, for the importation of foodstuffs into Belgium after the fall of Antwerp, these proposals were directly counter to every dictate of military prudence. The natural feeling of people here was, and long continued to be, that the Germans were in complete control of Belgium, and how could a dozen or two neutrals safeguard the supplies imported? It was only with the greatest anxieties and misgivings that we consented to allow importations, and I sometimes doubt whether the proposals would ever have been made or our consent given if we had known how long the work would have to last, or the extent to which it would grow. Yet, in spite of this, the work has gone on uninterruptedly for twenty-eight months and has grown from small beginnings into an undertaking which may be literally called gigantic.

Now the only thing which has made this possible has been the absolute confidence which Mr. Hoover and his colleagues have inspired in all the Allied Governments. They have been in the most difficult position and have borne the heaviest responsibilities that could possibly fall to the lot of any neutral, but their absolute frankness in discussion and their energy in carrying out their undertakings have led us to rely absolutely upon their word and upon their ability. How high a tribute this is, no one can perhaps understand who has not had actual experience of war conditions, but the American people may be confident that these American citizens leave behind them in Europe a reputation which, if I may say so, America may count on as a national possession in future years.

I do not speak of the financial help which the American people have given to the Relief, because this is a sort of farewell speech and I am sure that while we must say farewell to the American directors of the work, we need not do so to American interest in the work. On the contrary, I am sure that American interest will in the future be even keener than in the past and that the American people will take a pride in competing with the Allied nations in giving financial support to a great enterprise with which the name of America must forever remain associated.

A third type of reaction came from Merry del Val. Assuming that Poland, who, as head of our London office, had sent him the resignation message, was speaking with authority, he embraced the opportunity for the Spanish to take over the whole works. In a letter to the French Ambassador in London, Paul Cambon, he wrote:

SPANISH EMBASSY, LONDON
15 February 1917

My Dear Colleague:

The American members of the Commission for Relief in Belgium having signified to me their irrevocable decision to retire from the work, I have the honor to inform you, in my capacity of founder and President of the Commission, that it will be carried on under the administration of their Spanish colleagues.

Thus, Mr. José Roura . . . will take the direction of the Commission. He will place himself at your disposal for the information which you will be good enough to give him, in the belief that the Commission will continue to receive in the future the same support as it has hitherto received from the Government of the French Republic, and that it will maintain with Your Excellency and your Government the same good reputation as it has had in the past, resolute, as is the Government of His Majesty the King my August Sovereign, to do all that is possible for the relief of the occupied territories of France.

MERRY DEL VAL

The British Ambassador in Washington, Sir Cecil Spring-Rice, wrote to Secretary of State Lansing:

BRITISH EMBASSY
WASHINGTON, February 16, 1917

SIR:

I have the honour to inform you that I am in receipt of a cablegram from Mr. Balfour, His Majesty's Principal Secretary of State for Foreign Affairs, in which I am instructed to convey to you, in writing, an expression of the warm appreciation of His Majesty's Government of the manner in which American citizens have conducted the work of relief in Belgium for more than two years. His Majesty's Government deeply regret their enforced withdrawal which will, however, they feel sure, in no way affect the continuation of American interest in the work as it will in no way affect the determination of His Majesty's Government to proceed with it.

CECIL SPRING-RICE

It took me a few days to put an end to all this confusion.

Some of our C.R.B. staff members in Europe, worn out by constant frustration and outraged at the exiled Belgian Government's earlier effort to have me removed as C.R.B. Chairman, were strong for accepting Ambassador Page's advice at once. They had long wanted to hand over the whole works to the Spanish or Dutch or anyone who would give them an opportunity to return to their professions or to join the American forces in case of war.

I canvassed the directors of our principal offices and found that Poland, Kellogg, Chevrillon, Honnold, Brown, and White believed that we should go on. We exchanged a multitude of cables on the subject which, due to long delays in transmission, appeared inconsistent and added to the confusion. Warren Gregory, our Director in Belgium, and some of our subordinate staff decided to retire.

I told our staff that we would go on until something else happened, such as a declaration of war by the United States. We could then probably transfer the responsibilities inside Belgium and Northern France to Dutch and/or Spanish nations and continue functioning to the Belgian frontier.

I informed our Patron Ambassadors and the British Foreign Office that we would continue until something else happened which might necessitate our retirement. British Ambassador Spring-Rice wrote to me:

BRITISH EMBASSY, WASHINGTON
8 March 1917

MY DEAR MR. HOOVER:

The Foreign Office have telegraphed requesting me to communicate, confidentially, to yourself and to the State Department the following statement of the position in regard to Belgian Relief. . . .

After a discussion of the various alternatives and the fact that I was willing to go on with the work, the letter continued:

". . . Such a solution would be a great relief to us because the constitution of any competent new organisation at these two places would, we have found, inevitably create friction with the Spanish Government, owing to the ambiguous nominal constitution of the existing Commission. If

Americans will remain in control we shall of course be glad to arrange for it to be made clear that their responsibilities after the withdrawal of their delegates from the occupied territories are fundamentally different from their previous responsibilities and that they are fully and finally discharged from those previous responsibilities.

If the American Commission finally decides to adopt this course with the approval of the United States Government we should be glad to be placed in a position at once to notify the Spanish and Netherlands Governments of the fact."

In addition to the above message, the Foreign Office have instructed me to discuss with you the financial situation of the Commission. It appears that, while the British Government can, to a certain extent, increase the subsidies which they are now giving, they cannot undertake to provide an increase up to the full amount which would be required if the present programme of imports is to be maintained. The British authorities feel in the circumstances that it should be possible for a sum of at least five hundred thousand pounds a month to be provided in the United States, more or less on the same lines as the French and British subsidies. Perhaps you could let me know your views on this aspect of the situation, so that I can cable your opinion to London.

Believe me,

CECIL SPRING-RICE

Hymans, the Belgian Minister in London, expressed satisfaction that we would continue in this cable:

LONDON, 8 March 1917

HOOVER, NEW YORK

Following letter received: begins, "London March 7th. I have learned with deep satisfaction that Mr. Hoover and his colleagues have consented to maintain as far as is possible the present organization of the Commission for Relief. He himself and colleagues will continue to exercise their most useful functions at Rotterdam and at London even in case of complete rupture between the United States and Germany. I am charged by the Government of the King to inform the Commission that it approves this solution most earnestly. It seems to be the best solution to the efficient continuance of the work of ravitaillement since Mr. Hoover and the members of the Commission have directed this work since its inception with

such noble devotion and wherein they have shown such remarkable capac-
ities. It is once more an occasion for me to express to them the lively gratitude of the Government and the Belgian nation and I should be obliged
if you will kindly forward these expressions to your most distinguished
President. Hymans." Ends.

RELIEF COMMISSION

On March 12, the Marquis de Villalobar arranged that in the event
of war, our staff could withdraw:

BRUSSELS, March 12, 1917

To His Excellency the Marquis de Villalobar

. . . I have the honor to communicate that Monsieur the Governor General has consented that a safeconduct should be granted to the American
members of the C.R.B. designated in the annex of your above-mentioned
letter, whenever they should ask for them and whatever may be the position between Germany and the United States of America. In all cases a
quarantine of not exceeding four weeks duration is necessary before their
departure to satisfy military interests. . . .

LANCKEN

On April 4, two days after President Wilson asked the Congress
for a declaration of war, the French Foreign Minister took occasion
of the withdrawal of American C.R.B. staff members from the occupied territory to send me the following cable through Ambassador
Jusserand in Washington:

At the moment when the American members of the Relief Commission
are leaving the invaded territory and when the United States, at the call
of their President, inspired by their high sentiment of justice and liberty,
are ranging themselves on the side of the Allies in the struggle against the
German aggressor, I desire to ask you to express to the Federal Government all our gratitude for the assistance lent to the French population,
which has remained under the yoke of the enemy, by American citizens
who have given themselves to this charitable task with such devotion. It
is to their efforts, under the energetic direction of their Chief, Mr. Hoover,
that the North of France has been enabled to continue to subsist. We are
happy to think that, if it is henceforth impossible for him to continue to

control on the spot the working of the ravitaillement, at least Mr. Hoover will continue to direct and administrate with his tried colleagues, and in full accord with us and our Allies, as long as the French regions of the North are not liberated, the Ravitaillement Commission to which his name will remain attached.

BRIAND

I was in Washington on February 14 and 15 to consult with Secretary Lansing on Page's recommendation that we quit the Relief. I had no intention of bothering the President, but while I was there, Secretary of the Interior Franklin K. Lane, an old friend, sent me to see Mr. Wilson in the White House. Our discussion naturally touched upon the plight of the Belgians and of the Relief Commission. I told him of my hopes of restoring the German guarantees of safety for our ships but added that our financial outlook was desperate, since our loan, designed to secure dollar exchange, had necessarily failed. Upon a sudden thought, I suggested that possibly Congress could vote us an appropriation for expenditures in the United States and that I believed that the Allies would meet our European currency outlays. The President at once responded that he believed that this should be done and that at a favorable time he would recommend it. At this interview the President suggested that when I returned to Europe I make a report upon the economic and other questions which might arise in case we got into the war.

CHAPTER 35

I GET PASSAGE TO EUROPE
WITH ADVENTURES

It was urgent that I get back to Europe, and since all North Atlantic passenger traffic had been suspended, I finally secured passage for Cadiz on an ancient Spanish cargo jalopy with some passenger accommodations, the *Antonio López*. I was accompanied by Will Irwin of the *Saturday Evening Post* staff. We sailed on March 13, 1917, and after roaming around the Atlantic for twelve days, we arrived at Cadiz on March 25. Fortunately, the ship carried a radio operator, and our offices kept me advised on important matters. Since I could not deal with these questions effectively until I reached London, I defer discussing them at this point.

By the ship's wireless we received news of the U-boat sinking of several American vessels and of the revolution in Russia. We were of the opinion that this would remove one objection to the United States' joining the Allies by removing the fear that the war was a fight to sustain the Czar. It seemed certain that the United States would soon be in the war and that we would need to substitute other neutrals for our staff in Belgium and the North of France.

I have given an account in my *Memoirs* of the experiences which I encountered from Cadiz to London, and with slight revisions I reproduce it here because of its link with C.R.B. affairs.

At Cadiz I was met by an official who asked me to stop at Madrid to confer with the Spanish Minister of Foreign Affairs. Our landing being on Sunday, we made a thorough examination of Cadiz, although I was in no humor for sight seeing. The city was the emblem of the vanished glory of Spain. From here had radiated the great trade of the Conquest and the Spanish colonies. The entrancing white houses with their luxurious grounds, their beautiful grilles and their minarets spoke of a greater day. And the obvious present poverty confirmed the idea that nothing is very stable in civilization.

On arrival at Madrid next day, I went at once to find out what the Minister of Foreign Affairs had in mind. It happened that he had been apprised, through the Spanish Ambassador in London, of the possibility of our asking the Dutch and Spanish to take the place of Americans for the inside work in Belgium. After discussing that possibility, his next question was, "What is your salary?" And his next, "What salary will our nationals receive if the situation develops to require them?" He seemed stunned at the idea of no pay but possibly just expenses.

I felt he suspected that no Yankee ever worked for nothing or ever told the truth. The major importance of the interview, however, was his agreement that the Spanish Government would do its best to see that the Relief continued. The neutrality of the Spanish and the Dutch was still important to the Germans.

I finally reached Paris with no more inconvenience than sleeping five in a compartment built for four and spent the next days on relief matters with French officials and certain questions President Wilson had asked me to investigate.

The wireless to the *Antonio López* had indicated, the Germans had drawn the Hindenburg Line some miles back to a better prepared and more strategically located defense. The result was the recovery by France of some 50 communes out of the 1200 occupied by the German Army. The recovered soil included the municipality of Noyon. We were thus relieved of relieving by that much.

The French had arranged to celebrate this victory and this recovery of French soil on March 31st. There was to be a service in the partially-destroyed *hôtel de ville* at Noyon—the great cathedral had been too far destroyed for use. I was urged by the French officials to attend. A great number of notables were assembled, including Cabinet Ministers, Senators, the Cardinal, the Prefect of the Oise, the generals of that sector and other public officials.

A platform for the notables had been erected at one end of the great hall. The *maires* of the recovered communes were seated in front rows facing us. Fully half of them were women, most of whom I recognized.

It was a colorful and moving occasion. The *hôtel de ville* is an ancient mark of Gothic magnificence. The tempered light from the few stained-glass windows which remained was shot through by streams of sunshine from a shell hole in the roof. The magnificent music of the massed military bands, and the solemn and affecting sermon from the Cardinal stirred one's deepest emotions. Senator Noel paid a touching tribute to the Relief, and the Prefect spoke of his amazement at finding the efficiency of the Relief and the good health of the children.

Just as we were rising at the end, still under the spell of this intense spiritual expression of a great people, a raucous voice called out from fifty feet away, "Monsieur Hoover, où est l'argent pour les sacs?" (Where is the money for the sacks?) Most of those in my neighborhood looked at the grizzled old *maire* who was speaking, and then at myself. I was the only soul, aside from the *maires,* who knew what the unseemly remark was all about. I fear I broke the spell with a laugh.

However, I gave the necessary assurances to the *maire* and evaded further inquiries. The explanation was that some time before, the British had discovered on captured German trenches sandbags made from C.R.B. floursacks. The British indignation was only a little less violent than the French when they imagined our condensed milk tins were being used for hand grenades. The French Committees for "Benevolence" in the Communes had been making a little money for their charities by selling the empty sacks to dealers who, in turn, sold them to the Germans. After the discovery of this practice I had stopped it by requiring every *maire* to deposit 10 francs for each sack to be repaid when the empties were returned. We put the sacks into the clothing workrooms at Lille and Brussels and saw to it that they were turned into children's clothes, although the indelible words "Belgian Commission" appeared on many a youngster's front or back. Anyway, the old *maire* had a deposit of 500 francs with us. Despite his joy at being returned to France, his economic soul came to the surface.

But I can still hear the final words of the Cardinal's thanksgiving to the Almighty and his blessing on us all—then the mighty burst of La Marseillaise.

CHAPTER 36

WE SET UP SPANISH AND DUTCH
REPRESENTATIVES IN BELGIUM
AND NORTHERN FRANCE

I arrived in London on April 3, 1917. The attack by the German submarines on American ships had made our entry into the war inevitable. On April 2, President Wilson made his eloquent address to Congress requesting a declaration of war. At once our American staff began to come out of the occupied territory. Pending arrangements for neutrals to represent the Commission inside Belgium, I requested the Spanish Minister in Brussels to arrange for certain members of our staff to remain, particularly Prentiss Gray, who was now our Director in Brussels, until the Spanish and Dutch could take over.

Setting up neutral representation to take over the protection in Belgium and the North of France proved troublesome and long drawn out. There were international jealousies which I cannot attempt to explain. Chevrillon, as early as March 12, reported that the French Government insisted that the Swiss should take over in the North of France and the Dutch in Belgium. They did not want the Spanish.

On March 22, our London office received a copy of the British proposal to the French on the future organization of the Commission. They favored a Dutch staff in both Belgium and Northern France.

Foreign Office, London
22 March 1917

Ministry of Foreign Affairs, Paris

1. His Majesty's Government understand that the French Government would be glad to have a brief explanation of their precise view on the sub-

ject of the future organization of the Commission for Relief in Belgium and Northern France.

2. It is unnecessary to enter into any historical account of the organization of the Relief Commission. It is sufficient to say that the continuance of its work has been made possible by the fact that its establishment has fulfilled two requirements. These are: First, a thoroughly efficient business organization for the purchase, transport and distribution of supplies; and secondly, the presence in the occupied territories of thoroughly reliable delegates in free and constant communication with the head office of the Commission and in a position to report fully on the machinery of distribution and on the action and attitude of the German authorities.

3. Any future organization established to take over any part of the functions of the present American Commission must fulfil these two requirements. Provided that this is secured, the Allied Governments need not, and indeed ought not to trouble themselves as to the precise details of the Relief Commission's administrative arrangements.

4. His Majesty's Government, in agreement with the French and Belgian Governments, desire that the . . . organization . . . should remain unchanged in the hands of the present American managers. The offices of the Commission at Rotterdam, London and New York would thus undergo no alteration. . . .

5. On the other hand [should the U.S. enter the war], the American managers will be unable to exercise personal control over conditions in occupied territory, and they will thus neither be able to guarantee a sound method of distribution nor will they be able themselves to ensure a constant flow of information from the delegates in the occupied territories to the offices at Rotterdam and London. It is therefore necessary that some supplementary organization should be created with headquarters on neutral soil in Holland, to act as connecting link between the American managers on the one hand and the delegates and distributing agencies in Belgium and Northern France on the other.

6. His Majesty's Government believe that this function can best be discharged by a Dutch organization. . . .

8. In either event, it will be necessary to nominate some prominent neutral, preferably a Dutchman, with some experience of political business, who could carry out such part of the constant diplomatic business between the Relief Commission and the German authorities. . . . In the past it has been Mr. Hoover's ability and energy which have enabled the Allied Gov-

ernments to secure guarantees from the Germans which could never have been obtained by the ordinary methods of neutral diplomacy.

9. It must obviously be left to Mr. Hoover to select a man for this position with whom he feels that he can co-operate and on whose activity he can rely.

10. In general, it is desirable that the American managers of the Commission should keep in their own hands, so far as possible, the appointment of all delegates in the occupied territory. . . .

11. In order to obtain the necessary diplomatic support it unfortunately seems necessary to associate more than one neutral Government in the protection of the work. The Spanish and Netherlands Governments have already given their protection and it has been suggested that the Swiss Government should be associated with them. His Majesty's Government are perfectly ready to accept this latter proposal, but . . . it seems essential that so far as possible the actual administrative personnel of the relief work in the occupied territories should be of one nationality.

On March 28, Spanish Ambassador Merry del Val complained to Poland, our London Director, that his countrymen were being slighted.

Immediately on my arrival in London, I proposed a plan of organization, and it was approved by the British Foreign Office. It provided that the C.R.B. should deliver supplies up to the Belgian frontier and that a new committee of Spanish and Dutch members should be created and should preside in Belgium.

In the meantime, I had been asked by President Wilson to take charge of American food problems in Washington, which position I accepted on the condition that I also continue to direct the Relief Commission and complete the studies he had requested.

The Swiss Minister in London, in a letter to me dated April 13, requested that there be Swiss representation on the staff inside Belgium and Northern France. I replied to him on April 14 that we would welcome Swiss representatives (although in 1914 the Swiss had declined to become one of our sponsors), subject, of course, to approval by the Allied Governments.

The Spanish and Dutch refused to accept the relative positions I had suggested in my plan. I tried to reconcile their differences, but on April 25, I had to leave for Washington.

I appointed Poland our Director in Europe and left him to find the way to peace among our Patrons. Before leaving I appointed an eminent Belgian, Fernand Baetens, who had served on the C.R.B. staff, as our representative in Brussels.

The Spanish-Dutch conflict continued for nearly three months after I departed, but finally Poland found the way to peace and so advised the British Foreign Office:

LONDON, 12 July 1917

DEAR SIR HUGH DALY:

. . . I beg to advise that the slight difficulty in regard to Patrons of the Committee for Protection has now been adjusted. You will recall that there was some objection on the part of the Dutch to having the Spanish Minister at The Hague a joint Patron with the Queen of Holland. However, this has all been adjusted by withdrawing the Spanish Minister as Patron and also withdrawing the Jonkheer de Weede at The Hague, leaving as Patrons the Spanish Minister and the Dutch Minister Resident in Brussels, and the Spanish Ambassador and the Dutch Minister in London as the only active Patrons of the Committee. We have been advised that the King of Spain and the Queen of Holland have accepted the patronage of the Committee, but we assume that this is in an honorary capacity and that they should not appear upon letterheads, et cetera.

POLAND

CHAPTER 37

GERMAN TORPEDOES; SPANISH
AND BRITISH PROTESTS

Our most urgent problem during my stay in London from April 3 to 25 was ships. The unlimited submarine war was wreaking havoc in shipping. The ships lost from all causes amounted to:

	Gross Tonnage
January, 1917	365,000
February, 1917	537,000
March, 1917	591,000
April, 1917	867,000

Most of the ships were torpedoed, and these included neutral as well as Allied vessels. Seven of those torpedoed were C.R.B. ships.

In addition, we lost two sunk by mines. Five more were stranded or lost from the failure of the Germans to issue clear directions regarding the open channels. Two more ships were attacked by submarines but escaped.

On April 5, we telegraphed Spanish Minister Villalobar in Brussels:

The torpedoing within last two days of *Feistein* and *Trevier*, carrying 10,000 tons wheat having German safe-conducts and markings, pursuing supposed safe route laid down by German authorities, again jeopardizes whole relief. This makes five ships torpedoed since February carrying 23,000 tons grain, and unless we can get some definite and believable assurance we cannot induce a single ship, much less the crews, to pursue this work and I have serious doubts whether Allied Governments will

321

allow us to go on sacrificing ship after ship in constant violation of every sacred undertaking made by German authorities. We are doing our best to prevent this . . . coming [to the] point at which relief breaks and we are depending wholly upon your good self to see if you cannot find some solution that will again give reassurance that our ships can be protected and that we can continue.

HERBERT HOOVER

The same day, we also appealed to Ambassador Merry del Val to protest through the Spanish Ambassador in Berlin.

The next day, Villalobar replied to my telegram:

Entirely agreed with your telegram torpedoing of such ships is outrageous. . . . Returning tomorrow to Brussels where Lancken will also be back from Berlin. I will state officially all your just remarks. . . . Will also see on the matter Governor General in order to demand the guaranties which are more than ever necessary. . . .

VILLALOBAR

On April 8, von der Lancken replied to Villalobar that the *Storstad* had been torpedoed in the prohibited zone, which was not true.

That day, I reviewed the history of our ships torpedoed since the unlimited submarine war, all of which carried German safe-conduct passes, in a communication to our Spanish and Dutch Patron Ambassadors and Ministers:

LONDON, 8 April 1917

. . . On the 3rd of February we learned that the Belgian S.S. *Euphrates* of 4,250 tons, outward bound in ballast, provided with the Commission's markings and a safe-conduct pass from the German Minister in The Hague, had been torpedoed without warning and most of the crew drowned. This act occurred before the expiration of the period notified as safe to the 4th of February.

On February 6th the Danish steamer *Lars Kruse*, carrying 2,300 tons of maize, inward to Rotterdam, provided with the Commission's markings, was sunk and only one member of the crew saved. The German authorities assert that this ship struck a mine, but the evidence points the other way.

On March 8th the Norwegian steamer *Storstad,* en route to the newly agreed "safe" lane, carrying 10,000 tons of maize, with Commission's markings and safe-conduct pass from the German authorities in the Argentine, was stopped by a submarine and subsequently torpedoed without examination of the ship's papers. One of the crew died of exposure and another was drowned.

On March 16th the Belgian steamers *Haelen* and *Tunisie,* outward bound on the "safe lane" from Rotterdam in ballast for New York, carrying all the Commission's markings together with safe-conduct from the German Minister at The Hague, were shelled by a German submarine, and six members of the *Haelen* crew were killed. . . . [The ships] managed to escape, but the *Haelen* was so injured that she had to put into a Norwegian port for repairs.

On March 17th the Belgian steamer *Ministre de Smet de Naeyer* was shelled by a submarine in the North Sea, but managed to escape. She was outward bound in ballast and was provided with the Commission's markings and had as usual a safe-conduct pass from the German Minister at The Hague.

On March 31st the Norwegian steamer *Feistein,* inward bound within the "safe" lane, carrying 4,650 tons of wheat, was torpedoed and sunk without warning in broad daylight off the Dutch coast near Terschelling. She carried all the Commission's markings and safe-conduct pass issued by the Swiss Minister, Washington, on behalf of the German Government.

On April 2nd the Norwegian steamer *Anna Fostenes,* inward bound, loaded with 3,100 tons of wheat, was torpedoed near Rotterdam well within the "safe" lane. She carried full Commission's markings and safe-conduct pass issued by the Swiss Minister, Washington, on the authority of the German Government.

On the 4th of April the Belgian S.S. *Trevier,* carrying 4,396 tons of wheat, was torpedoed in broad daylight without warning ten miles off the Dutch coast within the "safe" lane. She carried full markings and safe-conduct pass from the Swiss Minister, Washington, issued with the authority of the German Government, and six members of the crew were seriously wounded by shell fire after they had taken to the boats.

On April 8th we received word that the Norwegian steamer *Camilla,* inward bound, with 2,600 tons of wheat, on the "safe" lane, had been torpedoed without warning. She carried as usual the Commission's markings and a safe-conduct pass issued by the Swiss Minister at Washington on the authority of the German Government.

Since resuming traffic with German assurances on February 28th, three steamers have arrived safely and five have been sunk.

It is impossible to express the indignation which we rightly feel over these acts, and we are at a loss to know whether this continued sinking of steamers in violation of their undertakings is a settled policy of the Imperial Government or whether it is due to the reckless irresponsibility of submarine commanders. In any event the immediate peril and loss of life of innocent seamen continuing resolutely in the service of helpless people is transcended only by the tragedy of suffering imposed on those millions of men, women, and children we are trying to preserve.

HERBERT HOOVER

On April 13, von Bissing replied to Villalobar through von der Lancken that the *Anna Fostenes* had been sunk by a mine and that the *Knudsen* had been ordered to sea by the British, which was not true. Von Bissing also claimed that the *Haelen* had tried to escape a summons by the submarine and had therefore been fired upon and that the *Trevier* was sunk in the prohibited zone, all of which was untrue according to testimony of the crews. He added:

Not doubting in the slightest the real desire of Messrs. the Patron Ministers to arrive by common accord at a satisfactory solution of the difficulties mentioned by Your Excellency, I do not hesitate to repeat that the Imperial Government is, as in the past, decided to facilitate, in conformity with the agreements come to, the ravitaillement of the population in the occupied territories of Belgium and Northern France. I can consequently assure Your Excellency that the Imperial Government will take all useful measures in its power to avoid C.R.B. boats being attacked by units of the Imperial Navy if these boats comply rigorously with the regulations laid down by the former.

Von Bissing, on the same day, also presented a long memorandum from the German Navy claiming that the *Storstad* had been in the danger zone, which was untrue. With regard to the *Feistein*, they produced a German newspaper dispatch stating that its sinking had been due to a mine or the "imprudence of the Captain." Concerning the *Smet de Naeyer*, they insisted that the attacking submarine had only taken a shot at it. As for the *Haelen*, they claimed that its captain had not stopped as ordered by the submarine. The *Anna Fostenes,* they claimed, had been sunk by a mine. They said that the *Trevier* had been sunk in the "danger" zone.

Von der Lancken's comment was:

Your Excellency will perceive from this summary sketch of news as yet unconfirmed officially . . . that the accidents which have happened to the ships of the C.R.B. seem in general and at first sight imputable, either to fortuitous circumstances, to acts of imprudence on the part of the Captains of these ships, or to insufficient instructions having been given them by the Commission for Relief. What is certain is that in no case has an error or fault yet been proved against the ships of the Imperial Marine. . . .

VON DER LANCKEN

My own conclusion was to place more confidence in the word of the surviving crews than in the word of the German Navy.

The Spanish Ambassador in London gave me this further information:

LONDON, April 16th 1917

SIR:

. . . besides your own protest and that of the British and French Governments, the Spanish Government has lodged another on their own account against the submarine attacks in question. I am also informed that the German political Dept. in Brussels is in active communication with the naval Dept. in Berlin and that the German Authorities both in Berlin and Brussels express the greatest displeasure at the occurrence. I hope, therefore, that we shall soon notice a change.

In any case I will hasten to transmit the German Government's reply as soon as I receive it.

A. MERRY DEL VAL

On April 17, von der Lancken again proffered an explanation of the sinkings of our ships to the Marquis de Villalobar, repeating the same German alibis. On April 20, our ship the *Kongsli* was torpedoed but was towed into a Norwegian port.

On April 23, the British Foreign Office notified us as follows:

Sir:

I am directed by Lord Robert Cecil to inform you that the Spanish Government have not only transmitted to the German Government the protest recorded by the Governments of Great Britain and France regarding attacks by German submarines on your Relief vessels, but have added thereto an expression of their own reprobation of such outrages.

I am now to suggest for your consideration that the Commission, on their part, should move their Spanish and Dutch Patróns to make it known, in the name of the Commission, both at Berlin and at Brussels, that, in view of these repeated attacks, which are in direct breach of the formal and solemn guarantees of the German Government, the Commission will be unable to assure the continuance of supplies unless the German Government take immediate steps to provide that their engagements are respected by their naval officers, *and not only replace the stores which have been lost, but also supply from their own merchant fleet a tonnage equivalent to that of the Belgian Relief vessels which have been torpedoed.*[1]

By adopting this course the Commission would free itself from any charge of interrupting the course of supplies and would place the responsibility of the due performance of this duty upon the German Government, who can hardly fail to appreciate the difficulties as to transport arising from the hesitation naturally felt by the Allies in providing vessels which run graver risks than those employed in their own service because they are navigated without armament and without special precautions.

Eyre A. Crowe

While I was no less indignant than the Foreign Office, I had no faith that demanding the replacement of stores and ships would have any effect on the German mind. And to make the demand and have it refused would have put us in the practical position of having to quit the Relief. The terrible consequences of this would have fallen on the Belgians and French and not on the Germans. Strange as it may seem, I believe that the civilian government in Berlin was sincere in wanting our ships protected but so far could not control their militarists.

The British now held up our ships at Halifax. Since I was compelled to leave for the United States on April 25, I drafted a letter

[1] Italics mine.

for Poland to be sent to the Foreign Office, which he did on April 30. After reviewing the recent sinkings and German replies to protests, the letter continued:

On the part of the Commission, in view of the foregoing and in view of other communications of the German authorities through neutral ministers of which the British Foreign Office is advised, I am willing to take the responsibility of saying that these occurrences do not yet indicate a purpose on the part of the German authorities to break down the Relief, and that despite the losses of our ships, we are amply justified in going ahead with the Relief work; and that we should continue to send forward our vessels with the utmost dispatch to Rotterdam.

I . . . attach copy of a communication just received through His Excellency the [Spanish] Minister for Belgium presenting a picture of the very distressing situation now arising in the occupied territories. This is only one of many communications of a similar character which we have received. I feel sure that the British Foreign Office will concur with us, not only that the situation demands the release of the vessels at Halifax and that we continue to forward relief cargoes from America, but that the greatest possible efforts must be made to increase by every means in our power the shipments to the people of Belgium and Northern France, among certain sections of whom starvation has indeed already commenced.

POLAND

The German Foreign Office protested the British holding of our ships at Halifax to the Spanish Ambassador in Berlin on April 29 and issued a long memorandum, again insisting that the sinking of our ships was not really their fault. The Spanish Ambassador in Berlin lodged another protest on May 5, to which the German Foreign Office again replied that they had done no wrong. On May 10, the Swiss Legation in Berlin sent the German Foreign Office the following protest in connection with the torpedoing of the *Anna Fostenes*:

This steamer was proceeding on its voyage with a safe conduct issued by the Swiss Legation in Washington and was announced to the Imperial Legation in Berne on March 7th by the Swiss Political Department. In view of this circumstance the Swiss Legation would be very much obliged to the Ministry of Foreign Affairs if a communication could be sent to this Legation as to the results of the investigations undertaken regarding the cause of the sinking of the aforesaid steamer.

Discouraging as all this was and as terrible as its consequences were, we still hoped that the energetic action of our Spanish Patrons might save the Relief. Our hopes were confirmed by the subsequent slowing down of sinkings.

CHAPTER 38

OUR CRISIS OF MAY 1917

On taking office as United States Food Administrator, I was confronted with an extremely discouraging situation concerning American supplies of food, the result of drought in our 1917 harvest, and the fact that all of our surplus from the 1916 harvest had already been exhausted. Consequently, we had no statistical surplus to export to anybody. Furthermore, because of the torpedoing of our ships, our C.R.B. transport was almost paralyzed. We were now dependent for ships on our small Belgian-flag ships and neutral charters. But the neutrals avoided charters to us. Aside from their charters to the Allies and beyond their own needs for imported supplies, they had four million tons of ships, most of them used in commercial traffic over the world. We determined to bring pressure on them to furnish us with the minor tonnage we needed.

On May 26, I wrote to Secretary of State Lansing about the neutrals' obligation to help us:

DEAR MR. LANSING:

As you are . . . aware, the Belgian Relief Commission is delivering about 60,000 tons of foodstuffs per month and it requires shipping to handle an additional 40,000 tons per month.

. . . you . . . have particulars from the British Embassy as to the amount of Swedish, Dutch, and Spanish shipping which is available over and above the needs of those countries. . . .

. . . I also understand that various neutrals are making inquiries here as to whether their food supply will be cut off under the embargo.

It seems to me that the time has arrived when we might consider some definite service from these . . . [neutrals] of a character which does not jeopardize their ships but which leads them into the path of a little humanity . . . that we should say to them that they should undertake to provide the transport of 100,000 tons of foodstuffs for the Belgian Relief . . . and that unless they are prepared to enter upon this path of decent dealing we shall reserve all the questions of the export of foodstuffs from this country to . . . [them] until further notice.

It seems to me that if this hint were given at the present moment it probably would be as effective as direct action under embargo legislation. The Belgian Relief Commission is prepared to pay the same price which is made in this work for employment of ships for the Allies, or in setting a figure the price of foodstuffs exported from the United States will also be considered. I think it would be desirable to have these ferments working in the neutral mind as soon as possible.

HERBERT HOOVER

The Secretary of State spread this idea about. During previous months, the Norwegians, Dutch, Danes, and Swedes had purchased large amounts of food in the United States, some of which was in storage and some on board ship. As soon as we received the embargo powers from the Congress, we halted the shipment of this food. As Food Administrator, I notified the neutrals that I was prepared to obtain export permits for them, provided that they delivered part of their accumulated food to Rotterdam for the Relief and provided also that they chartered us additional ships.

The first to accept these terms were the Norwegians, who were represented in Washington by the explorer Fridtjof Nansen. After long and tedious discussions, I confirmed an agreement with him:

WASHINGTON, 22 August 1917

MY DEAR MR. NANSEN:

In order that we may come to a definite understanding of the fulfillment of our agreement concerning the division of the Norwegian grain supplies now in the United States, and the allocation of Norwegian shipping for the purpose of transporting these supplies to Rotterdam and Norway, I review below the agreement as I understand it:

First: Your Government is to immediately transfer to the Commission for Relief in Belgium 16,000 tons of rye and 14,000 tons of wheat, now on the Atlantic seaboard, at original contract prices.

Second: The Norwegian Government will receive licenses for exporting 2,300 tons of wheat and 18,000 tons of barley.

Third: The Norwegian Government will charter to the Commission for Relief in Belgium . . . [six ships] making a total . . . 26,300 tons [of carrying capacity]. . . .

Fourth: It is understood that the Commission for Relief in Belgium will effect hull and war insurance on the above ships from Atlantic ports to Rotterdam. . . .

Fifth: It is understood that the charter rate will be Kr. 38 per quarter plus 25 per cent, which includes hull insurance, equivalent to the current rates between Atlantic ports and Norway. In view of the fact that the Commission for Relief in Belgium office will effect the insurance, the Norwegian Government will deduct from the total charter cost, the cost of the current hull insurance between Atlantic ports and Norway. Freight to be paid before departure in Kroner currency.

Sixth: It is understood that a steamer will be placed at the disposal of the Commission for Relief in Belgium immediately to lift the balance of the 30,000 tons, that is, 3,700.

Seventh: It is to be noted that the United States Government does not write insurance, and consequently the insurance offered by the Belgian Commission cannot be guaranteed by the United States Government.

We have already instituted inspection of the above named ships, and would be pleased to have your approval of this arrangement at the earliest possible date in order that we may complete the program.

HERBERT HOOVER

The Norwegians were at all times most co-operative with us. In early September, 1917, the Norwegian Minister secured us six charters.

However, the British, who were dreadfully short of ships, objected to these arrangements:

FOREIGN OFFICE, LONDON
3 October 1917

The Director
Commission for Relief in Belgium, London
SIR:

I am directed by Lord Robert Cecil to acknowledge the receipt of your letter of September 15th stating that the Commission for Relief in Belgium have chartered the Norwegian S.S. "Avona" for two and the Norwegian S.S. "Songa" for four consecutive voyages.

. . . the owners of these vessels have already been informed . . . that these charters cannot be approved. His Majesty's Government regret they cannot depart from the rule by which they have hitherto been guided that only charters for one voyage can be approved.

I am to ask you to be so good as to furnish a statement of the amount of tonnage now in the service of the Commission for Relief in Belgium or in sight for that service.

W. LANGLEY

On my instructions, Poland replied:

LONDON, 17 October 1917

The Under-Secretary of State for Foreign Affairs
DEAR SIR:

. . . You state that His Majesty's Government regret they cannot depart from the rule by which they have hitherto been guided that only charters for one voyage can be approved. I beg to say that no such rule has ever been applied to Relief charters. It has always been customary for us to charter ahead as far as possible, quite in accord with the Inter-Allied Chartering Executive. . . . You are of course well aware that the Belgian vessels, which are the only ones upon which we can count definitely in arranging our program from month to month, supply but about one-third of our required tonnage, and that the balance must be supplied from neutral or other charters. You will appreciate that in making provision for monthly shipments aggregating some 110,000 to 120,000 tons . . . can be subject to no variation upon . . . [this] depends whether the people of Belgium are or are not to starve, such arrangements cannot be made from month to month, but must be determined far ahead.

In protecting our future imports we have therefore made the . . . charters ahead. . . .

Inasmuch as the British Government, in accord with the French Government, have in principle guaranteed to make up to the Relief for tonnage necessary to carry its approved program, any interference with these charters effected would make necessary additional allocations by the Inter-Allied Chartering Executive, the final effect being merely an interruption and disturbance of arrangements without altering in any way the shipping requirements. . . .

POLAND

The British agreed that we should keep the ships. While we did not attain our minimum need, we did greatly improve our overseas arrivals for September and October.

We did not succeed as well with the Dutch as we did with the Norwegians. They had sixty ships in American harbors, about 95,000 tons of which were loaded with food. They had additional foodstuffs in warehouses. Upon their application for export licenses, I opened negotiations with the Netherlands Minister early in July, 1917. The Dutch proved most difficult and dilatory. However, we came to an agreement on August 13 by which a portion of their accumulated food was to be delivered to the Relief and we were to receive some charters. We had stipulated that the agreement was subject to inspection and to the good condition of the food. The Agriculture Department inspectors condemned it *in toto*. Some 95,000 tons of food was lost to a world where the wolf stood at the door.

The Swedes also had amassed about 1,000,000 bushels of wheat and rye in the United States and had sent the ships to load it. As a condition of issuing them export permits, I reached a settlement with them on August 22 by which they consented to sell the Relief 550,000 bushels and give us six charters.[1]

THE GERMANS PLEDGE NOT TO TAKE THE HARVEST OF 1917 IN BELGIUM AND NORTHERN FRANCE

I have already cited the view of Lord Grey, expressed to me in December, 1916, that despite all our difficulties the Commission should continue its work. I consulted President Wilson, and he agreed with Grey that we must continue.

On June 9, I suggested that negotiations to protect the forthcoming harvest in Northern France be undertaken with the German General Staff.

We . . . suggest that it is time to begin negotiations with Headquarters at Charleville, concerning the disposition of the French native crop of

[1] The documentation of these negotiations will be found in the subsequent volume on the United States Food Administration.

1917. We presume that this matter will be handled by the . . . [Dutch and Spanish] and that this agreement will read from the General Staff to them.

You have in your files . . . a copy of the agreement entered into between Dr. Kellogg and Major von Kessler in 1916 and we suggest that this be followed as nearly as possible. Please keep us advised of the progress of these negotiations.

On July 3, I asked our London office to urge more speed in the settlement of the harvest question in Belgium. That same day, our Director in London addressed the Director of our office in Brussels as follows:

MY DEAR MR. BAETENS:

. . . we know that everyone in Belgium has been working hard on the matter of the new agreements for the following harvest. . . .

While I am sure it is quite unnecessary to urge upon you the importance of having this question settled right away, we must tell you that there are certain political considerations here which make it gravely necessary that we have an undertaking from the Germans, along essentially the lines of last year, covering these distributions, and I beg that you will present this view to the Patron Ministers and do everything possible to get the information to us at the earliest date.

POLAND

At the end of July, our neutral representatives in Brussels were notified by the Germans that the North of France crops would be reserved for the civilian population:

BRUSSELS, 30 July 1917

To the Comité Hispano-Néerlandais, Brussels

I have the honor to advise the Comité Hispano-Néerlandais that, according to telegraphic communication from Count Wengersky, the total crop of bread grains, rye and wheat, in the occupied territories of Northern France and the Flanders Etape will be reserved to the civil population.

As the crop will be less important than that of last year it will be necessary to bring the flour ration down to 150 grams per day beginning September 1st.

Concerning the potato crop, nothing definite can yet be stated. Count Wengersky hopes, however, to be able to fix the ration at 200 grams per head per day.

REITH

Von Bissing agreed to this reservation of the harvest of 1917 for the civilian population in the Occupation Zone.

CHAPTER 39

FINANCING THE COMMISSION

During the third year, we had two separate finance problems. The first arose prior to the entry of the United States into the war, the second afterward. Our $150,000,000 loan had fallen through, and the British and French had suspended our subsidies on February 1 with the outbreak of the submarine war. We expended the funds we had earned from the sale of our marooned food in England and borrowed about £1,370,000 from the Banque Belge in London. The Banque demanded that we procure guarantees from the British to cover those sums. The Banque also required that the C.R.B. should endorse the obligation, and thus we volunteers were all personally liable for its repayment. We did not take this last demand too seriously. I directed our London office to allow this overdraft to "lie quiescent." Ultimately, it was met by the French and British Governments.

AMERICAN FINANCING FOR THE COMMISSION

As I have mentioned, early in this third year President Wilson had given me some encouragement that we might get some help from the Congress. I informed our influential C.R.B. Committee in New York of this hope in order that they might help if an appropriate time came. In late March, before the United States had declared war, they addressed this letter to the President:

29 March 1917

Sir:

Your Committee, appointed to co-operate with the Commission for Relief in Belgium, have the honor to submit for your consideration the following suggestions:

336

First: There is a prevailing report current in the press of the country that in the event of the United States entering into the war with Germany a credit of large magnitude will be created for the benefit of some or all of the Allied Governments. We suggest that in case this be done a portion of the credit so offered be specifically allocated . . . for expenditure by our Commission. . . . It would inure directly to the benefit of the Allies because to that extent it would relieve them of the monthly payments they are themselves making for the same purpose; at the same time it would give to this country an appropriate share in the responsibility and burden of financing . . . [this] work. . . .

It is not our opinion or desire that the advances thus made should be permitted to replace or diminish private relief. . . . In any event we propose to continue our efforts to stimulate charitable gifts. . . .

A. J. HEMPHILL

In the meantime, the Belgian Government at Le Havre contributed an idea. On April 18, they requested the American Government to expand our subsidy in order to eliminate all charity appeals. I did not agree with this idea because we would need expanded subsidies; moreover, our committees, raising charity all over the world, were a great source of moral strength.

On May 17, two days before I was formally appointed Food Administrator, I obtained an allotment of American "loans" to Belgium and France for the C.R.B. amounting to $75,000,000. By Congressional stipulation, all American loans had to be spent in the United States.

Although the British and French made good on our bank overdrafts and resumed subsidies to the Commission to cover our sterling and franc expenditures in April, they soon began to stir up difficulties:

FOREIGN OFFICE, LONDON
5 July 1917

The Secretary,
Commission for Relief in Belgium, London
SIR:

I am directed by Lord Robert Cecil to acknowledge the receipt of your letter of the 21st ultimo, in which you state that the French and British subsidies for April and May have been paid over to the Commission but that the whole amount received has not been expended.

I am to observe that sums actually spent after the end of May 1917 would appear to give rise to a claim against the Government of the United States of America. I am therefore to request that you will arrange to refund the unexpended balance, as on the 1st ultimo, of sums which the Commission has received from British credits.

MAURICE DE BUNSEN

I instructed Poland to take issue with this notion, and he protested to the Foreign Office:

LONDON, 13 July 1917

The Under-Secretary of State
DEAR SIR:

Replying to your letter of the 5th of July in regard to claims against the Government of the United States, the position of the British Government in this matter is not quite clear to me. There is of course no distinction in our accounts between funds received from the British or French Governments for the . . . [relief] of Belgium. Our subsidies, as you are aware, have always been made to us through the Belgian Government. . . . Our monthly transactions vary from £2,000,000 to £3,000,000, and our contingent liabilities usually are about £8,000,000 to £9,000,000. To obtain the unexpended balances on hand at any time, it would of course be necessary to close our accounts and completely liquidate our affairs. . . .

It was our understanding that there was to be no liquidation of the affairs of the C.R.B. but that the regular procedure would be carried on as usual with money supplied to us as usual . . . [through] the Belgian Government.

Since we are unadvised in regard to this, will it be possible for you to furnish us with the agreements upon which the claim against the United States is based, whereupon we will immediately refer the matter to Washington and endeavor to have it put in order.

POLAND

The British and French Governments apparently were not aware of Congressional limits on these funds, which were to be used exclusively in the United States. I cabled Poland:

WASHINGTON, 30 October 1917

. . . The terms of American loan do not permit remittance of these moneys abroad. . . . I am asking Mr. Lansing to take the matter up formally with the various governments concerned. . . . An appeal had been made to the President by the King of the Belgians, to which the President has replied that the American Government will give every assistance for expenditures in the United States, but he asks the King . . . to interest himself in securing the provision of the necessary funds from the European governments concerned to carry on European expenditures of Commission.

HOOVER

The settlement of this matter stretched into our fourth year. I take up the subject again in my account of that period.

CHAPTER 40

THE TROUBLED BELGIANS

Both the Belgians in Belgium and their exiled Government at Le Havre could not know our many difficulties of protecting the people in Belgium, dealing with the submarine war, squeezing exports from the American people from a statistical vacuum caused by drought and previous drains, and finding ships to carry the priority in supplies which we had established for them over all other nations.

Their anxieties came to the surface in a dispatch from King Albert to President Wilson on October 18, 1917:

HIS EXCELLENCY MR. WOODROW WILSON,
  President of the United States of America, Washington
During more than three years the American Commission for Relief under Mr. Hoover's able leadership has achieved with marked success and under the most trying circumstances the task of supplying the Belgian nation with the bare necessities of life. Moreover, Your Excellency's Government has lately assumed the burden of financing the Commission. Those unmistakable marks of sympathy make me feel confident that whatever the difficulties may be, the United States will never allow their noble work to be jeopardized. However, since several months the imports of foodstuffs have been inadequate and the last reports which reach me from the invaded territory are such that I consider it my duty to make a personal appeal to your intervention. The Belgian population is confronted not only with hardship and suffering but with actual famine; the death rate is steadily increasing. Infantile mortality is appalling. Tuberculosis is spreading and threatening the future of the race. Only by immediate and energetic action can the lives of many of my unhappy people be saved during the

impending winter. My Government has put all available ships at the disposal of the Commission and is unable to provide for more. For the additional transports as well as for cargoes and financial means Belgium must rely entirely upon the United States. I do not doubt but your Excellency will give to Mr. Hoover full power to meet the present emergency with adequate measures, and in such conditions we are confident that Mr. Hoover will assure the success of the great task he has nobly assumed in the name of the American nation.

ALBERT

The President was somewhat nettled by this dispatch, since he was familiar with what were, in fact, Herculean efforts on our side to keep the Belgian people alive. He requested that I draft his reply. I did so with a feeling that the King was simply uninformed. The President, however, introduced more emphatic expression into my draft. The following was the President's reply of October 26:

To His MAJESTY KING ALBERT

I have given most careful consideration to Your Majesty's cablegram, and I need not assure Your Majesty of the deep solicitude which I feel for the civil population of Belgium as conditions become incessantly more difficult and the obstacles to be overcome increase in number.

While the Commission has delivered some 400,000 tons of foodstuffs since the submarine warfare began, it has shipped an additional 250,000 tons which have failed to reach their destination either because of sinkings or because of inability to complete delivery of goods in transit through the war zone, besides which the delays to steamers in transit have entailed the loss in carrying capacity of over 100,000 tons. The Commission has been powerless to prevent these losses and no one feels more deeply the suffering entailed than do its members.

Frankness in making a complete statement of the causes of the shortage compels me to say that even the Belgian authorities have from time to time increased the difficulty by requisitioning Belgian ships under charter to the Commission at critical periods.

The relief work requires the regular movement of 220,000 tons of shipping, and while the losses of ships and the failure of neutrals and of the Allies to supply shipping last June reduced their regular fleet to 120,000 tons, the Commission have by the addition of steamers furnished by this

Government, and purchases of ships by this Government waived in their favor, now built up their fleet to 160,000 tons.

Furthermore, with my approval, Mr. Hoover has obtained from various governments certain tonnage for this purpose in return for food supplies. This has been done with an insistence we have felt could be justified only by the duty of maintaining the lives of these helpless civilians. For no other purpose have we gone to such length. We now have the hope through these means of securing sufficient additional neutral shipping, and with success in the negotiations now pending, there may be available a fleet of sufficient size.

Your Majesty is doubtless familiar with the financial difficulties of the Commission, which arise out of the inability of this Government to provide funds for expenditures outside of the United States, and the necessity of securing financial assistance from the other Governments for expenditures abroad, in which matter I trust Your Majesty will interest yourself.

The foregoing is but a general survey of the situation, but I trust it will convey to Your Majesty some idea of the difficulties with which the Commission has to contend. I need hardly reiterate that we are determined to do everything this Government can to meet the requirements of the civilian population of Belgium which has such a claim upon our sympathy and friendship, and that if we are unable to render them the full measure of services to be desired, it will be through no lack of effort or sympathetic understanding on our part.

WOODROW WILSON

On October 26, Secretary Lansing sent the following letter to Minister Whitlock, who was now stationed at Le Havre:

DEAR MR. MINISTER:

It is desired that you take an opportunity to impress upon the Belgian Government the fact that this Government has not only done all that could reasonably be expected of it to provide food for the civilian population of Belgium, but has exacted from neutral nations additional foodstuffs for the Belgians in return for concessions as to food and supplies. This has been done by Mr. Hoover with an insistence and severity that we have not exercised on our own behalf, and has caused resentment which we have willingly accepted in the interest of Belgium.

Furthermore, we have given Belgian food shipments from the United States priority over all the Allies.

Neither this Government nor Mr. Hoover has any obligation other than good will in the matter, and Mr. Hoover has repeatedly asked the Belgian Government to take over the purchase and transport of supplies.

For your confidential information, I may say that the tone of implied criticism in messages from Belgian sources and the apparent attempts to load responsibility upon individuals and this Government are difficult for us to understand. It is hoped that by taking every occasion to create an understanding of the true situation, and the difficulties before the Commission, you will succeed in ending the influence of those who apparently are seeking to convey an impression that the inadequacy of the food supply in Belgium is in any way attributable to negligence or lack of sympathetic understanding on behalf of this Government or its officials.

ROBERT LANSING

CHAPTER 41

OVERSEAS SUPPLIES
DURING THE THIRD YEAR

There can be no more telling evidence of the difficulties of the C.R.B. during its third year than the statistics of our ship arrivals in Rotterdam and our losses en route. With about 120,000 tons of supplies the drastic minimum need for Belgium and Northern France, the monthly figures became a grim and graphic record of the unlimited submarine war, the world shortage of ships and food, and the heroic efforts of our staff. Above all, they indicate the privations of the Belgians and Northern French.

Our third-year monthly deliveries to Rotterdam from overseas were:

From November 1, 1916 to the Unlimited Submarine War

November 1916 .... 65,494 tons
December 1916 .... 70,458 tons
January 1917 .... 90,019 tons

From the Unlimited Submarine War to the United States Declaration of War

February 1917 .... 24,294 tons
March 1917 .... 10,116 tons

From the United States Declaration of War to November 1, 1917

April 1917 .... 61,719 tons
May 1917 .... 19,742 tons
June 1917 ....133,520 tons
July 1917 .... 33,946 tons
August 1917 .... 43,473 tons
September 1917 .... 73,128 tons
October 1917 .... 98,266 tons

Total ....724,175 tons

Fortunately, we had accumulated about 70,000 tons in Rotterdam prior to the submarine war. This allowed us to ameliorate the situation somewhat during the worst months. From these stocks we shipped 43,089 tons into the occupied areas; the remainder was in process of loading.

Thus the imported commodities delivered from Rotterdam during the C.R.B.'s third year were as follows:

	Belgium (Tons)	North of France (Tons)
Wheat and rye grain	402,740	85,801
Flour	4,713	3,562
Meat, bacon and ham	13,430	18,718
Lard and lard substitutes	24,643	15,820
Maize	40,113	3,857
Rice and rice substitutes	27,378	14,105
Peas and beans	20,847	10,092
Yeast materials	8,428	——
Cocoa	1,834	1,898
Coffee	5,052	4,030
Fish	3,689	2,187
Condensed milk	2,393	10,615
Soap	3,622	3,958
Sugar	——	8,615
Clothing	117	1,053
Miscellaneous (mostly for children)	17,395	7,190
Total	576,394	191,501
Grand total		767,895

In addition, our agreements with the Germans regarding the protection of native food produced 302,503 tons of bread grains and a larger tonnage in potatoes and other vegetables and certain animal products. These deliveries did not include about 10,000 tons of food which we secured from Holland, some 1,000 tons of which were meats, fats, and eggs, the remainder mostly vegetables.

At one time during the year, we borrowed 15,000 tons of wheat from the Dutch Government which, as Food Administrator, I guaranteed to replace later, and did so. It proved a great help at our low point.

Aside from the supply difficulties engendered both by the submarine war, which made it impossible to secure ships, and by the world shortage of food, we lost directly 163,500 tons of supplies marooned in England and France and 66,000 tons torpedoed or wrecked—a total of 229,500 tons which we had had en route and which otherwise could have been delivered. Our ship losses were:

Sunk by German submarines:
  Euphrates (in ballast)
  Lars Kruse with 2,300 tons of food
  Storstad with 10,000 tons of food
  Camilla with 2,650 tons of food
  Anna Fostenes with 3,062 tons of food
  Trevier with 4,300 tons of food
  Kongsli (partial loss) 7,700 tons of food
  John Bakke with 2,000 tons of food
  Victoria II (in ballast)
  Berlanger with 4,500 tons of food
  Feistein with 4,400 tons of food

Sunk by Mines:
  C. R. Knudsen (in ballast)

Other Losses at Sea:
  Petra with 3,200 tons of food (fire and beached)
  Eftichia Vergotti with 5,400 tons of food (stranded)
  Radnorshire with 8,800 tons of food (cause unknown)
  Kittiwake with 2,700 tons of food (cause unknown)
  Eburoon with 3,000 tons of food (stranded)
  Ramfos with 4,600 tons of food (stranded)

WHAT HAPPENED TO THE PEOPLE IN BELGIUM

To those familiar with the science of nutrition, the intake in calories per capita is somewhat indicative. The average over the third year is a sufficient measure of the suffering of the people in Belgium and Northern France:

Imports	Calories
Bread	865.0
Bacon	12.3
Lard	81.0
Beans	0.5
Rice and rice flakes	35.7
Cerealine	8.0
Macaroni &c	8.0
Biscuits	3.4
Torrealine	6.9
Coffee	—
Cocoa	2.4
Soap	—
Onions	4.4
Native Supplies	
Potatoes	175.0
Sugar	60.0
Artificial honey	60.0
Jam	25.0
Meat (100-150 gr. per week)	25.0
Soup Kitchens	
Soup	150.0
Total	1,522.6

This total of 1,522 daily calories per capita was but an average for the year, and often it fell below. Those who did heavy work had to have a minimum of 2,500 calories a day or there would have been no economic life; thus the rations for others fell far below 1,500 calories. Moreover, this diet was totally inadequate in fats and proteins. The calory average, in fact, was less than one-half of the prewar normal.

But statistics of ships and tons and rations cannot convey the bitter human picture. My correspondence with Francqui gives some indication of it. In a letter dated May 8, 1917, which I received on May 20, 1917, he wrote:

My dear Hoover:

The famine is extending. . . . unfortunate people are daily reached by it. Not later than yesterday a clerk in my secretariat fell down with syncope in the office, having become enfeebled through being deprived for some time of sufficient nourishment. He fell as so many others fall, for what happens here happens everywhere.

Last Sunday at Antwerp, in a line of unemployed, waiting for their soup ration at the distribution door, 12 persons fainted away through weakness and this is a common sight in all large towns and industrial centres. . . .

Besides all the consequences of hunger which I have mentioned and which are apparent in the extension of sickness and death, the doctors have just made a new discovery. They noticed that numerous persons complained of eye trouble at twilight; many people lose their sight at nightfall and remain blind until the day has completely broken the next day, which phenomena, the doctors assert, has always been recognized in India when the country has been desolated by famine. That is the present state of affairs, my dear Hoover; pray report it to the governments. . . . Whatever the objects of war may be, let them understand at least that the Belgian population has done nothing to merit starvation. . . .

If the war is to continue all this year either our importation programme must be augmented and that as quickly as possible, by about 50%, or the Belgian population will succumb.

With a few exceptions, the population still remains optimistic and they hope, according to the assurances that we have always given them, that the importations are going to augment and everybody still has this hope. Its realisation should be hastened, however, for this mirage that we have had reflected before the eyes of the population should not too long delay its transformation into reality or the worst is to be feared. In certain places the population has already commenced stealing and pillaging shops of traders of the Comité.

And it is just when we are striving to delay the cataclysm which menaces the population that the British Foreign Office interdicts importations of bacon and lard under the pretext that the Germans purchase cattle here. That the occupying force does not always respect the guarantees he has given I will not dispute, particularly with you, but it must not be forgotten that the products which he takes away represent but very little to him. Notice, further, that the abuses committed are nearly always by German subaltern agents. . . .

Has not the war yet taught them [the Foreign Office] that it is not the few hundred or thousand kilos of meat purchased from time to time in Belgium, unknown to us, by the Germans that will influence the result of hostilities? On the contrary, it is bad policy for the Allies to forbid importations of bacon and lard and thus deprive a population famished but very courageous of the small amount of food which will permit them still to resist death. The Germans, indeed, profit by all such incidents as the suppression of the importation of bacon and lard, to spread the news that the Allies are losing interest in the Belgians. . . . We all rely on you, my dear Hoover, to draw us from these misfortunes.

P.S.—You should also know that the Germans are again commencing to carry away men. In the Province of Luxembourg 2,000 men, unemployed and otherwise, have been taken so far. In Hainaut, also, about 2,000.

These deportations, commenced a week ago, are being daily carried on. The men deported are from 16 to 45 years; all are taken, unemployed or not, workmen, clerks, citizens; only priests, doctors, barristers, pharmacists and teachers have been left alone. All these men have been sent into the North of France where they are made to work by force at the construction of trenches, roads and other constructions for military objects. It is slavery recommencing. . . .

FRANCQUI

Under the date of July 2, he wrote to me:

. . . I feel it is my imperative duty to make a pressing appeal to the generous and efficient devotion with which the distressing situation of my country has always inspired you. I beg you instantly to support with your great influence the repeated efforts which we are making in London to obtain an increase, an indispensable increase, in the programme of importation, principally in flour, peas, beans, rice and fats.

Four millions of Belgians, our working families and the Petit Bourgeoisie of the towns and industrial regions are wasting away most lamentably on account of insufficient nourishment. Those who survive are condemned to a physical debilitation without remedy, unless we very soon succeed in procuring at the least the ration of food which is physiologically indispensable, and even a surplus which should compensate the deficiency of the preceding months.

You have been able to judge for yourself, before your departure from Belgium, how deep was the misery of the lower classes, and that the ravitaillement, even with the programme of importations anticipated, was even then hardly sufficient.

Since your departure, the situation has grown increasingly worse. The winter was exceptionally long and severe and exhausted our last reserves in indigenous products. In the spring, the production of indigenous foods of general consumption was very restricted; for this reason and also because of the diminution in the importations, the demand made by the well-to-do classes was so heavy that the prices far surpassed the resources of the rest of the population.

It follows that, at present, about 45% of the population lives exclusively on the foods imported by the C.R.B.; thus, for example, according to the last census, the number of participants in the "Soupes" amounted to 2,687,-000 instead of the 2,100,000 at the end of 1916. A proportion of 30% approx. of the people depends *almost* exclusively on the imported foodstuffs, being still in a position to procure for themselves a small addition in the foodstuffs sold by the communal or intercommunal stores, or on the open market. The remainder, that is about 25%, live on their own produce; this is the case with farmers living on their farms (20%) or for a great part depending on purchases in the open market, these are the rich classes (5%).

The statistics of mortality show a constantly increasing percentage, following a regular progression. In certain comparative graphs, the curve of mortality rises on the same proportion as the curve of the importations descends!

Doctors from all parts of the country, especially from the industrial regions of the Hainaut and Liège, send us of their own accord, the most alarming reports on the terrifying progress of morbidity; principally through tuberculosis and various diseases caused by mal-nutrition. The heads of those rare industries which are still in activity (coal mines) implore us to put them into a position to feed their people better; they cannot work as they are too weak to do so.

The population is beginning to lose the patience and proud stoicism which you at one time so much admired. They send us petitions, sometimes imploring, sometimes threatening. In between times, they give most disquieting demonstrations at the markets and before the foodshops. We are perhaps on the eve of more serious outbreaks. . . .

On August 6, I received another appeal from Francqui, this time by telegraph:

I have sent you on several occasions, particularly on the 30th July last, reports showing the pressing necessity, under pain of disaster, of importing a strict minimum of 100,000 to 110,000 tons of supplies per month—70,000 for Belgium and 33,000 for the North of France.

From week to week, in spite of all our efforts, the situation is becoming more alarming. The last vital resources of the great majority of the population—reduced for over seven months to scarcely half a food ration capable of sustaining life—are on the eve of becoming exhausted. For many, life is nothing but slow death; now already many people are commencing to die of inanition.

We look with terror upon what the approaching winter will be if a sufficient ravitaillement is not assured, owing to lack of ships.

I make one supreme appeal to your energy and your devotion to Belgium, and hope that, thanks to your great influence with the American Government, you will succeed in solving the capital question of shipping.

The distracted Francqui could not know of the shortage of food faced by all of the Allied world or of the lack of transportation as a consequence of the unlimited submarine war. And I could not advise him of all this lest this revelation of trying times among the Allies fall into German hands.

And poor Francqui, isolated from the world, was blaming the British Foreign Office. The facts were that after the submarine war began on February 1, only the barbaric actions of the Germans, who sank our ships, prevented our food from reaching the Belgian people.

Cardinal Mercier called for daily prayers and special services throughout Belgium that the Commission be sustained in its stubborn fight for Belgian lives. We needed those prayers.

FOURTH YEAR

November 1, 1917 to the Armistice, November 11, 1918

INTRODUCTION

So that the reader may better understand the problems of our fourth year, I give a brief preliminary account of the background against which the C.R.B. had to operate.

With the United States' declaration of war in April, 1917, we had been compelled to withdraw our American staff from Belgium and Northern France and substitute Spanish and Dutch representatives. The C.R.B., however, continued to shoulder the major job of relief by delivering supplies up to the Belgian frontier. We maintained our offices in Brussels under Director Fernand Baetens, and we depended on the vigorous energies of our Spanish and Dutch Ambassadors and Ministers to protect us in our troubles with the Germans.

I have related in the narrative of the third year the measures which I had taken as Food Administrator to set up complete priority for the C.R.B. in exports of American food and the pressures which we had brought on neutrals to charter us their ships. By the end of the third year, these measures had improved the dreadful situation in Belgium and Northern France.

We entered the fourth year with high hopes that the suffering of the Belgians and Northern French would soon end. In November and December, 1917, we furnished them with their minimum monthly needs. But the shift in the tides of war was to plunge us into great difficulties again.

On the war front, Allied strategy did not initially contemplate the use of large American armies but was based on the Allies' holding the Western Front while they starved the Central Empires and their economy by blockade. But the German defeat of Russia in early 1918 enabled them to move to the Western Front. Their attacks extended from March to July. Their breakthroughs were ultimately checked but necessitated an entire reversal of Allied strategy. It now became essential to transport huge American armies and equipment to Europe. In addition to the demands this created on shipping, the accumulated loss of ships over the world from submarines and wrecks had totaled nearly 6,000,000 tons during 1917. It was followed by a further loss during 1918 of more than 3,000,000 tons. The great American ship-building program had bogged down and contributed little to alleviate the situation.

All this shipping destruction and the military demands on the tonnage still afloat seriously cut into the C.R.B. At this time, however, Allied requisitions of neutral ships drove the neutrals to charter to the C.R.B. as the lesser of perils. The result was that we had a fair-sized fleet from July, 1918, until the Armistice, in November.

In the narrative of the third year, I reviewed the desperate food situation in the United States when we came into the war in April, 1917. This plight lasted until the harvest of 1918. Our Food Administration measures for stimulating production in meats and fats began to effect surpluses in these commodities by March, 1918, and the stimulation of ground crops gave us the great grain harvest of 1918. Thus in our fourth year we were hard put to furnish the ten million people of Belgium and Northern France with meats and fats from November 1, 1917, to March, 1918, and with cereals until July, 1918.

In October, 1918, the sledgehammer attacks of the Allied armies and starvation combined to bring the collapse of the Central Empires. The surrender was signed on November 11.

As in my accounts of the former years, I have divided the fourth-year narrative into topics. Although this makes for some overlapping, a chronological account would be confusing.

THE PASSING OF WALTER HINES PAGE

One of our sad blows during the year was the retirement of Ambassador Walter Hines Page because of illness due to overwork. The C.R.B. would have failed had it not been for him. The personal affection our staff held for him was unbounded.

CHAPTER 42

THE INCREASING NEEDS
OF BELGIUM AND NORTHERN FRANCE

There had been a great decline in the native crops in the Belgian and French harvests of 1917. In late October, 1917, our American staff in Europe, under Poland, held a conference in Rotterdam with the representatives of the Comité National and the Comité du Nord, our Patron Ministers in Holland and Belgium, and the German representatives from the area. The significant paragraphs of Poland's report were as follows:

. . . Owing to a lesser area being planted and the considerably decreased unit production resulting from lack of fertilizers, improper cultivation, etc., the native crops in Belgium and France, as in most of Europe, are steadily decreasing. . . .

In Belgium we are endeavoring to provide, as heretofore, a ration of about 250 grams [of bread] per capita per day . . . to which are added extra amounts for child feeding, soups for the destitute, extra rations for heavy workers, etc. . . .

The total amount of wheat required . . . [by imports] is 68,000 tons per month.

. . . In France there are practically no native cattle . . . [or] milk . . . products . . . remaining. . . . The conditions in Flanders now closely approach those in France. . . .

In Belgium, owing to the lack of fodder, animal-fat products in the form of milk, butter, cheese, etc., and tallow have greatly decreased. . . .

Poor as the native crop of potatoes was last year, the prospects are that . . . it will be 25 per cent poorer this year. . . .

. . . If at any time the Holland importations are cut down, the overseas imports must be correspondingly increased. . . .

. . . Early in the year we made arrangements to import Norwegian herring . . . and have arranged to supply between 15,000 and 20,000 barrels [of] smoked herrings per month, which should produce from 1,000 to 1,500 tons net of fish. . . .

As all the reserves in Belgium, France and Rotterdam have been wiped out, it is essential that these be built up as rapidly as possible. . . .

POLAND

The C.R.B. program called for the import from overseas of a minimum of about 130,000 tons per month during our fourth year.

The conference succeeded in improving the management of the minor shipments from Holland. However, this operation was most troublesome. The Dutch had to be paid in guilders, of which the British and French could spare but few. Our Directors at one time negotiated a loan from the Dutch banks on the security of French bonds. The uncertainty of the financing made the supplies very irregular.

There was, however, an unusual run of herring on the Belgian coast at this time. The people not only used nets but waded into the surf with baskets. To the Belgians, it was a special intervention of the Almighty.

In July, 1918, trouble developed over the distribution of food in Northern France. The Comité du Nord had been greatly weakened by the departure or death of its principal members. We were therefore forced to reorganize the Comité, placing its central office in Brussels, where our Director, Baetens, and the protecting Spanish and Dutch Ministers could give more attention to its problems.

On August 14, under authority from the French Government, I issued the following directive:

The disorganization of the Comité . . . [du Nord] through the departure of so many of its members renders an immediate reorganization necessary. This reorganization will be effected as follows:

The representatives of the six districts, who are also presidents of the district committees, will comprise the Executive Committee of the Comité du Nord . . . together with the delegate of the Comité National . . . [of Belgium], who is at present Mr. Van Brée; the representative of the Commission for Relief in Belgium, at present Mr. Baetens; the general secretary and the secretary and the active president of the Comité [du Nord]. . . . This Executive Committee are to undertake the following duties:

1. The election of an active president, who should be resident in Brussels and for this office we nominate Mr. Le Blan. [And for president in the North of France, we nominate Mr. Labbé].

2. To fill all vacancies in the district representation in co-operation with the district committees.

3. While all general decisions as to matters of rationing, distribution policy, finance, and administration shall be subject to the approval of the C.R.B., the Executive Committee will have full authority and discretion in the [French] occupied territories to act to the best interests of the populations concerned, and for this purpose will give general instructions to the district committees, with discretionary powers as to the details of execution.

4. All communications with regard to the above matters, to and from the occupied territories, are to to be made exclusively through the channel of the C.R.B.

5. All questions involving the German guarantees and undertakings will, as at present, be under the protection of the Comité Hispano-Néerlandais.

Effective 1st September 1918.

HERBERT HOOVER

We often received kind words from the people we served. On September 21, the Comité du Nord, at a meeting in Brussels, dispatched this note to me:

The members of the Executive Committee of the Comité d'Alimentation du Nord de la France, meeting at Brussels, the 16th and 21st September 1918, once more express to the Commission for Relief in Belgium their feelings of real gratitude for the material and moral aid given to the inhabitants of Northern France during more than three years, and who, at the same time as they procure for the people the foodstuffs necessary to existence, permit them thus patiently to endure their unhappy fate;

The members of the Executive Committee address to their eminent President, Monsieur Herbert Hoover, and to all his devoted collaborators in the United States and in Europe, a testimonial of the profoundest admiration for the work accomplished;

They are conscious of the difficulties met with, particularly in the beginning of the last year, as well as of the almost superhuman efforts which had to be made to surmount them, and they express to the Commission for Relief in Belgium their sincere thanks and those of the inhabitants of the North of France, for all the efforts they have made in view of their ravitaillement, and are convinced that the general arrangements made to this effect have been dictated solely by the high interest of the cause in question.

The members of the Executive Committee place all their confidence in the Commission for Relief in Belgium, which has in its hands the fate of 1,600,000 French people remaining in the occupied territory, and for whom nine-tenth of their foodstuffs have to be imported from abroad.

CHAPTER 43

FINANCING THE COMMISSION

Our financial problems in the fourth year did not prove difficult as far as American subsidies were concerned. In November, 1917, I obtained an increase in our Congressional appropriations to $9,000,000 monthly for Belgium and $6,000,000 for the North of France. However, since the law provided that these funds had to be spent solely in the United States, we were constantly troubled by the problem of securing British and French funds sufficient to cover purchases of food in Holland and payments for neutral and Belgian shipping. At the beginning of the fourth year, we were in debt to the Banque Belge in London for more than £1,700,000.

In the meantime, Chevrillon was energetically working on the French Government for help and arranged a meeting for Poland and Shaler with French officials in Paris. At this conference the French Government agreed to contribute its share if Britain would do likewise. The gist of Poland's report to me was:

LONDON, 7 December 1917

MY DEAR HOOVER:

Shaler and I returned yesterday . . . we were successful in accomplishing every object of the journey.

The first and most important was to provide for the financing of the European expenditure along the lines indicated by your telegrams. Soundings of the British made it apparent that we could expect nothing from them until France had declared herself. . . . We . . . had a preliminary meeting with your friend Monsieur Homberg, who . . . presented to Minister Klotz a memorandum which had been drawn up. . . . The Minister finally agreed that France should assume the entire European cost of the ravitaillement of her own people, and one-half the cost of the ravitaillement of Belgium, provided England would do the same. He also authorized me, in order to protect the guilder exchange, to effect a loan in Holland in guilders for an amount which has since been fixed at 60,000,000 guilders at the best terms obtainable; France to put up the necessary collateral; England being requested to join with France in the transaction; the loan to be guaranteed by England, France, and Belgium. This seems the most satisfactory way of meeting the very difficult question of guilder exchange, but I must say I foresee great difficulties and think there is about one chance in ten of success. However, I shall proceed to Holland immediately and hope for the best.

We have not yet heard of England's acceptance of the French demand. . . .

. . . as a matter of fact we were in a perfectly desperate situation and for three or four days were absolutely bankrupt. We had to turn down an insurance cheque for £100,000 and had other payments of £90,000 and smaller amounts due which we were being urged to meet. . . .

POLAND

Finally, Poland and Chevrillon succeeded in getting the French Treasury to act independently of the British on the grounds that collapse of the Relief would not only bring infinite suffering to the Northern French but would also have political repercussions all over France. They obtained a check for £1,000,000 from the French Ministry of Finance.

Since Poland made no headway with the British Foreign Office on subsidies, we then instructed him from Washington to take up the matter with the Prime Minister Lloyd George. Poland's letters to the Prime Minister no doubt got lost in the crowded bureaucratic corridors of those intensely busy times. He received no replies.

In the meantime, however, Poland received a blow from the French Treasury; they canceled his £1,000,000 check, saying:

LONDON, 28 December 1917

DEAR MR. POLAND:

. . . In spite of my lively desire to help you under these terrible circumstances, and in spite of receiving the authorization given to me by Monsieur the Financial Minister to pay you £1,000,000 (one million pounds), to my great regret I find it impossible to advance to you even for two or three days the sum which is necessary to you. The end of the year is indeed burdened with such heavy payments that cannot be deferred and which will leave no margin to the sums at my disposal.

F. Avenol

Finally, I cabled the Prime Minister through Poland. With his usual good will, Mr. Lloyd George ultimately cleaned up the tangle. As a first step, on January 2, the Belgian Minister in London received a contribution from the British Treasury of £750,000 to our debt at the Banque Belge, as is shown in the following letter.

... London
2 January 1918

To His Excellency Baron Moncheur,
  Belgian Minister in London
Your Excellency:
  ... I am directed by the Lords Commissioners of His Majesty's Treasury to inform you that they are causing the sum of £750,000 to be transferred to the credit of the account of the Belgian Government at the Bank of England on the 2d inst.

John Bradbury

Eventually, no doubt on Lloyd George's intervention, the British, on January 5, agreed to provide a subsidy jointly with the French, albeit a reduced one.

CHAPTER 44

ANOTHER SHIPPING CRISIS

The measures of pressure on the neutrals which we had adopted enabled us greatly to increase delivery to the Belgians and the Northern French—temporarily—but we had to have more neutral charters for the coming months. Then a new obstruction was born. The Allied Governments and the United States had created an Inter-Allied Chartering Executive to handle all neutral charters. This Board took a dim view of our independent shipping arrangements with neutrals. They even attempted to take away some Swedish charters which we had obtained for the Relief in a trade for food from the United States.

The number of ships we needed was small compared to the total still in use by the neutrals for commercial trade. Poland complained of the interference of the Inter-Allied Chartering Executive to the British Foreign Office:

LONDON, 1 November 1917

The Under-Secretary of State for Foreign Affairs
DEAR SIR:

. . . I have just returned from an interview with the Secretary of the Inter-Allied Chartering Executive, who informs me that although we can rely on them to extend every assistance possible to the Relief, and that in view of the arguments presented it may be possible for them to confirm the several trip charters of the "Songa" and "Avona" which we had arranged, and to confirm the chartering of other Swedish vessels, still it is impossible for them to definitely assign, to the Relief, ships to make up the shortage of 10,000 tons for December and 40,000 tons for January.

364

In view of the above and the absolute necessity of this tonnage to insure the minimum living ration to the people of Belgium and Northern France, we beg that the Foreign Office will indicate to us how, in accordance with the understanding between the British and French Governments, the Relief is to be protected.

Action must be taken at once to avoid grave consequences.

POLAND

Because the C.R.B. was a sort of "stepchild" to all the shipping authorities at home and abroad, I concluded to appeal to a higher level. Colonel Edward M. House represented the United States on the Inter-Allied Council in Paris (later to be known as the Supreme War Council). I sent word to the Colonel through the State Department that we were in trouble and that I had directed Poland to go to Paris to explain our problems to him.

Poland arrived in Paris on November 22 and found Colonel House most helpful. Through his intervention and Poland's urging, the Inter-Allied Council passed the following resolution on November 29, 1917:

. . . The Allies declare that they give priority over all their own provisioning to the ravitaillement of the populations of Belgium and invaded Northern France, on the basis of the C.R.B. program, such as defined in the Conference held in London between the C.R.B. and the British Government. They guarantee the necessary tonnage for the execution of this program, taking into account the ships which the C.R.B. now have at its disposal and those which it may procure in the future either directly or with the help of the Allied Governments.

Colonel House arranged a meeting for Poland with Premier Clemenceau, and Poland reported to me on December 7 concerning these negotiations:

. . . At an interview with Monsieur Clemenceau, he expressed a desire to have the same evening a memorandum of some of the facts which were presented to him in regard to the Commission. . . .

We were told by various French officials that all of the evacués coming out of [Northern] France—and there are some 300,000 of them now—were united in praise of the American Commission and continually made statements that without our efforts the population would have succumbed.

It would have been impossible for the government officials or any of the French persons whom we met to have been more appreciative or sincere in their expressions of thanks. The gratitude of everyone was touching to the point of being embarrassing. . . .

I thought at the time that with this order from the Inter-Allied Council, our troubles were over. Not so. Any such thought implied that four nations, each with a dozen unco-ordinated departments engulfed in a veritable hurricane of clamor for ships, would mend their ways. The various Allied shipping committees, of course, promised daily to fulfill these demands.

We did not get the ships. To underscore the need for action on our behalf, Chevrillon prepared a long memorandum, which was transmitted to Premier Clemenceau. After reviewing the promises we had received, he continued:

. . . we have asked in vain that ships be assigned to us. For the last seven months the people of the invaded territories have only had three-quarters of the necessary living ration. The result has been actual or semi-starvation in many regions, a great increase in the death rate, a great decrease in the birth-rate, and, through hunger, the forcing of probably hundreds of thousands of high-class workmen and workwomen into the employ of the Germans, thereby releasing a corresponding number of recruits for the army. The morale of the whole population has necessarily been greatly reduced, and, despite the magnificent courage they have shown, almost they were forced to believe that their own compatriots and the Allies had ceased to care for them. We do not believe that the French, Belgian or English people can be held to a steadfast and indomitable prosecution of the war if this state of semi-starvation of the occupied territories ever again is allowed to recur.

Still we did not get the ships. I have mentioned in the Introduction to this fourth-year narrative the great shift in Allied strategy beginning in April, 1918, with their resulting imperative need for more ships. Nevertheless, I believed that it was an Allied duty to keep the ten million people of Belgium and Northern France alive. Moreover, the amount of shipping we needed was comparatively small in proportion to the whole Allied cargo fleet. On April 10, I made a vigorous protest to the President and the State Department about our treatment, demanding the promised sixty thousand tons of ships immediately. The State Department replied in these discouraging terms:

WASHINGTON, 15 April 1918

DEAR MR. HOOVER:

In Mr. Polk's absence I beg to refer again to your letter of the 10th instant to him with which you enclosed a copy of a letter that you had addressed to the President with reference to Belgian relief.

Pursuant to your request, cables were sent to the American Ambassadors at London and Paris and to the American Minister at Havre, requesting them to obtain the views of the governments to which they are accredited concerning the tonnage referred to in your letter.

The Department is in receipt this morning of cables from London and Paris, paraphrases of which I enclose herewith.

GORDON AUCHINCLOSS

The enclosures were:

From Paris.

The Ambassador was informed by the Foreign Office on April 13th that a conference would be called on the 23d instant in Paris for the purpose of settling the whole subject of tonnage. The necessity for administering relief to Northern France and Belgium is fully appreciated, although a preference was expressed for the use of the sixty thousand tons of shipping referred to for the transportation of troops.

From London.

I have just been sent the following answer from the Foreign Office:

"The Secretary of State for Foreign Affairs presents his compliments to the United States Ambassador, with reference to Mr. Page's memorandum number 514 of the 12th instant relative to a question of allocating 60,000 tons of shipping, either for the transportation of American troops and supplies to France or to the Belgian relief, has the honor to say that in the present circumstances it appears to His Majesty's Government to be of paramount importance that this tonnage should be devoted to military purposes. . . . There would be no objection on the part of His Majesty's Government to the Commission for Relief in Belgium being invited to charter further Swedish ships now in Sweden."

The recommendation regarding the Swedish ships had a hollow sound to us. The Swedes had already reminded us that despite the German guarantees, two Swedish ships in our employ had been torpedoed along our "safe" route to Rotterdam. Moreover, they had been losing ships in the Allied service and had concluded that they must retain their fleet for importing their own overseas supplies.

On April 18, Poland again submitted a memorandum reviewing our predicament to the Inter-Allied Council. After again explaining the desperate food situation in Belgium and Northern France, he pointed out our inability to get scarcely any charters for the coming months and added:

. . . The situation confronting the people of Belgium and France is the most serious since the war began.

By a decision of the Inter-Allied Council which met in Paris December 5th last, it was established that the relief requirements of Belgium and France, both as to food and ships, should have priority over all other Allied requirements. This has been put into practice as to foodstuffs [by the United States Food Administration] but in regard to shipping, while the principle has been acknowledged, the respective shipping executives have not given effect to the decision.

In the bare possibility that we might get Swedish ships, despite Sweden's earlier adamant stand, on May 1, I cabled Minister Whitlock at Le Havre as follows:

Under the present pressure for American troops to France there is no hope of saving Belgian relief except in one direction. There are some 300,000 tons of Swedish vessels idle in Swedish ports; all efforts to charter any of these for the Relief have so far failed. A personal appeal from King

Albert to the King of Sweden should be successful. We will secure full guarantees that if 120,000 tons are chartered to the Relief for six months or for longer they may return unmolested to Swedish ports on completion of their service, and bunkers will be provided. This is our only hope.

HOOVER

On instructions from me, Poland telegraphed Chevrillon on May 8:

. . . Urge Clementel insist through French representatives Maritime Council that action be taken. It becomes apparent real difficulty is that Ship Executives England, France and America are receiving equally imperative demands through War and other Departments and that we cannot expect results unless supreme authorities personally direct Relief requirements shall have preference in shipping. I believe it imperative that you secure that Monsieur Clemenceau himself shall inform State Department Washington and British Government that it is his desire Relief be given immediate priority. Similar effort being made Prime Minister England.

The Allies by now had moved to co-ordinate their own shipping more effectively and had reorganized their ship control through the creation of the Allied Maritime Council, of which the United States was a member. At a meeting in London, they referred us to another Inter-Allied body—the Wheat Executive—with pious words. At this, I instructed Poland as follows:

WASHINGTON, 8 May 1918

Poland, London

British authorities in London telegraphed British authorities here to help out Belgian Relief, and, as has been invariably case heretofore, this help consists in advising the American Government to do something when it is clearly obvious American Government has insufficient shipping to handle its own prime necessities. If the authorities really intend to carry out provisions Paris Conference the British authorities must instruct Guthrie [manager of the Wheat Executive] to turn over to Belgian Relief instantly specific neutral ships; otherwise you may take it that all expressions of priority or interest are absolutely valueless. . . . We require 40,000 tons deadweight shipping for May loading. . . .

HOOVER

On May 11, Poland cabled me this heartbreaking news:

LONDON, 11 May 1918

Hoover, Washington

. . . we understand on excellent authority that United States Shipping Board inquired of British War Office if they concurred in furnishing 60,000 tons required . . . and the British War Office replied they did not concur in this action.

It appears to us that this is the dividing of the ways and that the United States Government together with Great Britain has now to make the decision as to whether or not the people in Belgium and Northern France are to be fed. Purely as a war measure and independent of all considerations of humanity . . . we are sure the feeding of the people of the occupied territories is equally as important as the shipment of troops and food to Britain and France. We are sure that if this question were left to the decision of the public of Great Britain and the United States, Belgium and France would be fed. . . .

On May 15, Chevrillon advised Poland that

Clemenceau has telegraphed to Washington in most pressing terms [on continuation of the Relief], also to Lloyd George. Ministers Commerce and Foreign Office are jointly cabling High Commissioner Washington. . . .

Upon appealing to President Wilson, I learned that he, too, leaned toward the point of view of our own and Allied military leaders that the Relief came second to military needs. The situation seemed absolutely hopeless. I fully appreciated the military need, but I was responsible for ten million helpless people. I was confident that if I could get the matter to the attention of Prime Minister Lloyd George, I would get a different answer. Therefore I cabled our office in London to present to the Prime Minister the following message from me as Chairman of the Commission—not as an American Government official:

WASHINGTON, 16 May 1918

. . . "As Chairman of the Belgium Relief, I wish to again ask your personal intervention upon behalf of these suffering people. Three years ago, upon my personal appeal, you intervened to save the Relief and established it firmly as an unparalleled enterprise in humanity, with the full sympathy and generous financial support of the British peoples. That action, which cost much in sacrifice to the British people in its demonstration of their true and broad humane objectives in the war, became one of the most potent forces in the conviction of the American people of the Allies' just cause. At our adherence to the Allied cause our Government considered its obligations included a participation in the maintenance of these peoples who have suffered first and continue to suffer most from barbarism. . . . The problem today is ships. Our people have stripped to the bone to furnish transport of supplies and men for Allied support. We can furnish no tonnage unless sacrifice is made somewhere in these directions. The tonnage required is so pitiable . . . in the vast totals, as to seem to justify the risk. Today to consign the Belgian people to starvation after three and one-half years of almost unendurable suffering and steadfast loyalty and service in the Allied cause, is indeed a terrible fate. . . . I feel that without Your Excellency's intervention and positive instruction the Relief cannot be saved and a direction from yourself to your authorities and a communication of your approval of necessary diversions to our President would yield solution by our joint shipping authorities."

HOOVER

On May 20, I again pressed the matter with President Wilson, asking that the American Shipping Board provide half of the sixty thousand tons, little as that was. He agreed to help and gave the necessary orders. I cabled Poland:

WASHINGTON, 21 May 1918

Relief Commission, London

American Shipping Control in conformity with British 50-50 agreement have allotted steamers "Harold" 5,100, "Talbot" 11,700, "Storviken" 7,500, "Dicto" 6,000, and "Senta" 5,800. Also accept obligation additional 18,000 June-July loading, which will complete American quota. This sufficiently concrete evidence that British offer has been accepted. A ghastly situation in Belgium has thus been averted by the individual efforts of the C.R.B.

HOOVER

Lloyd George had again been our savior. I received the following cable from him:

LONDON, 23 May 1918

Herbert Hoover

I have received . . . your cable of May 16th. I had already conferred personally with the Belgian Prime Minister, Mr. Poland, and British officials, and I understand that you have since learned through the Allied Maritime Transport Council of our willingness to provide one-half of the tonnage necessary to make up the monthly shortages of the Commission for Relief. I am gratified to hear today that the United States Government have agreed to take similar action and that, therefore, there is now no necessity for me to communicate with President Wilson as suggested in your cablegram. . . .

His Majesty's Government maintain their deep solicitude for the people in occupied Belgium, and will spare no effort to relieve the privations they so gallantly endure. I am entirely in accord with the decision of the Inter-Allied Council that the relief requirements of Belgium and Northern France, both as regards food and ships, shall have priority over other Allied requirements, and I trust that the present joint action will assure the continuity of essential supplies.

I take this opportunity of saying how much I appreciate the lasting services you have rendered to all the Allies by your unfailing and effective efforts on behalf of the people of Belgium.

LLOYD GEORGE

As a matter of fact, it was the intervention of both Clemenceau and Lloyd George that saved the Relief—for a while.

Our real salvation came suddenly, from another quarter. The neutrals still had a great amount of tonnage beyond that needed to transport supplies for themselves, and they now concluded that C.R.B. voyages under German promises of immunity from attack were less dangerous than voyages for the Allies. The result was that by the first of June, 1918, the C.R.B. had obtained from the Norwegians, Dutch, Danes, and Swedes a fleet of 250,000 tons of shipping. At this point, the Allies suspended the "alternative," but from this moment on the Belgians were out of danger.

In July, 1918, I went to Europe to settle our food program for the coming year with the Allied Food Administrators. I relate those matters in detail in my narrative of the Food Administration.

Although there were delays in getting our new fleet in motion, we were able, thanks to our abundant American harvest of 1918 and this added shipping, to furnish adequate supplies to Belgium and Northern France until we were relieved of all anxieties by the German surrender.

To the gigantic attack of the Germans on the Western Front from March to July, 1918, the only answer was the immediate transport of the huge American armies from the United States to France, and that meant more and more ships. Since the neutrals held out on chartering their ships because of German threats, the only course open to the Allies, including the United States, was to requisition every neutral ship outside their home ports, making allowance for the imports they needed. There was ample moral justification for this action. The whole purpose of the Allies in the war was to preserve the rights and independence of the small nations. Some of these ships were obtained by the C.R.B., the neutrals being given the alternative of chartering to us or of serving the Allied military.

CHAPTER 45

OUR DIMINISHING TROUBLES
WITH THE GERMANS

All representation of the Relief Commission in matters connected with Germany had to be handled by our protectors, the Spanish and Netherlands Ministers and Ambassadors. In addition, Swiss Ministers and Consuls at our ports of departure issued the German safe-conduct passes for our ships, and the Swiss Government occasionally had to represent us at Berlin in these matters.

GERMAN TORPEDOES AND SEIZURES

During the first month of our fourth year, November, 1917, our ship *Haelen,* with a cargo of 4,299 tons of wheat, was seized by the Germans on the grounds that she was sailing in the prohibited zone. Through efforts of the Spanish Ambassadors, the case was tried in the German Prize Court, and on March 30, 1918, the equivalent of the *Haelen*'s cargo in food was furnished to the C.R.B.

On February 12, 1918, our ship the *Friedland,* carrying a cargo of 6,618 tons of wheat, was sunk by a German submarine. The statement by our London Office to Ambassador Merry del Val was as follows:

. . . The damage to the Relief Service by the violation of the German Authorities of their solemn agreement can hardly be measured in money, as it had the result of destroying confidence in the intentions of the German Government, of greatly increasing our insurance expenditure, and of rendering it almost impossible to effect neutral charters. The direct loss to the Commission, however, is estimated to have resulted in a minimum of $1,121,832.83.

The reply by the German Foreign Office to the Spanish Ambassador with regard to the *Friedland* was most evasive:

May 27, 1918

The Foreign Office has the honour to respectfully inform the Royal Spanish Embassy that, from the information received from the General Staff of the Navy in connection with the Note verbale of March 6, 1918 . . . no German submarine can come into question regarding the sinking of the Swedish steamer *Friedland*. The destruction therefore of the steamer can only be ascribed to mines and the vessel having struck one. . . . This being very probable for the reason that about two months later, almost in the same vicinity, another vessel belonging to the Commission for Relief, the *Flandres*, also struck a mine and foundered, and that no mines have been laid by German naval forces in the free channel.

The declarations of the crew, according to which they had observed the blow of a torpedo, are probably due to self-deception caused by fact that jets of water were forced up by the air which escaped from the vessel, which was on the point of sinking. . . .

The statement made that the second explosion occurred just at that point where the lifeboats lay clearly proves that a mine must have been the cause of this explosion and not a torpedo, as otherwise the course of the torpedo must have in any case been observed.

From our information we did not believe a word of this statement.

On March 18, our London office appealed to Ambassador Merry del Val to secure the release of one of our chartered ships, the *Prinsessen Ingeborg*, which had been seized by the Germans on her outward journey from Rotterdam and taken into Kiel. The Ambassador was successful in securing the return of the ship.

Mr. Poland furnished our Spanish Patrons with another incident of the Germans' firing on one of our ships:

On August 30, 1918 the Norwegian steamer *Bjornsterne Bjornson* sailed from New York with a cargo of 5,268 tons of wheat for the Commission in Rotterdam. The Captain was furnished with a German safe-conduct pass. The vessel was attacked by a German submarine outside the limits of the German danger zone on September 14th 1918 at 2:30 p.m. At the time of the attack there were displayed all the recognised markings of the Commission for Relief in Belgium, as above described.

The testimony shows that the attack could not be excused on the ground of mistake on the part of the German submarine commander, or of inattention or neglect on the part of the ship. In all, eight shots were fired, resulting in certain damage to the ship and entailing delay in her progress to Rotterdam.

When there arose in Belgium the question of the disposition of the 1918 crops, the Spanish and Dutch Ministers in Brussels secured the same undertakings as those of 1917.

By early October, 1918, it was evident that the German armies were cracking up. The Germans asked for an Armistice on October 4. Their demoralized armies were in full retreat, evacuating Lille on October 17. On October 18, the King of the Belgians returned to Ostend.

There now arose the problem of how to provision the population of Northern France and that of Southern Belgium behind the retreating Germans, since transport of supplies from Rotterdam was cut off. Poland obtained 20,000,000 military rations valued at about $4,500,-000 from the British Army. The British promptly demanded that these rations be paid for by the United States because they were partially comprised of food which had come from us. We arranged for payment by the United States.

The Germans made speedy retreat under President Wilson's ultimatums, and the C.R.B.'s troubles with them were over.

CHAPTER 46

STATISTICAL RESULTS FOR THE FOURTH YEAR

The following tables show the monthly deliveries of supplies (351 cargoes) to Rotterdam for both Belgium and Northern France during our fourth year. They indicate the privations of the people and their salvation at mid-year.

Month 1917	Tons Arrived Rotterdam
November	118,863
December	83,433
1918	
January	72,482
February	72,599
March	60,070
April	85,445
May	68,597
June	72,260
July	104,088
August	125,899
September	75,553
October	151,889
Total	1,091,178

The following were the commodities delivered, in tons:

Commodities	Belgium	Northern France	Other Destinations[1]
Wheat and Rye	331,744	80,878	89
Flour	127,739	47,773	10
Maize (corn)	95,035	17,430	202
Lard Oil, Grease	40,029	20,977	6
Peas and Beans	46,371	17,133	11
Rice and Rice Substitutes	27,278	14,685	9
Meat, Bacon, Ham	19,513	21,078	26
Barley	23,595	2,090	2,450
Condensed Milk	5,395	16,082	6
Sugar	—	14,500	—
Coffee	4,430	5,279	1
Fish	6,369	2,566	—
Soap	2,620	5,027	2
Cocoa	1,987	3,110	—
Clothing	2,661	742	—
Butter and Cheese	1,394	1,347	—
Yeast Materials	2,378	—	—
Automotive Supplies	151	126	42
Miscellaneous (mostly for Children)	13,185	18,560	72
Total	751,874	289,383	2,926

Stocks in Rotterdam totaled 89,987 tons on November 1, 1918.

NATIVE FOOD SUPPLIES OBTAINED

In addition, under the agreements with the Germans against requisitioning of native food production, the crops of 1918 in Belgium and Northern France yielded the Relief about 274,000 tons of grain, together with potatoes and other vegetables.

[1] The "Other Destinations" were sales from wrecked ships.

DUTCH SUPPLIES

We obtained from Holland about 10,000 tons—mostly vegetables and fish.

OUR SHIP LOSSES

During our fourth year, five of our ships were torpedoed by the Germans; four were sunk or damaged by mines; four were lost from other or unknown causes.

The detailed record was:

Steamer	Tons of Food Lost	Cause of Loss
Haelen[2]	4,299	Seized by the Germans
Clangula	100	Torpedoed by the Germans
Imo	In ballast	Explosion in Halifax
Friedland	6,618	Torpedoed by the Germans
Min'str de Smet	In ballast	Sunk by a mine
Flandres	In ballast	Sunk by a mine
Eole	3,649	Damaged by a mine
New Sweden	In ballast	Torpedoed by the Germans
Gasconier	4,433	Sunk by a mine
Sydland	In ballast	Torpedoed by the Germans
Mathilda	5,730	Torpedoed by the Germans
Keltier	In ballast	Disappeared
Tyr	3,579	Fire at sea
Syrie	3,580	Disappeared

We therefore lost about 30,000 tons of food en route during our fourth year. The loss of ships in ballast meant the loss of food which could have been transported by them on return and later voyages. Thus the real loss was greater than the tonnage of food actually sunk.

Bad as the situation was for the six months from January to June, there was little death from starvation, and the 2,500,000 children in our canteens were fully cared for.

[2] Through efforts of the Spanish Ambassadors, the cargo was released to the Commission on March 30.

CHAPTER 47

WHAT WENT ON INSIDE BELGIUM
AND NORTHERN FRANCE

We had constant insight into what was going on in Belgium and Northern France from our staff in Belgium through our Rotterdam office. That information was of daily value to us in Washington because it revealed the increasing failure of German food and raw-material supplies. They, however, held fairly well to their guarantees concerning the native food supplies and our imports.

From time to time, I was able to correspond with Francqui, and these letters have considerable interest for their summations of the problems of the C.R.B. and the Comité National. These communications were infrequent, since they could only be transmitted when an opportunity free from German perusal was possible.

WASHINGTON, 24 January 1918

MY DEAR FRANCQUI:

Our situation when we started the Relief was one of anxiety only as to finance; later on we added the anxiety of shipping, and now we have to add another and even greater anxiety than either of the other two—and that is the food supply. . . .

In the matter of foodstuffs, the exportable balance of wheat from America [statistically] is exhausted. We have not the shipping to go to more remote markets. . . . You will be astonished to realize that I [as United States Food Administrator] am now putting the American people on a practical rationing of many of the commodities most urgently needed in Europe. . . .

As my department practically controls the despatch of foodstuffs from the United States, you may be assured that the Belgian Relief will have full priority in shipments. . . . We must load whatever character of food we may have available at the time, and therefore you may expect to receive some shiploads of flour, some shiploads of corn, and some shiploads of wheat, but we will try to make up a total quantity sufficient for you to struggle through.

. . . [C.R.B.] has an office next door to mine in this department and is a matter of constant solicitude. You and I thought from time to time, in years gone by, that we had overcome almost overwhelming difficulties—I am afraid the difficulties ahead of us are even greater. . . . The next six months are the most difficult period that we will have to face, because every indication promises enormously increased production from . . . [the 1918 harvest] all of which will be realizable in the last half of this year.

I cannot speak too highly of the single-minded devotion which Messrs. Poland, Honnold, Brown, Gray, Rickard, and Shaler still give to the management of the Relief work after all these years. Positions much more attractive from a public point of view have been offered to these men, and the constancy with which they are giving this service without profit to themselves is beyond any experience that I have hitherto had in dealing with men.

I trust that you and your people may keep good courage. All that is humanly possible is being done for Belgium. . . .

HERBERT HOOVER

Francqui could not have known of our extreme difficulties in American food shortages.

April 2, 1918

MY DEAR HOOVER:

. . . Your letter arrived at the time when, owing to the progressive lack in the importation of cereals, we were forced to reduce the consumption of bread. This day, which we had seen coming with real anguish, has arrived. Since the 15th March the bread ration was reduced from 330 grammes to 250 grammes. This is all the more painful because this reduction of the ration had to be made at a period of the year when resources of native foodstuffs are at their lowest; this is particularly the case as regards potatoes, the stocks of which are completely exhausted, our populations in the large towns having been completely deprived of them for several months.

The Belgian population accepted the measure taken with the resignation which characterises the sick man who feels his end approaching. [You will understand] that under present circumstances the decision we have just taken is a calamity for the working and bourgeois population whose physical distress has become lamentable, particularly in the towns. This population had need, more than ever, of pulse and fats; to replace the lack of wheat, it is necessary therefore to send us, particularly, beans, rice and maize.

But it is no longer necesary for me to plead with you the cause of 7½ millions of Belgians and 2½ millions of French. You have made yourself their champion with the Allied Governments. . . .

The estimates of importations for April and May are not, unfortunately, reassuring. We are told of an importation of 50,000 to 55,000 tons of cereals for April and even less for May. . . .

We appreciate more than we can express the disinterested devotion of your London colleagues, and at Rotterdam. I also have seen them at work during over three years and I have had occasion several times to speak with them. They are men of noble heart and indefatigable energy—worthy of their Chief.

Your letter revived in my recollection our hopes and efforts at the commencement. Which of us would have dreamt at that time of the mountains of difficulties which we should have to surmount! And the more time passes the more difficult does the task become, particularly for you, my dear Hoover.

The political and military events which pass bring us continually fresh surprises. They prove to us that we can only congratulate ourselves, you and I, on having defended the cause of the ravitaillement of the Belgian population, for I hope that the day is not far when we shall see the apex of the work which has assured the existence and the future of the Belgian people more than any military decisions.

E. FRANCQUI

May 6, 1918

MY DEAR HOOVER:
. . . The crisis we are going through at present is certainly the worst since the debut of the Relief. You know already that for a month and a half the

ration of bread of the minimum programme was reduced 25%. We are on the eve of having to reduce it further, from 250 to 180 grammes. I know well, that in the neighboring countries they have not fared much better, as regards the bread ration. But there, failing bread, the population can at least eat other things. In Belgium, this compensation is no longer possible. For a long time now, the bread has been the element representing the greatest nutritive value of the ration. The day that we are forced to distribute no more than 180 grammes, the alimentary value of the general ration will be only 1,000 calories, hardly that, even allowing that the mass of the population can still procure for themselves some indigenous foodstuffs.

Moreover, this day is imminent. Our present resources in cereals for bread-making will barely suffice to furnish the ration of 250 grammes up to the end of May. As for new consignments of cereals which were announced to us, they could only be made into bread as for the first ten days of June. That is to say, if we maintain the reduced ration as at present at 250 grammes we risk being completely without bread a whole week in the beginning of the next month. . . .

The Belgian population depends on us more than ever, my dear Hoover, to deliver them from famine. For, I say it without the least exaggeration, it is real famine which reigns in Belgium. Never a day passes that some one does not die of hunger in Brussels. The hospitals are crowded with patients having no further illness but denutrition. I know your great heart. If you could, as do the gentlemen of the Spanish Dutch Committee, make a little tour amongst the populations of our towns and over industrial centres you would come back, as they do, with tears in your eyes. These people, our hope of tomorrow, are condemned to a slow decay.

May the months of June and those following bring us days of less anguish than the month of May seems to presage for us.

E. FRANCQUI

Francqui's anguish was soon to be relieved. With our greatly increased fleet and our abundant harvest, I was able, in July, to transmit cheer and assurance that ample supplies were at last assured.

I visited Britain and France in July to attend a conference of Allied Food Administrators, and while there, I received many messages of thankfulness and gratitude from our colleagues in Belgium and Northern France, including one from Cardinal Mercier.

With the retreat of the German armies in mid-October, the revolution in Germany, and the obviously approaching end of hostilities, the question of continuing the C.R.B. after the war was raised with Poland by both the Belgians and the French. I, however, postponed any decisions until my arrival in Europe in November, and thus these decisions appear in the narrative of our fifth year.

FIFTH YEAR

From the Armistice, November 11, 1918, to September 30, 1919

CHAPTER 48

PRESIDENT WILSON DIRECTS CONTINUED AID TO BELGIUM AND NORTHERN FRANCE

Even while the new German Republic was asking for the Armistice, a dying ember of their armies' brutalities flared up. In the Germans' retreat through Northern France, they destroyed the French coal mines. On November 2, I received word from Belgium that they had ordered the destruction of the Belgian coal mines. At once I addressed President Wilson as follows:

2 November 1918

DEAR MR. PRESIDENT:

I am informed through our correspondents this morning that the Germans in Belgium have given notice to the coal mines to the effect that all men and animals should be brought out of the pits, all raw materials in possession of companies to be delivered to the Germans and that the mines will be destroyed at once. They have already started in two places in Belgium.

I can scarcely express the concern that I feel over this matter. It means the loss of an absolutely vital necessity to these people over the coming winter. It will result in enormous loss of human life. It seems to me hardly in accord with the professions recently made by the German government in their communications to you.

I have not had a great deal of faith in protests but it does seem to me that if you could see your way to point out in a note to the Germans that this does not accord with their professions; that it means the most terrible of human hardships; that it is absolutely wanton and that the continuation of this policy will necessitate the imposition of a greater

387

burden upon the German people at the hands of the Allies. It might be that it would cause them to hesitate and at least appears to me could do no harm.

HERBERT HOOVER

The President sent word through the Allied Military Mission, then negotiating the Armistice, which stopped this villainy.

Although technically it belongs in the account of our fourth year, to provide an understanding of what follows, I include here a letter which I addressed to the President on October 21, making recommendations for continued operations by the C.R.B. and its finance in case we continued.

WASHINGTON, 21 October 1918

DEAR MR. PRESIDENT:

The task of the Belgian Relief Commission—the preservation of the life of 10,000,000 occupied Belgians and French over these four years—is now rapidly drawing to [a] conclusion, and questions as to what further assistance should be extended to these people and as to what organization should be set up are pressing. . . .

The released French population can be best cared for by their own Government . . . and I do not therefore consider that we need concern ourselves therewith.

The Belgian people, while more fortunate than the Serbians and Poles in that they are all alive, [will] come out of occupation undernourished, underhoused, underclothed, industrial plants ruined, without raw material, and without resources in shipping and money to find a remedy.

There is immediate need for 550,000 tons of shipping, of which 350,000 are now in use by the Relief Commission. The Allied Governmental aid needs to be at once increased from about $15,000,000 per month at present being given (of which our Government furnishes $9,000,000) to about $30,000,000 per month. With these resources over twelve to eighteen months I believe the people could be made self-supporting.

Assuming this must be accomplished, the problem of organization at once arises. . . . I need hardly mention that . . . myself and my colleagues . . . would like to have relief from this especially poignant anxiety that has now extended over four years.

With the present misery and economic difficulties facing Europe there can be little hope of Belgian recuperation without the major help coming from the United States. . . .

If the matter were undertaken by the Belgian Government alone, they would naturally have to take their position with the other needy Allied Governments under the various Allied controls; whereas, if a distinctly American organization, maintained by the American Government, were to be installed for this service, such an organization could easily secure the same [services] in obtaining priorities and supplies, and complete independence of action from other Allied control that it now possesses.

. . . If American participation in [the] organization of rehabilitation is to be maintained it would seem logical to continue it through the Relief Commission whose organization is in action and simply requires larger resources, and the use of these media would avoid discussion of any new instrumentality with the Allied Governments. It would represent the rounding out of an enterprise of our people toward another in which we could have lasting pride.

One of the objectives in peace conferences must be the repayment, in addition to other damages, to Belgium of the whole of the sums that have been spent by the Relief Commission, together with such further moneys as are spent on rehabilitation. It would appear to me that it would be a pointed and positive lesson to the world for all future time if it could be made a peace condition that the expenditures of the . . . Commission both in the past and in the future are made repayable by the Germans, directly to the Relief Commission, and that this Commission should refund the sums advanced by the various governments.

I should be glad to have your views in the matter, and if you consider [that] the Commission should be continued to this new purpose and that it will have the support of . . . [our] Government, it is desirable that its relations to [the] Belgian and other governments should be properly defined.

HERBERT HOOVER

On November 6, 1918, after verbal discussions, he addressed the following letter to Secretary of State Lansing:

DEAR MR. SECRETARY:

In view of the approaching evacuation of Belgium and the new problems that confront this unfortunate people, I have asked Mr. Hoover to expand the activities of the Commission for Relief in Belgium to cover the entire relationship of this Government, and possibly that of other governments, together with all American public charity, to the whole business not only of food but also clothing, raw material, tools, machinery, exchange and other economic relief involved in the reconstruction of Belgium.

I would be obliged if your Department would give him all support and cooperation in this matter and refer to him for guidance in all questions of an economic order that arise in any connection between Belgium and this country.

On November 7, 1918, the President approved the program I had proposed:

THE WHITE HOUSE, WASHINGTON
7 November 1918

DEAR MR. HOOVER:

The probable early evacuation of Belgium brings us face to face with the problem of this distressed people, not only in regard to continued food relief, but also with regard to the many questions of economic rehabilitation. The initial task of preserving the bare lives of the people during German occupation, undertaken four years ago under your direction, is now nearing completion. I believe that the American people will willingly accept a large share of the burden of assisting in the now all-important work of reconstruction and rehabilitation, pending repayment by Germany for the injury done.

In order that such assistance should be exerted in the most liberal, efficient, and comprehensive manner, I feel that it should be organized under a single agency, which may co-ordinate the whole effort of the American people and Government, in the furnishing of supplies, machinery, finance, exchange, shipping, trade relations, and philanthropic aid. I also feel that such an agency, in addition to being the sole vehicle of supplies, should also have some proper participation in the expenditure and distribution of assistance. Such unity of administration would give much greater assurance of proper assistance and should be effective in preventing profiteering.

The large experience of the Belgian Relief Commission, the character of its organization without profit, its established use of shipping, and the sympathetic bond which it now forms with the Belgian people point to its continuation and enlargement as the natural agency for this purpose. I should therefore be glad if you and your colleagues of the Commission would undertake this extended work.

I understand that it is also the wish and purpose of the English and French people to participate in carrying this burden. It would seem to me desirable to inquire if these Governments would not therefore continue and enlarge their present support to the Commission to these ends, so that we may have a comprehensive and efficient agency for dealing with the entire problem on behalf of all.

It is of course of primary importance that our assistance in this expenditure and organization shall be built upon co-operation with the Belgian Government and the use of such internal agencies and methods as may be agreed upon with them, to whom our whole solicitude is directed.

It is also of first importance that the expenditure of all the philanthropic aid of the American people toward Belgium, of whatever character, should be conducted by or under the control of the Commission, if duplication and waste are to be avoided.

With a view to the advancement of these ideas, I have addressed a note to the various departments of our Government, indicating my wish that all matters relating to these problems should be undertaken under your guidance and that they should give to you every co-operation.

I wish you to proceed at once with the undertaking so far as it relates to the United States, and I should be glad if you would, through the proper agencies, take up a discussion of these matters with the Belgian Government and with the English and French Governments as to their relationship and participation.

WOODROW WILSON

Not to bother the President any more than was necessary in the midst of his arduous negotiations for an armistice, I replied to him by letter:

November 9, 1918

DEAR MR. PRESIDENT:

In enlarging the functions of the Belgian Relief Commission to cover the entire reconstruction and relief programme for Belgium, I would like to suggest for your approval the following matters. . . .

Under the present powers of the government, the Treasury is able to make advances to the Allied governments. . . . It would seem to me a right interpretation of the law for the Treasury to undertake to furnish $200,-000,000 to the Belgian government and stipulate that the money is to be used for expenditures in the United States through the Relief Commission. It appears to me that the prevention of starvation and disturbances in this population is vital to the making of the status quo during armistice, and is therefore a legitimate advance under the present law. . . . I would propose that these advances should be subject to the Belgian Government's finding from other governments all monies necessary to pay transportation charges on any materials shipped from here and to find monies from other quarters for all purchases made outside the United States.

I would be very glad indeed to have your views in the matter.

HERBERT HOOVER

The President approved this proposal, and two days after the signing of the Armistice, I addressed Secretary of the Treasury William G. McAdoo, transmitting the President's directive of November 7 and outlining our requirements:

WASHINGTON, 13 November 1918

DEAR MR. SECRETARY:

In accordance with the approval of the President at today's conference, I beg to confirm that the Treasury will increase advances for food and clothing to the Relief through the Belgian Government up to a maximum of $20,000,000 per month and to make such provisions as would give three months' notice before termination of this arrangement.

. . . I realize the pulls on the Treasury at this time and, to some degree, the difficulties under which the Treasury operates . . . on the other hand, these measures are vital not only to the maintenance of the state of war, but in the continuance of our future policies in Europe. The advances would obviously need to be made to the Belgian Government through the Belgian Minister, and he is presenting a program of this order.

I believe that the Belgian Government should provide for the funds from other quarters for transportation and distribution of this program, and Mr. Davis[1] and I will endeavor to insist upon this provision in Europe.

HERBERT HOOVER

The Secretary made the necessary financial arrangements.

[1] Norman Davis had been appointed the Treasury Agent for Europe and accompanied me on my journey.

WE SETTLE C.R.B. RELATIONS WITH THE BELGIANS

I arrived in London on November 23, twelve days after the Armistice was signed, and was engaged there for several days negotiating the organization of the Reconstruction and Relief of Europe.

On November 28, I arrived in Brussels, accompanied by Poland, our European Director of the C.R.B., and Hugh Gibson, who had been delegated to my service by the State Department.

Six days before my visit, the King had returned to Brussels amid great acclaim. No leader of people merited it more. The same day, he assembled the Parliament and announced a new Ministry. All but five members of the old Le Havre Ministry were retired.

Leon Delacroix, a man of great distinction, became Prime Minister, with a Cabinet of eminent personalities. His Ministry embraced many men who had served with us in Belgium during the war. The most distinguished of them all was Emile Francqui.

We at once went into conference with the Prime Minister, Francqui, and Van Brée of the Comité National. We first reviewed the problems of Reconstruction. The Belgians did not place as much emphasis on their needs as I had expected before leaving Washington. They said that they had skilled and willing labor, that enough industry could be quickly restored to enable them to manufacture the industrial equipment which had been destroyed or taken away by the Germans, and that they could finance most of their internal costs. They stressed that their major need was the financing of continued imports of food and some raw materials until they could rebuild their exports and become self-supporting. The sums needed were much less than President Wilson's authorization.

WE PROPOSE A PLAN FOR WITHDRAWAL
OF THE C.R.B.

The members of our C.R.B. staff in Europe and at Le Havre all longed to return home to try to re-establish themselves in their professions. Moreover, we had no desire to impose American officials on the Belgians.

We therefore proposed that the Belgian Government and the Comité National appoint some Belgian to each position in the C.R.B. and that we simply take our pipes and walk out. The Belgians would thus have, ready made, a fleet of ships and an organization for the purchase and transport of raw materials and food. We also suggested that they could take our cash in hand and settle with the representatives of the American Treasury the details of further subsidies which our government was willing to give. They could liquidate our accounts with the subsidizing governments; they could apply any residues from our profits and our charity receipts to public purposes. All we wanted to take with us was our name—The Commission for the Relief of Belgium—and a guarantee against outstanding liabilities.

Alternatively, I suggested that Belgium could become a part of the new organization for the Relief and Reconstruction of Europe, which would purchase, transport, and finance the dollar cost of their supplies.

The Belgians insisted that they could not spare the outstanding men necessary to take over our jobs and added that they wanted to remain independent of any general scheme for the Relief and Reconstruction of Europe. They urged that they needed the continuation and protection of the C.R.B. in order not to be crowded out by other nations clamoring for postwar help. Finally, we reluctantly agreed to go on temporarily.

We believed that we would be able to get Belgium's industrial wheels moving within three months and then liquidate the C.R.B. But the liquidation, as it turned out, required years. However, we were soon able to simplify our operations by having the Belgians take over railway and canal transport, our warehouses, and the control of processing and distribution.

The C.R.B. no longer had to deal with or watch the Germans. We could ignore the process of obtaining permission from the Allies to pass through the blockade. With the abundant American harvest of 1918, we had no worry over food supplies.

For a time, we were relieved of shipping difficulties by loading

American supplies on return voyages of the ships which had brought home the men and equipment of the American Army. However, shipping troubles soon began again as all nations rushed to restore their commercial trades. I give an account of these difficulties in my later narrative of the Relief and Reconstruction of Europe.

The Relief organization quickly won relief for itself from another direction. In Belgium, at the time of the Armistice, at least 60 per cent of the labor force was unemployed, and more than four million people were destitute and on the charitable rolls of the Relief. Eager to work, these people started to clean up the German wreckage overnight. Factories and mines were opened, railways and canals repaired, and within sixty days the number of destitute decreased to a few hundred thousand. Thus our C.R.B. labors were reduced to finance, purchase, overseas transportation, supplies, and a vast amount of accounting.

We had no need for an extensive American staff in Belgium. I persuaded Poland to stay on as Director in London, Walter Brown as Director at our new base in Antwerp, and I appointed an old C.R.B. hand, Fred H. Chatfield, as our sole representative in Brussels, and Edgar Rickard continued in New York.

CHAPTER 49

WE CONTINUE THE C.R.B.
IN THE NORTH OF FRANCE

Gibson, Poland, and I returned to Paris from Belgium on November 30, 1918, and at once took up Relief matters with the French Minister of Agriculture, Victor Boret, his Food Administrator, Ernest Vilgrain, and the Minister of Blockade, A. Lebrun.

Since Vilgrain had a functioning organization which was looking after 93 or 94 per cent of the French people, we proposed that he stretch it to include the 6 or 7 per cent of the people then remaining in the North of France and that we should retire within a month.

The French presented many arguments on why the C.R.B. must continue. The whole political organization above the commune level, except in a few cities, had been destroyed, and the only co-ordinated organization existing was the C.R.B. and the remainders of our old French Committees. A further argument cited to us was that two million refugees would be returning home from Belgium or from German prison camps, along with deported French workmen.

The railways and canals north of the old Hindenburg Line had been destroyed by the Germans in their retreat, and supplies would have to reach the North of France via Belgian railways and canals. It was apparent that the French Government could not handle this situation for some months.

We finally agreed to go on but stipulated that the French should furnish us with the necessary wheat and other cereals from their stocks in the South of France and transport them to Antwerp and Dunkirk. We stipulated that the French Government should supply us with exchange to pay our European outlays for both Belgium and

Northern France and that they should arrange any necessary loans from the United States to finance our purchases in the United States, all of which they agreed to do—and did.

WE RESUME

Unlike the case of Belgium, where the machinery of government was now functioning vigorously, we were compelled to set up elaborate American supervision in the North of France. The population, having gone through four years of German occupation and the holocaust of the retreating German armies, seemed to have lost all energy and initiative. We had to reinvigorate our Communal Committees in their old job of rationing and care of the destitute.

With General Pershing's approval, I recruited our old C.R.B. Northern France hands, who had joined the American Army when we entered the war. All these men, because of their character and their knowledge of France and its language, had been given commissions in our Army. Many of them had distinguished themselves in the war.

I placed Hallam Tuck in charge in Northern France. Of former C.R.B. staff members who came back as Assistant Directors or in charge of districts were Perrin Galpin, C. G. Bowden, M. M. Brown, E. D. Curtis, F. Exton, A. C. B. Fletcher, G. S. Jackson, R. A. Jackson, T. B. Kittredge, C. N. Leach, A. L. Malabre, W. H. Sperry, F. D. Stephens, C. M. Torrey, L. C. Wellington, F. C. Wickes, and R. C. Wilson.

We arranged with the French Ministry to set up a new French Committee to replace the remnants of the old Comité du Nord, but we stipulated that it must include Labbé and Le Blan as President and Chairman. It was named the *Comité General de Ravitaillement des Regions Libérées (Comité Libérées* for short).

By a circuitous motor trip to and from Brussels, we were able to inspect the major part of the old areas where we would have to administer again. Many of the large towns, such as Ypres, La Basseé, Bailleul, St. Quentin, Lens, and Armentières, were either totally destroyed or uninhabitable. The beautiful old city of St. Quentin had scarcely one house left. There was hardly a factory standing in the whole region.

Almost all the locks and nearly all the bridges over the Lys and Scheldt canals had been blown up. Apparently, the entire network of railways and canals would be useless for months. There was a belt some fifteen miles wide and four hundred miles long following the old trenches across the whole of France in which there were scarcely any inhabitants, and the land would be unproductive for years to come.

To handle transportation, pending the restoration of the railroads and canals, General Pershing lent me a multitude of trucks, with the use of American drivers until we recruited Frenchmen.

We also had to cope with the returning refugees. These two million men, women, and children streamed down the broken roads from every direction, seeking their old homes, only to find many destroyed.

To solve the refugee problem, we sought aid from our never failing friend, Admiral W. S. Benson, Commander of the American Navy in Europe. The Admiral at once delegated to us Vice Admiral Thomas Craven and as many officers and sailors as were needed. He gave us a huge amount of lumber and unassembled barracks and furniture. Admiral Craven and his men began erection within ten days and in a month more had the whole refugee problem on the way to a temporary solution, with the C.R.B. furnishing trucks and food. In reply to a press inquiry from the United States, I summarized the situation in this statement:

PARIS, 28 December 1918

. . . The C.R.B. had hoped to surrender the Relief of Northern France to the French Government immediately upon German retreat. It has been found, however, impossible for the French Government to undertake the food supply of this area for some months to come, and upon the urgent request of the Government the C.R.B. has decided to continue.

After four years' paralysis of wholesale and retail business; with the destruction of the principal towns and shops, these trades have disappeared and the people are today dependent upon a ration issued directly to them just as before the German evacuation.

Twenty of the members of the C.R.B. who joined the American Army as officers have been released by General Pershing to undertake this work.

Transportation connection is maintained with the region through Dunkirk and through one Belgian canal still operating, supplemented by motor trucks originally installed by the armies and now being gradually taken over by the C.R.B.

The population in this area at the moment of the retreat was about one and a half millions, there also being about 300,000 [French] refugees in Belgium who are returning, and [also] some 500,000 refugees in [Southern] France, [together with the freed war prisoners from Germany] all of whom are anxious to return to their native soil.

The destruction of some twenty principal towns and literally hundreds of villages renders the return of these refugees a stupendous problem. Every effort is being made to restrain them from going back until some systematic prior provision of shelter can be made. They, however, evade all official urging and the roads are a continuous procession of these pitiable . . . [groups]. Thousands of them reach their villages to find every vestige of shelter destroyed and finally wander into the villages farther back from the acute battle area, which are already overcrowded to a heartbreaking degree.

In order to remedy this situation to some extent, the Relief Commission has secured 150 volunteers from the American Navy and is taking over a large amount of secondhand barrack material from the Navy and Army, and these barracks are in course of erection adjacent to the destroyed villages under the superintendence of naval volunteers.

A large amount of boots and shoes and warm clothing have been taken over from the Quartermaster's supplies, and are being distributed to the people. The French Government is endeavoring to obtain some cattle from Switzerland and horses from the various armies, which, together with the meager supply of agricultural implements, may enable the population to get in some portion of next year's crop in those areas that are not too badly destroyed by battle.

The entire industrial life of the region has been destroyed by the Germans. There is scarcely a single factory that can be operated without a very large portion of new equipment. The coal mines are totally destroyed, and the network of railways in this region rendered almost hopeless of reconstruction for many months. The German method of destruction was to bend every single rail by exploding a hand-grenade under it, rendering it useless for all time. The Grand Canal du Nord, which connects this section of France with the Belgian canal system and is the natural entreport for goods from Antwerp or Rotterdam, was itself practically the fighting line for months and is so badly destroyed that it will take fully a year for its complete reconstruction.

The relief is based upon the allowance of food to the value of about 35 cents per day to the destitute, those having any resources or employment being required to pay. The problem of destitution is not yet known but appears to be fully 60 per cent of the people.

The French Government is supplying some food from France to the Relief Commission and the imports required from the United States . . . [are very large].

On December 10, I established the headquarters of the United States Food Administration in Paris to correlate all American supplies to Europe. From this same office we conducted the Belgian Relief, the Relief of Northern France, and the Relief and Reconstruction of Europe.

THE C.R.B. BECOMES THE WORLD'S GREATEST GROCERYMAN—AND AT A PROFIT

The organizational structure of the Relief during the war had been built around the idea of selling rations to those who could pay and using this money to care for the destitute. In setting the prices of food under the rationing system, we had added a small margin to cover unexpected expenses or destruction and to enable us to level off rising world prices.

It will be remembered that our whole organization—Americans, Belgians, and French—were volunteers. About the only paid staff were accountants and clerks. The multitude of Belgian and French women who did the detailed distribution work received no more than free rations. Our office space was mostly free—from generous business firms. Our shipping and purchasing agents worked without their usual fees. The Belgian Government now sold our rations at no cost to us.

It quickly dawned on the population south of us in France that our prices on bread, fats, sugar, and so forth were much lower in the former occupied areas in the north. They complained to the Paris Government and commented caustically and critically on its Food Administration. The very direct French mentality quickly found a solution that was simple in nature. The French authorities in Paris requested that we raise our prices to the level of those of the people to the south of us. The Belgian Government, fearful of the rise in prices when normal commercial distribution was re-established, also asked us to raise our prices to the French level. We did so.

We could dispose of the flood of French francs which came to our hands in the North of France partly because of the widespread destitution and the dire needs of the refugees. However, the Belgian situation had a different complexion. Their population had flocked to work, and the number of destitute had so diminished in number that most of the Belgian receipts from sales accumulated into the hands of the Relief organization.

We were suddenly transformed into a gigantic grocery business with ten million customers, and we found ourselves with large "margins," or "profits," above costs—all in local currencies.

WE SELL BELGIAN FOOD TO THE GERMANS

In the Armistice Agreement, the Allies and "Associated Powers" (meaning the United States) promised that the Germans would have food, presumably at once. But the Allies maintained the blockade on Germany, despite American protests, for more than four months, until March 15, 1919. I describe this particular display of statesmanship in detail, with documentation, in my narrative of the Relief and Reconstruction of Europe. The effect of this action was to stimulate the rise of Communism (Spartacists) in Germany. Machine guns clattered in the streets of many cities. When the blockade was relaxed, it was touch and go on whether the representative government of President Ebert could survive.

In the earlier months of our fifth year, when shipping was relatively easy to obtain, we had built up large stocks of food in Belgium against possible eventualities. To alleviate the German situation, we at once, after March 15, furnished the Germans with about $45,000,-

000 worth of food from the C.R.B. stocks. It was only just that they should pay the same price that the C.R.B. received in the Relief areas. The Germans paid us in gold, and the profit, in dollars, totaled $1,568,412.88.

The net profit from the sale of food marooned in British ports at the time of the Germans' unlimited submarine war totaled $575,-420.47. With these and other trading profits and the residues in the hands of our supporting Committees, we had at our disposal more than $38,000,000.

CHAPTER 50

WINDING UP THE DELIVERY
OF SUPPLIES

On March 26, 1919, the C.R.B. formally advised Francqui that it would retire from purchase and transport of supplies to Belgium as of April 30:

PARIS, 26 MARCH 1919

MY DEAR FRANCQUI:

Apropos of the discussions we have had, I think we are in agreement that the time has arrived when we should undertake a further step in the demobilization of the C.R.B. and the Comité National. . . . it would seem to me desirable from the point of view of transportation of Belgian imports that the C.R.B. fleet should be placed in control of the Belgian authorities or Belgian merchants in such a manner as to allow . . . [it more] mobility in handling . . . [general imports] and exports. . . .

In order to carry this out, I understand that it is agreed that the Belgian Government will take over the outstanding charters of all steamers which arrive in New York after April 30th. . . .

It is desirable, I think, from the point of view of the American Treasury and the Belgian Government, that the C.R.B. should remain active for a certain further period which we may determine from time to time. . . .

There is one particular in this connection that I wish made emphatic: In any arrangements that the Belgian Government may set up to carry on this work, there must be no feeling on their part that they are under any obligation whatever to do business with men formerly associated with the C.R.B. Some of these men may be useful from their previous experience with Belgium, but I do not for one moment countenance any man trading on his association to obtain business ends.

HERBERT HOOVER

403

Less than two weeks later, we notified the French Food Administrator that the need for our food imports was rapidly reaching an end and that we would terminate the distribution of food on May 1 but would continue our charitable operations in the former occupied regions:

PARIS, 8 April 1919

MY DEAR VILGRAIN:

The relief of Northern France is now coming to its logical conclusion. Your Ministry has now so energetically spread its own organization over the invaded regions that the necessity for the foodstuffs imported through the C.R.B. is steadily diminishing. We have taken stock of the various food supplies and clothing in the hands of the local relief committees and find that with the transfer of certain stocks which we have in reserve at Antwerp, the people will require no further C.R.B. overseas shipments in order to complete the provisioning until the 1st of July. Therefore, I have instructed the C.R.B. to hand over stocks in Antwerp to the French committee and, so far as ravitaillement is concerned, to cease all connection therewith on the 1st of May.

In order that the directors of the C.R.B. may give evidence to the French people of their devotion . . . my . . . colleagues have decided that we will carry on . . . the child clinics and the special feeding of the 30,000 debilitated children until such time as they are in normal condition. This is, of course, undertaken from funds provided by the directors of the C.R.B. and does not involve French Government intervention.

We are also arranging for the completion of the distribution of some thousands of tons of gift clothing which we have imported in the north of France. The 300 barracks which have been initiated by the C.R.B. and carried on . . . with the assistance of the American Navy, will be completed early in May, so that after that date our sole connection with the North will be the care of the 30,000 debilitated children.

I wish to express again on my own and on behalf of . . . all my colleagues the sentiments of respect which we have derived from the four years of co-operation with the French Government and the admiration for the ability, courage, and fortitude of the two [and a half] millions of French people of the occupied . . . whose food supply was entrusted to our administration now over four and one-half years ago.

HERBERT HOOVER

THE TOTAL FOOD SUPPLY IN THE FIFTH YEAR

During our fifth year—from November 1, 1918, to the end—the C.R.B. provided the following supplies to Belgium and Northern France from overseas:

	Belgium (Tons)	Northern France (Tons)
Wheat, Rye and Barley..................	555,257	2,181
Flour	72,294	8,506
Meat, Bacon and Ham	29,908	6,210
Lard and Lard Substitutes..............	54,219	13,932
Maize	37,475	——
Rice and Rice Substitutes..............	38,868	12,823
Peas and Beans........................	19,065	5,163
Yeast Materials	411	——
Cocoa	2,061	1,980
Coffee	2,218	7,649
Cottonseed Oil Cake...................	2,014	——
Fish	6,405	433
Condensed Milk	14,834	14,535
Soap	8,247	7,423
Sugar	1,436	12,661
Vegetable Oil	2,037	——
Clothing	9,977	4,004
Miscellaneous	1,898	11,001
Total	858,624	108,501

In addition to the supplies to Belgium listed above, we secured for them the following commodities from the U.S. Army Liquidation Commission:

	Tons
Food	37,480
Clothing	8,184
Miscellaneous	50,774
Total	96,438

Thus the total supplies to Belgium during our fifth year were 955,062 tons.

These supplies were financed as follows:

United States subsidies to C.R.B.	$106,632,000
On credit from the Liquidation Board	28,549,672
Charity	12,100,644
Total	$147,282,316

The following supplies were furnished to the North of France from November 1 until the end:

	C.R.B.	French Government	U.S. Navy
Food	86,081	240,000	——
Clothing	4,004	——	——
Soap	7,423	——	——
Miscellaneous	6,001	——	40,000
Total	103,509	240,000	40,000 (building materials)

The total supplies were thus about 383,509 tons.

The 240,000 tons supplied by the French Government consisted of breadstuffs and were bought from the United States on a loan basis. These supplies for the North of France were financed as follows:

Loans:
Subsidies from U.S. Treasury to purchase C.R.B. supplies	$28,400,200
Loans from U.S. Treasury to France to finance breadstuffs	28,800,400
Total Loans	57,200,600

Charity:
Supplies by U.S. Navy at estimated cost	3,420,500
Trucks from U.S. Army at estimated cost	240,000
Charity through C.R.B.	5,050,504
Total Charity	8,711,004
Grand Total	$65,911,604

Life certainly had become more pleasant to ten million people during our fifth year.

CHAPTER 51

THE PROVISION OF CLOTHING

The provision of clothing was a secondary but essential operation throughout the history of the C.R.B. Because this aspect of our work cut across all three areas under our supervision—Occupied Belgium, the Belgian Etapes, and Northern France—I present here a comprehensive account of it covering all these areas over our entire four and a half years.

There was little production of textiles by the invaded people during the war. There were mills, but, except for a minor amount of native wool and some minor stocks of cotton on hand, there were no raw materials available during this whole war. Four and a half years is a long time to keep going with repairs and patches.

Since the Allied Governments were adamant against our importing textile raw materials (and indeed they needed them for their own military and civilian populations), we turned to imports of second-hand clothing, and later we added large amounts of manufactured materials. That we measured clothing in tons (24,384 tons or about five shiploads) is in itself evidence of a considerable operation. The number of items we imported probably exceeded 200,000,000, but even this was no extravagance for 10,000,000 people during a period of more than four years.

To manage the clothing problem, we set up a division of the Relief organization with its own Director and with his offices in New York, London, Brussels, and Lille.

The Belgian and French women created great workshops in the

407

cities. There, every scrap of our imports was turned to use, and these devoted women undertook the distribution of their renovated items.

So efficient were they that one could stop a small boy on the street and note the indelible number on the inside of the collar of his blouse. With no questions asked of him, but from the records these women made, one could know his name, his address, the members of his family, their monetary resources, the date the material had arrived at the work room, and the name of the woman who had made the blouse.

We organized drives for second-hand and gift clothing from over the whole neutral world. Devoted women began sending beautifully knit sweaters and socks. A rivulet began in Patagonia, and by the time it gathered strength over all South America and had reached Panama, it was a veritable river of knit goods. Likewise, a rivulet began in Alaska which by the time it had traversed Canada, the United States, and had reached New York was a flood. We never discouraged these world-wide knitters by informing them that the Belgian and French women at that time seldom wore sweaters and rather toilsomely unraveled them and re-knit the beautiful wool into shawls.

We received a mass of other beautifully made clothing, especially for children, from women all over the world. When the Western press reported that newly born babies had to be wrapped in paper, we received a welcome flood of layettes.

In collecting second-hand clothing, we found that it had to be carefully inspected before shipment overseas in order to eliminate useless items. We could not afford to waste valuable shipping space in ships crossing the Atlantic on inappropriate and worn-out articles. For instance, there was no need for silk hats—of which donors seemed to have had a great surplus. But almost every item was useful. Men's dinner suits reappeared as beautiful coats for children and adults. As mere men, we started eliminating what we believed useless, throwing out old evening gowns at the ports. Hearing of this, the Belgian and French women complained vigorously. They wanted these fine silks and fabrics especially for children.

Incidentally, as showing the innate gaiety of Belgian women, the

Brussels women, who had set up a gigantic work room in the Pole Nord, displayed a long line of dressmakers' dummies, clad in the various styles of evening gowns for more than thirty years, and arranged them in sequent order. The exhibit did not last long, for it disappeared to give the cheer of bright clothes to underclad girlhood.

A curious phenomenon developed with regard to the gift clothing. Either the donors had placed money in pockets or had neglected to take it out. We cashed several thousand dollars' worth of various world currencies and coins into francs for the women's work rooms.

An incident of the ingenuity of a people was the making of automobile tires into soles for shoes. By processing and the use of heavy presses, these soles were in many ways better than leather—but there were not enough of them for the ten million people who were constantly walking about.

Useful as these gifts of newly made and second-hand clothing were, they did not meet our problem. We were driven to importing cloth and material, needles, thread, buttons, shoes, and leather fittings. We started by buying "mill-ends," "out-of-style goods," and "market gluts." Soon we were obliged to give huge orders to manufacturers.

For the first two and a half years, the British Foreign Office had but little enthusiasm for our clothing activities and, in fact, at one time stopped our imports of even second-hand clothing (see Chapter 23). However, we developed two reports for them. One, from Belgian physicians, showed the rapid growth of respiratory diseases, especially in children, because of the lack of clothing; the other was a report of an extensive survey made by a member of our American staff—Milton Brown. These reports and our own urgings finally secured approval of the Foreign Office for one of the largest single textile orders in the world up to that time.

Of the 24,384 tons of clothing that we handled, 10,571 tons were gifts and 13,313 tons were purchased. Of this total, 15,870 tons went to Belgium and 6,639 tons to Northern France. After the Armistice, we sold 1,375 tons of second-hand clothing to the American Relief Administration for its use in other parts of Europe.

A rough estimate of the contents of these tons used in Belgium and

Northern France, made from reports of the work-room distribution, showed they had made up:

Single articles of clothing............................ 28,212,046
Pairs of boots, shoes and stockings.................... 1,453,291
Single blankets and quilts............................ 17,423

The C.R.B. totals were:

New clothing materials and supplies:
Made-up articles of new clothing................... 4,141,498
Yards of cloth..................................... 23,256,020
Buttons, buckles, hooks and eyes, etc. (in dozens) 29,620,202
Thread in spools and knitting wool (in pounds)...... 4,858,235
Boots, shoes and stockings (in pairs).............. 4,396,961
Leather soles, heels and shoe laces (in pairs),
    pieces, repair leather......................... 5,003,866
Single blankets, pillows and quilts................. 796,408

But statistics cannot show the glow of spirit from a warm or gay garment or the suffering from their scarcity.

BELGIAN LACE

A minor but noteworthy adjunct of the textile operation concerned the Belgian lace makers. For centuries, hand-made lace had been a home industry carried on in a few countries, but most extensively by the Belgian women. With the coming of the war, they had neither raw material nor an export market. We originally classed these women as unemployed, and they received relief as such.

But in 1915, a committee of Belgian women came to us, presenting the plight of the lace workers and the danger of their losing the art and skill. They proposed that we import linen thread and needles for them and that we make cash advances from our local currency on the pieces of lace produced sufficient to pay for their food and other essentials. They suggested that the lace be sold currently in the Allied countries or stored by the C.R.B. for sale after the war and that from the sales further payment be made to the lace workers. The entire project was beautifully managed by volunteer committees of Belgian women under the American-born Countess de Beughem. We secured permission from the British blockade authorities to import the materials and to export such lace as we could sell. By the end of the war, the C.R.B. had a store of lace on hand which I did not believe could ever be sold.

But Mrs. Hoover organized committees of American women in England and the United States who promoted the sales during and after the war. In the end, these indefatigable women sold all the lace, and the Belgian women's committee divided more than $1,000,-000 in net proceeds among the individual producers, each according to the value of her product.

CHAPTER 52

STATISTICAL SUMMARY OF THE
C.R.B.'S FIVE YEARS

To quiet forever any possible criticism of the operations of the C.R.B., we published several large volumes from the documents in the Hoover Institution on War, Revolution, and Peace.

One volume of 440 pages prepared by George I. Gay, one of our old hands, gives the content and the cost of every cargo and the record of its distribution to each commune in Belgium and Northern France. This volume contained every detail of our accounts and our final balance sheets. Another volume, compiled by Frank Surface, statistically covered all Relief operations in Europe during the First World War. Two other volumes, published by the C.R.B. and compiled by H. H. Fisher and G. I. Gay, reproduced a part of the documentation of the C.R.B.

ANNUAL DELIVERIES OF SUPPLIES DURING
THE ENTIRE PERIOD OF THE C.R.B.

Our yearly deliveries of imported supplies over the years from November 1 to November 1 were (in tons):

First year	983,808
Second year	1,300,322
Third year (the submarine war)......	724,175
Fourth year	1,091,178
Fifth year (10 months).............	1,074,948
Total	5,174,431

THE VARIOUS OVERSEAS COMMODITIES DELIVERED

Commodity (in tons)	To Occupied Belgium	To Belgian Refugees Holland & Havre	To Invaded France	To French Refugees Holland	To Other Desti-nations[1]	Total
Wheat, Barley, Rye.	2,397,456	——	466,027	150	59,558	2,923,191
Flour	335,608	——	75,788	25	16,683	428,104
Bacon	75,438	54	51,067	12	25,147	151,718
Lard	148,709	3	72,372	8	5,248	226,340
Maize	404,431	——	42,834	—	4,519	451,784
Rice	215,411	——	102,030	14	22,220	339,675
Beans, Peas	122,105	——	49,312	17	21,065	192,499
Yeast Materials	10,920	——	691	—	51	11,662
Butter, Cheese	3,632	——	3,165	—	6	6,803
Cocoa	5,882	——	6,988	—	261	13,131
Coffee	11,911	——	29,994	4	66	41,975
Fish	16,777	——	5,186	1	——	21,964
Meat	18,313	——	13,941	9	5,445	37,708
Milk	26,890	279	53,731	21	756	81,677
Soap	14,490	——	24,621	18	11	39,140
Sugar	1,517	——	49,505	2	220	51,244
Sundry Foodstuffs ..	65,018	——	25,973	—	751	91,742
Clothing	15,870	284	6,639	18	958	23,769
Miscellaneous	3,005	619	11,088	—	23,311	38,651
Benzine, Oil, Grease	1,558	——	628	—	96	1,654
Totals	3,894,941	1,239	1,091,580	299	186,372	5,174,431

NATIVE SUPPLIES SECURED

The C.R.B.'s agreements with the Germans, whereby the native food was protected, secured 910,642 tons of bread grains, which, on the basis of our delivered costs, were valued at more than $1,365,-000,000. In addition, the native food requisitioned or paid for by the Relief organization came to 524,000 tons, thus a total of about 1,889,-000 tons.

[1] Marooned cargoes sold in England and sales to Germany and other countries.

SHIPS LOST EN ROUTE

The Commission delivered 2,323 cargoes in its four and one-half years and incurred the following disasters:

Vessels torpedoed 17
Vessels mined 14
Vessels torpedoed or mined 3
Vessels fired on by submarines 3
Miscellaneous wrecks 15
Total accidents 52
Vessels lost 38
Vessels or cargoes damaged 14

Of the ships lost, fourteen were on outward voyages in ballast, with a total deadweight tonnage exceeding 200,000 tons. Since many of these were under charter for subsequent inward voyages, the C.R.B.'s difficulties amid the world-wide famine of ships were greatly increased.

SUPPLIES LOST EN ROUTE

Cargo lost at sea	114,000 tons
Cargo marooned in England and sold	95,000 tons
Food purchased or contracted for in Britain and France, canceled or sold in consequence of German refusal to permit shipping from those countries	68,000 tons
Total	277,000 tons

NUMBER OF WAREHOUSES AND COMMUNES

The number of warehouses maintained by the C.R.B. and the number of communes to which supplies were delivered were:

	Warehouses	Communes
Belgium	134	2,598
Northern France	106	2,133
Totals	240	4,731

THE NUMBER OF PERSONS ENGAGED

Associated with or employed by the organization were approximately:

American personnel	500
Belgian personnel (estimated)	40,000
French personnel (estimated)	15,000
Members of Charity Appeal Committees	
United States (estimated)	50,000
British Empire (estimated)	26,500
Elsewhere (estimated)	5,000
Approximate total	137,000

RECEIPTS AND EXPENDITURES
CALCULATED IN DOLLARS

RECEIPTS

Government Subsidies

United States Treasury	$386,632,260.44	
British Treasury	109,045,328.73	
French Treasury	204,862,854.21	$700,540,443.38

Charity

United States	34,521,026.99	
Great Britain	16,641,034.85	
Other Countries	1,128,733.67	52,290,795.51
Sales of supplies outside		
relief areas		54,700,732.24
Exchange, interest, and		
commercial remittances		8,217,757.88
Profits on sales to other nations		
and civil population		38,919,635.92
Free services[2]		75,849,312.00
Total		$930,518,676.93

[2] This sum was estimated by Edward Flesh, a Vice President of the United States Food Administration Grain Corporation in charge of purchases and transportation.

EXPENDITURES

Purchase and Transport	
Overseas Supplies	$864,656,414.92
Refunds of Working Capital to	
U. S. Treasury	23,033,683.45
Overhead and Administrative	
Services	3,908,892.74
Gifts to Belgium	33,869,635.42
Gifts to Northern France	5,050,050.40
Total	$930,518,676.93

TOTAL OF FINANCIAL OPERATIONS

These figures do not represent the full operations of the Relief organization because they do not include our internal purchases in Belgium and Northern France at a value of $1,889,000,000, making a total of over $2,800,000,000.

The total overhead and administration expenses of the C.R.B. were $3,908,892.74, or one-third of one per cent of the C.R.B. operations.

The estimate is based on the fact that the members of the Commission were volunteers, with allowances of expenses only to junior members, and that the Commission received its purchasing, shipping, insurance, and accounting services without profit to those who rendered them.

In this estimate, calculations were made on the basis of the usual overhead of governmental or commercial agencies. It is probably an underestimate. My own estimate was some $5,000,000 higher.

WINDING UP THE C.R.B.

CHAPTER 53

SETTLING OUR ACCOUNTS WITH
THE SUBSIDIZING GOVERNMENTS
AND THE BELGIAN DEBTS
TO THE UNITED STATES

Winding up the C.R.B. was a long and tedious job which took until February, 1927, when we received the auditors' final statement. Our first task after the completion of Relief deliveries was to settle our accounts with the subsidizing governments—that is, Britain, Belgium, France, and the United States.

As I have stated earlier, at the very beginning of the Commission in October, 1914, we had placed both its accounting and auditing in the responsible hands of Deloitte, Plender, Griffiths & Company, an international firm. They carried on this work until the very end without pay, except for the salaries of the men assigned to our offices.

We had two distinct sources of funds: on the one hand, those which came from charity and the profits made by the Commission, and on the other, the subsidies from governments.

On May 10, 1919, I sent the Treasury officials of Belgium, France, and the United States a long memorandum detailing how we proposed to liquidate our complicated accounts. The major points of my proposals were that the auditors should present a certificate covering in detail the application of all subsidies, separately for Belgium and Northern France, together with a statement of the supply shipments to each of them; that we should retain all "profits" for allocation to charitable purposes in the two countries as we might determine; that since after the Armistice the Relief had been mostly paid for by the

419

United States, any residues of American subsidies should be refunded by the C.R.B. to the United States Treasury to be applied to the reduction of the debts of Belgium and France. I also requested of each government that the Belgian, French, and American Treasuries each appoint a delegate to receive and approve the auditors' statement when presented.

THE BRITISH ACTION

The British Government took no action on our plan of settlement but released us from accounting to them by agreeing to settle the matter of their subsidies directly with the Belgian and French Governments, but they said that for the record, they would like to have copies of our final accounting, which we gave them.

THE BELGIANS ACCEPT OUR PLAN

The Belgian Government accepted our plan in the following letter:

BRUSSELS, 16 July 1919

My dear Francqui:

Replying to yours of June 26 last, I have the honor to inform you that I agree to the proposals of Mr. Hoover, President of the C.R.B., relative to the form of the final accounts of this organization and the method of closing them.

According to your suggestion I appoint to verify these accounts in agreement with certified accountants chosen by the United States Government, Mr. Fortin, Councillor at the Court of Accounts.

LEON DELACROIX

THE FRENCH DISAGREE ON ONE ITEM

The French Finance Minister, in a lengthy statement on July 17, 1919, approved our proposals, except that he refused to agree to the idea of returning the balance of American subsidies to the United

States Treasury. On July 19, I referred him to the Secretary of the Treasury for settlement of this question. They did not agree until the settlement of France's war debts with the United States in 1923.

On September 16, 1919, I returned home. But the problems of the Relief continued. I appointed two of our former Directors, Messrs. Rickard and Poland, as liquidators of the C.R.B., subject to my approval of their actions. Theirs proved a tedious and drawn-out task because of the vast amount of intricate detail which had to be threshed out with the various governments, litigation of insurance and damage claims which had arisen over the years, and the problem of the disposal of our "profits" for permanent charitable organizations in Belgium and Northern France. The task extended over eight years, until we finally closed our books on February 3, 1927, with an auditors' certificate which entirely approved them.

On June 19, 1920, I returned to the United States Treasury $17,246,490 in unspent working capital for Northern France Relief and $1,512,901.66 on the Belgian account. The Treasury approved this settlement on June 21, 1920, and on December 27 of that year, the Belgian Government approved. We received a final quittance from the United States Treasury on all accounts on April 26, 1922.

Under the laws of Britain, France, and the United States, all advances from one country to another during the war were treated as "loans." Although this practice was maintained with regard to the advances for the Relief, neither we of the C.R.B. nor the high officials of the three governments considered them to be other than "subsidies" and always referred to them as such in our discussions and negotiations.

The provisions of the Treaty of Versailles required that the responsibility for repayment of all Relief advances to Belgium be imposed upon Germany in priority over reparations to any other nation. But the United States did not ratify the Treaty. Also, we abandoned the idea of any reparations from Germany. By our failure to sign the Treaty, we denied ourselves German payment for the Relief costs and in consequence laid the cost on the Belgians. In the Belgians' view, the United States thus had little moral claim to repayment of the Relief "loans."

PRESIDENT WILSON'S ATTEMPT TO OBTAIN CONGRESSIONAL CANCELLATION OF THE BELGIAN RELIEF LOANS

On February 22, 1921, President Wilson sent a message to Congress recommending that the United States accept German obligations for the American pre-Armistice loans to Belgium as the other governments had done. His message was:

To THE SENATE AND HOUSE OF REPRESENTATIVES:

I herewith call your attention to an agreement with Belgium made by the British and French Premiers and myself, which is embodied in the following letter:

June 16, 1919

M. Hymans, Ministre des Affairs Estrangères,
SIR:

The Reparation Clauses of the draft Treaty of Peace with Germany obligate Germany to make reimbursement of all sums which Belgium has borrowed from the Allied and Associated Governments up to November 11, 1918, on account of the violation by Germany of the Treaty of 1839. As evidence of such an obligation Germany is to make a special issue of bonds to be delivered to the Reparation Commission.

Each of the undersigned will recommend to the appropriate governmental agency of his Government that, upon the delivery to the Reparation Commission of such bonds, his Government accept an amount thereof corresponding to the sums which Belgium has borrowed from his Government since the war and up to November 11, 1918, together with interest at 5 per cent unless already included in such sums, in satisfaction of Belgium's obligation on account of such loans, which obligation of Belgium's shall thereupon be cancelled.

G. CLEMENCEAU
WOODROW WILSON
D. LLOYD GEORGE

In recommending to you that Congress take appropriate action with regard to this agreement, certain facts should be brought to your attention.

After reciting the history of the pre-Armistice loans to Belgium, the President stated that the total amount was $171,780,000 on all accounts, including Relief, but did not include Relief subsidies subsequent to the Armistice. His message continued:

. . . A recommendation at this time that suitable legislative action should be taken may appear somewhat premature, but in view of the approaching termination of my Administration I have brought this matter to your attention, hoping that suitable action may be taken at the appropriate time.

WOODROW WILSON

The Congress took no action on the President's recommendation.

SETTLEMENT OF THE BELGIAN DEBTS TO THE UNITED STATES

The whole problem of the repayment of advances to Belgium was imposed on the United States World War Foreign Debt Commission created by the Congress in 1922. I was a member of this Commission, together with two Cabinet colleagues and two representatives from each House of the Congress.

I at once proposed that all pre- and post-Armistice "loans" to Belgium for Relief purposes be canceled. I pointed out the sentimental background of these loans, in that the American people had considered the advances to the C.R.B. as a gift. I argued further that we had deprived the Belgians of the repayment of these sums, which might have been the case had we not wiped out the special Treaty provision agreed to by President Wilson. And I produced President Wilson's message to Congress of February 22, 1921.

My six colleagues, however, were five to one against me, since they felt that cancellation of the loans to Belgium might establish a precedent which could affect debt settlements with other countries. Also, they did not believe that they could carry such a proposal with the Congress, which by this time had become very anti-European and had already denied President Wilson's recommendation.

When the Dawes Commission revised the German reparations payments in January, 1925, continuous priority of reparations was assigned to pay the various nations' advances to Belgium. The Belgians thus continued to receive payments from the Germans on British and French Relief advances, which relieved them of the necessity to make those payments for Relief.

On August 10, 1925, a Belgian Commission, of which Francqui was Chairman, came to Washington to settle the question of the loans which Belgium had received from the United States. On August 18, an agreement was signed. The Debt Commission's report to the Congress on this settlement was divided into two parts: the pre-Armistice loans and the post-Armistice loans. The Commission's recommendations to the Congress bearing upon the pre-Armistice loans were:

In the settlement arrived at, the Belgian debt was divided into two parts. It will be recalled that at the time of the Peace Conference at Paris in 1919, Belgium advanced a claim for war damages as a prior charge on reparations amounting to $1,000,000,000 in gold; that she also claimed that Germany should be compelled to redeem in gold 6,200,000,000 paper marks forced into circulation in Belgium during the period of German occupation, which marks had been redeemed by the issuance of Belgian francs by Belgium; and that she also maintained that France, Great Britain, and the United States should cancel her war debts, representing sums advanced prior to November 11, 1918. During a critical period of the Peace Conference, largely at the instance of President Wilson, Belgium was induced to reduce her claim for war damages from $1,000,000,000 to $500,-000,000, and to abandon her claim for 6,200,000,000 gold marks on the condition that France, Great Britain, and the United States would forgive her prearmistice debts and would look to Germany for repayment of the sums due. On June 16, 1919, M. Clemenceau, President Wilson, and Mr. Lloyd George signed a letter addressed to the Minister of Foreign Affairs of Belgium stating that each would recommend to the appropriate governmental agency of his Government that upon delivery to the Reparation Commission of bonds of Germany to be issued in reimbursement of all sums which Belgium had borrowed from the three Governments prior to the armistice, each Government would accept a proportionate share of the bonds on account of Belgium's obligation to repay the loans, which obligation was thereupon to be cancelled. This arrangement was incorporated in article 232 of the treaty of Versailles. Although France and Great Britain ratified the treaty, it was not ratified by the United States. The question of the release of Belgium from her obligation to repay the prearmistice advances was separately submitted to Congress by President Wilson in a communication dated February 22, 1921, a few days before the close of his administration, but never came up for consideration.

Although the representatives of Belgium at the Peace Conference understood that the action of President Wilson in negotiating the peace treaty and making the agreement was subject to ratification, it was not anticipated that he would experience any difficulty in securing ratification in the United States. The man in the street in Belgium always regarded the failure of the United States to confirm the agreement of President Wilson as a breach of faith.

While the commission was aware of the fact that no legal obligation rested upon the United States as a result of the assurances given Belgium at the time of the Peace Conference, it nevertheless felt that there continued a weighty moral obligation upon this Government, since, as a result of the action taken by President Wilson, Belgium had waived rights which otherwise it might have obtained. This differentiated the prearmistice debt of Belgium from all other debts due the United States from foreign countries.

The provisions of article 232 of the treaty of Versailles were not carried out by Germany. The failure of Germany to fulfill its reparation obligations finally resulted in the adoption of the Dawes plan of August, 1924. In an agreement of January 14, 1925, signed at Paris, apportioning the Dawes plan receipts among the several countries entitled to reparations it was provided that 5 per cent of the annual payments by Germany available for reparations (first deducting certain priorities, such as service of the German external loan of 1924, army costs, and the like) was set apart to provide repayment of the Belgian prearmistice debt. France and Great Britain agreed to accept their proportion of the amounts to be received, and Belgium has been relieved to this extent as a debtor of these two nations. The portion of these receipts which would have been payable to the United States if the treaty of Versailles had been ratified by this Government is being paid to Belgium by reason of her prearmistice debt to the United States, and Belgium agreed to pay over such amounts immediately to this country. The commission did not accept the Belgian proposal that amounts to be received from Germany be substituted by Belgium for repayment of the prearmistice debt.

The commission, however, felt that under all the circumstances *the*

United States should not ask Belgium to repay more than the principal of the prearmistice advances. A schedule of annual installment payments over a period of 62 years, without interest, the payments to be a direct obligation of Belgium irrespective of receipt of payments from Germany, was finally agreed upon by the two commissions.

The installments on the pre-Armistice debt began at $1,000,000 for 1926, rising to $2,900,000 in 1932, and scheduled to continue at that level until 1987.

This settlement of the pre-Armistice debts of $171,780,000 by installments over sixty-two years, without interest, could have been met by the Belgians by a simple investment in United States bonds. What this settlement meant can be indicated by assuming that the Belgians at that time had invested about $20,000,000 in United States bonds. On this basis of calculation, the settlement canceled about 87 per cent of the pre-Armistice Relief subsidies.

SETTLEMENT OF POST-ARMISTICE BELGIAN RELIEF DEBTS

The total of the post-Armistice "loans" to Belgium amounted to $175,430,808.68. Of this sum, $104,642,122.66 was for Relief. The majority of the Debt Commission were most rigorous over this segment. They insisted upon adding compounded interest arrears to the principal, bringing the amount up to about $246,000,000. This compounding of interest on Relief loans brought the United States the name "Uncle Shylock." I protested against the inclusion of the Relief segment at all and argued that it ought to be canceled or at least placed on the same basis as the pre-Armistice Relief advances. However, my colleagues asserted that the Congress would endorse no such concessions and voted five to one against me. The payments on the post-Armistice segment were to be started in 1926, with installments on principal and interest beginning at $1,970,000 annually and rising to $5,200,000 in 1931 and to $12,200,000 in 1987.

The total payments of the post-Armistice debt, spread, as they were, over sixty-two years, if subjected to a valuation by a compound discount table at 4½ per cent (the current U.S. Government rate), would indicate a reduction of the debt to about 40 per cent of the total.

THE FRENCH DEBT SETTLEMENT

The French debt settlement did not discriminate between Relief and other purposes. Together with accrued interest, the principal was fixed at $4,025,000,000. The installments, including current interest, began at $30,000,000 in 1926 and were scheduled to rise to $113,-694,786.74 in 1987. If the French had invested about $2,000,000,000 in United States bonds at this time—at their current rate of interest—this amount would have met the whole installment plan. In other words, the settlement amounted to a debt reduction of about 50 per cent.

THE MORATORIUM AND THE END OF PAYMENTS

Since all payments on intergovernmental debts, including German reparations, were stifling the world's economy and thrusting it deeper and deeper into the world-wide depression in 1931, I, as President, proposed and secured a moratorium on all debt payments until December, 1932. Later, in 1932, I proposed to the Congress a revision of all the World War debts. They were not only a continuing depressant but in volume exceeded the capacity of nations to pay either in goods or in gold. The Congress refused, and in January, 1933, all World War debtors to the United States, except Finland, abandoned their payments for good. The total which had been repaid by the Belgians on all accounts was about $20,000,000, or less than 5 per cent of the original debt.

When the French, in 1933, abandoned payments, the total which the United States had received in principal and interest from them was about $163,000,000 on the agreed debt of over $4,000,000,000, or a payment of under 5 per cent.

THE END RESULTS

The net total advanced by the United States for the Relief of Belgium and Northern France was $386,632,260.45, less $23,033,683.43 returned to the United States by the Commission, or $363,578,577.02. The total payment by the Belgians on their debt amounted to about $20,000,000. To have canceled the Relief debts from the beginning would have brought great satisfaction to the American people. But all the inspiration to the world, which surely would have come from such an act, was sacrificed on the altar of Congressional appeasement.

CHAPTER 54

WE CREATE GREAT INSTITUTIONS

When we terminated the Commission's work, we had balances of more than $38,000,000 available for charitable purposes under the agreements with the various governments.

BELGIUM

The charitable funds applicable to Belgium included:

(1) The large "profits" in francs from sale of food during the Armistice;

(2) The profits in sterling from the sale of marooned food during the submarine war;

(3) The profits in dollars from sale of food to the Germans from C.R.B. stocks at the time the blockade was relaxed;

(4) Dollar and sterling balances in the hands of our charitable committees.

The total of these funds available to Belgium would be the equivalent of more than $33,000,000 in dollars, sterling, and Belgian francs.

I went to Brussels in mid-August, 1919, to confer with our colleagues, Francqui and Van Brée, and Prime Minister Delacroix to settle disposal of these funds. I suggested that we assign these sums to the Belgian Government, which should apply them to charitable purposes through such agencies as they might select. The Prime Minister strenuously objected, arguing that his Cabinet was sufficiently divided over other problems without taking on a new one. He insisted that these funds belonged to the C.R.B. and that we should designate the purposes for which they were to be used.

Shortly afterwards, I submitted a tentative plan to Delacroix, having discussed it with Francqui. The plan had been revolving in Francqui's and my mind for a year. Our great concern was the plight of the Belgian universities and technical schools, which had little permanent endowment and would come out of the war with destroyed buildings and demoralized finances. The Belgians had little in the way of scientific-research institutions or scholarships in their schools and colleges. Moreover, I wished to establish a fund, the service of which would contribute to continued friendship of our two countries.

The Prime Minister and Francqui requested me to draft a plan along these lines. I prepared the original document in my own handwriting. The original text hangs on the walls of the *Fondation Universitaire* (one of our foundations) in Brussels.

The original document is of some interest, and I reproduce it here, including some scratched-out passages and bad grammar—the result of midnight toil. The parts in brackets were the scratched-out passages.

M. DELACROIX
Your Excellency—

The Belgian Government formally approved (as also have the other Governments concerned) the method that I proposed [I presented] for settling the accounts of the Commission for Relief in Belgium.

[This mem] The Section IV "e" of that Memorandum provided as follows. . . .

We [now find upon] have now made a preliminary [study] inspection of the accounts [but will] not complete owing to the volume of transactions—exceeding four' milliards of francs they will not be in final form for some months. In the meantime it is evident that the sums disposable [under that] will be realized for Belgium under the above agreement [and including the profits earned by the Comité National] amount to [approximately] a minimum of 150,000,000 francs. This sum includes the profits of the Comité National who have acted as the agents of the Commission for

Relief in Belgium and [they] must account to the Commission for these profits and therefore are included in these proposals.

During the last four years of association [of] with the Belgian people and [with] from many discussions with my colleagues in the Comité National [of] with the members of the government [and] universities and the public it has become evident that no greater [purpose could be] service could be performed for [rendered] the Belgian people than that these funds should be applied to strengthen the extension of higher education in Belgium—The war and the present economic situation have demonstrated the [great role that] extreme importance [the extension] of wider distribution of higher education among [the common people] all classes regardless of means [played on has and will be play in the justice]. In order to compass this end it is necessary first to undertake such measures as will open the institutions of higher learning freely to [those who] the sons and daughters of those who have not the means to undertake [such] the expenses of [such] higher training. And second, to strengthen the financial resources of the institutions themselves so that they may not only render more efficient service to the community as a whole but also that they may undertake the additional burden of this increased attendance.

Therefore, [after careful discussion with—I wish to] I propose that the funds mentioned above should be applied as follows:

(a) as to 43% to the creation of [a few a fe a joint American and Belgian] a foundation the income of which shall be applied [by loans scholarships or gifts to students] in principle to enable to children of persons who not the means to otherwise [provide] to secure them to [get] secure higher education. This may be accomplished by loans, gifts, scholarships, or otherwise to secure these ends. This foundation to be vested in a board of joint American and Belgian trustees to be initially selected by the Directors of the Commission for Relief in Belgium and the Comité National. Such [minor] portions of this fund as the trustees may consider advisable may to be applied to [the of] education looking toward the protection of child life.

(b) Direct payment of 57% of the total francs available to the trustees of the following institutions in the following proportions:

Brussels University	12%
Louvain University	12%
Ghent University	12%

Liège University	12%
Mons Technical Inst.	3%
The Colonial School	6%

These funds to be at the free disposition of these institutions [and the] but generally for the purpose of increasing their efficiency and ability to serve the community.

3. If the above proposals should prove acceptable I would propose to authorize the Comité National to make [pay] immediate payment of 20,000,000 francs to the purposes and in the proportions mentioned under "b" in order to enable them to immediately overcome some of the disabilities imposed by the war.

After some discussion with my colleagues, this original draft was amended in some details, and my actual statement to the Prime Minister was as follows:

BRUSSELS, 28 August 1919

M. Delacroix, Prime Minister, Brussels
YOUR EXCELLENCY:

The Belgian Government on 16th July formally approved (as also have the other governments concerned) the method that I proposed for settling the accounts of the Commission for Relief in Belgium.

Section IV (*e*) of that memorandum provided as follows:

"The amounts contributed for charity in cash or in kind, the profits created by voluntary service in handling foodstuffs, being the free charitable aspects of the Commission to be shown by statements of amount and the purpose to which these sums have been applied in charity. Further the basis of such charitable sums which may be decided by the Commission as unexpended and applicable to the subsequent charitable operations now being continued by the Commission will also be shown. Such balances will be appropriated or invested for the benefit of the population in Belgium and Northern France as shall be determined by the Commission."

We have now made a preliminary inspection of the accounts, but owing to the volume of transactions—exceeding four milliards of francs—they will not be in final form for some months. In the meantime, it is evident that the sums that would be realized for Belgium under the above paragraph amount to a minimum of Frs. 150,000,000. This sum includes the unexpended gifts and the profits of the Commission for Relief in Belgium applicable to Belgium in all its agencies, in America, England, Holland, and in Belgium through the operations carried on by Comité National as the agents of the Commission for Relief in Belgium.

During these last four years of association with the Belgian people and from discussions with my colleagues in the Comité National, with the members of the Government and the universities, and the public, it has become evident that no more democratic service could be rendered to the Belgian people than that these funds should be applied to the extension of high education in Belgium. The war and the present economic situation have demonstrated the extreme importance of the widest distribution of high education amongst all classes, especially those of limited means. In order to compass this end, it is necessary:

1st. To undertake such measures as will open the institutions themselves so that they may not only render more efficient service to the community as a whole but also that they may undertake the additional burden of this increased attendance.

Therefore I propose that the funds mentioned above should be applied as follows:

a) As to the 37 per cent to the creation of a foundation, the income from which shall be applied in principle to enable the children of families who have not the means to otherwise secure such education, to obtain it, this may be accomplished by gifts, scholarships, or otherwise to obtain this general principle. I would propose that this foundation should be vested in a board of half each Belgian and American trustees, the American trustees to be selected by the Directors of the Commission for Relief in Belgium. Some minor proportion of this fund, as the trustees may consider advisable, could well be applied to the extension of such education as will look toward the protection of child life.

b) Direct payment of 63 per cent of the total funds available to the trustees of the following institutions, proportionally as under:

Brussels University	13⅓%
Louvain University	13⅓%
Ghent University	13⅓%
Liège University	13⅓%
Mons Mining School	3 %
The Colonial School	6⅔%

These funds to be at the free disposition of these institutions but generally for the purpose of increasing their efficiency and ability to serve the community. The total of these sums, however, not to exceed 95,000,000 francs, any excess reverting to fund *a*.

If the above proposals should prove acceptable, I would propose to authorize the Comité National from the funds belonging to the Commission for Relief in Belgium, to make immediate payment of 20,000,000 francs to the proportions mentioned under *b*, in order to enable them to overcome immediately some of the disabilities imposed by the war. The arrangements under *a* to be set up as quickly as the organization can be perfected.

HERBERT HOOVER

The Prime Minister promptly approved our proposal:

BRUSSELS, 5 September 1919

Herbert Hoover
DEAR SIR:

The honor falls to me of addressing to you the thanks of the Belgian Government for the generous intentions expressed in your letter of the 28th August 1919.

How many times have you not justified the title of "Friend of the Belgian Nation." For five years you have consecrated your inexhaustible activity to victualling our populations in distress, and now you are about to give a new proof of the ties of profound sympathy which unite you to us, by showing your solicitude for higher education and for all the more advanced studies of our population so sorely tried, and also by assuring the future of the organizations for the protection of childhood founded during the war.

The Council of Ministers, at their sitting of the 5th September, accepted with thanks the project of which you have sketched the broad outlines. They will submit to the . . . [Legislature] a project for a law granting a civil entity to the universities of Ghent and Liège, to permit these to receive the liberalities of the Commission for Relief, and they ask you—counting on your agreement in this matter—to let all the interested parties benefit by your generosity, in whatever language, French or Flemish, they wish to pursue their higher studies.

While awaiting the vote on this projected law the Government will accept willingly, for the universities of Ghent and Liège, the first sums which you place at their disposal to permit them to supply the most urgent necessities.

L. DELACROIX

THE ESTABLISHMENT OF TWO SEPARATE BENEVOLENT FOUNDATIONS

On December 19, 1919, I wrote the Prime Minister and Francqui presenting a proposal for disposal of our remaining balances to a new foundation. Subsequently, it seemed desirable to split the fund into two foundations—one in Belgium and the other in the United States. On March 11, 1920, we cabled the following to Francqui:

... [Mr.] Hoover ... [believes] that a return to the original idea is in the best Belgian interest, that is, to create one legal foundation in Belgium and another legal foundation in the United States. The whole of the present franc resources to be transferred to the Belgian Foundation. Its directors to comprise two representatives from American Foundation and the entire distribution of income arising from the Belgian Foundation to be carried out by Directors of Belgian Foundation. That the Directors of American Foundation shall comprise the former Directors of the C.R.B. together with two representatives of Belgian Foundation one of whom to be the Belgian Ambassador and that the invested funds of the American Foundation to consist of the dollar residues of the C.R.B. These dollars can be invested either in the United States or, if desirable, invested . . . in Belgium. . . . It appears to him that this arrangement would be the most consonant with a desire for complete stability free from any national or political influence, and the American Foundation would later on attract to itself further support from American public and can be used as a continuous instrument of good feeling for Belgium in the United States. If the whole of the Foundation is set up under purely Belgian auspices the project will at once have lost all American interest. Essential motive of entire proposal is to build up a permanent bridge of fine and high relationship between the two countries to become a permanent force in both communities. . . .

RICKARD

On March 26, Francqui cabled his warm agreement to the arrangement.

The liquidation being further along, the total allocations as of May 24, 1924, were calculated in dollars:

To University of Brussels	$ 3,818,897.64
To University of Ghent	3,818,897.64
To University of Liège	3,818,897.64
To University of Louvain	3,818,897.64
To School of Mines, Mons	954,724.39
To Colonial School, Antwerp	1,909,448.84
To Ecole de Carillonneurs, Malines	3,000.00
To Fondation Universitaire	6,846,080.88
To C.R.B. Educational Foundation	7,686,065.17
Total	$32,674,909.84

A part of the funds above assigned to the C.R.B. Educational Foundation were subsequently used to establish the Fondation Francqui in Belgium.

Balance (May 1924) reserve against claims; liquidation expenses; residue to be paid to C.R.B. Educational Foundation	1,091,129.78
Grand total	$33,766,039.62

THE BELGIAN AMERICAN EDUCATIONAL FOUNDATION

The original C.R.B. Educational Foundation was in 1938 renamed the Belgian American Educational Foundation. The income on the roughly $3,000,000 endowment finally retained for this Foundation has been applied to the exchange of educational material, post-graduate students, and professors between Belgium and the United States. This American Foundation, from its start to December 31, 1955, expended a total of $13,718,960, and the market value of its remaining securities was $3,885,954. Some twelve hundred students and professors have been exchanged, and other activities have been supported. Of the Belgian students sent to the United States, four have become

Prime Ministers and fifty Cabinet officers. Twenty to twenty-five per cent of the professors in Belgian universities today are C.R.B. Fellows. Many professional men of great competence in both countries have benefited.

DISPOSAL OF NORTH OF FRANCE PROFITS

Soon after the Armistice, we were making "profits" on the sales of food to the Northern French. The total "profits" in French francs distributed by the C.R.B. for charity during the Armistice and after, at the adopted rates of exchange, amounted to $5,050,504.40. During the time previous to the withdrawal of our staff, the C.R.B. expended a large amount of these funds on the destitute and returning refugees. After the C.R.B. withdrawal at the end of April, 1919, we continued to work with the Comité d'Assistance, using the residues of our "profits."

On February 11, 1921, Poland wrote a detailed review of this activity, of which the following is a condensation:

In April 1919 it was evident that conditions had again become sufficiently normal to justify the . . . [C.R.B.] in winding up its work of feeding the 2,000,000 people of the occupied regions of Northern France, which had been undertaken in 1915 at the request of the French Government and was continued at their request after the Armistice.

It was also foreseen that the charitable activities of the Commission should be terminated so far as concerned direct intervention by an American staff. In order to avoid interruption when we withdraw . . . definite steps were taken to place the C.R.B. benevolent activities exclusively in the hands of the French [Committees].

The Comité d'Assistance des Régions Libérées d'Acord de la C.R.B. was therefore organized with Mr. Hoover as Chairman and Mr. Poland, Mr. Rickard, Mr. Shaler, and Mr. Tuck, Directors, and Mr. Chevrillon, Treasurer, representing the American group, Monsieur Labbé and a distinguished body of French doctors and men of affairs, representing French interests. Regional centers were established, which, in turn, organized local distribution committees, composed in large part of those who had been identified with the C.R.B. organization for the past four years. The Regional Directors formed an Executive Committee with M. Labbé as President. . . .

In 1919 some 7,000 children and in 1920 over 10,000 children were sent to health camps along the North Coast. . . . The way in which they recovered under this treatment was a matter of wonder. The results were so good that this work has now been taken over by the Government.

In 1920 "Consultation Nourisson" was started all over the devastated regions. This concerns itself with the care of very young children from birth to . . . two years, as well as care of mothers. The mothers receive expert medical advice and a donation of food, money, or medicine, as the circumstances require. The cost works out to about twelve to fifteen francs per child per month, and the results up to date, in reducing infant mortality, have been remarkable. In the Liberated Regions . . . as of December 1st, 1920, there were 441 "Consultations [Centers]" at which were employed 383 doctors, 120 nurses, 435 "Sage Femmes," 392 secretaries—a personnel of 1,330. There were 34,000 children being cared for at these centers, at a total cost to that date of Frs. 4,526,000.

Other expenditures for "Goûtes," "Vacance Scolaire," Child Clinics, "Assistance Discrète," and Special Relief, have amounted to Frs. 5,676,412, making a total already expended of Frs. 10,203,000. The funds which have been made available to December 1st, 1920, through the Comité d'Assistance and the earlier distributions of the C.R.B. Benevolent Fund amounted approximately to Frs. 26,595,000, of which a balance remained of approximately Frs. 16,392,000. . . . The number of children cared for will very soon reach 45,000. . . .

The benefits of the "Vacance Scolaire" were so apparent that the Department Bienfaisance of the Liberated Regions has taken over the whole activity. The results obtained by the "Consultation Nourisson" in the reduction of infant mortality, the raising of the standard of child life, and the education of the mothers are so remarkable that it has been strongly endorsed in the French Assembly, a resolution of thanks to Mr. Hoover having been passed by that body. . . .

The approximate financial position of the Comité d'Assistance, as of 1st December 1920, is as follows:

Made available from C.R.B. Benevolent Fund, C.R.B. allocations from "profits," transfers from the Comité de Ravitaillement of C.R.B. allocations and other funds . . . . Frs. 26,585,000

Balance, as of 1st December 1920 (subject to correction) ....Frs. 16,392,000

POLAND

At the adopted rate of exchange, these sums expended after our staff retired amounted to about $2,500,000. As the liquidation of the C.R.B. proceeded, we made some further small contributions to the above-mentioned French charities which we had created.

THE AUDITORS' FINAL STATEMENT

What with the involvement of governments, ship losses, and litigation over claims, the process of accounting proved a lengthy one. After certifying to the accuracy of our final accounts, the Auditors' Report read:

The Commission for Relief of Belgium

NEW YORK, 3 February 1927

DEAR SIRS:

Our firm acted as auditors of the Commission from the inception of its active operations until the termination thereof, some five years later. In addition to our duties as auditors, at Mr. Herbert Hoover's request, we arranged a method of account-keeping and selected the accountants who supervised the handling of the funds and accounts in its principal offices. Thus the records covering expenditures by the Commission of nearly a billion dollars were under our scrutiny.

Now that those records are passing into history, we are glad to emphasize the thorough and consistent attention of the Commission's Managers to the business of the Commission, and their cooperation, which enabled the records to be so maintained that all the transactions of the Commission could be fully verified, thus preventing any charge being sustained against the integrity of the administration of the Commission's affairs.

The records are evidence of the important services rendered by the Commission's principal officials, which services were given without remuneration. In this connection, we would state that Mr. Hoover set an example by not accepting, directly or indirectly, any form of remuneration from the Commission and by refusing, throughout the period of the

Commission's activities, to take from the funds of the Commission the cost of his traveling or other out-of-pocket expenses while engaged on the business of the Commission.

We consider it an honor to have been selected as auditors of the Commission and to have been able to make a contribution to so great a work. We did not charge for the time of any of our principals during the whole of the term of our service, and so far as our assistants were concerned, we added only a nominal percentage to the cost of their salaries. Therefore, no profit whatever accrued to our firm as a result of the arduous services rendered by our firm over a long term of years.

DELOITTE, PLENDER, GRIFFITHS & CO.

CHAPTER 55

EXPRESSIONS OF APPRECIATION
TO THE C.R.B.

FROM THE FRENCH

Already included in Chapters 19 and 34 are statements of appreciation from President Poincaré, and Foreign Minister Briand. M. Edmond Labbé, who had been the real leader of our French Comité du Nord during the entire life of the Commission, wrote Poland:

LILLE, 24 December 1919

DEAR SIR:

. . . You know, as well as Mr. Hoover, what gratitude your concerted labors have awakened in our hearts. Let us express it once more, fully conscious of the service that the C.R.B. rendered to our populations during the interminable duration of this horrible war. The C.R.B. has given us the means of resisting physiological deterioration, and, what is of even greater value, of fighting against the weakening of our morale.

This task once accomplished, the Committee might have considered its work completed. . . . [The work continued] for the young and adolescent who had been so hindered in their development by insufficient food, and for the . . . mothers . . . to prepare the way for robuster generations. . . .

For four years, in spite of our anguish, in spite of our fears, in spite of our mourning and misery, the C.R.B. furnished us with the means of making every Christmas a little less somber, of giving back to every family a little joy for this festival, and reminding them, for at least one day in the year, that they should keep their faith in the future and yet hope for a happy issue. How could we lose such memories? . . .

We send it [the Commission] the expression of our gratitude, to all

441

without exception, uniting in the same feeling of sympathy its President, Herbert C. Hoover, its Director, W. Babcock Poland, and every American citizen who lent it their help and their support. . . .

E. LABBÉ

Appreciative letters of gratitude came to us from our other French colleagues—Maurice Le Blan and Louis Chevrillon. At a reception given for many of my colleagues and me at the Hotel de Ville in Paris in August, 1918, the French officials again and again gave expression to their gratitude. The members of the Commission and I personally received thousands of letters of gratitude from the local French committees, the Communes, and many individuals.

FROM THE BRITISH

In many places this narrative has indicated the consideration shown to us by Prime Ministers Asquith and Lloyd George and by Foreign Minister Lord Grey and his associate, Lord Robert Cecil. There is one letter I received from a great Englishman which I have valued all of my life. On leaving England in January, 1917, for a visit to the United States, I had written a note of appreciation for the particular and devoted service of Lord Eustace Percy of the Foreign Office. Prior to my departure in April to take up my duties as United States Food Administrator, I received the following letter from him, which, in effect, constituted an answer by the British Foreign Office to the militarists, who had opposed and obstructed us at all times:

THE FOREIGN OFFICE
April 10, 1917

DEAR HOOVER:

When you left England last you wrote me a letter to which I never have replied. I do so now. You are mistaken in thinking that our association has involved any personal sacrifice on my part—for some inscrutable reason I seem to be condemned to pass through the horrors of these years with no sacrifice that can be dignified by that name.

But what I have learnt in these years I have learnt from my association with you. . . . This is not a subject I can dilate upon—I have not the words. But I have watched a great work accomplished by a great American—with a concentration of purpose and a devotion to duty which I cannot forget. I hope the years to come will give me some opportunity of showing the respect—and something more—that I feel. You know that you can always command my services at every place and time, and my hope is that some day I may be able to render you some service of that greater kind which is rendered because it cannot be asked for.

EUSTACE PERCY

FROM AMERICANS

This paragraph is from a letter to me from President Wilson:

Nothing that the American people had had the privilege of doing during the war has more deeply enlisted their interest and sympathy than the relief of the suffering of the stricken population of Belgium.

WOODROW WILSON

And for the satisfaction it will give to my old colleagues, I reproduce an editorial from the *New York Times* of September 25, 1925, under the title "America at Its Highest":

The story of the Commission for Belgian Relief just published in statistical form, with a brief interpretation, makes a glorious chapter in the history of the Great War and the two years immediately following. It is an account not only of philanthropic enterprise, but also of business venture and management without parallel in history. No Argonautic legend or Arthurian romance can match this story of the succor of a whole people by an organization conceived and directed by one man—having many of the attributes of a government and yet remaining on a temporary basis, having no well-defined legal status and carrying on its gigantic work without incorporation even. This little republic of relief, it might be called, flew its own flag, issued its own passports, operated a fleet of ocean vessels, owned and worked a great number of canal boats, entered with immunity many countries, requisitioned native food supplies as well as carrying them from other countries, rationed populations, operated mills and factories and lines of transportation, and, in fact, maintained "the whole economic cycle of a nation." Was ever such an ideal state erected on the earth with no other thought than of serving humanity? Well might those who saw its ships come up out of the sea wonder if there were not an Atlantis, after all, out to the westward of Europe. . . .

We are becoming callous to amounts in the millions. It is the infinite care with which this vast scheme of relief was organized and administered down to the last detail, so that every one helped should have enough for bare subsistence and no more, lest some one else should suffer. It was a marvelous machine operated at an administrative expenditure of less than one-half of one per cent of the total amount of the financial program. Who the master engineer of the project was no one needs to be told, for his name is known throughout the earth, not only because of what he did for Belgium, but also because of what he did for other starving millions all the way from the North Sea to the Urals.

It is all an illustration of what such a directing mind as that of Herbert Hoover can do when left to work out its plans for human betterment without political interference and when assisted by men and women of such competence and loyalty as surrounded him in this adventure on an earth-scale for relief of the neediest.

Whatever Mr. Hoover may do . . . he may have the consciousness that he has written the brightest chapter that any one man has written in the history of the war. And so far from creating a debt, other than of gratitude on the part of those lives he prolonged or whose children he saved, he had a surplus of over thirty millions which he left for the education of those whose lives he helped save. This chapter might well be entitled *America in Excelsis*.

FROM THE BELGIANS

I have reserved the remarks of appreciation from the Belgians until the last for it was here that the heart of our labors lay. I could assemble an entire volume of expressions of Belgian appreciation for the Commission's service. They would include messages from the King, the Prime Minister, and members of Parliament, as well as literally hundreds of thousands of letters and testimonials from adults and children.

On July 3, 1919, I received the following telegram from the Comité National, with which we had had our daily contacts:

The Delegates of the Provincial Committees of the National Committee, assembled today for the last time and deeply impressed at the remembrance of the miseries of occupation, send a last homage of imperishable gratitude to their great friend, Herbert Hoover; to the Commission for Relief in Belgium, and to their Government, for the great services they rendered during the long period of suffering.

FRANCQUI

I replied:

July 8, 1919

Will you convey my gratitude to the members of the Comité National for their most kind expressions to the members of the Commission for Relief in Belgium on the occasion of the final dissolution of the Comité? It is impossible to express the affection and admiration which everyone on the C.R.B. holds toward our Belgian colleagues. It is based upon an intimate experience and association over four and one-half years of the greatest tragedy and triumph that has ever come to a nation. Their fortitude, courage and ability in those dark days have contributed far more to that ultimate triumph than the world can ever know.

HERBERT HOOVER

On September 13, 1919, I received this telegram from Francqui:

MY DEAR HOOVER:

In the meeting of the 10th of September of the Chamber of Deputies, M. Delacroix, the Prime Minister, informed the assembly of the magnificent gift made to the Universities and Institutions of higher learning from the balance of the funds of the Commission for Relief in Belgium. The reading of your letter to the Prime Minister and the reply which he has sent to you, created much applause. Among the public and in the papers, talk of this happy event and praise of the C.R.B. and its president are on all lips.

I had the opportunity in connection with this gift, to meet the authorities of our Universities and I wish I could tell you of the emotion and joy with which they expressed their gratitude. At the moment when your great country received Cardinal Mercier so warmly and when it prepares to receive our King, the act of the C.R.B. in endowing our higher education reveals a characteristic which is indeed a kind to make more solid than ever the links which the trial of 1914-1918 has formed between our two countries.

I wish particularly to inform you of the feelings of our fellow citizens on these days when, more especially Americans and Belgians feel their hearts beat in union.

E. FRANCQUI

During the war, King Albert had proposed to confer upon me their highest order decoration. I had explained my personal feeling that I should accept no decorations. I did mention that many of my colleagues would value them as marking their service, and each of them was so honored.

However, upon the King's return to a freed Belgium, one of his first acts was to convene a special session of the Parliament, where a new order was created, with no insignia and with only one member—"The Friend of the Belgian People."

EPILOGUE
AND
APPENDIX

EPILOGUE

I must jump twenty years ahead to continue the story of Belgian appreciations. In 1938, I responded to many urgings by King Leopold, the Prime Minister, and many Belgian friends to revisit their country. It is of no purpose to describe the many courtesies extended to me by the King, the Ministry, the Parliament, and the thousands who lined the streets.

The most touching reminder of Relief days was a convening, for the first time in twenty years, of the C.R.B. and Comité National in our old Board room in a leading bank in Brussels. We had met there monthly to determine major policies until the American withdrawal when we declared war. With Belgian meticulousness, the chairs at the Board table had been marked for each member. After the final meeting dissolving the Comité in 1919, we had never met again, even for social purposes.

On my visit to Belgium in 1938, the Vice-President of the Comité National, Emmanuel Janssen, and the Secretary, Firmin Van Brée, summoned a special meeting, with the exact old protocol, at the Comité's former meeting hour and place. Of the Americans, Hugh Gibson, now Ambassador to Belgium, Hallam Tuck, Perrin Galpin, Millard Shaler, Milton Brown, and I were present.

The Chairman declared that the agenda for the day contained only three items—to call the roll, to honor the dead, and to renew friendships built in time of trial.

I have seldom been more affected than by that roll call and the frequent reply of the clerk, "Passed beyond." More than one-half of the chairs were empty. Many of the chairs were occupied by men obviously feeble with age, all of them under great emotion at so vivid a reminder of those who had passed on.

It was then I realized that while I had been in my early forties during the war, our Belgian colleagues had been old and tried men, often twenty years my senior.

Every article in the room and every word revived memories of men who had risen to great acts and great days. Somehow, a great spirit flowing with human devotion flooded the room.

I journeyed again to Belgium in July, 1958, at the request of President Eisenhower to deliver the address on American Independence Day, which the Belgians, through their Exposition, had set apart in honor of the United States. In addition, the Belgians had declared July 5 Hoover Day. The major event was to reconvene the survivors of the C.R.B. and the Comité National in the same Board room and around the same table in our second meeting after nearly forty years. Addresses were made by the Prime Minister and our surviving Belgian colleagues. I can present the scene no better than to reproduce parts of my address in reply to them:

Your Excellency, the Prime Minister, to my friends in Belgium and especially my old colleagues of the C.N., C.F., H.N., and the C.R.B.

No doubt the meaning of these cryptic letters has long been forgotten. They are, however, precious to some of us as the short names of our four organizations of forty-four years ago.

There are scarcely a dozen of the Old Guard in this audience. The inexorable passage of time probably makes this our last meeting.

Therefore, I have thought for this occasion and this audience [mostly] of a later generation, it would be appropriate that I speak of some incidents of many years ago. And also I should point out some extraordinary influences which have flowed from these Belgian relief organizations to the whole world down to this very day. . . .

This is an occasion and a setting which reaches into the depths of our memories and our emotions. Here in this very room at this very table we worked together for long years in the First World War. Here we managed the supply of food for 10,000,000 people. We cared for the [children, the] ill, the aged and the destitute. And beyond that our organizations sustained the morale, the unity and the spiritual strength of a people during those four dreadful years.

Only twice since have we met here. Twenty years after the First World War, I revisited Belgium at the invitation of His Majesty King Leopold. On that occasion, now twenty years ago, the survivors of the C.N., the C.F. and the C.R.B. came together again in this very room and at this very table for the first time since we had finished our task in the First World War.

Those great Belgians—Ernest Solvay and Emile Francqui—the Chairman and the President of the Comité National had passed away. When our surviving members convened here in their accustomed chairs an acting Chairman Baron Janssen and old war-time Secretary, Firmin Van Brée, presided. With a formality which for the moment covered our emotions the Chairman declared the agenda for the day contained but three items: to call the roll, to honor the dead, and to renew the friendship of those of us who were still living.

Many chairs were empty. In others were men feeble with age. At the roll-call came a somber reminder of the passing years in the secretary's oft repeated answer "Passed beyond." Not until that moment did I realize that my American colleagues and I were in our thirties and our early forties, while the Belgian and French members were experienced leaders, twenty years our elders.

Every word and every article in the room breathed of the great men of Belgium and France who had risen to transcendent courage and unsurpassed devotion to the survival of their countrymen.

And today this second meeting of the C.N., the C.F., H.N., and C.R.B. after still another twenty years has the same agenda—to mention those who still live, to honor those who have passed on, and to renew old friendships. Our memories of our former colleagues and our emotions here are undimmed by the passing of more than forty years.

But the joint efforts of our old Belgian, French, and American colleagues over the years since the First World War have not been confined to these two reunions.

When in the Second World War, for a second time, Belgium was ground between the millstones of enemy occupation and the Allied blockade, our American and Belgian colleagues came into action. . . .

And again with the world-wide famine which inevitably followed the Second World War, my old C.R.B. colleagues and I were given the mission from President Truman to co-ordinate the effort of all nations to defeat the approaching death from hunger of more than a billion human beings in fifty nations.

Belgium and France were again involved in that desperate plight of the world. . . . in this crisis our old Belgian, French, and American colleagues came into action again. . . .

And my mind still thrills with memories of every one of my more than twenty war-time visits to Belgium and Northern France. Again and again I witnessed the devotion and courage of those 60,000 Belgian and French men and women who worked in the relief. At most their remuneration was a free ration.

I should also pay tribute to the great officials of governments who made our work possible. The ambassadors and ministers of the United States, Spain, and the Netherlands, as our honorary chairmen, gave us unfailing encouragement and support—and they included the beloved Hugh Gibson.

In our undertakings we received the support of the Presidents, the Prime Ministers, and the Ministers of Foreign Affairs of Britain, France, Belgium, and the United States. It was they who responded to our appeals for financial support, when the unprecedented outflow of charity from the world proved insufficient for our needs. And I would be remiss did I not also include the German Minister of Foreign Affairs and other German civilian officials who aided us in many crises.

Lasting benefits have come to the world from the experience we gained in those years of the First World War. . . .

The Belgian Relief Organization was unprecedented in history. It pioneered the war Food Administrations in the modern world. It pioneered the methods of relief of great famines. . . .

Among our problems at that time of grim rations was the appalling spread of disease and degeneration in 2,500,000 children in Belgium and Northern France. Our joint organizations developed a system for their maintenance and rehabilitation through an extra meal a day of special food in canteens for all the affected infants, children, expectant mothers, aged and ill. The job was done by thousands of devoted women.

When the Armistice of the First World War came the group of Americans who had served in Belgium were given by the Allied governments the responsibility of relief and reconstruction for most of Europe. We expanded this same system of rehabilitation to 13,000,000 more children under direction of the same Americans who had served in Belgium.

Again, after the Second World War, the same group of Americans from that original staff in Belgium secured the adoption of the C.R.B.-C.N. system of rehabilitation of world-wide war-debilitated children under the United Nations. And the organization is still directed by one of our First World War American Delegates in Belgium. It has served the cause of more than 100,000,000 children.

And there has been another consequence which flowed from our joint activities at that time. At the end of our operations in August 1919, the Relief Organization had handled more than $1,300,000,000. And incidentally, in these forty years there has never been a challenge to the integrity of any person in its administration.

At that time we found ourselves with about $39,000,000 in a special fund built up from the residues of world charity and from our trading with other nations.

Of the $5,000,000 on the French side, we endowed certain charities in the north of France.

Your speakers have recounted what we did. Out of the fund of about $34,000,000 on the Belgian side, we in 1919 replenished the endowments of the Belgian Universities. And in 1920, with these large sums remaining in the Belgian fund we established in Belgium the Fondation Universitaire, a center of academic and scientific cooperation, and in the United States the Belgian American Educational Foundation, to carry on intellectual exchanges between our two countries. We later established the Fondation Francqui. The C.R.B. and C.N. survivors still participate in the management of these foundations. These organizations have contributed greatly to the advancement of science, education and public welfare.

I need to mention here only one of the endeavors of these organizations which are so alive in service today.

For thirty-eight years the Belgian American Educational Foundation, in cooperation with the Fondation Universitaire, has given nearly 2,000 fellowships to Belgian and American graduate students, professors and scientists, for study in the other country. Amongst the Belgians who studied in American universities there have been four Prime Ministers and some forty have been members of ministries. Many of your teachers and professional men have received training in America. On our side, many Americans have attended Belgian institutions and many of them have risen to eminence in our universities and our professions.

We have the special honor of having a Prime Minister, a former C.R.B. student, here today. Is it any wonder that from all this common background of our two nations that an affection and an understanding exist between us unparalleled between any other two nations in the world?

It is difficult for me to express my pleasure at this occasion. It especially comes to me who has so intimately known the Belgian people in times of defeat, trials and suffering and intrepid recovery.

The greatness of a nation does not lie in the numbers of its people, nor in their economic and industrial accomplishments. It lies in the spiritual and moral foundations of its people.

Perhaps as few other men, I know the indomitable spirit, the courage and the character of the Belgian nation with the glorious record of its long past.

THE AMERICAN STAFF
OF THE C.R.B.

There is no eloquence that can portray the loyalty and devotion of the American staff of the C.R.B. Theirs was a service at the command of pure idealism. They were men who sacrificed their positions and came to the service of saving the lives of ten million men, women, and children.

The men and women on the following list received no remuneration. Only to some of the youngsters did we allow traveling expenses. Many gave service during the whole four years, the others for varied periods, but always a sacrifice to human service.

Theirs was a task of difficulties by day and lasted far into the nights. They seldom lived as they were accustomed at home. Winter storms and contagious diseases were but minor discomforts. Their abilities and tact in preserving the lives of ten million, amid the conflicts of a great war, are proved by their successes. The only tribute a historian can offer them is to preserve their names and terms of service in this volume. To each of them, I owe a debt of gratitude for their friendship, which has extended all of their lives.[1]

The list below is the volunteer staff. They carried all the major responsibilities. We employed large paid clerical and accounting staffs, and they were no less devoted to the Commission and its purpose than the volunteer staff.

[1] The list below is not complete, since in the hurry of war we kept no formal register. The term "withdrawal" refers to the removal of our staff in Belgium and Northern France at the United States' declaration of war in April, 1917. As the text shows, some of them were retained longer in their tasks by agreement with the Germans.

Frank Angell	January–August 1916
Robert Arrowsmith	December 1915–December 1918
Fernand Baetens	December 1914–May 1919
David P. Barrows	January–March 1916
Griffin R. Barry	August 1915–December 1916
Lindon W. Bates	November 1914–November 1915
Jarvis E. Bell	October 1914–January 1915
Louis Belrose	June–August 1916
Paul Beri	October 1917–August 1919
S. Reading Bertron	July 1915–November 1918
Carleton G. Bowden	December 1914–January 1916;
	June–October 1916;
	December 1918–May 1919
Frank P. Brackett	July–December 1916
Henry P. Bradford	January–May 1916
Bennett H. Branscomb	December 1914–February 1915
Walter Lyman Brown	December 1915–October 1923
Milton M. Brown	February 1916–April 1918;
	December 1918–June 1919
Floyd S. Bryant	December 1914–January 1915
German Bulle	Beginning to December 1916
Oliver C. Carmichael	December 1914–April 1915
Charles H. Carstairs	January 1915 to withdrawal
Philip H. Chadbourn	February–December 1915
William H. Chadbourn	March–July 1915
H. Gordon Chasseaud	November 1914–August 1915
F. H. Chatfield	January–August 1916;
	December 1918–May 1919
Louis Chevrillon	January 1915–December 1922
Oswald Chew	February–July 1916
Albert W. Clark	December 1915–June 1916
Archibald D. Clark	December 1914–December 1915
Arthur Clark	January 1914–January 1915
R. Stanley Clark	December 1914–August 1916
Charles R. Clason	December 1914–January 1915
Albert N. Connett	January–April 1915
Thomas O. Connett	January–April 1915
Morris W. Croll	June–September 1915
Oscar T. Crosby	May–September 1915

Edward D. Curtis	Beginning to withdrawal; January–June 1919
Henry F. Cutler	August 1916–January 1917
R. Fulton Cutting	July 1915–November 1918
Paul Dana	April–June 1915
J. Dangerfield, Jr.	December 1914 to withdrawal
Thomas B. Dawson	June–August 1915
Armand Dulait	December 1914–November 1918
Harry L. Dunn	July 1916 to withdrawal
William McKee Dunn	February–June 1916
Robert M. Dutton	April 1915–November 1916
Richard T. Dyer	December 1916–February 1917
William C. Edgar	November 1914–November 1918
Frederick Exton	February–August 1916; November 1916 to withdrawal; January–July 1919
J. H. Fleming	January 1915–February 1916
Alfred C. B. Fletcher	February 1916–February 1920
Horace Fletcher	February–November 1915
William W. Flint, Jr.	December 1914–January 1915
Samuel A. Forter	December 1918–May 1919
John A. Gade	September 1916–January 1917
Frank H. Gailor	December 1914–July 1915
Perrin C. Galpin	November 1914–May 1915; December 1918–August 1922
Carleton B. Gibson	December 1914–April 1915
John L. Glenn	December 1914–September 1915; June–October 1916
Prentiss N. Gray	March–April 1917
Joseph C. Green	October 1915–July 1917
Donald M. Gregory	October 1916 to withdrawal
Warren Gregory	November 1916–March 1917
William M. Gwynn	June 1916 to withdrawal
Guillermo F. Hall	February 1916–April 1917
William C. Hall	July 1916–July 1917
Herbert F. Hamilton	February–July 1916
George M. Harper	May–June 1915
Charles F. Hawkins	December 1914–April 1915
James A. Healy	November 1914–January 1920

Dannie N. Heineman	October 1914 to withdrawal
Alexander J. Hemphill	November 1914–December 1920
Nathaniel Peter Hill	January–June 1919
Emile F. Holman	December 1914–February 1915
William L. Honnold	October 1915–November 1918
Roy T. House	February–May 1916
W. Hulse	October 1915–November 1918
Millard Hunsiker	October 1914–March 1915
Edward E. Hunt	December 1914–March 1916
John G. Iliff	May–September 1915
Will Irwin	From beginning to end
George S. Jackson	November 1914–November 1915; February–July 1919
Robert A. Jackson	May 1915 to withdrawal; December 1918–August 1919
William B. Jackson	December 1915 to withdrawal
Rene L. Jensen	January 1915–November 1918
A. C. Jenson	December 1914–March 1915
Amos D. Johnson, Jr.	December 1914–July 1915
Thomas H. Jones	December 1914–April 1915
Vernon Kellogg	June–November 1915 July–August 1919
St. Alban Kite	November 1915–August 1916
Tracy B. Kittredge	November–December 1918
J. W. Krueger	December 1918–August 1919
C. N. Lathrop	September–December 1915
Dr. Charles N. Leach	March 1916 to withdrawal; November 1918–July 1919
Ernest T. Liefeld	July 1916 to withdrawal
W. C. Lowdermilk	December 1914–January 1915
Dr. William P. Lucas	May–August 1916; February–March 1919
John F. Lucey	October 1914–November 1918
R. Ridgeley Lytle, Jr.	May–August 1915
Charles H. Macloskie	Beginning to January 1915
Dr. Alfred L. Malabre	January–April 1916; December 1918–July 1919
Arthur B. Maurice	January 1917 to withdrawal
Robert W. Maverick	September 1916 to withdrawal

Robert D. McCarter	November 1914–November 1915
Frederick W. Meert	November 1914 to withdrawal
Dudley S. Morgan	June 1916 to withdrawal
D. S. Murdock	January–July 1915
David T. Nelson	December 1914 to October 1915
Thomas E. Oliver	September 1915–May 1916
Earl D. Osborn	October 1915–April 1916; September 1916 to withdrawal
Scott H. Paradise	December 1914–April 1915
Maurice Pate	July 1916–June 1917
William A. Percy	December 1915 to withdrawal
Dr. Philip S. Platt	June 1916 to January 1917
William B. Poland	September 1915–August 1925
Francis H. Potter	February–October 1916
Philip B. K. Potter	February 1916 to withdrawal
Henry S. Pratt	September 1916–January 1917
Lewis Richards	January 1915–June 1919
Gardner Richardson	May 1915 to withdrawal; December 1918–July 1919
Edgar Rickard	October 1914–August 1925
A. B. Ruddock	July 1916 to April 1917
Samuel S. Seward, Jr.	June–December 1915
Millard K. Shaler	October 1914–August 1922
John L. Simpson	December 1915–July 1917; October–December 1918
Richard H. Simpson	December 1914–April 1916
Robert P. Skinner	October 1914–July 1, 1919
Robinson Smith	December 1914–October 1919
George F. Spaulding	December 1914–January 1915
William H. Sperry	December 1914 to withdrawal; November 1918–August 1919
T. Harwood Stacy	December 1914–March 1916
F. Dorsey Stephens	January 1915–April 1916; December 1918–May 1919
William C. Stephenson	June–October 1915
Gilchrist B. Stockton	April 1915–January 1916; July–October 1916
Carlos H. Stone	December 1916 to withdrawal
Melville E. Stone	October 1914–November 1918

William W. Stratton	January–July 1915
Oscar S. Straus	July 1915–November 1918
Lewis L. Strauss	September 1917–August 1922
William M. Sullivan	December 1914–January 1915
Roscoe Stubbs	November 1914–December 1915
Clare M. Torrey	December 1915–October 1916
E. Coppee Thurston	December 1914–August 1916
Frederick C. Thwaits	August 1916 to withdrawal
William Hallam Tuck	September 1915–December 1916; December 1918–August 1922
Julius A. Van Hee	January 1915 to withdrawal
John B. Van Schaick	September 1915–September 1916
Robert H. Warren	December 1914–May 1915
L. C. Wellington	December 1914–May 1915; August 1915–September 1916; November 1918–June 1919
John Beaver White	October 1914–November 1918
Almon C. Whiting	September 1916 to withdrawal
Caspar Whitney	May 1915–April 1916
Francis C. Wickes	August 1915–June 1917; December 1918–October 1919
Edgar Williams	June 1916–February 1917
Dr. Percy H. Williams	December 1914–January 1915
Randolph C. Wilson	September 1916–January 1920
Robert Withington	March–December 1916
Carl A. Young	December 1914–June 1916

Served in Rotterdam

W. C. Ames	July–October 1919
Robert A. Mann	December 1914–July 1915

Served in London

Ben S. Allen	October 1914–May 1919
H. Foster Bain	June 1915–September 1916
C. T. Brodrick	December 1914–January 1915
J. W. Dickson	November 1914–January 1915
George Inness Gay	July 1916–December 1929
Charles A. Smith	March–August 1916
Louis J. Mayreis	January–June 1916

Served in New York

George Barr Baker	October 1915–August 1919
Julius H. Barnes	July 1918–September 1919
Edwin P. Shattuck	July 1917–August 1922

OUR CHARITY COMMITTEES IN THE UNITED STATES

As was noted earlier in these pages, with the co-operation of the Governors of all forty-eight states, we established a committee in each state to solicit funds for our work. There were probably fifty thousand members of these committees, and our accounts demonstrate the great help which we got from them—more than $34,-800,000.

Those who worked for these committees contributed tremendously, and I regret that space prevents my listing them here.

Upon the American declaration of war, some thirty of our men enlisted in the American Army and served with distinction. Later in their lives, many rose to high positions in their professions and in public life.

INDEX

INDEX